McGraw-Hill Ryerson
Foundations of Mathematics 10

Authors

Barbara J. Canton
B.A. (Hons.). B.Ed., M.Ed.
Limestone District School Board

Steve Etienne
B.Sc., B. Admin., Ed. Cert.
District School Board of Niagara

Honi Huyck
B.Sc. (Hons.), B.Ed.
Belle River, Ontario

John Santarelli
B.Sc.,B.Ed.
Hamilton-Wentworth Catholic
District School Board

Ken Stewart
B.Sc. (Hons.), B.Ed.
York Region District School
Board

Contributing Authors

Derrick Driscoll
B.Sc., B.Ed.
Thames Valley District School
Board

Ann Heide
B.A., B.Ed., M.Ed.
AHA Educational Activities
Ottawa, Ontario

Sandy Szeto
B.Sc., B.Ed.
Toronto District School Board

Consultants
Senior Consultant

Steve Etienne
B.Sc., B. Admin., Ed. Cert.
District School Board of Niagara

Assessment Consultant

Lynda M. Ferneyhough
B.Math., C.F.P., M.Ed.
Peel District School Board

Literacy Consultant

Nina Purba Jaiswal
B.A., B.Ed., M.Ed.
Peel District School Board

Pedagogy Consultant

Jacqueline Hill
B.Sc., B.Ed.
Durham District School Board

Technology Consultant

Derrick Driscoll
B.Sc., B.Ed.
Thames Valley District School
Board

Advisors

Jacqueline Hill
B.Sc., B.Ed.
Durham District School Board

Janet Moir
B.A.(Hons.), B.Ed
Toronto Catholic District School
Board

Colleen Morgulis
B.Math. (Hons.); B.Ed.
Durham Catholic District School
Board

Larry Romano
B.A. (Hons.); B.Ed.
Toronto Catholic District School
Board

Cheryl Warrington
B.Sc., B.A., B.Ed.
District School Board of Niagara

McGraw-Hill
Ryerson

Toronto   Montréal   Boston   Burr Ridge, IL   Dubuque, IA   Madison, WI   New York
San Francisco   St. Louis   Bangkok   Bogotá   Caracas   Kuala Lumpur   Lisbon   London
Madrid   Mexico City   Milan   New Delhi   Santiago   Seoul   Singapore   Sydney   Taipei

The McGraw-Hill Companies

McGraw-Hill Ryerson
Foundations of Mathematics 10

ISBN-13: 978-0-07-097768-6
ISBN-10: 0-07-097768-2

www.mcgrawhill.ca

4 5 6 7 8 9 10   TCP   1 5 4 3 2 1 0

Printed and bound in Canada

Care has been taken to trace ownership of copyright material contained in this text. The publishers will gladly accept any information that will enable them to rectify any reference or credit in subsequent printings.

CBR™ is a trademark of Texas Instruments.

The Geometer's Sketchpad®, Key Curriculum Press, 1150 65th Street, Emeryville, CA 94608, 1-800-995-MATH.

PUBLISHER: Linda Allison
ASSOCIATE PUBLISHER: Kristi Clark
PROJECT MANAGEMENT: Pronk&Associates, Jim Rogerson
DEVELOPMENTAL EDITORS: Write On!: Marg Bukta, Susan Lishman,
                        Rachelle Redford, JJ Wilson
MANAGER, EDITORIAL SERVICES: Crystal Shortt
SUPERVISING EDITOR: Christine Arnold
COPY EDITORS: Write On!: Erin Bardua, John Green, Christine Hobberlin
PHOTO RESEARCH: Pronk&Associates
PERMISSIONS: Pronk&Associates
EDITORIAL ASSISTANT: Erin Hartley
REVIEW COORDINATOR: Jennifer Keay
MANAGER, PRODUCTION SERVICES: Yolanda Pigden
PRODUCTION CO-ORDINATOR: Zonia Strynatka
COVER DESIGN: Liz Harasymczuk
INTERIOR DESIGN: Pronk&Associates
ART DIRECTION: Pronk&Associates
ELECTRONIC PAGE MAKE-UP: Pronk&Associates
COVER IMAGE: Courtesy of Getty Images

Acknowledgements
Reviewers of Foundations of Mathematics 10

The publishers, authors, and editors of *McGraw-Hill Ryerson Foundations of Mathematics 10*, wish to extend their sincere thanks to the students, teachers, consultants, and reviewers who contributed their time, energy, and expertise to the creation of this textbook. We are grateful for their thoughtful comments and suggestions. This feedback has been invaluable in ensuring that the text and related teacher's resource meet the needs of students and teachers.

Dan Bruni
York Catholic District School Board

Ian Charlton
Thames Valley District School Board

Chris Dearling
Mathematics Consultant
Burlington, Ontario

Mary Ellen Diamond
Niagara Catholic District School Board

Emidio DiAntonio
Dufferin-Peel Catholic District School Board

Wayne Erdman
B.Math., B.Ed.
Toronto District School Board

Karen Frazer
Ottawa-Carleton District School Board

Doris Galea
Dufferin-Peel Catholic District School Board

Mark Guindon
Industrial Consultant-Sheetmetal Journeyman
Bath, Ontario

Beverly A. Hitchman
Upper Grand District School Board

Raymond Ho
Durham District School Board

Mike Jacobs
Durham Catholic District School Board

Alan Jones
Peel District School Board

Travis Kartye
Thames Valley District School Board

Alison Lane
Ottawa-Carleton District School Board

Edward S. Lavor
Toronto Catholic District School Board

Jane Lee
Toronto District School Board

David Lovisa
York Region District School Board

Paul Marchildon
Ottawa-Carleton District School Board

Donald Mountain
Thames Valley District School Board

Andrzej Pienkowski
Toronto District School Board

Richard Poremba
Brant Haldemand Norfolk Catholic District School Board

Clyde Ramlochan
Toronto District School Board

Sharon Ramlochan
Toronto District School Board

Julie Sheremeto
Ottawa-Carleton District School Board

Robert Sherk
Limestone District School Board

Susan Siskind
Toronto District School Board

Robert Slemon
Toronto District School Board

Victor E. Sommerkamp B.Sc., B.Sc (Honours), B.Ed., M.A.
Dufferin-Peel Catholic District School Board

Joe Spano
Dufferin-Peel Catholic District School Board

Carol Sproule
Ottawa-Carleton District School Board

Michelle St.Pierre
Simcoe County District School Board

Laura Stancati
Toronto Catholic District School Board

Tony Stancati
Toronto Catholic District School Board

Tara Townes
Waterloo Catholic District School Board

Chris Wadley
Grand Erie District School Board

Anne Walton
Ottawa-Carleton District School Board

Terrence Wilkinson
Simcoe County District School Board

Peter L. Wright B.Sc (Hons), M.Sc, B.Ed.
Grand Erie District School Board

Contents

Scavenger Hunt

Explore Your Textbook!

1. Your textbook has nine chapters. In each chapter there are a number of sections. How many sections are there in the whole book?

2. List what comes after Chapter 9.

3. Suppose you wanted to find out where graphing calculators are used, where would you look to find the exact pages?

4. What is the title of Chapter 1?

5. Find the Get Ready! pages in Chapter 1. Read the Chapter Problem. What problem is Darren trying to solve?

6. What is the title of Section 1.1?

7. What two terms are defined in the margin on page 6?

8. What are the Key Concepts of Section 1.3?

9. Suppose you are working on problem 4 on page 33 and you got stuck. Where could you find help?

10. In Chapter 1, find a MathConnect that has a web address. What is the Web address?

11. Find the Chapter 1 Review. How can this help you to study for a test for this chapter?

12. Look at the list of Key Terms at the beginning of Chapter 1. Pick a Key Term and look it up in the Glossary at the end of the book. Write the term and the definition.

13. Suppose you are having trouble with the use of technology, where would you look for help?

14. Suppose you need to review specific math skills that you find difficult, where would you find helpful information?

Get Started!

Welcome to *Foundations of Mathematics 10*

Before you begin to explore the new math concepts and skills presented in this textbook, think about all the ways you use mathematics every day. Look at the examples on the mind map below. How would you use math to answer these questions? Think about other situations in your life that involve mathematics.

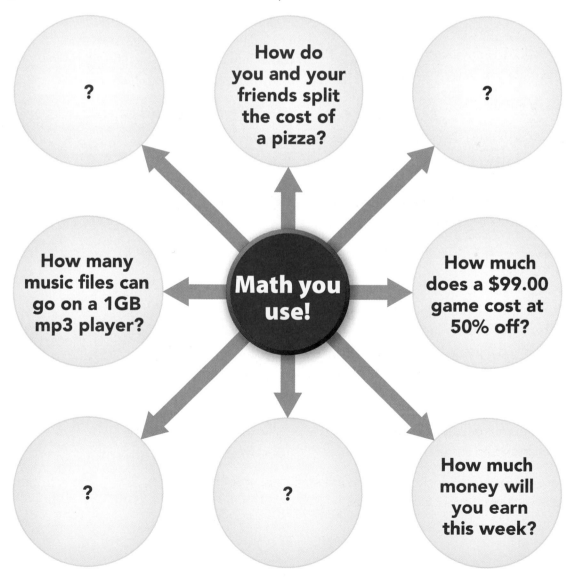

?

How do you and your friends split the cost of a pizza?

?

How many music files can go on a 1GB mp3 player?

Math you use!

How much does a $99.00 game cost at 50% off?

?

?

How much money will you earn this week?

Problem-Solving Strategies

How can you solve problems like the four below? Compare your ideas with the strategies that are shown on the following pages.

Problem 1

In the first round of a soccer tournament, each team must play each other team once. How many games are necessary if there are 12 teams in the tournament?

Problem 3

Sasha is comparing cell phone plans. Company A charges $40 per month for the first 250 min or less plus $0.25/min for each additional minute. Company B charges $30 per month for the first 250 min or less plus $0.30/min for each additional minute. Sasha thinks she will use about 20 min each day. Which plan should Sasha choose? Why?

Problem 2

What is the sum of the first 99 consecutive positive odd numbers?

Problem 4

Tatjana is building a wood fence to enclose a rectangular field with dimensions 72 ft by 112 ft. She will place a fence post at each corner and every 8 ft along the sides. How many fence posts does Tatjana need?

People solve mathematical problems at home, at work, and at play. There are many different ways to solve problems. In *Foundations of Mathematics 10*, you are encouraged to try different methods and to use your own ideas. Your method may be different but it may also work.

A Problem-Solving Model

Where do you begin with problem solving? We suggest the following four-step process.

Understand

Read the problem.
- Think about the problem. Express it in your own words.
- What information do you have?
- What further information do you need?
- What is the problem asking you to do?

Plan

Select a strategy for solving the problem. You may sometimes need more than one strategy.
- Consider other problems you have solved successfully. Is this problem like one of them? Can you use a similar strategy? Strategies that you might use include
  - Draw a diagram
  - Make an organized list
  - Look for a pattern
  - Make a model
  - Work backward
  - Make a table or chart
  - Act it out
  - Use systematic trial
  - Make an assumption
  - Find needed information
  - Choose a formula
  - Solve a simpler problem
- Decide whether any of the following might help. Plan how to use them.
  - tools such as a ruler or a calculator
  - materials such as grid paper or a number line

Solve!

Solve the problem by carrying out your plan.
- Use mental math to estimate a possible answer.
- Do the calculations and record your steps.
- Explain and justify your thinking.
- Revise your plan if it does not work out.

Look Back

Examine your answer. Does it make sense?
- Is your answer close to your estimate?
- Does your answer fit the facts given in the problem?
- Is the answer reasonable? If not, make a new plan. Try a different strategy.
- Consider solving the problem a different way. Do you get the same answer?
- Compare your method with that of other students.

Problem-Solving Strategies

Here are some different ways to solve the four problems on page x.
Often you need to use more than one strategy to solve a problem. Your
ideas on how to solve the problems might be different from any of these.

PROBLEM 1	In the first round of a soccer tournament, each team must play each other team once. How many games are necessary if there are 12 teams in the tournament?

Strategy	Example	
Solve a simpler problem	**Number of Teams**	**Number of Games**
Draw a diagram	2	1
Make an organized list	3	3
Look for a pattern	4	6
	5	10

The number of teams start at 2 and increase by 1 each time.
The number of games starts at 1 and increases according to the
pattern 1, 3, 6, 10. The *difference* between consecutive numbers
of games increases by 1 each time. Continue the pattern to find
the number of games for 12 teams.

Number of Teams	Number of Games
6	15
7	21
8	28
9	36
10	45
11	55
12	66

Conclusion: There will be 66 games if each of the 12 teams plays each
other team once.

PROBLEM 2	What is the sum of the first 99 consecutive positive odd numbers?
Strategy	**Example**
Find needed information	The first 99 consecutive odd numbers are the odd numbers from 1 to 197.
Solve a simpler problem	Find the sum of the first 5 consecutive odd numbers:
Look for a pattern	$1 + 3 + 5 + 7 + 9$ $= (1 + 9) + (3 + 7) + 5$ $= 10 + 10 + 5 = 25$ *Notice that the sum of the first and last numbers equals the sum of the second and second-last numbers.*

Use the pattern that the sum of the first and last numbers equals the sum of the second and second-last numbers to find the sum of the first 8 consecutive odd numbers. Find the sum to check if the pattern works.

The first 8 consecutive odd numbers are 1, 3, 5, 7, 9, 11, 13, and 15. The sum of the first and last numbers is 16. There are 8 numbers, so multiply by 8, then divide by 2.

$$\frac{8 \times 16}{2}$$

Divide by 2 because you have added the numbers twice.

$$= 64$$

So, $1 + 3 + 5 + 7 + 9 + 11 + 13 + 15 = 64$

The pattern works. Use the pattern to find the sum of the first 99 consecutive odd numbers, that is the odd numbers from 1 to 197. The sum of the first and last numbers is 198. There are 99 numbers, so multiply by 99, then divide by 2.

$$\frac{99 \times 198}{2}$$

$$= 9801$$

Conclusion: The sum of the first 99 consecutive odd numbers is 9801.

Problem-Solving Strategies

	PROBLEM 3	Sasha is comparing cell phone plans. Company A charges $40 per month for the first 250 min or less plus $0.25/min for each additional minute. Company B charges $30 per month for the first 250 min or less plus $0.30/min for each additional minute. Sasha thinks she will use about 20 min each day. Which plan should Sasha choose? Why?

Strategy	Example
Make an assumption	Assume Sasha will use the same number of minutes each day, 20.
	There are about 30 days in one month.
	$20 \times 30 = 600$
	Sasha will use about 600 min per month.
Find needed information	Calculate the total cost for each plan.

Company A

$C = 40 + 0.25(600 - 250)$
$\quad = 127.5$

The first 250 min are paid for by the monthly fee. Sasha must pay the per minute charge for the remainder of the minutes.

The total cost for Company A will be $127.50 per month.

Company B

$C = 30 + 0.30(600 - 250)$
$\quad = 135$

The total cost for Company B will be $135.00 per month.

Conclusion: Sasha should choose Company A because it will cost her about $7.50 less per month if she uses her phone for 20 min each day.

PROBLEM 4	Tatjana is building a wood fence to enclose a rectangular field with dimensions 72 ft by 112 ft. She will place a fence post at each corner and every 8 ft along the sides. How many fence posts does Tatjana need?
Strategy	**Example**
Find needed information	The width of the field is 72 ft. Since fence posts are to be placed every 8 ft, the width will be divided into 8-ft sections. $$\frac{72}{8} = 9$$ The length of the field is 112 ft. It will also be divided into 8-ft sections. $$\frac{112}{8} = 14$$
Draw a diagram	There will be 9 sections of fence along the width of the field and 14 sections along the length. 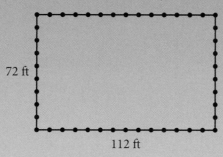 **Conclusion:** Tatjana needs 46 fence posts.
Choose a formula	The dimensions of the field are 72 ft by 112 ft. Find the perimeter of the field. $$P = 2l + 2w$$ $$= 2(112) + 2(72)$$ $$= 224 + 144$$ $$= 368$$ The perimeter of the field is 368 ft. Fence posts will be placed every 8 ft. $$\frac{368}{8} = 46$$ **Conclusion:** Tatjana needs 46 fence posts.

1

Measurement Systems and Similar Triangles

Have you ever wondered how tall a cliff or a mountain is, or how far across it is to the other side of a river or ravine?

In this chapter, you will explore the properties of similar triangles. You will use these properties to find heights of very tall objects. You will also explore the imperial and metric measurement systems.

In this chapter, you will

- verify, through investigation, properties of similar triangles
- determine the lengths of sides of similar triangles, using proportional reasoning
- solve problems involving similar triangles in realistic situations
- use the imperial system when solving measurement problems
- perform everyday conversions between the imperial system and the metric system and within these systems, as necessary to solve problems involving measurement

Reasoning and Proving

Representing | Selecting Tools

Problem Solving

Connecting | Reflecting

Communicating

Key Terms

corresponding angles	metric system	ratio
corresponding sides	proportional	similar triangles
imperial system		

Literacy Link

Start your own Word Wall. Update your Word Wall at the beginning of each section with the Key Terms covered in that section.

Definition:	Characteristics:
Examples:	**Non Examples:**

A draftsperson prepares technical drawings and plans that are used to build everything from industrial machinery to skyscrapers. The drawings provide visual guidelines showing details of the structures specifying the dimensions, materials to be used, and the procedures to be followed. A strong mathematics background is critical to this and many other careers.

Get Ready!

Fraction and Number Sense

1. Order the fractions in each set from least to greatest. The first part has been done for you.

   a) $\dfrac{3}{8}, \dfrac{5}{32}, \dfrac{1}{2}, \dfrac{3}{4}$

   $\dfrac{3}{8} = \dfrac{12}{32}$

   $\dfrac{1}{2} = \dfrac{16}{32}$

   $\dfrac{3}{4} = \dfrac{24}{32}$

   Therefore, from least to greatest, they are $\dfrac{5}{32}, \dfrac{3}{8}, \dfrac{1}{2}, \dfrac{3}{4}$.

   b) $1\dfrac{1}{2}, \dfrac{5}{16}, \dfrac{1}{4}, \dfrac{7}{5}, \dfrac{11}{32}$

   c) $\dfrac{9}{16}, \dfrac{5}{64}, \dfrac{3}{8}$

2. Simplify. The first part has been done for you.

   a) $\dfrac{3}{8} + \dfrac{3}{16}$

   $= \dfrac{6}{16} + \dfrac{3}{16}$

   $= \dfrac{9}{16}$

   b) $\dfrac{5}{32} + \dfrac{3}{64} + \dfrac{5}{8}$

   c) $\dfrac{5}{16} - \dfrac{3}{8}$

   d) $\dfrac{3}{4} \times \dfrac{1}{2}$

   e) $\dfrac{3}{4} \times \dfrac{1}{8}$

   f) $3\dfrac{1}{4} + 5\dfrac{1}{2}$

   g) $\dfrac{3}{16} \times 2$

   h) $26 \div \dfrac{1}{2}$

   i) $\dfrac{1}{2} + \dfrac{3}{4} + \dfrac{5}{8}$

   j) $\dfrac{7}{8} - \dfrac{1}{2}$

Ratio and Proportion

3. Write each ratio in simplest form. The first part has been done for you.

   a) 54:18

   $54 \div 18 = 3$

   $18 \div 18 = 1$

   $54:18 = 3:1$

   b) 36:9

   c) 24:36:72

4. Solve. The first part has been done for you.

   a) $\dfrac{x}{3} = \dfrac{1}{5}$

   $5x = 3$

   $x = \dfrac{3}{5}$

   b) $x:9 = 5:3$

   c) $4:1 = p:3$

   d) $1.5:s = 9:15$

   e) $8:6:10 = 12:p:q$

Chapter Problem

Darren is a tree surgeon. He has to cut down a large tree that has become diseased. Darren must determine the height of the tree and figure out where the top of the tree will land when the tree is cut down. In this chapter, you will learn some of the mathematics needed to solve Darren's problem.

Angle Properties

5. Find the measure of each indicated angle. The first one has been done for you.

a)

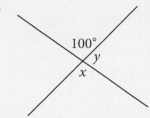

x = 100° (opposite angles)
y = 80° (supplementary angles)

b)

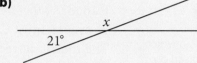

c)

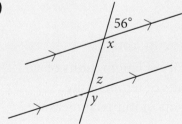

d)

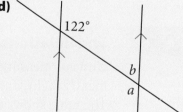

e)

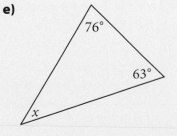

f)

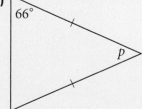

Imperial Measure

How tall are you? Did you answer in feet and inches or in centimetres? How cold is it outside? Did you answer in degrees Fahrenheit or in degrees Celsius?

Canada's official measurement system is the **metric system**. However, most Canadians use both the metric and **imperial systems**. The metric system is used in most countries. The United States, Canada's closest neighbour and largest trading partner, uses a measurement system that is based on the imperial system.

Different measurement systems are used in different industries. In science and medicine, metric is the system of choice around the globe. But in construction and cooking, for example, the imperial system is still commonly used.

metric system
- a system of measurement in which all units are based on multiples of 10

imperial system
- a system of measurement based on British units

Investigate

Tools

- gallon container
- imperial measuring cup
- imperial measuring spoons
- imperial scale
- pint container
- quart container
- sand or water
- yardstick

The Relationships Among Imperial Units

Units of measure are grouped into units of length, units of mass/weight, units of volume, and units of temperature. The table shows the most common units of imperial measure.*

Category	Units of Measure	Abbreviation
Length	inch, foot, yard, mile	in. or ", ft or ', yd, mi
Volume	teaspoon, tablespoon, fluid ounce, cup, pint, quart, gallon	tsp, tbsp, fl oz, c, pt, qt, gal
Weight	ounce, pound, ton	oz, lb, tn
Temperature	degree Fahrenheit	°F

*Unless otherwise noted, all references to imperial measures in this student text will be U.S.

Part A: Units of Length

1. a) Use a yardstick. Determine the number of inches in one foot, and the number of feet in one yard.

b) What is the smallest fraction of an inch shown on the yardstick?

Math Connect

The British imperial pints, quarts, and gallons are larger than U.S. pints, quarts, and gallons. The British fluid ounce is less than the U.S. fluid ounce.

Part B: Units of Volume

2. Use a measuring cup, measuring spoons, and pint, quart, and gallon containers. Explore how the units of volume are related to one another. Record your results.

Part C: Units of Weight

3. a) Use a scale. Find the weight of a variety of objects both in pounds and in ounces. How are ounces and pounds related? Record your results.

b) Research the relationship between pounds and tons. Record your findings.

Reflect Review your findings. Design a table to show how the units of length compare, how the units of volume compare, and how the units of weight compare. Share your findings with a partner. Are your unit comparisons accurate?

Example 1

Measure to a Fraction of an Inch

Find the length of each object to the smallest fraction of an inch.

Math Connect

A ruler cannot show 32nds or 64ths of an inch accurately. Calipers are used to make more precise measurements.

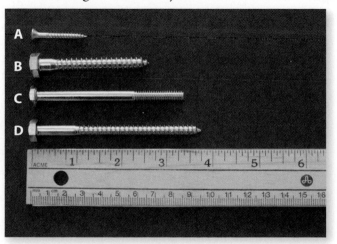

Solution

The bolts/screws measure

a) $1\frac{1}{4}$ in.

b) $2\frac{1}{2}$ in.

c) $3\frac{3}{8}$ in.

d) $3\frac{3}{4}$ in.

Example 2

Working With Volume

Steve owns a restaurant in Arizona. He bought a 55-gal drum of ketchup at a wholesale store. For the tables, he has $\frac{1}{2}$ pint squeeze bottles that he fills with ketchup from the drum. How many bottles can Steve fill from this drum of ketchup?

Solution

Find the number of pints in the drum.

$= 55 \times 8$ *There are 8 pt in a gallon, so multiply*
$= 440$ *the number of gallons by 8.*

There are 440 pt in 55 gal.

Each bottle will hold half a pint, so the number of bottles that can be filled is double the number of pints in the drum. Steve can fill 880 squeeze bottles from this drum of ketchup.

Example 3

Find the Cost to Carpet a Room

Calculate the cost, including taxes, to carpet the floor shown. The carpet costs $24 per square yard.

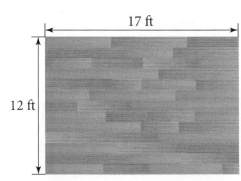
17 ft
12 ft

Solution

Calculate the area to be carpeted:
$A = l \times w$
$\quad = 17 \times 12$
$\quad = 204$

The area to be carpeted is 204 sq ft.

There are 3 ft in a yard and 9 ft in 1 sq yd. Divide by 9 to convert the area in square feet to square yards:

$$A = 204 \div 9$$
$$= 22\frac{2}{3}$$

The area to be carpeted is $22\frac{2}{3}$ sq yd.

Calculate the cost of the carpet:

$$= 22\frac{2}{3} \times 24 \qquad \text{\textit{The cost is \$24 per square yard, so}}$$
$$= 544 \qquad\qquad \text{\textit{multiply the area by 24.}}$$

Find the total after adding 14% tax (8% PST plus 6% GST):

$$= 544 \times 1.14$$
$$= 620.16$$

It will cost \$620.16 to carpet this room.

Key Concepts

- The basic units of imperial measure are the foot, gallon, pound, and degree Fahrenheit.
- There are fixed relationships among the different units for length, volume, and weight.

Discuss the Concepts

D1. List the imperial measures and their abbreviations that are used to measure the following.
    a) length   **b)** volume
    c) weight   **d)** temperature

D2. Describe how the imperial units for length are related.

D3. Describe how the imperial units for weight are related.

Practise the Concepts (A)

For help with question 1, see Example 1.

1. Measure the perimeter of each figure as precisely as possible.

   a)   **b)**    **c)**

For help with questions 2, 3, and 4, refer to Example 2. All measures are in U.S. imperial units.

2. Convert each measure to pints and to quarts.
   a) 32 fl oz
   b) 24 c
   c) 10 c
   d) 108 fl oz

3. Convert each measure to gallons.
   a) 64 qt
   b) 104 c
   c) 50 pt

4. Express each measure in fluid ounces.
   a) 5 qt
   b) 16 c
   c) 3 gal
   d) 5 pt

5. Convert each measure to pounds.
   a) 32 oz
   b) 456 oz

6. Express each weight in ounces.
   a) 3 lb
   b) 5.6 lb

7. Work with a partner. Discuss which units you would use to measure in each case. Explain your choices.
   a) the size of a book, a desk, a lawn, an airfield
   b) the volume contained in a thimble, a glass, a swimming pool, an ocean
   c) the weight of a sheet of paper, a book, a person, a car

Apply the Concepts B

8. A recipe calls for 7 tbsp of oil. How many fluid ounces of oil do you need?

9. Chris is sewing drapes and needs 20 ft of fabric. The local fabric store sells fabric by the yard. How many yards of fabric does Chris need?

10. Cindy is catering a dinner for a conference with 225 guests. She plans to serve a pasta course and figures she needs 6 oz of pasta per guest. How many pounds of pasta will she need to order?

11. A Canadian football field is 110 yd long and an American football field is 100 yd long. How many feet longer is the Canadian field?

For help with question 12, refer to Example 3.

12. Jamila's dining room is 13 ft long by 10 ft wide. She plans to install bamboo flooring that costs $18.50 per square yard. How much will Jamila pay for the flooring, including taxes?

Literacy Connect

13. Although the metric system is Canada's official measurement system, many Canadians know their weight and height in imperial measure. With a partner, discuss why this is the case.

Chapter Problem

14. Darren has to remove some dead branches at the top of a tree. The tree is approximately 15' tall. Darren stands 5' 10" tall. He has a ladder that reaches up 8' 5". Will Darren be able to use his ladder to trim the branches or will he need to rent scaffolding?

Extend the Concepts **C**

Use this floor plan for questions 15 to 17.

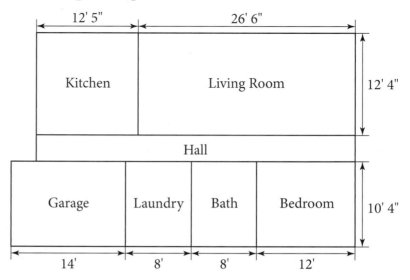
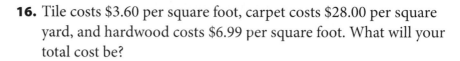

15. You plan to put carpet in the bedroom of your new home, hardwood floors in the living room, and ceramic tile in the kitchen, bathroom, and laundry room. Calculate the number of square feet of each type of flooring you will need.
   a) carpet   **b)** tile   **c)** hardwood

16. Tile costs $3.60 per square foot, carpet costs $28.00 per square yard, and hardwood costs $6.99 per square foot. What will your total cost be?

17. You need to buy primer to paint the three walls in the garage. The walls are 8' high. The garage door, the fourth wall, will not be painted.
   a) Calculate the total area to be primed.
   b) Suppose one quart of primer covers 110 sq ft. How many gallons of primer will you need?

1.2

Conversions Between Metric and Imperial Systems

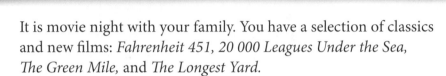

It is movie night with your family. You have a selection of classics and new films: *Fahrenheit 451, 20 000 Leagues Under the Sea, The Green Mile,* and *The Longest Yard.*

Is 451°F hot? How long is a league? A mile? A yard?

In movies and in real life, there are many references to distance, temperature, volume, and mass and weight. Making a quick mental conversion helps keep things in a context you understand. In some careers, it is often necessary to be able to make exact conversions between the imperial system and the metric system. In space exploration, for example, calculation errors can mean a failed mission, such as with the Mars Climate Orbiter.

Investigate

Tools
- graduated cylinders or measuring cups with both fluid ounces and millilitres
- metre stick
- scale with both pounds and kilograms
- thermometer with both Celsius and Fahrenheit
- yardstick

The Relationships Between Metric and Imperial Units

The table shows the most common units in each measurement system.

	Metric	Imperial
Length	millimetre (mm)	
	centimetre (cm)	inch (in.)
	kilometre (km)	mile (mi)
Mass (Metric)/ Weight (Imperial)	gram (g)	ounce (oz)
	kilogram (kg)	pound (lb)
	tonne (t)	ton (tn)
Liquid Volume	millilitre (mL)	fluid ounce (fl oz)
		pint (pt)
		quart (qt)
	litre (L)	gallon (gal)
Temperature	degree Celsius (°C)	degree Fahrenheit (°F)

Part A: Units of Length

Use a yardstick and a metre stick.

1. Approximately how many centimetres are in one inch?

2. a) Which is longer, a yard or a metre? By how much?
   b) Approximately how many yards are in one metre?

Part B: Units of Mass and Weight

The imperial unit, the pound, is a measure of weight. The weight of an object is affected by gravity. The metric unit, the kilogram, is a measure of mass. Mass is a measure of the amount of matter an object contains. It is not affected by gravity. An object weighs less on the moon than it does on Earth, but it has the same mass. However, when measuring how heavy something is on Earth, weight and mass are essentially equivalent.

Use a scale.

3. a) Which is heavier, one kilogram or one pound?
   b) Approximately how many pounds are in one kilogram?

4. Approximately how many grams are in one pound?

Part C: Units of Volume

Use graduated cylinders to explore how units of volume are related.

5. a) Which is larger, one cup or one litre?
   b) Approximately how many cups are in one litre?

6. Approximately how many millilitres are in one cup?

Part D: Units of Temperature

7. Select five different temperatures in degrees Celsius.
   a) Use a thermometer to find each equivalent temperature in degrees Fahrenheit.
   b) Work with a partner. Compare the temperatures in degrees Celsius to the equivalent temperatures in degrees Fahrenheit. Describe a method you could use to estimate a temperature in degrees Fahrenheit given a temperature in degrees Celsius.

8. Choose two different temperatures in degrees Celsius.
   a) Use the method you described in question 7b) to estimate the equivalent temperatures in degrees Fahrenheit.
   b) Use a thermometer to find each equivalent temperature in degrees Fahrenheit. Compare your results to your estimates in part a). How close were your estimates?

Math Connect

Find out your weight in pounds and your mass in kilograms. Then calculate your weight on the moon by multiplying your weight by $\frac{1}{6}$. What would your mass on the moon be? Go to www.mcgrawhill.ca/links/foundations10 and follow the links to find out your weight on other planets.

Often, an estimate is all that is needed when converting between the metric and imperial measurement systems. Here are some benchmarks for the most common estimates:

There are about 1.6 kilometres in 1 mile.
There are about 2.5 centimetres in 1 inch.
One yard is approximately equal to 1 metre.
There are about 450 grams in 1 pound.
There are about 2.2 pounds in 1 kilogram.
There are about 4 litres in 1 gallon.
One tablespoon is approximately equal to 15 millilitres.
There are about 30 millilitres in 1 fluid ounce.

A quick way to estimate a temperature in degrees Fahrenheit given a temperature in degrees Celsius is to double the temperature and add 30. Remember that an estimate is NOT an accurate result.

Example 1 Estimating

A Chan finds that when he estimates a volume in gallons given a volume in litres, his estimate is always low, and when he estimates a volume in litres given a volume in gallons, his estimate is always high. Explain why this happens.

B When Beatta estimates a distance in kilometres, given a distance in miles, she multiplies by 6, moves the decimal one place to the left, then adds the original number. Explain why Beatta's method works.

Solution

A Four litres is a little less than one gallon. So, when Chan divides by 4 to estimate the volume in gallons given the volume in litres, the estimate will always be too low. Similarly, when he multiplies by 4 to estimate the volume in litres given the volume in gallons, his estimate will always be too high.

B When Beatta multiplies by 6 and moves the decimal one place to the left, she is actually finding 0.6 times the value. By adding the result to the original values, she is taking 1 (the original value) plus 0.6 of the original value, which is the same as multiplying by 1.6.

Example 2 — Estimate or Calculate?

A Blueprints for a new amusement park ride were prepared using imperial units. The axles are to be manufactured in a metric facility. The blueprints indicate the diameter of the axles is to be $1\frac{3}{4}$". Is it sufficient to estimate the diameter of an axle in metric units? Why or why not? What is the diameter of the axles in millimetres?

B At Nitusha's most recent checkup, her mass was 55 kg. How many pounds does Nitusha weigh? Is an estimate good enough?

Solution

A An estimate is not sufficient in this situation. For safety, the conversion should be exact, so the axles will fit. There are 25.4 mm in one inch. Find the diameter of the axle in millimetres.

$$= 1\frac{3}{4} \times 25.4$$ *Convert $\frac{3}{4}$ to 0.75 and multiply 25.4 by 1.75.*

$$= 44.45$$

The diameter of the axles is 44.45 mm.

B Adults are usually weighed to the nearest pound. In this case, an estimate is sufficient.
There are 2.2 lb in 1 kg.
$55 \times 2.2 = 121$
Nitusha weighs approximately 121 lb.

> **Math Connect**
>
> Why are infants measured in smaller units than adults? Why are more precise measurements important in this case?

Example 3 — Convert Temperatures

Suppose the forecast high temperature today is 23°C. Estimate the temperature in degrees Fahrenheit.

Solution

To estimate the temperature, double and add 30.
$2 \times 23 = 46$
$46 + 30 = 76$
Therefore, 23°C is approximately 76°F.

Practise the Concepts

For help with question 1, refer to Examples 1, 2, and 3.

1. Estimate each measure in the indicated units.

   a) 10 mi   kilometres

   b) 3 m   yards

   c) 6 gal   litres

   d) 156 lb   kilograms

   e) 2 tbsp   millilitres

   f) 60 cm   inches

   g) 4 L   quarts

   h) 600 g   pounds

   i) 20°C   degrees Fahrenheit

   j) 80°F   degrees Celsius

2. The weather forecast calls for 12 cm of snow. How many inches can you expect?

3. Yesterday, the high temperature in Orlando, Florida, was 87°F. The high temperature in Stouffville, Ontario, was 28°C. Which city had the greater high temperature? How do you know?

4. You have a 1.5 gal jug. How many litres will it hold?

5. Joe is travelling in the United States. A road sign indicates he is 228 mi from his destination. How many kilometres is Joe from his destination?

6. Work with a partner. For each situation, discuss which would be more appropriate: an exact measure or an approximation. Explain your choices.

a) the distance to a hole on a golf course

b) the dose of a medicine

c) the outside temperature when you are deciding what to wear

d) the length of a car trip

e) the dimensions of parts of a machine

f) your height

7. A metric tonne is 1000 kg. Which is heavier, a metric tonne or an imperial ton? Explain.

Chapter Problem

8. The city Roads and Parks Maintenance Department has called Darren in to consult. Trees are to be planted around a new park. Hydro poles run along one side of the park. The hydro wires are 5 m above the ground. The table shows the maximum heights of the varieties of trees city planners wish to plant around the park. Which varieties can be planted beneath the hydro wires? How do you know?

Variety	Maximum Height (feet)
Amur maple	15 to 20
Blackhaw viburnum	12 to 15
Blue ash	40
Paperbark maple	20 to 30
Serviceberry	15 to 25

9. Ilya was watching an American news broadcast. It spoke of gas prices being \$3.20/gal. What was the price per litre?

Literacy Connect

10. You have a $\frac{5}{16}$ in. drill bit. Will it drill a hole large enough to fit a 5 mm bolt? Explain.

11. Eric found his great-grandmother's recipe for red currant jelly. All the measures are given in imperial units. Eric has metric measures. Work with a partner. Convert all of the measures to metric.

Red Currant Jelly

3 lb fresh red currants

3 c sugar

1 c + 1 tbsp water

1 tbsp cornstarch

12. Marcel can buy cheese at the farmers' market for $3.06/lb. At the grocery store, cheese sells for $6.59/kg. Which is the better buy? Why?

13. Masum's trainer recommended that she drink 2 qt of water a day. Masum bought a case of 500 mL bottles of water. How many bottles of water should she drink each day?

14. a) The temperature range in which most bacteria grow is from 5°C to 60°C. What is this range in degrees Fahrenheit?

   b) *Salmonella* bacteria are destroyed at cooking temperatures above 150°F. What is this temperature in degrees Celsius?

Achievement Check

15. You are having a party and want to make a fruit punch for the group. The recipe calls for
1 large bottle of pineapple juice (1.89 L)
2 cans of frozen concentrated orange juice (355 mL each)
2 large bottles of ginger ale (2 L each)
1 package of frozen strawberries (600 g)

   a) This recipe makes enough punch for 25 people. How many litres of punch is needed for a group of 85 guests?

   b) What size of container is needed to hold one recipe worth of punch?

   c) If the punch is mixed beforehand and stored in emptied and cleaned 4 L milk jugs, how many jugs of punch will be needed for 85 guests?

Extend the Concepts **C**

Reasoning and Proving

Representing | Selecting Tools

Problem Solving

Connecting | Reflecting

Communicating

16. The manufacturer of a new car claims it will use 9 L of gas per 100 km. How many miles per gallon is that?

17. Gunilla's baby is ill. The dosage indicated on the medication's label is 2.5 mL/kg every 4 hours. The baby weighs 9 lb 6 oz, and Gunilla has measuring spoons in these sizes: $\frac{1}{8}, \frac{1}{4}, \frac{1}{2}$, and 1 tsp. How much medication should she administer every 4 hours? Would it be wise for Gunilla to estimate? Explain.

18. Raj drove 550 km and used 30 L of gas. How many miles per gallon does his car get?

1.3 Similar Triangles

The Great Hall of the National Gallery of Canada in Ottawa has an impressive glass ceiling. The design of the Great Hall is intended to mimic the design of the nearby Library of Parliament.

Architects use similar figures in scale drawings and scale models as they design buildings.

Investigate

Tools

- grid paper
- protractor
- ruler

Properties of Similar Triangles

Method 1: Use Pencil and Paper

1. On grid paper, draw triangles ABC, DEF, and GHI.

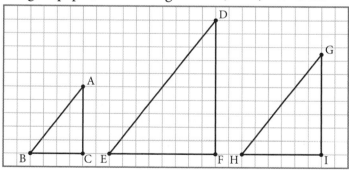

2. Copy and complete the table.

∠A =	∠D =	∠G =
∠B =	∠E =	∠H =
∠C =	∠F =	∠I =
AB =	DE =	GH =
BC =	EF =	HI =
AC =	DF =	GI =

3. Which measures are equal?
Which are different?

4. Find the ratios of lengths of pairs of corresponding sides.
How do the ratios compare to one another?
How do the measures of corresponding angles compare?

Tools

▪ computers
▪ *The Geometer's Sketchpad*®

Method 2: Use *The Geometer's Sketchpad*®

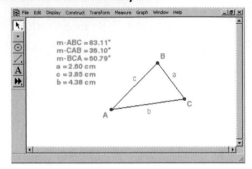

1. Open *The Geometer's Sketchpad*®. Open a new sketch.

2. From the **Edit** menu, choose **Preferences**. Click the **Text** tab. Make sure that the **Show labels automatically from all new points** check box is selected.

3. Use the **Segment** tool to construct a small triangle in the centre of your screen.

4. Measure angle ABC: use the **Selection** tool to select points A, B, C (in that order). Then, from the **Measure** menu, choose **Angle**. Measure angles CAB and BCA.

5. Use the **Text** tool to label sides a, b, and c of the triangle ABC. Side a is opposite angle A, side b is opposite angle B and side c is opposite angle C.

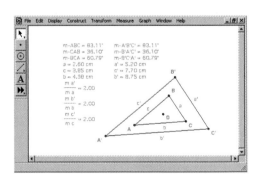

Using the **Selection** tool, select each line segment. Then, from the **Measure** menu, choose **Length**. Record the side lengths.

6. Use the **Point** tool to construct a point inside your triangle.

Select this point. From the **Transform** menu, choose **Mark Center**. Select every point and line segment on your triangle.

From the **Transform** menu, choose **Dilate**. Use a fixed ratio of 2 to 1. Click Dilate. You should have a new larger triangle on your sketch. This new triangle is similar to triangle ABC.

Use the **Text** tool to label the sides of the new triangle.

7. Using the same method you used for the smaller triangle, measure each of the angles and side lengths of the new, larger triangle.

What do you notice about the measures of **corresponding angles**?

How do you think the **ratios** of the lengths of **corresponding sides** compare?

8. To check your prediction about the ratios of lengths of corresponding sides, select one of the sides of the larger triangle and the corresponding side of the smaller triangle. From the **Measure** menu, choose **Ratio**.

Repeat for the other pairs of corresponding sides.

How are these ratios related to each other?

Do you think this is true for all pairs of similar triangles?

9. Repeat step 6 using a different fixed ratio to construct another pair of similar triangles.

Measure the angles and sides of the new triangles and find the ratios of the lengths of corresponding sides.
Compare your results with your classmates' constructions.
What patterns do you see?

Make a conclusion about the measures of the corresponding angles of similar triangles.

Make a conclusion about the ratios of lengths of corresponding sides of similar triangles.

Similar triangles

Triangles are similar if
- corresponding angles are equal
- corresponding sides are **proportional** in length

When naming similar triangles, list the letters of the corresponding angles in the same order for both triangles. For example, given similar triangles ABC and MNP, ∠A corresponds to ∠M, ∠B corresponds to ∠N, and ∠C corresponds to ∠P.

---

corresponding angles
- have the same relative position in a pair of similar triangles
- are equal

ratio
- a comparison of two quantities measured in the same units

corresponding sides
- have the same relative position in a pair of similar triangles

similar triangles
- triangles in which the ratios of the lengths of corresponding sides are equal and corresponding angles are equal

proportional
- two quantities are proportional if they have the same constant ratio
- the side lengths of two triangles are proportional if there is a single value which will multiply all of the side lengths of the first triangle to get the side lengths of the second triangle

Example 1

Find Missing Side and Angle Measures

Given $\triangle ABC \sim \triangle DEF$, find the measure of $\angle C$ and the length of DE to the nearest tenth of a unit.

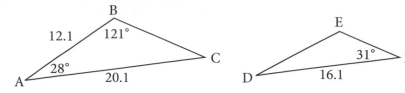

Solution

Since $\triangle ABC \sim \triangle DEF$, corresponding angles are equal.
Therefore, $\angle C = \angle F$
$$= 31°$$

Corresponding sides are proportional in length.

Therefore, $\dfrac{DE}{AB} = \dfrac{DF}{AC}$

The numerators are the side lengths of one triangle; the denominators are the side lengths of the other triangle.

$$\dfrac{DE}{12.1} = \dfrac{16.1}{20.1}$$

$$DE = \dfrac{12.1 \times 16.1}{20.1}$$

Multiply both sides by 12.1.

$$\doteq 9.7$$

The measure of $\angle C$ is 31° and the length of DE is 9.7 units.

Example 2

Use Opposite Angles and Similar Triangles to Find Missing Measures

Find the length of FG to the nearest tenth of a unit.

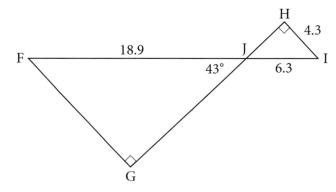

Solution

If △FGJ ~ △IHJ, then the lengths of corresponding sides are proportional.

∠HJI = 43° (opposite angles)
∠GFJ = 180° − (43° + 90°)
     = 47°
∠HIJ = 180° − (43° + 90°)
     = 47°

Since ∠GFJ = ∠HIJ, ∠FGJ = ∠IHJ, and ∠FJG = ∠HJI, then △FGJ ~ △IHJ.

$$\frac{FG}{HI} = \frac{FJ}{IJ}$$

$$\frac{FG}{3.8} = \frac{18.9}{6.3}$$ *Multiply both sides by 3.8.*

$$FG = \frac{3.8 \times 18.9}{6.3}$$ *Use a calculator.*

$$\doteq 11.4$$

The length of FG is 11.4 units.

Example **3**

Use Parallel Lines and Similar Triangles to Find Missing Measures

In the diagram, DE is parallel to AC.
Find the length of AC.

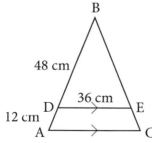

Solution

Draw the triangles separately.

AD = 12 cm and DB = 48 cm. AB is the sum of the two lengths. So, AB = 60 cm.

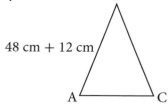

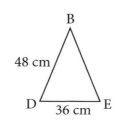

Since AC is parallel to DE, ∠A = ∠D and ∠E = ∠C.

Remember that with two parallel lines and a transversal, corresponding angles are equal. This is sometimes called the F pattern.

The angle at B is common to both triangles.

Since corresponding angles are equal, △ABC ∼ △DBE and the lengths of the corresponding sides are proportional.

$$\frac{AC}{DE} = \frac{AB}{DB}$$

$$\frac{AC}{36} = \frac{60}{48}$$

$$AC = \frac{36 \times 60}{48} \qquad \textit{Multiply both sides by 36.}$$

$$AC = 45$$

The length of AC is 45 cm.

Example **4** **Use Side Lengths to Determine if Triangles are Similar**

In △MNP, $m = 7$ cm, $n = 6$ cm, and $p = 4$ cm. In △HJK, $h = 17.5$ cm, $j = 15$ cm, and $k = 10$ cm. Show that △MNP ∼ △HJK.

Solution

Sketch and label the triangles.

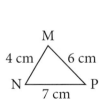 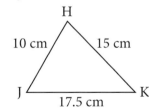

Write ratios comparing the longest sides, the shortest sides, and the third sides.

$$\frac{h}{m} = \frac{17.5}{7} \qquad\qquad \frac{k}{p} = \frac{10}{4} \qquad\qquad \frac{j}{n} = \frac{15}{6}$$

$$\frac{h}{m} = 2.5 \qquad\qquad\qquad \frac{k}{p} = 2.5 \qquad\qquad\quad \frac{j}{n} = 2.5$$

Since the ratios of corresponding sides are equal, △MNP ∼ △HJK.

Practise the Concepts Ⓐ

For help with question 1, refer to the Investigate.

1. For each pair of similar triangles:
List the corresponding angles.
List the corresponding sides.
List the ratios of the corresponding sides.
Write the proportionality statement for the corresponding sides.
   a) △ABC ∼ △DEF   **b)** △PQR ∼ △STU

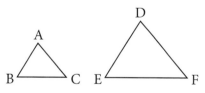

For help with question 2, refer to Example 1.

2. For each pair of similar triangles find all the missing measures.
   a) △DEF ∼ △XYZ

b) △ABC ~ △BDE

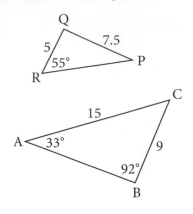

c) △ABC ~ △PQR

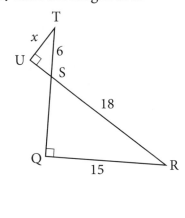

For help with question 3, refer to Example 2.

3. Find the length of the indicated side to the nearest tenth of a unit.

a) Find the length of side DE.

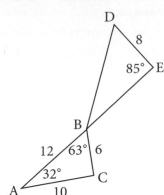

b) Find the length of x.

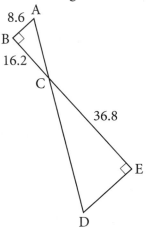

For help with questions 4 and 5, refer to Example 3.

4. Given that DE is parallel to AC, AD = 6.8, DB = 9.3, and BC = 12.8, find the length of BE to the nearest tenth of a unit.

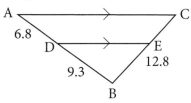

5. In the diagram, DE is parallel to AC. BD = 4, DA = 6, and BE = 5. Find the length of BC to the nearest tenth of a unit.

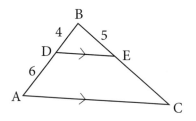

For help with question 6, refer to Example 1.

6. Given △ABC ~ △DEF, $a = 2.1$ cm, $c = 5.8$ cm, $e = 8.7$ cm, and $f = 6.9$ cm. Work with a partner. Discuss how you would find the length of d and b. Find the lengths of d and b to the nearest tenth of a centimetre.

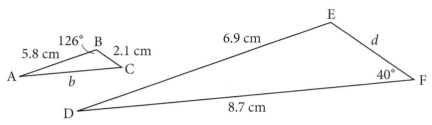

Literacy Connect

7. Explain how two sisters who look very much alike but are different ages can be compared to similar triangles.

Apply the Concepts **B**

For help with question 8, refer to Example 4.

8. In △VWX, WX = 28 cm, VX = 35 cm, and VW = 14 cm. In △PQR, QR = 20 cm, PR = 25 cm, and PQ = 10 cm. Are triangles VWX and PQR similar? How do you know?

9. Given that two triangles ABC and PQR are similar and that ∠A = 50°, ∠B = 90°, PQ = 12 cm, AB = 4 cm, and BC = 5 cm, find the measures of all the missing sides and angles.

10. Given △DEF ~ △RPQ, EF = 10 in., DF = 9 in., DE = 8 in., and RQ = 0.5 ft. Find the length of side PQ.

11. Triangles ABC and XYZ are similar. Angles A and C are equal, XZ is 21 cm long, AB is 7 cm long, and AC is 35 cm long.
a) Find the length of YZ.
b) Compare your answer to part a) with that of a classmate. Did you get the same answer? If your answers are different, work together to find which answer, if either, is correct.

12. Use *The Geometer's Sketchpad*®.
a) Open a new sketch, and construct a triangle.

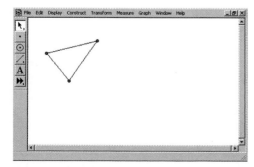

b) Construct a line passing through two sides parallel to the third side as shown.

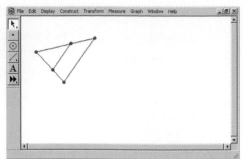

c) Measure the triangles to determine if they are similar. Drag the vertices to see if the result continues to hold true.

d) Label the triangles.

e) Use the **Text** tool and other *The Geometer's Sketchpad*® capabilities to show the appropriate measures and ratios. Write a statement of your conclusion.

f) Repeat parts b) and c) with a line parallel to a different side of the triangle.

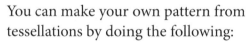

Achievement Check

13. M.C. Escher (1898–1972) was a Dutch artist best known for his mathematical representations. One series of his work dealt with transformations and tessellations.

You can make your own pattern from tessellations by doing the following:

- Start with a piece of cardboard three inches square.
- Along any two edges of the square, cut out a design.
- Attach the cut-out designs to the other edges of the square.
- Use your shape to trace figures to cover a piece of paper. The figures will fit together.
- Colour as desired to make an interesting picture.
- Explain how similar figures are featured in your design.

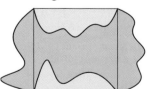

Math Connect

Doctors use similar triangles to calculate the position of radiation treatments for cancer patients. To learn more, visit www. mcgrawhill.ca /links/ foundations10 and follow the links.

14. Copy these triangles on grid paper.

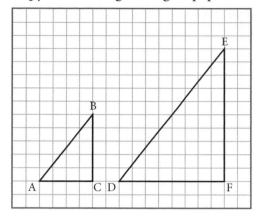

a) Determine if the triangles are similar. Show your work.

b) Find the area of each triangle.

c) Write a ratio comparing the areas of the triangles. How does this ratio relate to the ratio comparing the lengths of corresponding sides?

d) Make a statement about how the ratio comparing the areas of two similar triangles is related to the ratio comparing the corresponding sides.

e) Draw other pairs of similar triangles. Use these triangles to check your statement from part d).

15. $\triangle$PQR is similar to $\triangle$WXY. PQ = 12 cm, WX = 9 cm, and the area of $\triangle$WXY is 72 cm^2. Find the area of $\triangle$PQR.

16. The corresponding sides of two similar triangles are 4 cm and 6 cm in length. Find the ratio of the areas of the triangles.

Solve Problems Using Similar Triangles

One of the world's tallest totem poles was raised in Alert Bay, British Columbia in 1972. It would be very difficult to measure the height of this totem pole directly. One way to find its height is to use shadows. First, the length of the shadow of the totem pole is measured. At the same time, the shadow cast by a vertical object of known height is measured. Since the lengths of the two shadows and the length of the vertical object are known, similar triangles can be used to find the height of the totem pole. This totem pole stands approximately 173 feet tall!

Investigate

Find the Height of Your School's Flagpole

Tools

- long measuring tape
- metre or yard stick

Work in a group. Use a metre stick for the vertical object with known height.

1. Measure the length of the shadow of your school's flagpole.

2. Hold a metre stick at right angles to the ground. Have a member of the group measure the length of the shadow cast by the metre stick.

3. Sketch and label a diagram similar to the one shown. Include triangles showing the locations of the objects and their shadows.

4. Explain why the two triangles are similar.

5. Calculate the height of the flagpole. Show your work.

Example 1 — Find the Height of a Tree

A pole 3 m tall casts a shadow 4 m long. A nearby tree casts a 15 m shadow. What is the height of the tree?

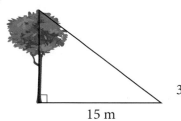

Solution

Use h to represent the height of the tree. The two triangles are similar, so corresponding sides are proportional.

$$\frac{h}{3} = \frac{15}{4}$$

$$h = \frac{3 \times 15}{4}$$

$$h = 11.25$$

The tree is 11.25 m tall.

Example 2 — Find the Length of a Pond

To find the length of a pond, a surveyor took some measurements. She recorded them on this diagram. What is the length of the pond?

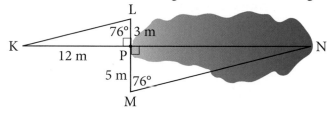

Solution

The triangles are similar, so the corresponding sides are proportional.

$$\frac{NP}{12} = \frac{5}{3} \qquad \textit{Multiply both sides by 12.}$$

$$NP = \frac{12 \times 5}{3}$$

$$NP = 20$$

The pond is 20 m long.

Example 3

Use a Mirror to Find Height

Elizabeth's eyes are 150 cm from the floor. She places a mirror on the floor 18 m from the base of a climbing wall. She walks backward 120 cm, until she sees the top of the wall in the mirror. What is the height of the climbing wall?

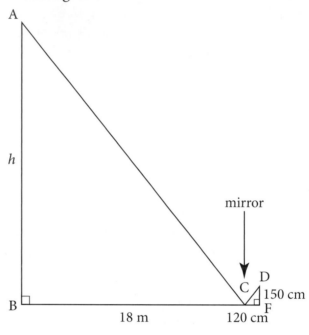

Solution

Let h represent the height of the climbing wall. When a beam of light hits a mirror, the angle at which the light hits the mirror, $\angle ACB$, equals the angle at which the light reflects off the mirror, $\angle DCF$.

$\angle ABC = \angle DFC = 90°$

$\angle BCA = \angle FCD$

So, $\angle BAC = \angle FDC$

Since corresponding angles are equal, $\triangle ABC \sim \triangle DFC$.

So, $\dfrac{AB}{DF} = \dfrac{BC}{FC}$

$\dfrac{h}{150} = \dfrac{1800}{120}$ *Make sure all measures are given in the same units. 18 m = 1800 cm.*

$h = \dfrac{150 \times 1800}{120}$

$h = 2250$

The height of the climbing wall is 2250 cm, or 22.5 m.

Practise the Concepts A

1. List at least five objects whose measure could be found using similar triangles.

2. Choose one of the objects you listed in question 1. Explain how you would use similar triangles to measure this object.

Literacy Connect

3. Sherlock Holmes uses similar triangles to determine the height of a tree in *The Adventure of the Musgrave Ritual*. Look up the story, and explain why it was necessary to use this method instead of measuring.

Apply the Concepts B

For help with question 4, refer to Example 1.

4. On a sunny day Josée's shadow is 2.9 m long, while the shadow of a tower is 11.3 m long. If Josée is 1.8 m tall, calculate the height of the tower.

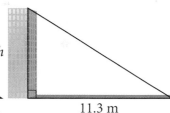
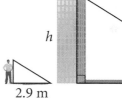

For help with question 5, refer to Example 2.

5. To calculate the length of a marsh, a surveyor produced the following diagram. Find the length of the marsh to the nearest tenth of a unit.

For help with question 6, refer to Example 3.

6. A hiker, whose eye level is 2 m above the ground, wants to find the height of a tree. He places a mirror horizontally on the ground 20 m from the base of the tree, and finds that if he stands at a point C, which is 4 m from the mirror B, he can see the reflection of the top of the tree. How tall is the tree?

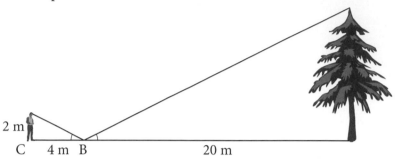

2 m

C   4 m   B   20 m

7. Two ladders are leaned against a wall so that they make the same angle with the ground. The 10' ladder reaches 8' up the wall. How much further up the wall does the 18' ladder reach?

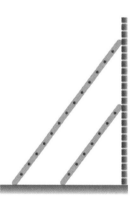

8. At a certain time of the day, the shadow of your friend who is 5 ft tall measures 8 ft. At the same time, the shadow of a tree measures 28 ft. Draw a diagram to represent the situation. How tall is the tree?

Chapter Problem

9. To find the height of a tree, Darren measures the shadow of a metre stick to be 90 cm and the shadow of the tree to be 3.2 m. Draw a diagram to represent the situation. How tall is the tree?

10. To find the width of a river, Jordan surveys the area and finds the following measures. Find the width of the river.

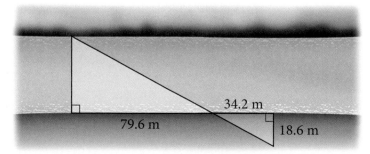

34.2 m

79.6 m   18.6 m

11. Light travels in a straight line. The pinhole camera, or camera obscura, makes use of this fact. When rays of light reflect off an object, and pass through the pinhole in a camera, they cross and form an upside-down image.

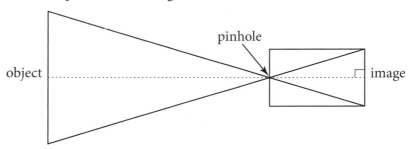

An object is 3.6 m from the pinhole. Its image is 4.2 cm from the opposite side of the pinhole. The height of the image is 0.8 cm. What is the height of the object?

For help with question 12, refer to Example 3.

12. Logan places a mirror on the floor 220 cm from the base of a wall. He holds a flashlight 130 cm above the ground, and shines the beam onto the mirror. How far must Logan stand back from the mirror so that the height at which the light shines on the wall is 100 cm greater than the height at which Logan holds the flashlight?

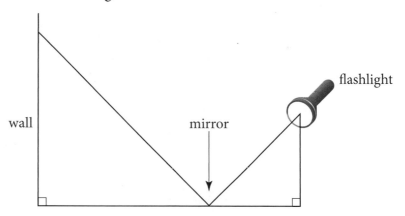

13. Use *The Geometer's Sketchpad*® to simulate finding the height of a tree.
a) Draw a horizontal line to represent the ground.
b) Place two points on the line; one will represent your feet, the other will represent the base of the tree trunk.
c) Construct perpendicular lines through these points.

d) Construct a point on each line, one to represent the top of your head, the other to represent the top of the tree.

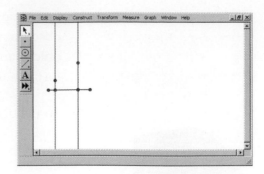

e) Construct segments joining the two points to the ground. Hide the original perpendicular lines.

f) Construct a line from the sky above the tree to the ground. This will represent a ray of sunlight.

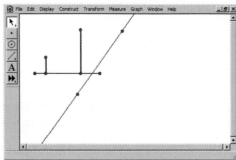

g) Construct two lines parallel to the ray of sunlight, one through the point representing the top of the tree, the other through the point representing the top of your head.

h) Construct the points on the ground where the rays of sunlight intersect the ground.

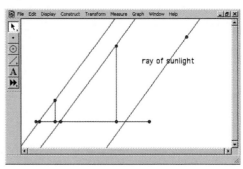

ray of sunlight

Reasoning and Proving

Representing | Selecting Tools

Problem Solving

Connecting | Reflecting

Communicating

i) Construct segments representing the shadows.

j) Use the **Measure** menu to measure the lengths of the line segments representing the heights of the person and of the tree, and the lengths of their shadows. Then, find the ratios comparing corresponding sides of the triangles.

k) Click and drag the line that represents the ray of sunlight to change the angle of elevation of the sun. What happens to the ratios from part j)? Explain.

14. A ski tow rises 39.5 m over a horizontal distance of 118.8 m. What vertical distance have you risen if you have travelled 750.2 m horizontally?

15. In the diagram, $\angle D = \angle A$, AB = 20 cm, CB = 12 cm, and DF = 10 cm. What is the measure of AF?

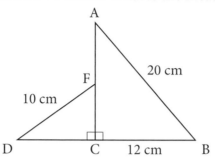

16. Eratosthenes was a mathematician who lived around 230 B.C.E. While living in Egypt, he learned that at noon on the first day of summer (approximately June 21 on the modern calendar), the sun shone directly down into a deep well in the city of Syene. This meant the sun was directly overhead. At the same time, in Alexandria, approximately 800 km almost due north of Syene, the sun's rays hit the ground at an angle of 7.2° from the vertical. Eratosthenes used this information to estimate the circumference of Earth.

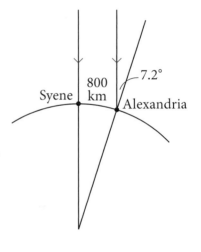

He set up the proportion $\dfrac{7.2°}{360°} = \dfrac{800}{\text{circumference of Earth}}$

a) Solve the proportion to estimate the circumference of Earth.

b) The actual circumference of Earth is approximately 40 000 km. How close was Eratosthenes' estimate?

c) Use your answer from part a) to estimate the diameter of Earth.

Chapter 1 Review

Review of Key Terms

corresponding angles	proportional
corresponding sides	ratio
imperial system	similar triangles
metric system	

1. Copy each sentence, then select the term from the box that best completes the sentence.

   a) A collection of British units is called the _____.

   b) A _____ is one value divided by another.

   c) Two triangles are said to be similar if _____ are equal and the ratios of the lengths of _____ are equal.

   d) Two quantities are _____ if they are related by a constant ratio.

2. Use words and diagrams to explain

   a) corresponding sides.

   b) corresponding angles.

1.1 Imperial Measure, pages 6 to 11

3. Express each measure using the indicated units.

   a) 2.5 ft   inches
   b) 200 fl oz   quarts
   c) 200 oz   pounds

4. A field measures 12' 4" by 26' 6". Find the length of fence needed to surround the field.

5. Taylor is mixing fruit punch for a party. The recipe calls for 2 tsp of sugar for each 8-oz glass of punch. Taylor has a 3 gal punch bowl. How many cups of sugar are needed to fill the bowl with punch?

1.2 Conversions Between Metric and Imperial Measures, pages 12 to 18

6. Express each measure using the indicated units.

   a) 6 km   miles
   b) 6 L   gallons
   c) 22°C   degrees Fahrenheit
   d) 8 m   feet

7. Elle can buy milk at a local farmers' market for $3.58 per gallon or at the grocery store for $3.79 for 4 L. Which is the better buy?

8. The carpet Danil has chosen for his new recreation room costs $8.99 per square metre. The room measures 15 ft by 18 ft. How much will it cost Danil to carpet this room?

9. Caleigh is using an American product to make protein shakes at home. The container calls for 2 tbsp of protein powder in 6 fl oz of milk. How much powder should she use in 1 L of milk?

1.3 Similar Triangles, pages 19 to 29

10. In the diagram, $\triangle ABC \sim \triangle DEF$.

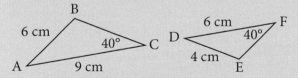

a) List the corresponding angles.

b) List the corresponding sides.

c) State the ratios of the corresponding sides.

d) Write the proportionality statement for the ratios of corresponding sides.

11. Find all the missing measures, given that $\triangle ABC \sim \triangle FED$.

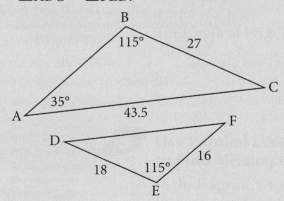

12. In the diagram, DE is parallel to XY, XD = 14.6 cm, ZX = 24.8 cm, and DE = 6.8 cm. Name the similar triangles and find the measure of XY.

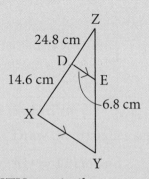

13. Triangles ABC and STU are similar. BC = 30 cm, AB = 40 cm, and TU = 25 cm.

What is the length of side ST?

1.4 Solve Problems Using Similar Triangles, pages 30 to 37

14. To calculate the height of a cliff, a surveyor takes the following measurements. The cliff's shadow is 12 m, while at the same time the shadow of a metre stick is 2 m. Draw a diagram to represent the situation. Find the height of the cliff.

15. To find the width of the White River near where it is spanned by the White River Suspension Bridge, Tina takes the measurements shown in the diagram. What is the width of the river?

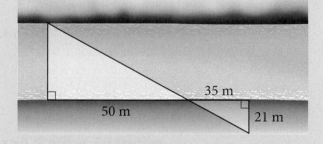

16. Tanesha needs to measure the height of a flagpole. She is 5' 9" tall. She finds that if she stands 12 ft from the base of a flagpole, the top of her head touches the guy wire holding the flagpole up. The guy wire is anchored 15 ft from the base of the pole. How tall is the pole?

1. Approximately how many inches is 10 cm of snow?

2. Approximately how many pounds is 450 g of barley?

3. How many inches is 4 yd?

4. Will a $\frac{3}{8}$" bit drill a hole large enough to fit a 9 mm bolt? Explain.

5. Mingmei is purchasing a new car and would like the gas mileage to be at least 33 mi/gal. She really likes a vehicle whose brochure says it uses 6.5 L/100 km. Does this car meet her minimum requirement? Explain.

6. It is recommended that you consume 1000 mg of calcium daily. One cup of milk contains 300 mg of calcium. If you drink 1 L of milk, will you have consumed the recommended daily amount of calcium? Explain why or why not.

7. Triangles QRS and XYZ are similar.
   a) List the equal angles.
   b) List the corresponding sides.
   c) State the ratios of the corresponding sides.
   d) Write the proportionality statement for the corresponding sides.

8. In the diagram, AB = 2.8 cm, CD = 3.5 cm, CE = 4.4 cm, and ∠A = ∠C. Name the similar triangles. Find the length of AE.

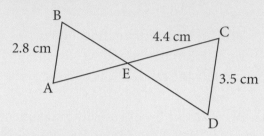

9. In the diagram, DE is parallel to AC, BD = 5, BE = 4, EC = 10. Name the similar triangles. Find the length of BA.

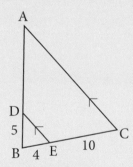

10. Carlos is trying to find the height of a tree. He measures a smaller tree to be 3 m tall. The smaller tree casts a shadow 1.5 m long, while at the same time the shadow of the taller tree is 5 m long. Sketch a diagram to represent the situation, and find the height of the taller tree.

Chapter Problem Wrap-Up

Darren has to cut down a large tree that has become diseased. To do this safely, he must determine the height of the tree and figure out where the top of the tree will land when it falls. Darren marked a horizontal cut line on the tree 50 cm from the ground. Then, Darren cut a stick and held it vertically at arm's length in front of him. He moved away from the tree until he could sight the top of the tree over the top of the stick and the cut line at the bottom of the stick. Darren's reach is 0.8 m, the stick is 0.7 m long and he stood 30 m from the base of the tree.

a) Find the height of the tree.

b) How far from the trunk will the top of the tree land?

c) Describe a different method that Darren could have used to calculate the height of the tree.

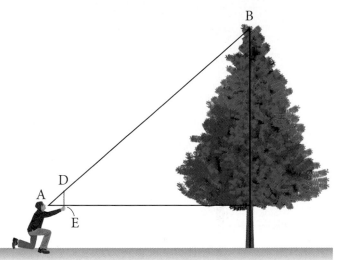

---

11. Sean needs to know the height of a cliff he is about to climb. He places a mirror on the ground 30 ft from the base of the cliff and walks backward until he can see the top of the cliff in the mirror. He walked back 10 ft from the mirror. Sean's eye level is 6 ft above the ground. Sketch a diagram to represent the situation and find the height of the cliff.

12. In the diagram,
BC = 7.2 mm,
CE = 9.3 mm,
and DE = 12.4 mm.
Name the similar
triangles and find
the length of AB.

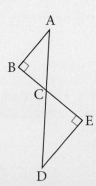

13. Draw a small, simple design on grid paper or using geometry software. Double all the dimensions, and draw a new symbol, similar to the first. Estimate the area of each figure or calculate using geometry software. Is the area of the larger figure double the area of the smaller figure? Now, draw a different large symbol on grid paper. From your previous work, how would you change the dimensions to draw a similar figure with half the area of the first? Explain your deductions and prove by estimating the area of each figure.

2 Right Triangle Trigonometry

Triangles provide strength and stability to structures. Right triangles are frequently used in structures such as bridges and roofs. In this chapter, you will investigate the Pythagorean theorem and the relationships among the side lengths of right triangles. You will apply these relationships to solve problems involving right triangles.

In this chapter, you will

- determine, through investigation, the relationship between the ratio of two sides in a right triangle and the ratio of the two corresponding sides in a similar right triangle, and define the sine, cosine, and tangent ratios
- determine the measures of the sides and angles in right triangles, using the primary trigonometric ratios and the Pythagorean theorem
- solve problems involving the measures of sides and angles in right triangles in real-life applications, using the primary trigonometric ratios and the Pythagorean theorem
- describe, through participation in an activity, the application of trigonometry in an occupation

Reasoning and Proving

Representing | Selecting Tools

Problem Solving

Connecting | Reflecting

Communicating

Key Terms

adjacent side	hypotenuse	sine ratio
angle of depression	legs	tangent ratio
angle of elevation	opposite side	trigonometry
cosine ratio	Pythagorean theorem	

Literacy Link

Use a KWL Chart to organize what you **K**now about the topic you are about to study, what you **W**ant to know about this concept and what you have **L**earned about this topic when you have completed the chapter.

| K
What Do I
KNOW? | W
What Do I
WANT to KNOW? | L
What Have I
LEARNED? |
|---|---|---|
| | | |
| | | |

Cordell works as a carpenter and uses mathematics every day. He uses the relationships in right triangles to ensure corners form 90° angles. There may be a woodworking or sheet metal course offered at your school. Talk to the teacher about the mathematics used in construction projects.

Get Ready!

Solving Proportions

1. Solve each proportion. The first part has been done for you.

a) $\dfrac{x}{15} = \dfrac{1}{5}$

   $5x = 15$

   $x = 3$

b) $\dfrac{x}{3} = \dfrac{18}{27}$ **c)** $\dfrac{12}{42} = \dfrac{x}{14}$

d) $\dfrac{4}{35} = \dfrac{x}{7}$ **e)** $\dfrac{10}{12} = \dfrac{5}{x}$

f) $\dfrac{11}{x} = \dfrac{33}{9}$ **g)** $\dfrac{2}{5} = \dfrac{22}{x}$

h) $\dfrac{24}{15} = \dfrac{x}{5}$ **i)** $\dfrac{34}{x} = \dfrac{17}{45}$

j) $\dfrac{16}{x} = \dfrac{64}{72}$

2. Solve for *x*. Express each answer as a decimal. The first part has been done for you.

a) $\dfrac{x}{18} = \dfrac{3}{15}$

   $15x = 18(3)$

   $15x = 54$

   $\dfrac{15x}{15} = \dfrac{54}{15}$

   $x = 3.6$

b) $\dfrac{4}{48} = \dfrac{x}{9}$ **c)** $\dfrac{32}{6} = \dfrac{5}{x}$

d) $\dfrac{18}{x} = \dfrac{45}{20}$ **e)** $\dfrac{9}{54} = \dfrac{22}{x}$

f) $\dfrac{27}{x} = \dfrac{15}{33}$ **g)** $\dfrac{12}{50} = \dfrac{x}{10}$

h) $\dfrac{27}{12} = \dfrac{x}{5}$ **i)** $\dfrac{4}{x} = \dfrac{45}{36}$

Rounding

3. Round to the nearest degree. The first part has been done for you.

a) 43.66°

   0.66 is closer to 1 than to 0, so 43.66° rounded to the nearest degree is 44°.

b) 12.8°   **c)** 79.2°

d) 58.14°   **e)** 77.6°

f) 90.3°   **g)** 42.18°

4. Round to one decimal place. The first part has been done for you.

a) 4.87

   0.87 is closer to 0.9 than to 0.8, so 4.87 rounded to one decimal place is 4.9.

b) 2.311   **c)** 9.567

d) 3.33   **e)** 5.41

f) 1.99   **g)** 26.98

5. Round to four decimal places. The first part has been done for you.

a) 2.346 11

   0.346 11 is closer to 0.3461 than to 0.3462, so 2.346 11 rounded to four decimal places is 2.3461.

b) 0.099 67   **c)** 3.462 33

d) 0.856 34   **e)** 0.909 11

f) 3.756 432 2   **g)** 31.605 846

Chapter Problem

A resort is located on a rocky ledge, 10 m above the waterfront. Jeff is building an elevator for the convenience of resort guests.

Jeff will have to use mathematics to help him plan and build the elevator system. The Pythagorean theorem and the trigonometric ratios will help Jeff design and construct the elevator.

Jeff needs to think carefully about the materials he will need. Suppose Jeff has a piece of metal 1 m long and he needs two pieces each 0.35 m long. How should he round the lengths in order to cut them and still have some extra to file off?

Squares and Square Roots

6. Find each square. The first part has been done for you.

a) 24^2

$= 24 \times 24$
$= 576$
Alternatively, on your calculator, press 24 $\boxed{x^2}$.

b) 56^2 **c)** 71^2

d) 12^2 **e)** 38^2

f) 19^2 **g)** 27^2

7. Find each square root. Round all answers to one decimal place. The first part has been done for you.

a) $\sqrt{27}$

On a scientific calculator, press $\boxed{\sqrt{\ }}$ *27 or 27* $\boxed{\sqrt{\ }}$.

b) $\sqrt{35}$ **c)** $\sqrt{188}$

d) $\sqrt{287}$ **e)** $\sqrt{1143}$

f) $\sqrt{63}$ **g)** $\sqrt{542}$

8. Evaluate. The first part has been done for you.

a) $3^2 + 6^2$

$= 9 + 36$
$= 45$

b) $7^2 + 1^2$ **c)** $5^2 + 4^2$

d) $12^2 - 8^2$ **e)** $10^2 - 9^2$

f) $6^2 + 11^2$ **g)** $13^2 - 2^2$

2.1

The Pythagorean Theorem

Pythagoras (c. 530 B.C.E.) was a mathematician, philosopher, and astronomer. He believed that everything could be predicted and measured in patterns or cycles. Pythagoras is credited with one of the most useful relationships in mathematics, the **Pythagorean theorem**. The Pythagorean theorem is useful when building structures, such as the International Space Station.

Do you think Pythagoras ever imagined we would still be using the Pythagorean theorem more than 2500 years later ... and in space?

Investigate

Tools

- 1-cm grid paper
- coloured paper
- protractor
- ruler
- scissors
- tape

The Pythagorean Relationship

1. On 1-cm grid paper, draw the three squares in each set. Label the squares with the set number, then cut the squares out. Find the area of each square in square centimetres, and record the area on the square.

   Set 1   squares with each side length: 3 cm, 4 cm, and 5 cm

   Set 2   squares with each side length: 5 cm, 12 cm, and 13 cm

   Set 3   squares with each side length: 6 cm, 8 cm, and 10 cm

   Set 4   squares with each side length: 4 cm, 5 cm, and 6 cm

   Set 5   squares with each side length: 4 cm, 12 cm, and 14 cm

2. Arrange the squares in each set to form a triangle. One side of each square forms one side of the triangle. Tape each arrangement onto a piece of coloured paper.

3. Use a protractor to determine whether any of the triangles contain a right angle.

4. Copy and complete the table based on your observations of the five triangles.

Set	Side Lengths (cm)			Areas of Squares (cm²)			Type of Triangle (right, acute, or obtuse)
1	3	4	5				
2	5	12	13				
3	6	8	10				
4	4	5	6				
5	4	12	14				

5. Look for a pattern in your results. Compare the areas of the squares on the sides of each triangle. Write a sentence to describe the relationship.

6. Look at the last two triangles. Does this relationship hold true for these triangles? How are these two triangles different from the first three?

legs
- the two shorter sides of a right triangle
- the sides adjacent to the right angle

hypotenuse
- the longest side of a right triangle
- the side opposite the right angle

Pythagorean theorem
- the square of the hypotenuse is equal to the sum of the squares of the legs
- for a right triangle with legs a and b and hypotenuse c, $c^2 = a^2 + b^2$

In a right triangle, the two shorter sides are called the **legs**. The **hypotenuse** is the side opposite the right angle; it is the longest side. The **Pythagorean theorem** states that in a right triangle, the square of the hypotenuse is equal to the sum of the squares of the legs.

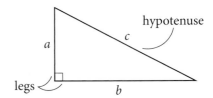

Example **1** **Find the Length of a Roof Truss**

Find the length of a slanting side of this roof truss.

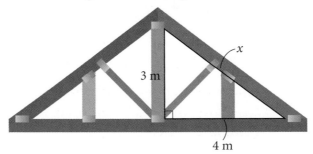

Solution

Part of the roof truss is in the shape of a right triangle. The lengths of the legs are 3 m and 4 m. Use the Pythagorean theorem to find the length of the hypotenuse.

$x^2 = 3^2 + 4^2$
$x^2 = 9 + 16$
$x^2 = 25$
$x = 5$

The slanting side of the roof truss has a length of 5 m.

Example **2** **Find How High a Ladder Will Reach**

Nirmala is planning to wash the windows on her house. She rests a 3-m-long ladder against the side of the house. The foot of the ladder is 1 m from the house. How high up the house will the ladder reach? Round your answer to the nearest hundredth of a metre.

Solution

Draw a diagram to represent the situation.

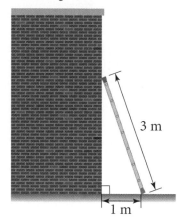

$3^2 = 1^2 + h^2$
$1 + h^2 = 9$
$h^2 = 9 - 1$
$h^2 = 8$
$h = \sqrt{8}$
$h \doteq 2.828$

The ladder will reach approximately 2.83 m up the side of the house.

Key Concepts

- In a right triangle, the hypotenuse is the longest side.

- The square of the hypotenuse is equal to the sum of the squares of the legs.

- You can use the Pythagorean theorem to find the length of one side of a right triangle given the lengths of the other two sides.

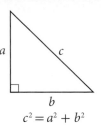

$$c^2 = a^2 + b^2$$

Discuss the Concepts

D1. Explain how you would find the length of w. Compare your answer with that of a classmate.

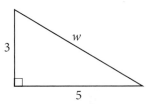

D2. When you look at a right triangle, how can you tell which two sides are the legs? How can you tell which side is the hypotenuse?

Practise the Concepts Ⓐ

For help with questions 1 and 2, refer to Example 1.

1. Find the length of each hypotenuse. Round your answers to one decimal place.

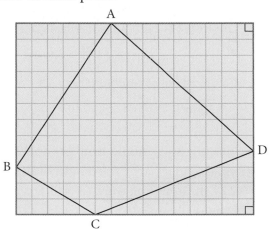

2. Find the length of the hypotenuse to the nearest tenth of a unit.

a)

15 m, 25 m, x

b)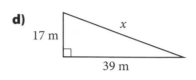

x, 6 cm, 10 cm

c)

12 in., x, 4 in.

d)

17 m, x, 39 m

For help with questions 3 and 4, refer to Example 2.

3. Find the length of the indicated side.

a)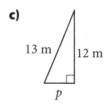

x, 25 m, 15 m

b)

d, 10 m, 6 m

c)

13 m, 12 m, p

d)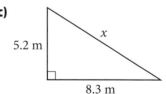

39 m, 15 m, f

4. Find the length of x to the nearest tenth of a metre. Compare your answers with those of a classmate. Did you both get the same answers? Is each answer reasonable?

a)

x, 4 m, 2.2 m

b)

x, 6 m, 3.1 m

c)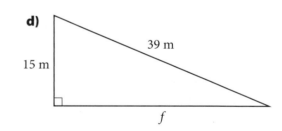

5.2 m, x, 8.3 m

5. Jie-ling walks home from school by walking around two sides of a rectangular park. The length of the park is 125 m and the width is 121 m. If Jie-ling were to walk diagonally across the park, how far would she walk?

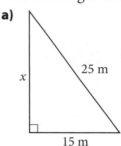

Math Connect

Watch an animation proving the Pythagorean Theorem. Then, demonstrate the Pythagorean Theorem yourself. Go to www.mcgrawhill.ca/links/foundations10 and follow the links.

Reasoning and Proving

Representing | Selecting Tools

Problem Solving

Connecting | Reflecting

Communicating

6. a) The school has to build a wheelchair ramp outside the front doors. The current stairs go through a vertical rise of 1 m. If the ramp is to be 14.6 m long, how far from the school will the ramp start? Round your answer to the nearest tenth of a metre.

b) If there is a wheelchair ramp at your school, with a partner, measure the length of the ramp and its vertical height. Use the Pythagorean theorem to calculate the horizontal distance from the school to the end of the ramp. Then, measure the horizontal distance and compare it to your calculated result.

Literacy Connect

7. A television is described as a 20" television if the screen has a diagonal length of 20".

a) If the screen of a 20" flat-screen television has a height of 12", what is the width?

b) If a new 55" plasma television screen has a height of 35", what is the width of the screen?

c) Do you feel the practice of sizing a television by referring to the diagonal width of its screen is a fair one? Explain.

d) What misconceptions might a customer have when going to buy a television?

e) Explain why you think this practice was started. Do you think it benefits the manufacturer, the retail storeowner, or the customer? Explain your reasoning.

f) In small groups, discuss your answers.

8. Samir is finishing his basement. He needs sheets of drywall that are 4' by 8'. His basement doorway is 85" tall and 36" wide. There is a landing at the top of the basement stairs, so Samir must carry the drywall with the longer side up. Will the drywall fit through the basement door? How do you know?

9. Sam is quilting a table runner of length 38 cm and width 22 cm. Sam will stitch along the diagonal, and then stitch lines parallel to the diagonal.

a) To the nearest centimetre, how long is the diagonal?

b) Build a model of Sam's table runner. Measure the diagonal on your model. Compare the value with the one you calculated in part a) above.

10. Natalya is playing baseball. She catches a ground ball at third base. The player on the opposing team is running toward first base. How far does Natalya have to throw the ball to throw the runner out?

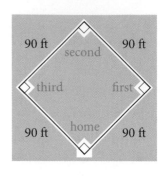

11. Sue and Greg are laying new laminate flooring in their living room. To check that the walls are square, Sue makes marks 3' from the corner along one wall and 4' from the same corner along the other wall. She measures the distance between the marks to be 5' 3". Do the walls in this corner meet at right angles? How do you know?

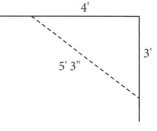

12. Daniel is building a wooden bridge for his daughter's model railroad. He sketches a plan for the bridge. What length of wood does Daniel need to build the bridge?

13. Darlene goes camping with her children. As they set up the tent, they discover that the vertical support poles are missing. What length of pole does Darlene need to buy?

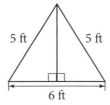

14. Jeff wants to make the cage portion of the elevator (the part in which passengers will ride). He knows he will have to brace each side of the cage.

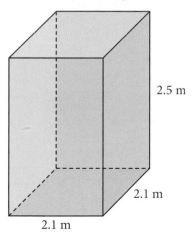

2.5 m

2.1 m

2.1 m

a) If each side of the cage is 2.1 m wide by 2.5 m high, how long will the brace piece be if Jeff wants the brace to go the full diagonal of the side?

b) The base of the cage will be 2.1 m square. What length will the diagonal brace piece for the base of the cage be?

Extend the Concepts **C**

15. A loading ramp is 2.8 m long. One end rests on a loading dock 0.7 m above the ground, and the other end leads into the back of a tractor trailer 1.2 m above the ground. Find the horizontal distance between the back of the truck and the loading dock, to the nearest tenth of a metre.

2.8 m

0.7 m

1.2 m

Explore Ratio and Proportion in Right Triangles

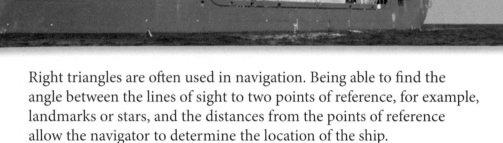

Right triangles are often used in navigation. Being able to find the angle between the lines of sight to two points of reference, for example, landmarks or stars, and the distances from the points of reference allow the navigator to determine the location of the ship.

Investigate

The Ratios of Side Lengths in Similar Right Triangles

Method 1: Use Paper and Pencil

Tools
- calculator
- grid paper
- protractor
- ruler

Work with a partner.

1. Follow these steps to draw a series of similar right triangles:

   a) Draw a horizontal line 20 units long. Label the point on the left A and the point on the right B. From B, extend the horizontal line 10 more units and label the new endpoint C. From C, extend the line 10 more units and label the new endpoint D. The length of AD is 40 units.

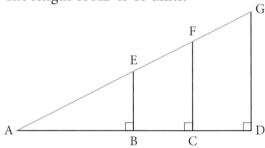

   b) Next, draw vertical line BE 10 units long, CF 15 units long, and DG 20 units long. Draw a line from A to form triangles ABE, ACF, and ADG.

   c) Use the protractor to measure the angle at A.

2. Measure the lengths of AE, AF, and AG. Record the lengths in a table.

3. Use a calculator to write the ratios of side lengths as decimals. Round each answer to two decimal places. Record the ratios in your table.

Triangle	Side Lengths	Ratio 1	Ratio 2	Ratio 3
ABE	AB = BE = AE =	$\dfrac{BE}{AE} =$	$\dfrac{AB}{AE} =$	$\dfrac{BE}{AB} =$
ACF	AC = CF = AF =	$\dfrac{CF}{AF} =$	$\dfrac{AC}{AF} =$	$\dfrac{CF}{AC} =$
ADG	AD = DG = AG =	$\dfrac{DG}{AG} =$	$\dfrac{AD}{AG} =$	$\dfrac{DG}{AD} =$

4. What do you notice about the values in your table?
  a) How are the values in the ratio 1 column related?
  b) How are the values in the ratio 2 column related?
  c) How are the values in the ratio 3 column related?

5. Compare the interior angles in the triangles. What do you notice?

6. Triangles ABE, ACF, and ADG are similar. How do the ratios of side lengths of similar triangles appear to be related?

Method 2: Use *The Geometer's Sketchpad* ®

Tools

- computer
- *The Geometer's Sketchpad* ®

1. Point to the **Straightedge** tool. Click and hold the mouse button to display the three line-drawing tools (**Segment**, **Ray**, and **Line**, in order from left to right). Choose the **Line** tool.

2. Construct line AD so that point D is below and to the right of point A. To do this, click first in the upper left region of the sketch to mark the first point. Then, click in the lower right region of the sketch to mark the second point.

3. Choose the **Text** tool. Click the first point to auto-label it. If the first point does not get labelled A, double-click the label and change it to A. Label the second point D. Drag the label below the line.

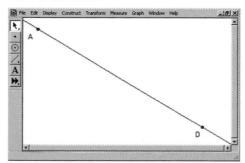

4. Construct horizontal line AC so that point C is to the right of point A. Label point C.

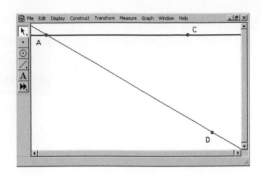

5. Choose the **Selection** tool. Select point C and line AC. Point C and line AC should now both be selected. From the **Construct** menu, choose **Perpendicular Line** to construct a line perpendicular to AC through C.

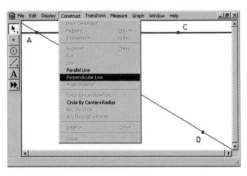

6. Select line AD and the perpendicular line. From the **Construct** menu, choose **Intersection**. Label point of intersection B.

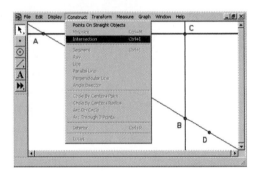

7. Choose the **Selection** tool. Point B is still selected. To deselect, click anywhere in the white background of the sketch. Select points C, then A, and then B. From the **Measure** menu, choose **Angle**. The angle will automatically be measured and will appear selected.

8. To deselect the angle measure, click in the white background of the sketch. Select points A, then C, and then B. From the **Measure** menu, choose **Angle**. The angle measure will appear below the previous angle measure and be selected. Verify that this angle measures 90°.

9. Deselect the previous angle measure. Select point A and then point B. From the **Measure** menu, choose **Distance**. The distance between the two points will automatically be measured and will appear selected. Drag this measure to side AB of the triangle.

10. Repeat step 9 to measure the distance between points B and C. Drag this distance measure to side BC of the triangle.

11. Repeat step 9 to measure the distance between points A and C. Drag this distance measure to side AC of the triangle.

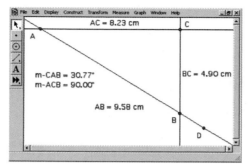

12. Deselect the last measurement by clicking anywhere in the white background of the sketch. Select point C and note that the pointer has become horizontal with the arrowhead pointing at the current location of point C. Press and hold the right arrow key and point C will move to the right. Notice that the pointer has not moved and still marks the original location of point C before you moved it. Do the measures of the angles change? Do the lengths of the sides change? Press and hold the left arrow key to return point C to its original location (tip of arrowhead).

13. Point C should still be selected. Use the arrow keys to move point C to four different positions, making sure not to change the size of the angles. Copy the table, and complete using a calculator. Round all values to two decimal places.

	Lengths			Ratios		
Triangle	AB	BC	AC	$\dfrac{BC}{AB}$	$\dfrac{AC}{AB}$	$\dfrac{BC}{AC}$
1						
2						
3						
4						

14. Complete this statement to summarize your findings: "Although each triangle has side lengths that are different, the ratios ..."

Example 1   Name the Sides and Angles in a Right Triangle

Name the sides of the triangle relative to the angle at A.

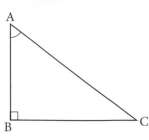

adjacent side
- the side that forms one of the arms of the angle being considered, but is not the hypotenuse

opposite side
- the side that does not form one of the arms of the angle being considered
- across from the angle being considered

Solution

Two sides of the triangle form the arms of ∠A. They are the hypotenuse, AC, and one of the legs, AB. Because side AB forms one of the arms of ∠A, it is the **adjacent side** to ∠A. The third side, BC, is across from ∠A. It is the **opposite side**.

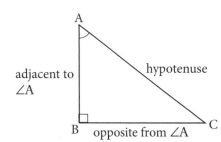

Example 2   Find the Ratio Comparing Side Lengths

Given △GHJ, write a ratio comparing the length of the side opposite ∠G to the length of the hypotenuse. Then, express the ratio as a decimal, rounded to three decimal places.

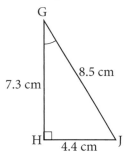

Solution

Side HJ is opposite ∠G. The length of HJ is 4.4 cm.
Side GJ is the hypotenuse. The length of GJ is 8.5 cm.

$$\frac{HJ}{GJ} = \frac{4.4}{8.5}$$
$$\doteq 0.518$$

Key Concepts

- The opposite side and the adjacent side of a right triangle are named relative to the angle being considered.

- In a right triangle, the hypotenuse is always the side opposite the right angle.

- Ratios comparing the side lengths of right triangles can be expressed as fractions or as decimals.

Discuss the Concepts

D1. Explain how to tell which side in a right triangle is the hypotenuse.

D2. Your friend missed class and wants to know an easy way to decide which side is opposite and which is adjacent to an angle in a right triangle. What would you say to your friend to help?

Practise the Concepts **A**

For help with questions 1 and 2, refer to Example 1.

Math Connect

Ancient Egyptian surveyors used a length of rope that was divided into 12 equal parts using 11 knots. Forming a triangle with sides in the ratio 3:4:5 created a right angle, which was used extensively in surveying and building.

1. Copy each triangle. Label the hypotenuse, the opposite, and the adjacent sides relative to the marked acute angle.

a)

b)

c)

d)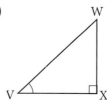

e)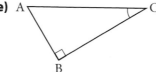

f)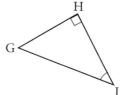

2. Copy each right triangle. Label the hypotenuse, the opposite side, and the adjacent side relative to the marked angle.

a)

b)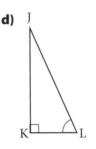

c)

d)

For help with questions 3, 4, and 5, refer to Example 2.

3. Write the ratio comparing the length of the side opposite the marked angle to the length of the hypotenuse. Then, express the ratio as a decimal, rounded to three decimal places.

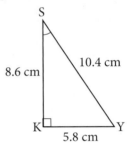

4. Write the ratio comparing the length of the adjacent side to the length of the hypotenuse for the marked angle. Then, express the ratio as a decimal, rounded to three decimal places. Compare answers with a classmate.

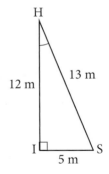

5. Write the ratio comparing the length of the opposite side to the length of the adjacent side for the marked angle. Then, express the ratio as a decimal, rounded to three decimal places.

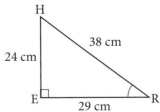

6. Write the ratio comparing the length of the opposite side to the length of the hypotenuse for the marked angle. Then, express the ratio to two decimal places.

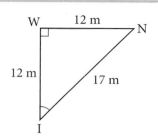

7. Write the ratio comparing the length of the adjacent side to the length of the hypotenuse for the marked angle. Measure the side lengths to the nearest tenth of a centimetre. Then, express the ratio to two decimal places.

a)

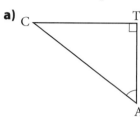

b)

8. **a)** Draw triangle XYZ with a right angle at Y and side lengths XY = 3 m, YZ = 4 m, and XZ = 5 m.
   b) Write the ratio comparing the length of the adjacent side to the length of the hypotenuse with respect to angle X.

Literacy Connect

9. **a)** Make up your own example to find the ratio comparing the length of the opposite side to the length of the hypotenuse.
   b) Build a model of your example.
   c) Trade your example and model with a classmate.

10. **a)** Draw a rectangle 3 cm by 3 cm. Label the vertices A, B, C, and D.
    b) Draw diagonal AC.
    c) For each of the right triangles formed, identify the side opposite ∠A, the side adjacent to ∠A, the side opposite ∠C, and the side adjacent to ∠C.
    d) For each triangle, write the ratios comparing the lengths of the sides opposite and adjacent to ∠A and of the sides opposite and adjacent to ∠C. What do you notice?
    e) Will the result you found in part d) be the same for rectangles of any size? Explain your answer.

11. Jeff has now built the elevator cage that he began in Section 2.1. The floor of the cage is 2.1 m square with a diagonal brace piece. The sides of the cage are 2.1 m by 2.5 m, also with diagonal braces.

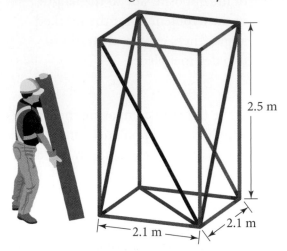

a) For the base, find the ratio of the length of the horizontal piece to the length of the brace.
b) For the side, find the ratio of the length of the vertical piece to the length of the brace.
c) For the side, find the ratio of the horizontal piece to the length of the brace piece.

Extend the Concepts

12. Draw △ABC with a right angle at B and legs each of length 17 units.
a) Find the length of the third side. Round your answer to the nearest tenth.
b) Write the ratio comparing the length of the opposite side to the length of the adjacent side with respect to angle A.

13. Draw triangle XYZ with a right angle at Y and legs each of length 1 unit.
a) Find the length of the third side. Round your answer to the nearest tenth.
b) Find the ratio comparing the length of the opposite side to the length of the hypotenuse with respect to angle X.
c) Find the ratio comparing the length of the opposite side to the length of the hypotenuse with respect to angle Z.

2.3 The Sine and Cosine Ratios

On breezy days, you can often find people flying kites. You might even find a kite-flying competition at your local park or beach. The height the kite reaches depends upon the length of the string and the angle of the string to the ground. **Trigonometry**, or *triangle measurement*, is the study of angles and triangles. In this and the next three sections, you will use trigonometry to calculate side lengths and angles in right triangles.

trigonometry
- means *triangle measurement*
- used to calculate lengths of sides and measures of angles in triangles

Investigate

Tools
- calculator
- grid paper
- protractor
- ruler

The Sine and Cosine Ratios

Method 1: Use Paper and Pencil

Work with a partner.

1. Use a ruler and a protractor to construct three similar right triangles, ABC, DEF, and GHJ. Label the vertices of the triangles so that the right angles are at B, E, and H. The angles at A, D, and G are corresponding angles. Label the angles at A, D, and G as x. Label the angles at C, F, and J as y.

2. Measure and record the side lengths and angles in each triangle.

3. Copy and complete the table. Write the ratios of side lengths as decimals, rounded to four decimal places.

Triangle	Ratio 1 — Length of side opposite x / Length of hypotenuse	Ratio 2 — Length of side adjacent x / Length of hypotenuse	Ratio 3 — Length of side opposite y / Length of hypotenuse	Ratio 4 — Length of side adjacent y / Length of hypotenuse
ABC				
DEF				
GHJ				

4. The sine ratio compares the length of the side opposite the angle being considered to the length of the hypotenuse. Ratios 1 and 3 are sine ratios.

$$\sin x = \frac{\text{length of side opposite } x}{\text{length of hypotenuse}}$$

$$\sin y = \frac{\text{length of side opposite } y}{\text{length of hypotenuse}}$$

Compare sin x and sin y. What do you notice?

5. The cosine ratio compares the length of the side adjacent to the angle being considered to the length of the hypotenuse. Ratios 2 and 4 are cosine ratios.

$$\cos x = \frac{\text{length of side adjacent to } x}{\text{length of hypotenuse}}$$

$$\cos y = \frac{\text{length of side adjacent to } y}{\text{length of hypotenuse}}$$

Compare cos x and cos y. What do you notice?

6. Compare sin x and cos y. What do you notice? Explain. Is this true for sin y and cos x? Explain.

Method 2: Use *The Geometer's Sketchpad* ®

Tools

- computer
- *The Geometer's Sketchpad* ®

1. Choose the **Segment** tool. Construct a vertical line segment AB by creating two points, one directly above the other. Choose the **Text** tool. Click each of the endpoints to label them A and B.

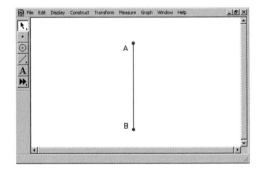

2. Choose the **Selection** tool. Select line segment AB and point B. From the **Construct** menu, choose **Perpendicular Line**. This will create a line perpendicular to AB through point B.

3. The perpendicular line will be selected. From the **Construct** menu, choose **Point On Object**. Choose the **Text** tool, and label this point C. The point will be selected. If the point is **not** on the right side of point B, press and hold the right arrow key until point C is on the right side of point B. If point C is already on the right side of point B, go to the next step.

4. Choose the **Selection** tool. Select points A and C. From the **Construct** menu, choose **Segment**. This will construct line segment AC.

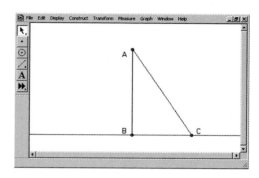

5. Click somewhere in the white background of the sketch to deselect line segment AB. Click the line passing through BC to select it. From the **Display** menu, choose **Hide Perpendicular Line** to hide the line.

6. Select points B and C. From the **Construct** menu, choose **Segment** to construct line segment BC.

7. From the **Edit** menu, choose **Preferences**. Click the **Units** tab and set **Precision** for **Angle**, **Distance**, and **Other** (**Slope**, **Ratio**, ...) to **hundred thousandths**. Click **OK**.

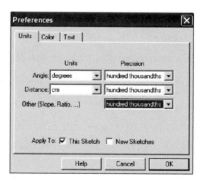

8. Click anywhere in the white background of the sketch to deselect line segment BC. Select point A, then C, and then B. From the **Measure** menu, choose **Angle**.

9. Deselect the previous angle measure. Select point C, then point A, and then point B. From the **Measure** menu, choose **Angle**.

10. Deselect the previous measure. Select point A and then point B. From the **Measure** menu, choose **Distance**. Drag the measurement to side AB of the triangle.

11. Repeat step 10 to determine the distance measures of line segments BC and AC. Drag the measurements to the appropriate sides of the triangle. Deselect the last distance measure.

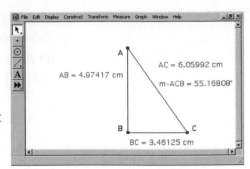

12. Select point C, and drag the point left and then right. Do the angles being measured change? Do the lengths of the sides change?

13. Copy the table. Record the lengths of sides AB, BC, and AC, and the measures of ∠ACB and ∠CAB in your table for triangle 1 (first row only).

Triangle	AB	BC	AC	∠ACB	∠CAB	$\dfrac{AB}{AC}$	sin ∠ACB	$\dfrac{BC}{AC}$	cos ∠ACB
1									
2									
3									
4									

14. From the **Measure** menu, choose **Calculate**. Click the distance measure of AB, then click the division button, and then click the distance measure of AC. Click **OK**. The ratio $\dfrac{AB}{AC}$ will be displayed. Record the value of the ratio in the table. Drag the ratio to the left of the sketch.

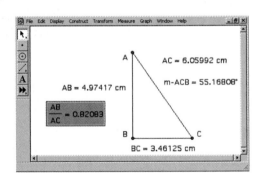

sine ratio

• the ratio comparing the length of the side opposite the angle to the length of the hypotenuse in a right triangle

• $\sin A = \dfrac{\text{length of side opposite } A}{\text{length of hypotenuse}}$

15. From the **Measure** menu, choose **Calculate**. Click **Functions**, and then click **sin**. Click the measure of ∠ACB. Click **OK** to calculate the **sine ratio** for ∠ACB. Record sin ∠ACB in your table.

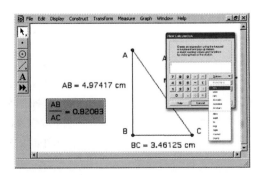

16. Repeat step 14 to find the ratio $\dfrac{BC}{AC}$. Record the value of the ratio in your table.

17. From the **Measure** menu, choose **Calculate**. Click **Functions**, and then click **cos**. Click the measure of $\angle ACB$. Click **OK** to calculate the **cosine ratio** for $\angle ACB$. Record cos $\angle ACB$ in your table.

cosine ratio
- the ratio comparing the length of the side adjacent to the angle to the length of the hypotenuse in a right triangle
- $\cos A = \dfrac{\text{length of side opposite } A}{\text{length of hypotenuse}}$

18. Drag vertices A and C to change the distance measures of all the sides and the angle measures. Record the side lengths, the measures of the angles, the ratios of side lengths, sin $\angle ACB$, and cos $\angle ACB$ in the next row of the table.

19. Repeat step 18 two more times to complete the last two rows of your table.

20. Use the data in your table. For each triangle, compare the value of the ratio $\dfrac{AB}{AC}$ with the value of sin $\angle ACB$. Compare the value of the ratio $\dfrac{BC}{AC}$ with the value of cos $\angle ACB$. What do you notice in each case?

21. Extend your table to add two more columns at the right with headings cos $\angle CAB$ and sin $\angle CAB$. Use a calculator to calculate cos $\angle CAB$ and sin $\angle CAB$ for the four triangles. Make sure that your calculator is in Degree Mode. Complete the table for the data that has been recorded.

cos $\angle CAB$	sin $\angle CAB$

22. Compare the value of sin $\angle ACB$ and the value of cos $\angle CAB$ for each row of the table. What do you notice? Compare the value of sin $\angle CAB$ and the value of cos $\angle ACB$ for each row of the table? What do you notice?

Example 1 — Find the Length of a Side

Find the length of side AB, to the nearest tenth of a centimetre.

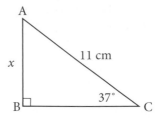

Solution

In the diagram, the length of the hypotenuse is 11 cm. AB is the side opposite ∠ACB. Use the sine ratio.

$$\sin 37° = \frac{x}{11}$$

$$11 \sin 37° = x$$

$$x \doteq 6.619$$

On a scientific calculator, enter 11 × sin 37 =.

The length of side AB is approximately 6.6 cm.

Example 2 — Let's Go Fly a Kite

Jamie's kite string is 35 m long. It makes an angle of 50° with the ground. Let x be the horizontal distance, in metres, to the kite. What is the horizontal distance between the kite and Jamie?

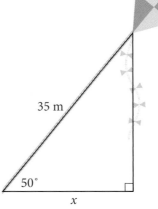

Solution

The length of the hypotenuse is 35 m. The side x is adjacent to the 50° angle. Use the cosine ratio.

$$\cos 50° = \frac{x}{35}$$

$$35 \cos 50° = x$$

$$x \doteq 22.497$$

On a scientific calculator, enter 35 × cos 50 =.

The horizontal distance between Jamie and the kite is approximately 22.5 m.

Example 3

Install an Escalator

Jay is supervising the installation of an escalator at a new office building. The escalator will make an angle of 30° with the ground and will rise a vertical distance of 20 ft.

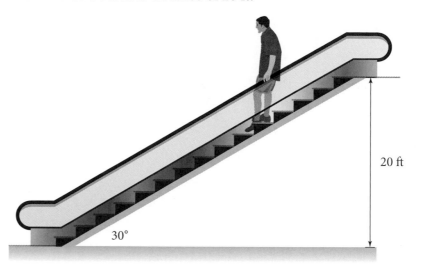

20 ft

30°

a) What is the length of the escalator?

b) Suppose the escalator travels at a rate of 100 feet per minute. How long will it take to travel from the lower floor to the upper floor?

Solution

a) The length of the side opposite the 30° angle is 20 ft. The length of the escalator is the hypotenuse. Use the sine ratio.

$$\sin 30° = \frac{20}{x}$$

$$x \sin 30° = 20$$

$$x = \frac{20}{\sin 30°}$$

On a scientific calculator, enter 20 ÷ sin 30 =.

$$x = 40$$

The escalator is 40 ft long.

b) The escalator will take $\frac{40}{100} \times 60 = 24$ s to reach the upper level.

Example **4** **Find the Measure of an Angle**

A storm caused a 13.5-m hydro pole to lean over. The top of the pole is now 11.8 m above the ground. Find the measure of the angle between the hydro pole and the ground, to the nearest degree.

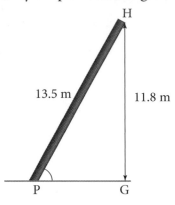

Solution

The length of the hypotenuse is 13.5-m. The length of the side opposite ∠P is 11.8 m. Use the sine ratio.

$$\sin P = \frac{11.8}{13.5}$$
$$\angle P \doteq 71.468$$

On a scientific calculator, enter
2nd sin (11.8 ÷ 13.5)= or
(11.8 ÷ 13.5) 2nd sin =.

The hydro pole makes an angle of 71° with the ground.

Key Concepts

- The sine and cosine ratios compare the lengths of the legs of a right triangle to the length of the hypotenuse.

$$\sin A = \frac{\text{opposite}}{\text{hypotenuse}} \qquad \cos A = \frac{\text{adjacent}}{\text{hypotenuse}}$$

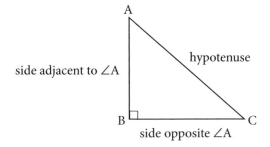

- The sine and cosine ratios can be used to find side lengths and angle measures in right triangles.

Practise the Concepts (A)

For help with question 1, refer to Example 1.

1. Use a scientific calculator to find each value to four decimal places.

  a) sin 42°   **b)** sin 33°   **c)** cos 19°

  d) sin 88°   **e)** cos 74°   **f)** cos 38°

  g) sin 45°   **h)** cos 42°

2. Use a scientific calculator to find the measure of each angle A to the nearest degree.

  a) sin A = 0.6092   **b)** cos A = 0.4067   **c)** sin A = 0.1425

  d) sin A = 0.7777   **e)** cos A = 0.3907   **f)** sin A = 0.2861

  g) cos A = 0.5736   **h)** cos A = 0.7193

For help with questions 3 and 4, refer to Examples 1 and 2.

3. Find x to the nearest tenth of a centimetre.

a)   **b)**

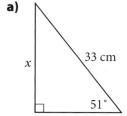

4. Find the length of side AB, to one decimal place, in △ABC.

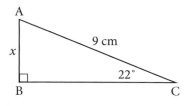

> **Math Connect**
>
> Geoscientists use their understanding of angles and their ability to manipulate trigonometric expressions in coastal geology, mineralogy, and geologic mapping.

For help with question 5, refer to Example 3.

5. In △XYZ, ∠X = 90°, ∠Z = 51° and XY = 15 cm. Find the length YZ.

For help with question 6, refer to Example 4.

6. Find the measure of angle K to the nearest degree.

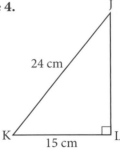

24 cm

K — 15 cm — L

Apply the Concepts **B**

7. In △DEF, ∠E is a right angle and length DF is 13.4 cm. If ∠F is 33°, what is the length of DE, to the nearest tenth of a centimetre?

8. A 5-m-long ladder is leaning up against the side of a barn. It reaches 4.2 m up the side of the barn wall. Find the angle the ladder makes with the ground.

9. Ron is building a skateboard ramp for his granddaughter Alexis. Ron wants the ramp to rise at an angle of 12°. If he also wants the ramp to rise vertically 0.5 m how long will the ramp need to be?

Reasoning and Proving

Representing | Selecting Tools

Problem Solving

Connecting | Reflecting

Communicating

10. A custodian secures a ladder of length 10 m against the side of the school. The ladder makes an angle of 70° with the ground. Will the custodian be able to reach a window that is 7.5 m above the ground? Justify your answer.

11. Hannah wants to make a lean-to shelter against a tree. She starts with a plank that is 2.1 m long. If she wants to have a 45° angle between the ground and the lower end of the plank, how far away from the base of the tree should the lower end of the lean-to be?

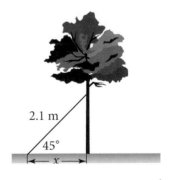

2.1 m

45°

x

Chapter Problem

12. Jeff will use right triangles in his design for the elevator to take resort guests down the cliff. He plans to have an angle of 45°, and a diagonal length of 1.2 m. How long will the vertical piece for this part of the elevator be?

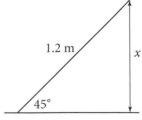

1.2 m

x

45°

Literacy Connect   **13.** Explain how the sine and cosine ratios are related.

14. Hugo has his own small plane. He is planning his approach to the Kingston airport. He wants to descend at an angle of 22° from horizontal. If he starts his descent at an altitude of 10 000 ft, how long is his glide path to the runway?

....

Achievement Check

15. The Canadian Standards Association states that the angle between a ladder and the ground must be between 70° and 80° for safety.

  a) If you have a 6-m ladder, find the maximum and minimum heights the ladder can reach.

  b) A 12-m ladder is leaning against a building so that it reaches a height of 11.5 m. Is this ladder positioned safely according to the Canadian Standards Association? Explain.

  c) Compare your answers to parts a) and b). Can you solve part b) without using trigonometry, by using the answer to part a)? Explain.

Extend the Concepts

16. The hypotenuse of a right triangle is 17.9 cm long.

  a) How long is the side opposite an angle that measures 27°, to the nearest tenth of a centimetre?

  b) What is the measure of the third angle in this triangle?

  c) How long is the side opposite the angle found in part b), to the nearest tenth of a centimetre?

17. a) If an isosceles triangle has base angles that measure 50°, and the height of the triangle is 3.2 cm, how long are the equal sides, to the nearest tenth of a centimetre?

  b) Confirm your answer to part a) by constructing this isosceles triangle.

18. Construct an isosceles triangle with equal sides 6 cm long and base 9 cm long. What is the measure of each base angle, to the nearest degree?

2.4 The Tangent Ratio

Kakabeka Falls on the Kaministiquia River near Thunder Bay, Ontario, is often called The Niagara of the North. It is the largest waterfall in the area surrounding Lake Superior. The falls plunge over sheer cliffs that contain some of the oldest fossils in the world. Measuring the height of the falls directly would be very difficult. In this section, you will explore another trigonometric ratio that is useful for finding distances that are difficult or impossible to measure directly.

Investigate

Tools

- calculator
- grid paper
- protractor
- ruler

The Tangent Ratio

Method 1: Use Paper and Pencil

Work with a partner.

1. Use a ruler and a protractor to construct a triangle MNP with the right angle at N.

2. Measure and record the side lengths and angles in the triangle.

3. The tangent ratio compares the length of the side opposite a particular angle to the length of the side adjacent to that angle.

$$\tan A = \frac{\text{length of side opposite A}}{\text{length to side adjacent to A}}$$

Find tan M. Round your answer to four decimal places.

4. Construct triangles STU and PQR similar to MNP so the angles at S and P correspond to the angle at M. Measure and record the side lengths and angles in each triangle.

5. Find tan S and tan P. Round your answers to four decimal places.

6. How do tan M, tan S, and tan P compare? Explain.

Tools

- computer
- *The Geometer's Sketchpad* ®

Method 2: Use *The Geometer's Sketchpad* ®

1. Choose the **Segment** tool. Construct a vertical line segment AB. Use the **Text** tool to label the points A and B.

2. Choose the **Selection** tool. Select line segment AB and point B. From the **Construct** menu, choose **Perpendicular Line**. This will create a line perpendicular to AB through point B.

3. The perpendicular line will be selected. From the **Construct** menu, choose **Point On Object**. Use the **Text** tool to label this point C. The point will be selected. If the point is **not** on the right side of point B, press and hold the right arrow key until point C is on the right side of point B. If point C is already on the right side of point B, go to the next step.

4. Choose the **Selection** tool. Select points A and C. From the **Construct** menu, choose **Segment**. This will construct line segment AC.

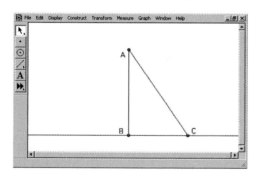

5. Click anywhere in the white background of the sketch to deselect line segment AB. Select the line passing through BC. From the **Display** menu, choose **Hide Perpendicular Line** to hide the line.

6. Select points B and C. From the **Construct** menu, choose **Segment** to construct line segment BC.

7. From the **Edit** menu, choose **Preferences**. Click the **Units** tab and set **Precision** for **Angle, Distance,** and **Other** (**Slope, Ratio, ...**) to **hundred thousandths.** Click **OK.**

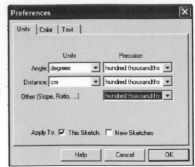

8. Deselect line segment BC. Select point A, then C, and then B. From the **Measure** menu, choose **Angle**.

9. Deselect the previous angle measure. Select point C, then point A, and then point B. From the **Measure** menu, choose **Angle**.

10. Deselect the previous measure. Select point A and then point B. From the **Measure** menu, choose **Distance**. Drag the measurement to side AB of the triangle.

11. Repeat step 10 to determine the distance measures of line segments BC and AC. Drag the measurements to the appropriate sides of the triangle. Deselect the last distance measure.

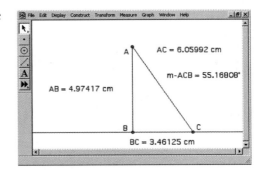

12. Select point C, and drag it left and then right. Do the angle measures change? Do the side lengths change?

13. Copy the table. Record the lengths of sides AB and BC, and the measures of ∠ACB and ∠CAB in your table for triangle 1 (first row only).

Triangle	AB	BC	∠ACB	∠CAB	$\frac{AB}{BC}$	tan ∠ACB	$\frac{BC}{AB}$	tan ∠CAB
1								
2								
3								
4								

14. From the **Measure** menu, choose **Calculate**. Click the distance measure of AB, then click the division button, and then click the distance measure of BC. Click **OK**. The ratio $\dfrac{AB}{BC}$ will be displayed. Record the value of the ratio in the table. Move the ratio to the left of the sketch.

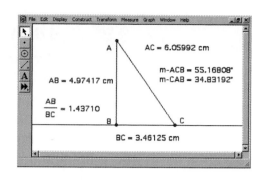

15. From the **Measure** menu, choose **Calculate**. Click **Functions** and then click **tan**. Click the measure of ∠ACB. Click **OK** to calculate the **tangent ratio** for ∠ACB. Record tan ∠ACB in your table.

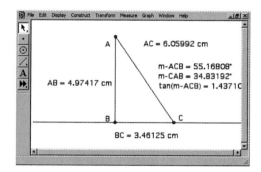

tangent ratio
- the ratio comparing the length of the side opposite the angle to the length of the side adjacent to the angle in a right triangle
- $\tan B = \dfrac{\text{length of side opposite } B}{\text{length of side adjacent to } B}$

16. Repeat step 14 to find the ratio $\dfrac{BC}{AB}$. Record the value of the ratio in your table.

17. Repeat step 15 to calculate the tangent ratio for ∠CAB. Deselect the measure. Record tan ∠CAB in the table.

18. Drag vertices A and C to change the distance measures of all the sides and the angle measures. Record the side lengths, the measures of the angles, the ratios of side lengths, tan ∠ACB, and tan ∠CAB in the next row of the table.

19. Repeat step 18 two more times to complete the last two rows of the table.

20. Use the data in your table. For each triangle, compare the value of the ratio $\dfrac{AB}{BC}$ with the value of tan ∠ACB. Compare the value of the ratio $\dfrac{BC}{AB}$ with the value of tan ∠CAB. What do you notice in each case?

21. Is there an angle for ∠ACB and ∠CAB for which tan ∠ACB = tan ∠CAB? Manipulate your sketch to explore this question. Explain the significance of your findings.

Example 1

Find the Height of a Waterfall

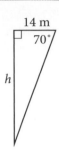
14 m
70°
h

Anysha stands 14 m to one side of the top of Kakabeka Falls. Her line of sight to the base of the falls forms a 70° angle down from the horizontal. What is the height, h, of the falls, to the nearest metre?

Solution

The length of the side adjacent to the 70° angle is 14 m.
h is the length of the side opposite the 70° angle.
Use the tangent ratio.

$$\tan 70° = \frac{h}{14}$$

$14 \tan 70° = h$ *On a scientific calculator, enter 14 × tan 70 =.*

$40.464 \doteq h$

The height of Kakabeka Falls is approximately 40 m.

Example 2

Find the Horizontal Distance for a Wheelchair Ramp

Elena is building a wheelchair ramp to a deck that is 90 cm high. The angle between the ramp and the ground must not be greater than 6°. Find the minimum allowable horizontal distance, d, between the start of the ramp and the deck, to the nearest tenth of a metre.

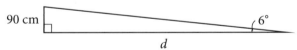
90 cm
6°
d

Solution

The length of the side opposite the 6° angle is 90 cm.
d is the length of the side adjacent to the 6° angle.
Use the tangent ratio.

$$\tan 6° = \frac{90}{d}$$

$d \tan 6° = 90$

$$d = \frac{90}{\tan 6°}$$ *On a scientific calculator, enter 90 ÷ tan 6 =.*

$d \doteq 856.292$

The minimum horizontal distance between the start of the ramp and the deck is approximately 856 cm or 8.6 m.

| **Example** | **3** | **Find the Angle Between a Wire and the Ground** |

A tower is supported by a wire. The wire is attached to the tower at a height of 19 m and to the ground 8.1 m from the base of the tower. Calculate the measure of the angle formed by the wire and the ground, to the nearest degree.

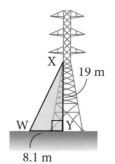

Solution

19 m is opposite ∠W. 8.1 m is adjacent to ∠W. Use the tangent ratio.

$$\tan W = \frac{19}{8.1}$$

On a scientific calculator, enter 2nd tan (19 ÷ 8.1) =.

$$\angle W \doteq 66.911$$

The wire makes an angle of approximately 67° with the ground.

Key Concepts

- The tangent ratio compares the lengths of the legs of a right triangle.

$$\tan A = \frac{\text{opposite}}{\text{adjacent}}$$

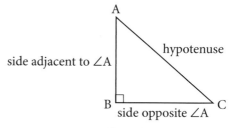

- The tangent ratio can be used to find side lengths and angle measures in right triangles.

Discuss the Concepts

D1. Explain why the tangent ratio for any right triangle depends only on the measure of the angle and not on the size of the triangle.

D2. Explain how you would use the tangent ratio to find the length of a side in a right triangle.

Practise the Concepts **A**

1. Use a scientific calculator to find each value to four decimal places.
   a) tan 28°   **b)** tan 36°
   c) tan 45°   **d)** tan 72°

2. Find the measure of each angle A to the nearest degree.
   a) tan A = 0.3443   **b)** tan A = 2.2460
   c) tan A = 28.6363   **d)** tan A = 1.5399

For help with question 3, refer to Example 1.

3. Find the height of the tower to the nearest tenth of a metre.

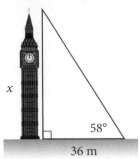

x

58°

36 m

For help with question 6, refer to Example 2.

4. Find the distance from the boat to the base of the lighthouse, to the nearest metre.

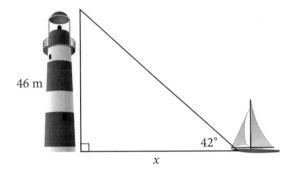

46 m

42°

x

Apply the Concepts **B**

5. In a right triangle, the side adjacent to an angle of 44° is 45 cm long. Draw the triangle. How long is the side opposite the angle, to the nearest centimetre?

6. In a right triangle, the side opposite an angle that measures 34° is 12 cm long. Draw the triangle. How long is the side adjacent to the angle, to the nearest centimetre?

7. To improve traffic flow in a city, a bridge will be built over a ravine. A surveyor stands 35 ft to one side of the site of the proposed bridge. From this point, he measures a 47° angle between his lines of sight to the two ends of the proposed bridge. Find the length of the bridge to the nearest foot.

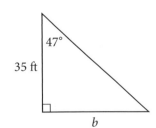

47°

35 ft

b

8. A mnemonic is a memory aid. A commonly used mnemonic for the trigonometric ratios is SOH CAH TOA.
   a) Explain the meaning of the letters in SOH CAH TOA.
   b) Write your own mnemonic to help you remember the trigonometric ratios. Explain how your mnemonic works.

9. A ship's navigator observes a lighthouse on a cliff. She locates the lighthouse on a chart, and notes that the top of the lighthouse is 23.9 m above sea level. She measures the angle from the sea to the top of the lighthouse to be 0.6°.

According to the chart, the area at the base of this cliff is very dangerous. For safety, ships are advised to remain at least 2 km from the base of the cliff. Is the ship safe? How do you know?

10. A carpenter is building trusses for a roof. The height at the centre of the truss needs to be 32.2 cm. If the angle at the base of the truss is to be 17°, what is the full length of the base of the truss? Does this answer seem reasonable? Explain.

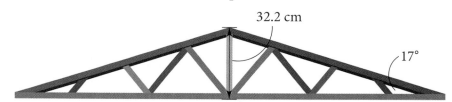

For help with question 11, refer to Example 3.

11. An airplane flying at an altitude of 7.5 km starts its descent 200 km from the airport. At what angle down from the horizontal will the airplane descend?

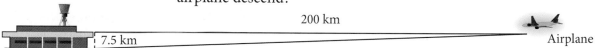

12. A ladder leans against a vertical wall and makes an angle of 76° with the ground. The foot of the ladder is 1.8 m from the base of the wall. How high up the wall is the top of the ladder, to the nearest tenth of a metre?

13. Jeff decides to put some extra bracing in the elevator shaft section. The width of the shaft is 1.2 m, and he decides to place bracing pieces so they reach a height of 0.75 m. At what angle from the horizontal must Jeff put the brace?

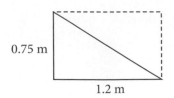

Achievement Check

14. The Cathedral Bluffs in Toronto, Ontario, are eroded sandstone cliffs that rise 90 m above Lake Ontario. Natalie is 1.4 m tall. From her position at the top of the cliffs, the angle between the surface of the lake and her line of sight to a boat is 39°. Find the distance between the boat and the base of the cliffs to the nearest tenth of a metre.

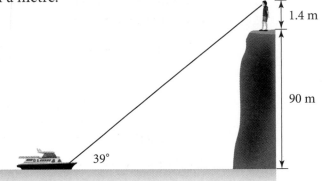

Extend the Concepts C

15. A cone just fits inside a can. The diameter of the can is 7.6 cm and its height is 10.4 cm. Find the angle at the vertex of the cone.

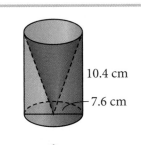

16. A roof truss spans a width of 36' and has a height of 8'. The sides that join at the top of the truss are equal in length.

a) Find the angle formed by the two sides that join at the top of the truss.

b) Find the length of the equal sides.

2.5 Solve Problems Using Right Triangles

Surveyors use an instrument called a transit to find lines of sight and measure angles.

Another tool that can be used to measure angles is a clinometer. In the Investigate, you will build a clinometer and use it to find the height of an object, such as a tall tree or your school building.

Investigate

Tools
- drinking straw
- measuring tape
- paper clips
- protractor
- tape
- thin string

Math Connect

A clinometer is a similar device to a mariner's quadrant. How could a mariner's quadrant tell ancient mariners their latitude?

Use a Clinometer to Measure Angles

Work with a partner.

1. Follow these steps to build your clinometer:

   a) Tie a paper clip to one end of a piece of thin string.
Tie the other end around the middle of a drinking straw.

   b) Tape the drinking straw along the base of a protractor, carefully making sure that the string is at the centre.

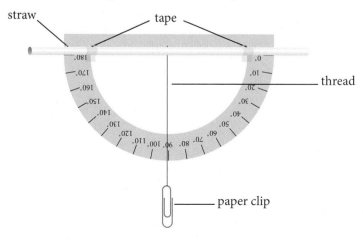

straw · tape · thread · paper clip

2. Choose a tall object, such as a tree. Follow these steps to find the height of the object:
   a) Measure and record the horizontal distance between you and the base of the object.
   b) Hold the clinometer with the straw on top and the paper clip hanging down. Tip the clinometer up until you can see the top of the object through the straw. Record the measure of the angle between the string and the straw.
   c) The angle between the string and the straw and the angle between the horizontal and the line of sight to the object are complementary angles. To find the angle of elevation, subtract the angle found in part b) from 90°.
   d) Use a trigonometric ratio to calculate the height of the object.

3. Compare your results with those of another pair of students who measured the same object.

To talk about angles, we need to have a reference point. Sometimes, we use an **angle of elevation** or an **angle of depression** .

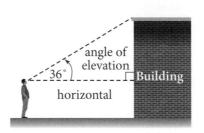

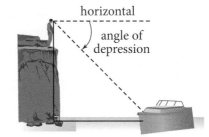

Example	1	**Find the Height of a Tree**

From a point 8.5 m from the base of a tree, the angle of elevation to the top of the tree is 36°. Find the height of the tree to the nearest tenth of a metre.

Solution

Sketch and label a diagram. 8.5 m is the length of the side adjacent to 36°. The height of the tree, x, is the length of the side opposite 36°. Use the tangent ratio.

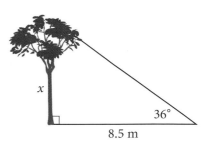

$$\tan 36° = \frac{x}{8.5}$$

$$8.5 \tan 36° = x$$

$$x \doteq 6.175$$

The tree is approximately 6.2 m tall.

Example 2

Find the Heights of Two Buildings

Two buildings are 41.6 m apart. From the roof of the shorter building, the angle of elevation to the top of the taller building is 44° and the angle of depression to the base of the taller building is 29°. Find the heights of the buildings to the nearest tenth of a metre.

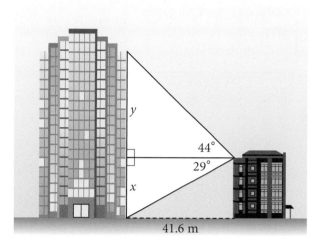

Solution

Find the height of the shorter building.

$$\tan 29° = \frac{x}{41.6}$$

$$41.6 \tan 29° = x$$

$$x \doteq 23.059$$

Find the vertical distance from the top of the shorter building to the top of the taller building.

$$\tan 44° = \frac{y}{41.6}$$

$$41.6 \tan 44° = y$$

$$y \doteq 40.172$$

The height of the taller building is the height of the shorter building plus the vertical distance from the top of the shorter building to the top of the taller building.

$$x + y = 23.059 + 40.172$$

$$= 63.231$$

The height of the shorter building is approximately 23.1 m, and the height of the taller building is approximately 63.2 m.

Key Concepts

- The trigonometric ratios and angles of elevation or depression can be used to find hard-to-measure distances.
- When solving problems involving right triangles, sketch and label a diagram then identify the angle of interest, the hypotenuse, and the sides opposite and adjacent to the angle of interest.

Discuss the Concepts

D1. What is the difference between an angle of elevation and an angle of depression?

Practise the Concepts (A)

1. Find the length of BC to the nearest tenth of a metre.

A

12.2 m

33°

B   x   C

For help with questions 2 to 4, refer to Example 1.

2. 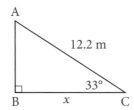 From a point 4.5 m from the base of a wind turbine, the angle of elevation to the top of the turbine is 87°. Find the height of the wind turbine to the nearest tenth of a metre.

3. From a point 9.3 m from the base of a billboard, the angle of elevation to the top of the billboard is 28°. Find the height of the billboard to the nearest tenth of a metre.

4. A forest ranger is in a fire tower 120 ft above the ground. She sights a fire at an angle of depression of 3°. How far is the fire from the base of the tower, to the nearest foot?

5. From the top of a 38.5 m-high cliff, the angle of depression to a boat is 38°. How far is the boat from the base of the cliff, to the nearest metre?

6. A 4-m long ladder is leaning up against the side of a garage. It reaches 3.8 m up the side of the garage wall. Find the angle the ladder makes with the ground, to the nearest degree.

Reasoning and Proving

Representing | Selecting Tools

Problem Solving

Connecting | Reflecting

Communicating

7. A lighthouse sits at the top of a cliff. The top of the lighthouse is 41 m above the water. The angle of depression to a small sailboat is 22°. Describe how you would find the distance from the sailboat to the base of the cliff.

8. Tonya is standing 17 m from the base of a tower. She measures the angle of elevation to the top of a tower to be 33°. What is the height of the tower, to the nearest metre?

9. A flagpole casts a shadow 22 m long when the sun's rays make an angle of 30° with the ground. How tall is the flagpole, to the nearest metre?

10. Marlene is making a pen in her backyard for her daughter's pet rabbits. She makes the pen in the shape of a right triangle. Two sides of the pen each measure 3 m. What is the length of the third side?

For help with question 11, refer to Example 2.

11. Two buildings are 15 m apart. From the top of the shorter building, the angle of elevation to the top of the taller building is 48°, and the angle of depression to the bottom of the taller building is 34°. Find the heights of the two buildings to the nearest tenth of a metre.

12. The horizontal distance between two hydro poles is 86 m. The angles of elevation to the tops of the poles are 14° and 17° as measured from a point halfway between the poles. What is the difference in the heights of the hydro poles, to the nearest tenth of a metre?

13. The plan shows the specifications for a fastener. At what angle from the horizontal should the cut be made to form the tapered end of the fastener?

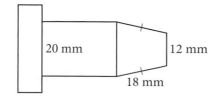

Review of Key Terms

Copy each definition, then write the word or phrase that best matches the definition.

1. A formula relating the lengths of the hypotenuse and the two legs of a right triangle.

2. The ratio comparing the length of the side opposite a particular angle to the length of the hypotenuse.

3. The ratio comparing the length of the side adjacent to a particular angle to the length of the hypotenuse.

4. The ratio comparing the length of the side opposite a particular angle to the length of the side adjacent to the same angle.

   A. the sine ratio

   B. the tangent ratio

   C. the Pythagorean theorem

   D. the cosine ratio

2.1 The Pythagorean Theorem,
   pages 46 to 53

For all questions, answer to the nearest degree or the nearest tenth of a unit.

5. As part of basic training, Chandra must climb a slanted net to reach the top of a wall. The net is 120 ft long and is anchored to the ground 100 ft from the base of the wall. How high is the wall?

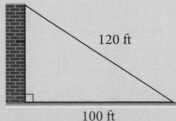

6. A rectangular piece of material 150 cm wide by 45 cm long was cut along the diagonal to form two congruent triangles. What is the length of the longest side of one of the triangles?

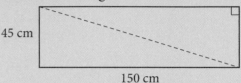

45 cm

150 cm

7. Brian enjoys hang-gliding. On his last flight, he jumped off a cliff 520' high. He landed 450' from the base of the cliff. How far did Brian travel?

2.2 Explore Ratios and Proportions in Right Triangles, pages 54 to 62

8. Copy △VWX into your notebook.

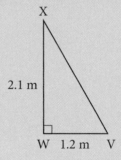

X

2.1 m

W   1.2 m   V

   a) For ∠V, find the ratio of the length of the opposite side to the length of the adjacent side.

   b) For ∠X, find the ratio of the length of the adjacent side to the length of the opposite side.

   c) What do you notice about these two ratios?

2.3 The Sine and Cosine Ratios, pages 63 to 73

9. Find the measure of the indicated angle.

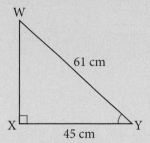

10. A meteorologist is tracking a cloud formation. The angle of the line of sight from the weather station to the cloud formation is 28° and the slant range is 65 km. Find the horizontal distance to the cloud formation.

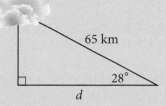

11. A firefighter leans an 11-m long ladder against a building. If the ladder makes an angle of 72° with the ground, how high up the building does the ladder reach?

2.4 The Tangent Ratio, pages 74 to 82

12. Find the length of side EF.

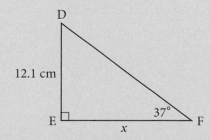

13. An airplane climbing at a constant angle relative to the ground has reached an altitude of 4 km. At this point, the plane has travelled a horizontal distance of 14 km. What is the angle at which the airplane is climbing?

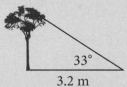

14. A spotlight is aimed at an angle of 50° up from the ground. It is 50 ft from the base of a signpost and shines on a sign at the top of the signpost. How high is the sign?

2.5 Solve Problems With Right Triangles, pages 83 to 87

15. From a point 3.2 m from the base of a tree, the angle of elevation to the top of the tree is 33°. Find the height of the tree.

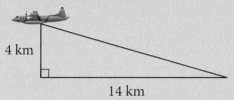

16. The angle of elevation to the top of the school is 37° from where you are standing 11.2 m from the wall of the school. Find the height of the school.

17. From a spot 60' from the base of a building, Shanav measures the angle of elevation to the top of the building to be 48°, and the angle of elevation to the top of an antenna on top of the building to be 56°.

a) Find the height of the building.

b) Find the height of the antenna.

1. State the Pythagorean theorem and draw a triangle to illustrate the theorem.

2. a) Copy the diagram. Label the sides as hypotenuse, opposite, and adjacent relative to angle A.

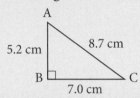

   b) Find sin A. Round your answer to four decimal places.

3. a) Copy the diagram. Label the sides as hypotenuse, opposite, and adjacent relative to angle M.

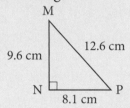

   b) Find cos M. Round your answer to four decimal places.

4. a) Copy the diagram. Label the sides as hypotenuse, opposite, and adjacent relative to angle S.

   b) Find tan S. Round your answer to four decimal places.

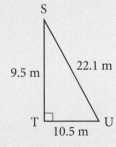

5. Find the length of the indicated side to the nearest tenth of a centimetre.

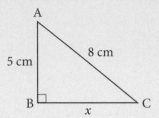

6. Find the length of the indicated side to the nearest tenth of a centimetre.

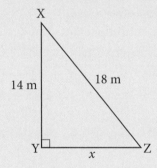

7. In a right triangle, the side opposite the 43° angle is 5 cm long.

   a) How long is the hypotenuse, to the nearest tenth of a centimetre?

   b) How long is the third side, to the nearest tenth of a centimetre?

8. In a right triangle, the side adjacent to the 55° angle is 7 cm long.

   a) How long is the hypotenuse, to the nearest tenth of a centimetre?

   b) How long is the third side, to the nearest tenth of a centimetre?

Chapter Problem Wrap-Up

Jeff is finally ready to begin building the elevator. He needs to calculate how much material he will need. He wants each side of the passenger cage to be 2.1 m wide and 2.5 m tall. He plans to put a brace on each diagonal.

a) How long will the brace be?

b) What angle will the brace make with the ground?

c) Which ratio did you use to calculate this angle?

d) Check that you have the correct angle by using each of the other two possible ratios to find the angle the brace makes with the ground.

9. The Leaning Tower of Pisa is approximately 55 m tall. Over the years, the tower tipped until it was approximately 4.5 m out of vertical alignment.

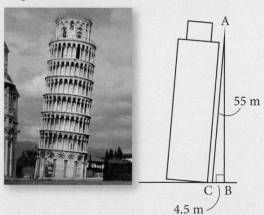

a) Find the measure of the angle between the tower and the ground to the nearest degree.

b) Find the vertical height of the tower to the nearest tenth of a metre.

10. The walls of Miles Canyon in the Yukon Territories rise about 50' above the Yukon River. From a spot on the edge of the canyon wall, Lia measures the angle of depression to a boulder to be 46° and the angle of depression to a second boulder to be 51°. Both boulders lie in the same line of sight. What is the horizontal distance between the boulders, to the nearest foot?

Task

Fix Up a Neighbourhood Park

The city has given a school a project to fix up a local community park. The entire park property is rectangular, measuring 30 m by 40 m.

1. A fountain will be installed in the centre of the park. Water will fall down three tiers of triangular plates, which are similar isosceles triangles. The diagram below shows a top view of the fountain.

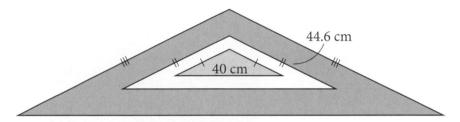

44.6 cm

40 cm

a) The smallest tier has area 196 cm². Find the height and the lengths of the equal sides of the smallest triangle.

b) The area of the middle tier is four times the area of the smallest tier. Find the length of the base of the middle tier.

c) The lowest tier has four times the area of the middle tier. Find the lengths of the sides of the bottom tier.

2. The park design will include wheelchair ramps to make the park accessible. Each ramp has an angle of elevation of 4.5°. There are two entrances to the park. The curb at one entrance is 16 cm high and the curb at the other entrance is 28 cm high.

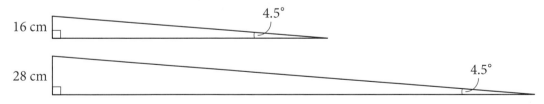

16 cm

4.5°

28 cm

4.5°

a) How far from the curb must each ramp start?

b) What is the length of each ramp?

3. In the park, there is a dead tree where the fountain will be placed. The tree will be removed. Three benches and a hedge surround the tree. At 3 p.m. the length of the shadow cast by the tree is 4.3 m. At the same time, the shadow cast by an object 1.6 m tall is 1.2 m long. The hedge is 4.9 m from the tree. Can the tree be cut at ground level, or does it need to be taken down in pieces to avoid damaging the hedge and benches? How do you know?

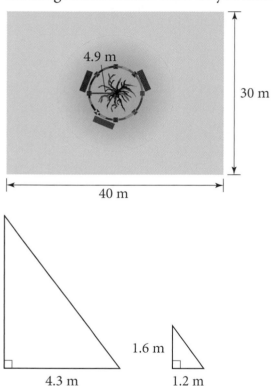

4. Make a scale drawing or three-dimensional model of the park. Add any extra features you think are needed. Include all the dimensions and any calculations involved in your design.

Chapter 1
Measurement Systems and Similar Triangles

1. A room measures 20 ft by 12 ft. The new floor will have ceramic tiles that are 9 in. by 9 in.
   a) Find the area of the room in square feet.
   b) Find the area of a tile in square feet.
   c) Use your answers from a) and b) to find how many tiles are needed.
   d) A box contains 24 ceramic tiles. How many boxes of tiles are needed for the floor?
   e) If each box of tiles costs $116, how much will the tiles cost, before taxes?

2. Adam is travelling in North Carolina at 80 km/h. He sees this sign: Myrtle Beach 225 mi. How long will it take him to get to Myrtle Beach if he maintains his current speed?

3. Which is the better buy for ground beef: $2.29/lb or $4.90/kg?

4. Find the missing side length and angle measures. Round to one decimal place where needed.
   a) Given △ABC ~ △DEF.

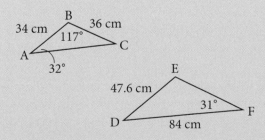

b) Given △GHI ~ △KJI.

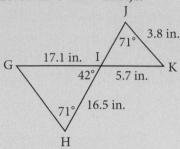

5. On a sunny day, Albert, who is 1.85 m tall, casts a shadow 0.76 m long. At the same time, a nearby flagpole casts a shadow 14.2 m long. How tall is the flagpole to the nearest tenth of a metre?

6. Albert places a mirror 7.2 m in front of the flagpole in question 5. How far back from the mirror does he have to be to see the top of the flagpole in the mirror? Give your answer to the nearest tenth of a metre.

7. The distance across a gorge is 63 ft. Susan stands at the front of the elevated observation deck, 6 ft back from the edge of the gorge. Her eye level is 8 ft from the ground. She can just see the bottom of the cliff on the other side. How deep is the gorge, to the nearest foot?

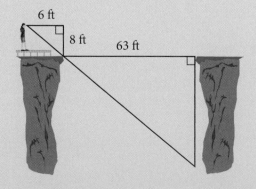

Chapter 2
Right Triangle Trigonometry

8. Use the Pythagorean theorem to find the length of the indicated side to the nearest tenth of a centimetre.

a)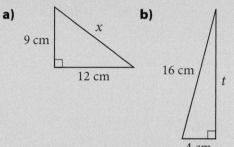

b)

9. A 10 ft extension ladder is positioned to reach 7.4 ft up a wall.

a) How far away from the base of the wall is the ladder?

b) Anthony extends the ladder to 16 ft and lays it back against the wall, without moving the base. How far up the wall will the ladder reach now?

10. Write the three trigonometric ratios for the marked angles.

a)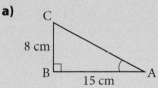

b)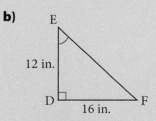

11. A ramp is being built to roll barrels onto a platform. The platform is 6 ft high and the angle of the ramp is to be 30° from the horizontal. How long will the ramp be?

12. The angle of elevation from a boat, 100 m from the base of a cliff to the top of the cliff, is 42°. How high is the cliff?

13. Two buildings are 30 m apart. From the top of the shorter building, the angle of elevation to the top of the second building is 37°. The angle of depression to the bottom of the second building is 47°. Find the height of the second building.

14. A zip line is attached to two platforms of different heights. The horizontal distance between the platforms is 50 m. From the higher platform, the angle of depression of the zip line is 20°. How long is the zip line?

3 Linear Relations

Many situations can be modelled by a graph that is a straight line: for example, the distance travelled by a high-speed train moving at a constant rate of speed, the total cost of printing digital pictures, and the relationship between the side length and the perimeter of a square. In this chapter, you will build on many of the concepts of linear relations developed in previous grades.

In this chapter, you will

- connect the rate of change of a linear relation to the slope of the line, and define the slope as the ratio $m = \dfrac{\text{rise}}{\text{run}}$
- identify, through investigation, $y = mx + b$ as a common form for the equation of a straight line, and identify the special cases $x = a$, $y = b$
- identify, through investigation with technology, the geometric significance of m and b in the equation $y = mx + b$
- identify, through investigation, properties of the slopes of lines and line segments, using graphing technology to facilitate investigations, where appropriate
- graph lines by hand, using a variety of techniques
- determine the equation of a line, given its graph, the slope and y-intercept, the slope and a point on the line, or two points on the line

Reasoning and Proving

Representing | Selecting Tools

Problem Solving

Connecting | Reflecting

Communicating

Key Terms

coefficient	rate of change	run	y-intercept
linear relation	rise	slope	

Literacy Link

Create a Verbal/Visual T-chart using pictures and/or words to help you model linear relations.

Picture/Word	Description
slope	

A truck driver works with linear relationships in many ways. Preparing for the slope of an approaching hill, calculating earnings related to the number of kilometres driven, and using the scale of a map to calculate distances are just a few. Developing a good sense of linear relations is a valuable skill for the job.

Get Ready!

Common Factors

1. Find the greatest whole number that divides evenly into the numbers in each pair. The first part has been done for you.

   a. 18, 21

   The factors of 18 are 1, 2, 3, 6, 9, and 18. The factors of 21 are 1, 3, 7, and 21. The greatest whole number that divides evenly into both 18 and 21 is 3.

   b) 5, 20

   c) 6, 9

   d) 8, 12

   e) 9, 12

   f) 5, 11

   g) 49, 84

   h) 24, 36

Operations With Fractions and Decimals

2. Express each fraction in lowest terms. The first part has been done for you.

   a) $\dfrac{16}{12}$

   $= \dfrac{16 \div 4}{12 \div 4}$

   $= \dfrac{4}{3}$

   b) $\dfrac{4}{10}$

   c) $\dfrac{2}{12}$

   d) $\dfrac{6}{24}$

   e) $\dfrac{15}{45}$

   f) $\dfrac{8}{15}$

3. Copy and complete the table.

	Fraction	Decimal
a)	$\dfrac{1}{2}$	
b)	$\dfrac{3}{5}$	
c)	$\dfrac{3}{8}$	
d)		0.25
e)		0.05
f)		0.625

Operations With Integers

4. Subtract. The first part has been done for you.

   a) $5 - (-8)$

   $= 5 + 8$

   $= 13$

   b) $4 - 6$

   c) $-2 - 2$

   d) $-5 - 7$

   e) $-2 - (-6)$

   f) $4 - (-9)$

5. Evaluate. Simplify each numerator and denominator first.

   a) $\dfrac{6 - 4}{3 - 7}$

   b) $\dfrac{2 - 5}{4 - 3}$

   c) $\dfrac{-4 - 8}{2 - 6}$

   d) $\dfrac{0 - 8}{-3 - 1}$

   e) $\dfrac{3 - (-2)}{-12 - (-2)}$

   f) $\dfrac{-7 - (-4)}{6 - (-5)}$

Chapter Problem

Jim drives a tractor-trailer. His job takes him throughout eastern Canada and through much of the eastern United States. Throughout this chapter, you will see how Jim uses mathematics to solve problems and how having knowledge of linear relations is a requirement of his job.

Graphing on a Coordinate Grid

6. Write the coordinates of each point. The first one has been done for you.

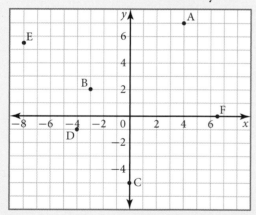

The coordinates of point A are (4, 7).

Working With Variables

7. Solve for x. The first part has been done for you.

a) $-3x = 6$

$$\frac{-3x}{-3} = \frac{6}{-3}$$
$$x = -2$$

b) $4x - 16 = 0$

c) $2.5x = -15$

d) $\frac{1}{2}x = -7$

e) $-\frac{1}{4}x = -3.5$

f) $0.6x = 2.4$

8. Evaluate each expression for $x = -3$.

a) $4x + 3$

b) $-2x + 7$

c) $-6 - x$

d) $2 - 1.5x$

e) $14x - 4$

f) $\frac{1}{2}x + \frac{3}{2}$

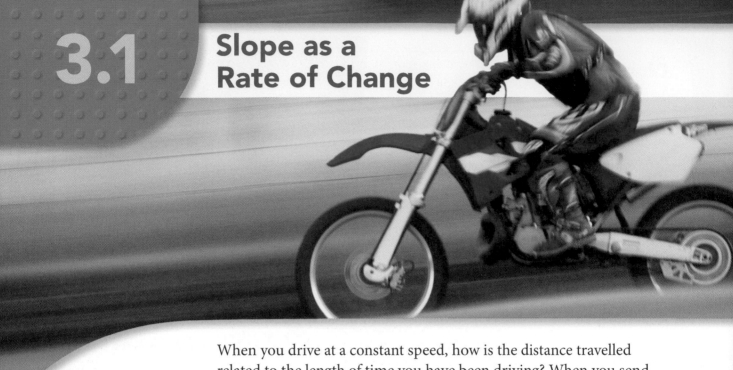

3.1

Slope as a Rate of Change

When you drive at a constant speed, how is the distance travelled related to the length of time you have been driving? When you send text messages, how is the total cost related to the number of text messages sent? These situations can be represented using a table of values, a graph, or an equation. In this section, you will make connections between each of these different representations by solving problems that involve constant rates of change.

Investigate

Tools

- grid paper
- graphing calculator
- ruler

Text Messaging

A wireless communications company charges its customers 15¢ per message for text messaging.

1. a) Make a table of values like the one shown. Copy and complete the table for 10 text messages.

Number of Messages Sent	Total Cost ($)	Rate of Change in Total Cost ($)
0	0	
1	0.15	$0.15 - 0 = 0.15$
2	0.30	$0.30 - 0.15 = 0.15$
3	0.45	$0.45 - 0.30 = 0.15$

rate of change
- a change in one quantity relative to the change in another quantity

b) What do you notice about the values for the **rate of change**? Why do you think this is the case?

2. Calculate the cost of sending each number of text messages.

a) 20   **b)** 30   **c)** 40

d) 50   **e)** 100   **f)** x

3. In each case, suppose you have sent the given number of text messages. Predict the change in the total cost if you send one more text message. Justify your answer.

a) 10   **b)** 49   **c)** 98

4. a) On grid paper, draw a graph comparing the total cost to the number of messages sent. Plot total cost on the vertical axis with scale increasing by increments of $0.15 from $0 to $1.50. Plot the number of messages sent on the horizontal axis with scale increasing in increments of 1 from 0 to 10.

b) Describe the shape formed by the points on the graph. Why does the graph have this shape?

5. a) Enter data from the table into a graphing calculator.

- Press [STAT]. Select **1:Edit**. Enter the values for number of messages sent in LIST 1 (L1) and enter the values for total cost in LIST 2 (L2).
- Press [2nd] [STAT PLOT]. Press [ENTER]. Set up Plot 1 as shown.
- Press [ZOOM]. Select **9:ZoomStat**.

b) Compare this graph to the graph you drew in question 4.

c) Press [Y=] and in Y1 enter 0.15X. Press [GRAPH]. What do you notice?

6. a) Draw a line through the points on your graph from question 4.

b) Choose any two points on the line. Find the **rise** and the **run**. Calculate the **slope** of the line.

c) Calculate the slope of the line using two other points on the line. How does this result compare to your result from part b)? Explain.

d) In question 5, you graphed the line $y = 0.15x$ on the same set of axes as the data from the table of values. Explain how the slopes you calculated in parts b) and c) relate to the equation of the line $y = 0.15x$ and to the rate of change of total cost.

In the Investigate, the change in total cost relative to the change in the number of text messages sent is constant. This is an example of a **linear relation**.

---

rise
- the vertical distance between two points on a line

run
- the horizontal distance between two points on a line

slope
- the steepness of a line
- compares the vertical distance to the horizontal distance between two points
- the slope of a line is equal to $\dfrac{\text{rise}}{\text{run}}$

linear relation
- a relation between two variables that appears as a straight line when graphed

| Example | **1** | **Calculate the Slope of a Given Line** |

The graph shows the number of squares used in each part of this pattern. The points are joined to show the trend.

Diagram   1   2   3   4   5

a) Determine the rise from point M to point N.

b) Determine the run from point M to point N.

c) Calculate the slope of the line.

d) What information about the pattern does the slope give? Explain.

Solution

a)

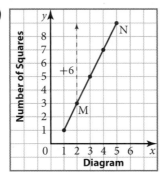

The rise is 6 units.

b)

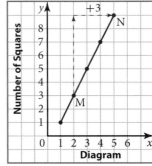

The run is 3 units.

c) slope $= \dfrac{\text{rise}}{\text{run}}$

$= \dfrac{6}{3}$

$= 2$

The slope of the line is 2.

The slope of this line is +2. This means that each time the x-value increases by 1, the y-value increases by 2. On the graph, the line goes up from left to right.

d) The slope shows the rate of change in the number of squares. Each diagram in the pattern has 2 more squares than the previous diagram.

Remember, the slope represents a rate of change. It shows how quickly the y-values are changing compared to the x-values.

Example **2**

Calculate Rates of Change

For the linear relation $y = 3x + 1$, create a table of values, then determine the rate of change in the y-values.

Solution

Choose values for x, then substitute them into the equation and solve to find the corresponding y-values.

x	y
0	1
1	4
2	7
3	10
4	13
5	16

For $x = 1$

$$y = 3x + 1$$
$$= 3(1) + 1$$
$$= 4$$

For $x = 2$

$$y = 3x + 1$$
$$= 3(2) + 1$$
$$= 7$$

Find the difference between consecutive y-values to determine the rate of change in the y-value each time the x-value increases by 1. Add a column to the table of values to record the rate of change.

x	y	Rate of Change
0	1	
1	4	$4 - 1 = 3$
2	7	$7 - 4 = 3$
3	10	$10 - 7 = 3$
4	13	$13 - 10 = 3$
5	16	$16 - 13 = 3$

The rate of change in the y-value is 3 each time the x-value increases by 1.

Example 3

Calculate the Slope for a Given Equation

For the line $y = -2x + 4$, make a table of values and graph the line. Then, use the graph to find the slope of the line.

Solution

Choose values for x, then find the corresponding y-values.

x	y
−2	8
−1	6
0	4
1	2
2	0
3	−2

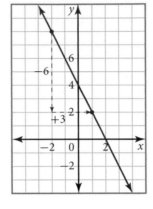

The rise is the vertical distance from (−2, 8) to (−2, 2), which is −6. The run is the horizontal distance from (−2, 2) to (1, 2), which is +3.

$$\text{slope} = \frac{\text{rise}}{\text{run}}$$

$$= \frac{-6}{3}$$

$$= -2$$

The slope of the line $y = -2x + 4$ is −2.

The slope of this line is −2. This means that each time the x-value increases by 1, the y-value decreases by 2. On the graph, the line goes down from left to right.

Example 4

Find the Rate of Change in Earnings

Sam earns $8 per hour babysitting the children next door.

a) Make a table of values showing Sam's total earnings for up to 5 hours of babysitting.

b) Determine the rate of change in Sam's total earnings.

c) Graph Sam's earnings.

d) Find the slope of the line. How is the slope related to the rate of change from part b)? Explain.

Solution

a)

Hours Worked	Total Earnings ($)
0	0
1	8
2	16
3	24
4	32
5	40

Sam earns $8 for each hour of babysitting, so multiply the hours worked by 8 to find the total earnings.

b) Determine the rate of change in Sam's total earnings each time the number of hours of babysitting increases by 1. Add a column to the table of values to record the rate of change.

Hours Worked	Total Earnings ($)	Rate of Change
0	0	
1	8	$8 - 0 = 8$
2	16	$16 - 8 = 8$
3	24	$24 - 16 = 8$
4	32	$32 - 24 = 8$
5	40	$40 - 32 = 8$

The rate of change is $8 per hour. This is Sam's hourly rate.

c) Graph the data. Plot hours worked along the horizontal axis, and total earnings along the vertical axis. Connect the points with a straight line.

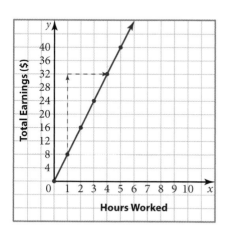

d) Use the graph. Choose any two points on the line. Using the points (1, 8) and (4, 32), the rise is 24 and the run is 3.

$$\text{slope} = \frac{\text{rise}}{\text{run}}$$
$$= \frac{24}{3}$$
$$= 8$$

The slope of the line is 8. This is equal to the rate of change; it is Sam's hourly rate of pay.

Discuss the Concepts

D1. When you are given the graph of a line, how can you tell, without calculating, whether the slope of the line is positive or negative?

D2. How can you determine the rate of change from a table of values?

D3. When finding the slope of a line from the graph, does it matter which points are selected? Explain.

Practise the Concepts **A**

For help with question 1, refer to Example 1.

1. For each graph, determine the rise and the run between the pairs of points shown, then calculate the slope.

a)

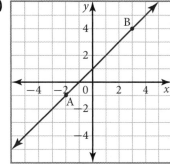

b)

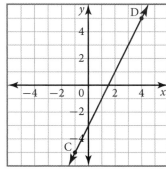

c)

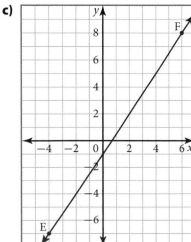

d)

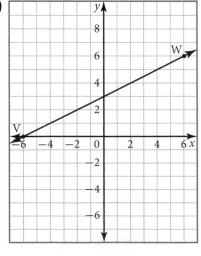

For help with question 2, refer to Example 2.

2. For each linear relation, create a table of values for $x = 0, 1, 2, 3,$ and 4. Then, determine the rate of change in the y-values.

a) $y = 2x + 5$

b) $y = x + 3$

c) $y = 4x - 2$

For help with questions 3, 4, 5, and 6, refer to Example 3.

3. Graph the relation in each table of values.

a)

x	y
0	−3
1	−1
2	1
3	3
4	5

b)

x	y
0	7
1	4
2	1
3	−2
4	−5

c)

x	y
−4	1
−2	2
0	3
2	4
4	5

4. For the tables of values in question 3 parts a) and b), determine the rate of change in the y-values for each increase of 1 in the x-values.

5. A downtown parking garage charges $2.50 per hour after 6 p.m.

PARKING RATES
Rates include GST and PST

30 min or less	$3.75
1 h or less	$7.50
1 h 30 min or less	$15.00
2 h or less	$22.50
Over 2 h	$8.00 per hour

NIGHT RATE
| After 6 p.m. | $2.50 per hour |

WEEKENDS and HOLIDAYS
| from 6 a.m. to 10 p.m. | $7.00 per hour |

a) Create a table of values that shows total charges for up to 5 h of parking.

b) Show the rate of change in total charges for each hour parked.

6. For each linear relation, create a table of values and graph the line.
   a) $y = x - 2$
   b) $y = 2x - 3$
   c) $y = 3x + 1$

7. Determine the rise and the run between the given endpoints, then calculate the slope of each line segment.

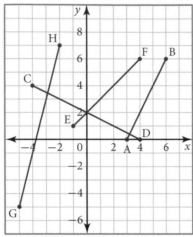

For help with questions 8 and 9, refer to Example 4.

8. Bim picked peaches last summer. His potential earnings are displayed in the table.

Baskets Picked	1	2	3	4	5	6
Earnings ($)	$1.50	$3.00	$4.50	$6.00	$7.50	$9.00

   a) Determine the rate of change in Bim's earnings for each basket picked.
   b) Graph the data from the table.
   c) Determine the slope of the line.
   d) How does the slope relate to your answer for part a)?

Apply the Concepts B

9. Each minute of a song in MP3 format takes up approximately 1.4 MB of disk space.
   a) Create a table of values and determine the rate of change in disk space used for each minute of music, up to 10 min.
   b) Graph the results from part a).
   c) Draw a line through these points. Determine the slope of the line.

10. The profile of a ramp is shown below. Determine the rise and the run between the end points of the ramp, and calculate the slope.

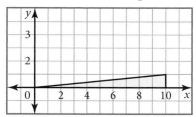

Chapter Problem

11. Jim drives a tractor-trailer. His job takes him throughout eastern Canada and much of the eastern United States. He earns $0.45 for each kilometre he drives.

a) Copy and complete the table of values.

Distance Driven (km)	0	100	200	300	400
Earnings ($)					

b) Enter the data from the table into a graphing calculator.
- Press [STAT]. Select **1:Edit**. Enter the distances in LIST 1 (L1) and enter the earnings in LIST 2 (L2).
- Press [2nd] [STAT PLOT]. Set up Plot 1 to graph a scatter plot.
- Press [ZOOM]. Select **9:Zoomstat**.

Literacy Connect

c) In Y1, enter the equation of a line you think would pass through all the points. Explain how the equation of this line relates to Jim's earnings. In what units is each variable measured?

12. For each linear relation, create a table of values for $x = 0, 1, 2, 3,$ and 4. Then, determine the rate of change in the y-values.

a) $y = \dfrac{1}{2}x - 3$

b) $y = -3x - 5$

c) $y = -0.5x$

13. On separate sets of axes, graph each linear relation from question 12.

14. Use the $\dfrac{\text{rise}}{\text{run}}$ method to determine the slope of each line from question 12.

15. A-frame chalets are built so that the steep slopes of the roofs do not allow snow to pile up on them.

a) Find the slopes of the two sides of the roof.
b) Is one side steeper than the other?
c) Are the signs of the slopes significant?
d) If each unit on the graph represents 0.5 m, how tall is the chalet?
e) How wide is the chalet?
f) Find the slopes using the measurements. Are the slopes different than the ones found before? Explain.

Extend the Concepts

16. Grace has a bank account that she rarely uses. On the last day of each month, the bank charges $4.50 as a service charge for managing the account. On January 1, Grace had $67.00 in her account. She made no deposits or withdrawals in this account for 6 months.

a) Create a table of values that displays the amount of money in her account on the first day of each month from January 1 to July 1.
b) Graph the data in the table from part a) to show a trend line.
c) Calculate the slope of the line.
d) Use a graphing calculator. Create a scatter plot of the data from part a). Determine the equation of a line of best fit for the data.

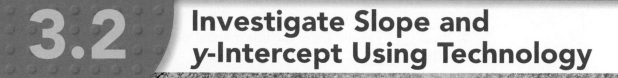

3.2 Investigate Slope and *y*-Intercept Using Technology

Rates of rain or snowfall, equipment rental costs, and potential earnings can often be modelled by using the properties of linear relations. Previously, you graphed linear relations by creating a table of values. You have also connected the slope of a line with the rate of change of a linear relation. In this section, you will use graphing technology to investigate two important properties of linear relations.

Investigate **A** Slope Using a Graphing Calculator

Tools

- graphing calculator

1. Press [WINDOW]. Use the standard window settings.

   - Press [2nd] [TBLSET] to set the table of values display. Set TblStart equal to 0 and set △**Tbl** equal to 1. This feature will cause the table of values to start with *x* = 0 and have the *x*-values go up by 1.

   - Press [MODE]. Cursor down to the last line and cursor over to **G-T**. Press [ENTER]. This will display the graph and the table of values in a split screen.

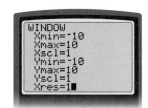

2. Press [Y=]. Enter the linear equation *y* = *x* in Y1. Press [GRAPH].

   a) Notice the direction and steepness of the line.

   b) In the table, what happens to the *y*-values as the *x*-values increase by 1?

   c) What is the slope of the line *y* = *x*?

3. Press ⌜Y=⌝ again. Enter the linear equation $y = 2x$ in Y2.
- Press ⌜GRAPH⌝.

a) Notice the direction and steepness of this line.

b) Is this line more or less steep than $y = x$?

c) In the table, what happens to the y-values as the x-values increase by 1? Press ⌜2nd⌝ [TABLE] to move the cursor to the table part of the screen. Use the left and right arrow keys to move between Y1 and Y2 columns.

d) What is the slope of the line $y = 2x$?

4. Repeat question 3 for $y = 3x$, $y = 4x$, $y = 10x$, and $y = \frac{1}{2}x$.

5. Repeat question 3 for $y = -x$, $y = -2x$, $y = -3x$, and $y = -4x$.

6. What can you conclude about the relationship between a linear equation, the slope of the line, and the rate of change in the y-values?

Investigate B   Explore the y-Intercept Using a Graphing Calculator

Tools

- graphing calculator

1. Set up the graphing calculator the same way you did in Investigate 1.

2. Press ⌜Y=⌝ enter the linear equation $y = x$ in Y1. Press ⌜GRAPH⌝.

a) Notice the direction and steepness of the line.

b) In the table, what is the value of y when $x = 0$? Locate this point on the graph.

c) What is the **y-intercept** of the linear equation $y = x$?

y-intercept
- the y-coordinate of the point where the graph intersects the y-axis
- the value of y when $x = 0$

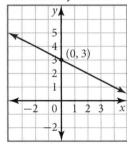

3. Press ⌜Y=⌝ again. Enter the linear equation $y = x + 2$ in Y2.
- Press ⌜GRAPH⌝.

a) Notice the direction and steepness of the line.

b) What is the steepness of this line relative to $y = x$?

c) In the table, what is the value of y when $x = 0$?

d) What is the y-intercept of the linear equation $y = x + 2$?

4. Repeat question 3 for $y = x + 3$, $y = x + 5$, $y = x - 2$, and $y = x - 7$.

5. Repeat question 3 for $y = -x + 1$, $y = -x + 4$, and $y = -x - 5$.

6. What can you conclude about the relationship between a linear equation and its y-intercept?

In a linear equation of the form $y = mx + b$, m represents the slope of the line (or the rate of change), and b represents the y-intercept (or initial value). A line with a positive slope goes up from left to right, and a line with a negative slope goes down from left to right. Ignoring the sign, the greater the slope, the steeper the line.

Example **1**

Identify the Slope and *y*-Intercept of a Linear Relation

For each linear relation, identify the slope and the *y*-intercept.
Confirm your results by graphing the relation on a graphing calculator.

a) $y = 4x$ **b)** $y = x + 9$

c) $y = x - 9$ **d)** $y = -3x + \dfrac{5}{2}$

Solution

a) Compare $y = 4x$ to $y = mx + b$.

Since *m* represents the slope of the line, the slope is 4.
The equation $y = 4x$ is the same as $y = 4x + 0$.
The *y*-intercept is 0.
In the table, the *y*-values are 0, 4, 8, 12,… .
The rate of change in the *y*-values is
constant, $+4$, so the slope of $y = 4x$ is 4.
The graph appears to pass through the
origin, (0, 0). The table of values shows that
when $x = 0$, $y = 0$, so the *y*-intercept is 0.

b) $y = x + 9$ is the same as $y = 1x + 9$.
The slope is 1 and the *y*-intercept is 9.
In the table, the *y*-values are 9, 10, 11,
12,… . The rate of change in the *y*-values
is constant, $+1$, so the slope of $y = x + 9$
is 1. The graph appears to pass through the
point (0, 9). The table of values shows that
when $x = 0$, $y = 9$, so the *y*-intercept is $+9$.

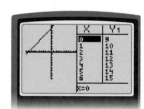

c) The slope is 1 and the *y*-intercept is -9.

In the table, the rate of change in the
y-values is constant, $+1$, and $y = -9$ when
$x = 0$. Therefore, the slope of $y = x - 9$ is 1
and the *y*-intercept is -9.

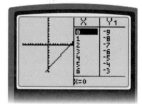

d) The slope is -3 and the *y*-intercept is $\dfrac{5}{2}$.
The rate of change in the *y*-values is
constant, -3, and $y = 2.5$ when $x = 0$,
which is the same as $\dfrac{5}{2}$. Therefore, the
slope of $y = -3x + \dfrac{5}{2}$ is -3 and the
y-intercept is $2\dfrac{1}{2}$.

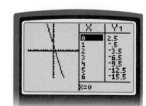

Example **2** **Identify the Slope and _y_-Intercept of a Linear Relation Involving Temperature**

For the linear relation, identify the slope and the _y_-intercept. Confirm your result by graphing the relation on a graphing calculator.

$F = 1.8C + 32$

Solution

The slope of the line is 1.8 and the vertical intercept is $+32$.

The relationship between temperatures in degrees Fahrenheit and degrees Celsius is linear. The equation can be written y = 1.8x + 32, where x is in degrees Celsius and y is in degrees Fahrenheit. 0°C converts to +32°F.

The rate of change in the _y_-values is consistently $+1.8$, and when $x = 0$, $y = 32$. Therefore, the slope of $F = 1.8C + 32$ is 1.8 and the F-intercept is $+32$.

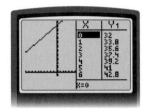

Example **3** **Equations of Lines**

The graph shows the total cost for an ice cream sundae with different numbers of toppings. If _x_ represents the number of toppings and _y_ represents the total cost in dollars, write the equation of the trend line by first determining the slope and the _y_-intercept.

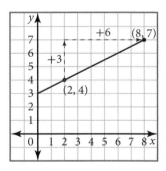

Solution

First, calculate the slope, _m_, of the line using the two points shown. In this case, $(2, 4)$ and $(8, 7)$ have been chosen.

$$m = \frac{\text{rise}}{\text{run}}$$
$$= \frac{3}{6}$$
$$= 0.5$$

The slope represents the cost per topping.

The _y_-intercept is 3. This is the initial value, which is the cost of a sundae with no toppings.

The equation of the line is $y = 0.5x + 3$.

Key Concepts

- Any linear relation can be modelled by an equation of the form $y = mx + b$, where m represents the slope of the line and b represents the point where the line crosses the y-axis, the y-intercept.
- Conversely, if m and b can be determined, a linear equation can be generated.
- The G-T setting on a graphing calculator allows you to view the graph and the table of values on a split screen.

Discuss the Concepts

D1. Describe how the appearance of a line changes if the slope increases.

D2. How can you tell the value of b in $y = mx + b$ by looking at the graph of a linear relation.

Practise the Concepts **A**

For help with questions 1 to 3, refer to Example 1.

1. Identify the slope of each linear relation.
   - **a)** $y = 3x + 6$
   - **b)** $y = -\dfrac{1}{4}x + 5$
   - **c)** $y = 0.25x - 0.10$
   - **d)** $y = 7 + 2x$

2. Identify the y-intercept of each linear relation.
   - **a)** $y = x + 4$
   - **b)** $y = -\dfrac{1}{2}x + \dfrac{3}{4}$
   - **c)** $y = 3x$
   - **d)** $y = 1.45 - 0.10x$

3. For each relation
   - graph the equation using a graphing calculator with the standard window settings
   - sketch the graph in your notebook
   - calculate the rate of change by looking at the TABLE
   - determine the value of y when $x = 0$
   - **a)** $y = 2x - 3$
   - **b)** $y = 1.5x + 3.5$
   - **c)** $y = 6 + x$
   - **d)** $y = -4 + \dfrac{1}{2}x$

For help with question 4, refer to Example 2.

4. Write the equation for each line given the slope and the *y*-intercept.

   a) slope: 3, *y*-intercept: 7

   b) slope: 1, *y*-intercept: -1

   c) slope: $\dfrac{3}{4}$, *y*-intercept: $\dfrac{1}{2}$

   d) slope: -4, *y*-intercept: 0

   e) slope: 0, *y*-intercept: 4

5. Use a graphing calculator to graph each equation from question 4. Sketch each graph in your notebook, and record the table of values for *x*-values from 0 to 6.

Apply the Concepts ⒷB

6. Write the equation for each line by first determining the slope and the *y*-intercept.

a)

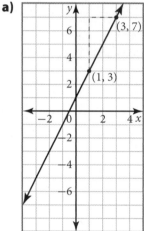

b)

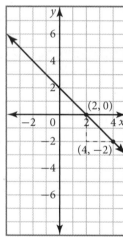

c)

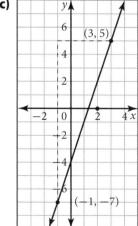

d)

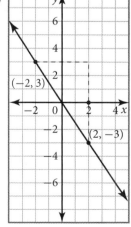

7. A graph of Marina's college fund is shown.

a) What is the slope of this line?

b) What does the slope represent?

c) What is the y-intercept?

d) What does this number represent?

e) Write an equation that represents the amount in Marina's college fund.

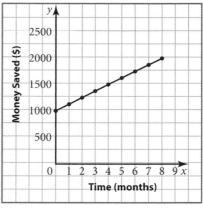

Chapter Problem

8. When Jim travels long distances, his average speed is approximately 90 km/h. On a return trip from Thunder Bay, 1500 km from home, Jim uses the equation $y = 1500 - 90x$ to determine his distance from home after x hours of driving.

a) What is the y-intercept of this equation? What does this number represent?

b) What is the slope of this equation? What does this number represent?

c) Input the equation into a graphing calculator and look at the table. How far away from home is Jim after driving for 6 h?

9. The cost of renting a car can be modelled by the equation $C = 19.99 + 0.27d$, where C is the total cost in dollars and d is the distance driven, in kilometres.

a) Explain the significance of the number 19.99 to the total cost of renting a car.

Literacy Connect

b) Explain how the graph of this linear relation would change if the charge per kilometre increased to 29¢.

Extend the Concepts

10. Graph the equation from question 9 using a graphing calculator with the standard window settings.

a) Explain why no line appears.

b) Which setting must be changed in order for the line to become visible? Why?

3.3 Properties of Slopes of Lines

A yurt is a tent built on a platform. In the photo you can see two slopes of the roof of the yurt. These slopes are related to each other, like those of the roof of a house. Of course, some things have no slope. In this section you will look at some other properties involving the slopes of linear relations.

Investigate

Tools

- computer
- *The Geometer's Sketchpad®*

Properties of Slope

Method 1: Use *The Geometer's Sketchpad®*

1. Choose the **Segment** tool. Construct a horizontal line segment AB. Choose the **Text** tool. Click the left endpoint and then the right endpoint of the line segment. The labels should automatically appear.

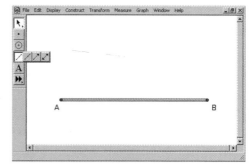

2. Line segment AB should be selected from the previous step. If it is *not* selected, choose the **Selection** tool and click the line segment. Select point B. From the **Construct** menu, choose **Perpendicular Line**. This will create a line perpendicular to AB through point B.

3. The perpendicular line will be selected. From the **Construct** menu, choose **Point On Perpendicular Line**. Use the **Text** tool and label this point C. The point will now be selected. If the point is already above point B, go to the next step. If the point is not above point B, press and hold the UP ARROW key until point C is above point B.

4. Choose the **Selection** tool. Since point C is already selected, now select point A. This will cause points A and C to both be selected. From the **Construct** menu, choose **Segment**. This will construct line segment AC.

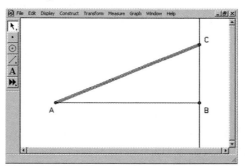

Math **Connect**

Yurts are eight-sided tent-like structures mounted on a wooden deck floor. You can rent a yurt in Algonquin Park with electric heat and an insulated floor, which makes for comfortable camping in all seasons.

5. Click somewhere in the white background of the sketch to deselect AC. Click the line passing through BC to select it. From the **Display** menu, choose **Hide Perpendicular Line** to hide the line.

6. Select points B and C. From the **Construct** menu, choose **Segment** to construct line segment BC.

7. Click somewhere in the white background of the sketch to deselect the previous measure. Select point B and then point C. From the **Measure** menu, choose **Distance**. Drag the measurement to side BC of the triangle.

8. Click somewhere in the white background of the sketch to deselect BC. Select point A, and then point B. From the **Measure** menu, choose **Distance**. Drag the measurement to side AB of the triangle.

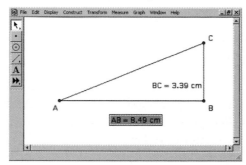

9. Use *The Geometer's Sketchpad®* to calculate a ratio. Click anywhere in the white background of the sketch deselect AB. From the **Measure** menu, choose **Calculate**. Click the distance measure of side BC, click the division button, and then click the distance measure of side AB. Click **OK** to calculate the ratio. Drag the measure of the ratio calculated to the left side of the triangle if necessary.

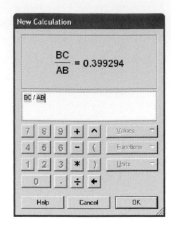

10. Deselect the previous measure. Select line segment AC. From the **Measure** menu, choose **Slope**. The slope of AC will be measured and a grid inserted. The slope measurement will appear under the previous measure.

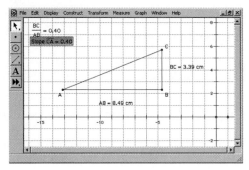

11. How are the slope of AC and the ratio of BC to AB related? Explain why this relationship exists.

12. Drag point C upward. Describe what happens to the slope of CA as C moves upward. Explain what is happening to the lengths of AB and BC as C moves upward that may account for the changes in the slope of CA.

13. Drag point C below AB. What do you notice about the slope of CA? What do you notice about the value of the ratio and the value of the slope of CA? Explain what is happening to the lengths of AB and BC as C moves downward that may account for the changes in the slope of CA.

14. How can you make the slope of CA equal 0? What is the length of line segment BC when the slope of CA is 0?

Tools

- graphing calculator

Method 2: Use a Graphing Calculator

1. Press WINDOW . Use the standard window settings.

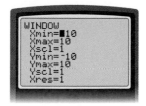

- Press 2nd [TBLSET]. Set **TblStart** equal to 0 and set △**Tbl** equal to 1. This feature will cause the table of values to start with $x = 0$ and have the x-values go up by 1.

- Press MODE , scroll down to the last line and choose **G-T**. This will display the graph and the table of values at the same time.

2. Graph $Y1 = 2x$. Notice the steepness of the line.

Graph $Y2 = 1x$ on the same axes and notice the steepness of this line.

Graph $Y3 = \frac{1}{2}x$ on the same axes and notice the steepness of the line.

What happens to the line as the **coefficient** of x decreases?

coefficient

- a number that is multiplied by a variable
- in $y = \frac{1}{2}x$, the coefficient of x is $\frac{1}{2}$

3. Write an equation that would produce a horizontal line. What is the coefficient of x?

Graph this equation as Y4. Use a thick line.

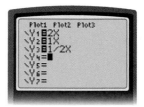

Math Connect

To change the line style on a graphing calculator, press Y= . Using ◄ , move your cursor to the slanted line before the function Y1 you are working on. Press ENTER to scroll through the available line styles. When you find the style you want, use ► to return to the function, or press GRAPH to graph the function.

4. Write an equation that would produce a line that goes down from left to right. What must be true about the coefficient of x?

Use Y5 to Y7 to graph lines that "mirror" the lines graphed in Y1 to Y3.

What do the equations of all lines with a positive slope have in common?

What do the equations of all lines with a negative slope have in common?

5. a) Clear the equations from above and graph $Y1 = \frac{1}{2}x$. Notice the steepness and location of the line. What is the slope of the line? What is the y-intercept of the line?

b) Graph $Y2 = \frac{1}{2}x + 3$. How does this line compare to the line in part a)?

Graph $Y3 = \frac{1}{2}x + 7$. Describe the pattern that is emerging.

Graph $Y4 = \frac{1}{2}x - 6$. Is the pattern holding?

c) Look at the lines from parts a) and b). Will any of these lines ever intersect? Explain your answer.

d) What is the name given to lines that never intersect? What do you notice about the slopes of these lines?

Example **1** **Positive and Negative Slopes**

Determine the slope of each object.

a)

30 in.   10 ft

b)

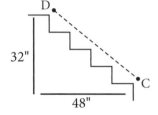

32"

48"

Solution

a) The rise, from the road to the point where the ramp enters the van, is 30". The run, from the point where the ramp touches the road to a position at the back of the van, is 10'. Convert 10' to inches. The run is 120".   *There are 12 in. in 1 ft.*

$$m = \frac{\text{rise}}{\text{run}}$$

$$= \frac{30}{120}$$

$$= \frac{1}{4} \text{ or } 0.25$$

The slope of the ramp is $\frac{1}{4}$.

Math Connect

Explain why the measure 5'11" cannot be entered into a calculator as 5.11.

b) The rise from the foot of the stairs to the top is 32". The run, from right to left, is −48". The slope of the stairs is indicated by CD.

$$m = \frac{\text{rise}}{\text{run}}$$

$$= -\frac{32}{48}$$

$$= -\frac{2}{3} \text{ or } -0.667$$

Since the rise is being measured from the top down, it is negative. The sign on the rise or run indicates direction. A positive number indicates up or to the right, and a negative number indicates down or to the left.

The slope of the stairs is $-\frac{2}{3}$.

The negative value indicates the stairs go down from left to right.

Example **2** **Parallel Lines**

Write the equation of the line that is parallel to each line.

a)

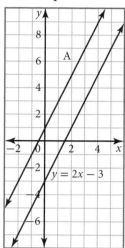

b)

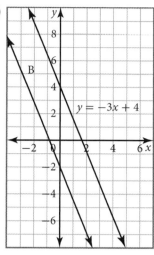

Solution

a) Line A is parallel to $y = 2x - 3$, so it has slope 2. Line A intersects the y-axis at $y = 1$, so it has y-intercept 1. The equation of line A is $y = 2x + 1$.

b) Line B is parallel to $y = -3x + 4$, so it has slope -3. Line B intersects the y-axis at $y = -2$, so it has y-intercept -2. The equation of line B is $y = -3x - 2$.

Key Concepts

- A line with a positive slope goes up from left to right; a line with a negative slope goes down from left to right.
- A horizontal line has a slope of zero.
- Parallel lines have the same slope.
- Ignoring the sign on the coefficient of x, the greater the coefficient of x, the steeper the line.

Discuss the Concepts

D1. Explain how you can determine whether a linear relation has a positive slope or a negative slope by looking at a graph.

D2. How does the steepness of a line relate to the coefficient of x?

D3. How does the y-intercept relate to the steepness of a line?

For help with questions 1 to 5, refer to Example 1.

1. Which side of this roof has a positive slope?
Which side has a negative slope?

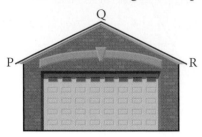

2. State whether the slope of each line is positive, negative, or 0.

a) $y = 2x + 5$ **b)** $y = -x + 3$

c) $y = 4 - 3x$ **d)** $y = 3$

e) $y = \frac{1}{4}x - 1$ **f)** $y = -0.5x + 0.5$

g) $y = -5$ **h)** $y = 12 + \frac{5}{2}x$

3. For each line on the graph, indicate which of the equations listed below represents the line.

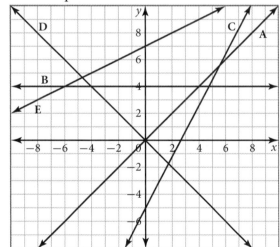

a) $y = 4$ **b)** $y = -x$

c) $y = x$ **d)** $y = \frac{1}{2}x + 7$

e) $y = 2x - 5$

4. Write the equation of a line that has a steeper slope than the given line.

a) $y = 3x + 2$ **b)** $y = x$

c) $y = -2x + 1$ **d)** $y = \frac{1}{4}x + 10$

5. Write the equation of a line that is less steep than the given line.

a) $y = -x$ **b)** $y = -4.5 + 2.5x$

c) $y = 5000 + 8.5x$ **d)** $y = -3x - 8$

For help with questions 6 and 7, refer to Example 2.

6. State whether the lines in each pair are parallel. Explain. Use graphing technology to confirm your answer.

a) $y = 3x + 4$ $y = -3x + 4$

b) $y = x + 6$ $y = x + 7$

c) $y = -2x + 5$ $y = 3 - 2x$

d) $y = \dfrac{1}{2}x$ $y = 0.5x + 2.25$

e) $y = \dfrac{1}{4}x - 2$ $y = \dfrac{1}{4}x + 2$

f) $y = 4$ $y = 0$

g) $A = 5000 + 0.08x$ $A = 5000 + 0.8x$

h) $C = 100 + 90x$ $C = 100x$

7. Write the equation of a line that is parallel to each line.

a) $y = -\dfrac{4}{3}x + 2$ **b)** $y = 6 + 0.9x$

c) $y = 7$ **d)** $y = 1 - x$

Apply the Concepts

8. Determine whether the lines represented by each pair of tables of values are parallel. Show your work.

a)

x	y
0	5
1	7
2	9
3	11
4	13

x	y
−2	8
−1	10
0	12
1	14
2	16

b)

x	y
2	4
3	1
4	−2
5	−5
6	−8

x	y
0	10
1	7
2	4
3	1
4	−2

c)

x	y
0	1
1	2
2	4
3	7
4	11

x	y
0	1
1	2
2	4
3	8
4	16

d)

x	y
0	−3
1	−1
2	1
3	3
4	5

x	y
−2	0
0	4
2	8
4	12
6	16

9.

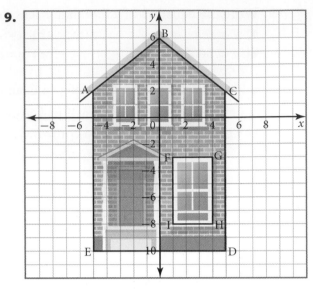

a) Which pairs of line segments are parallel?

b) Calculate the slope of AB.

c) Calculate the slope of BC.

d) Without calculating, determine the slopes of DE, GF, and HI.

Chapter Problem

10. On a job that takes him to Hamilton, Jim sees a sign warning of a hill with a 5% grade. The grade of a road is a measure of the steepness of the road.

a) Calculate the vertical change in this section of the highway if the horizontal change is 100 m.

b) Copy and complete the table of values.

c) Graph the data from the table using graphing technology.

d) Calculate the rate of change to determine the slope of the line that would pass through these points.

e) Determine the equation of the line passing through these points. Graph this line.

5%

Horizontal Change (m)	Vertical Change (m)
0	
1000	
2000	
3000	
4000	
5000	

11. Dylan borrowed $1000 from her parents so she could get her G1 driver's license and take a driver training course. Dylan has an after-school job, and she has agreed to pay her parents back at a rate of $50 per week.

a) Copy and complete the table of values for the amount owing to Dylan's parents each week from the time she borrowed the money until the 8th week.

x (weeks)	y (amount owing in $)
1	
2	

b) On grid paper, graph the data.

c) What is the y-intercept of this linear relation?

d) What is the rate of change in the y-values?

e) Explain why the slope of the line is negative.

f) Write the equation of this line in $y = mx + b$ form.

12. a) Using a graphing calculator, create a scatter plot of the data in question 11.

b) Input the equation from part f) as Y1 and graph the line. If the equation is correct, the line will intersect every point on the scatter plot. If the equation is not correct, check your work in question 11.

Extend the Concepts C

13. Use a graphing calculator. Graph the lines in each pair in the same window. Press , and select **5:ZSquare** to "square" the viewing screen. Complete parts a) to c) for each pair of lines.

i) $y = 2x$ $y = -\dfrac{1}{2}x$

ii) $y = 4x$ $y = -\dfrac{1}{4}x$

iii) $y = \dfrac{3}{4}x$ $y = -\dfrac{4}{3}x$

iv) $y = \dfrac{2}{3}x - 4$ $y = -\dfrac{3}{2}x + 2$

a) At what angle do the lines in each pair appear to cross? What is the name given to lines that intersect at this angle?

b) Find the slope of each line. How do the slopes compare?

c) What is the relationship between the slopes of each of the pairs of lines?

14. Write the equation of a line that is perpendicular to each line. Check your answer by graphing each pair of lines.

a) $y = 3x - 1$ **b)** $y = -2x + 5$ **c)** $y = -0.4x$

15. Write the equation of a line that is perpendicular to $y = 4$.

3.4 Determine the Equation of a Line

Many different situations can be represented by linear relations. A linear relation can be used to make predictions. For example, if you make regular deposits into a savings plan, you can write an equation and use it to predict how much money you will have at a later date. In this section, you will determine the equations of lines in a variety of ways, depending on the given information.

Investigate

Tools
- graphing calculator
- grid paper
- ruler
- toothpicks

Build Triangles

1. Arrange 3 toothpicks to form a triangle.

2. a) Add 2 more toothpicks to build a second triangle.

   b) Create a table of values. Record the number of triangles and the total number of toothpicks needed in the table.

Number of Triangles	Total Number of Toothpicks
1	3
2	

   c) Continue this pattern, adding toothpicks until you have 5 triangles. Record each number of triangles and the total number of toothpicks in your table.

3. Refer to your table of values. Explain how you know that the relationship between the number of triangles and the total number of toothpicks can be modelled with a linear relation.

Method 1: Use Paper and Pencil

1. On grid paper, plot the data in your table of values. Let x represent the number of triangles and y represent the total number of toothpicks needed.

2. What is the slope of this line?

3. What is the y-intercept?

4. Write the equation of the line that models the relationship.

5. How many toothpicks would be needed to make 5500 triangles?

Method 2: Use a Graphing Calculator

1. Enter the data from the table into L1 and L2. Use the window settings shown.

Create a scatter plot of the data in your table of values.

2. Press ⎡ Y= ⎤. Enter Y1=x, then press ⎡GRAPH⎤.

3. What changes need to be made to the equation so the line passes through all of the points on the scatter plot? Write the equation of the line that models the relationship between the number of triangles and the total number of toothpicks needed.

4. How many toothpicks would be needed to construct 5500 triangles?

Example 1 Determine the Equation of a Line From a Given Graph

Write the equation of each line in the form $y = mx + b$.

a)

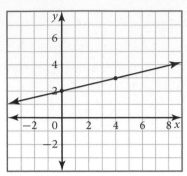

b)

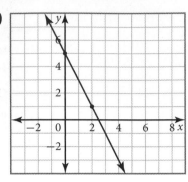

Solution

a) The graph intersects the y-axis at $+2$, so the y-intercept, b, is 2.

Find the slope.
Between the chosen points, the rise is $+1$ and the run is $+4$, so

$m = \dfrac{\text{rise}}{\text{run}}$

$\quad = \dfrac{1}{4}$ or 0.25

Substitute $m = \dfrac{1}{4}$ and $b = 2$
into $y = mx + b$.

The equation of the line is $y = \dfrac{1}{4}x + 2$.

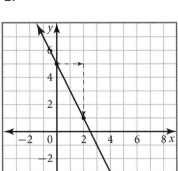

b) The graph intersects the y-axis at $+5$, so the y-intercept, b, is 5.

Between the chosen points, the rise is -4 and the run is $+2$, so

$m = \dfrac{\text{rise}}{\text{run}}$

$\quad = \dfrac{-4}{+2}$

$\quad = -2$

Substitute $m = -2$ and $b = 5$ into $y = mx + b$.
The equation of the line is $y = -2x + 5$.

Example **2** **Determine the Equation of a Line Given the Slope and a Point on the Line**

A line with slope 2 passes through the point (4, 3). Determine the equation of the line.

Solution

Make a table of values. Include the given point in the table.

x	y
0	
1	
2	
3	
4	3

Recall that the y-intercept is b in the y = mx + b form of the equation of a line. The y-intercept is the value of y when x = 0.

Since the slope of the line is +2, as the value of x increases by 1, the value of y increases by 2. Conversely, as the value of x decreases by 1, the value of y decreases by 2. Work backward from the point (4, 3) to find the value of y when $x = 0$.

x	y	Rate of Change
0	−5	
1	−3	−3 − (−5) = 2
2	−1	−1 − (−3) = 2
3	1	1 − (−1) = 2
4	3	3 − 1 = 2

So, when $x = 0$, $y = -5$.

The y-intercept, b, is -5. So, the equation of the line is $y = 2x - 5$.

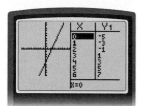

Use a graphing calculator to check your work. Graph y = 2x − 5 using the standard window settings and G-T mode.

Example	3

Determine the Equation of a Line Given Two Points on the Line

At the gym near her house, Sierra notices a chart that shows that the relationship between people's ages and their heart rates at different levels of exercise is linear. Sierra records the rates for herself and her mother, at the same exercise level.

Age	Heart Rate (bpm)
20	138
45	123

Solution

Two points in the relation are (20, 138) and (45, 123). Plot the points on a coordinate grid and use them to find the slope. From the graph, the rise is -15 and the run is 25.

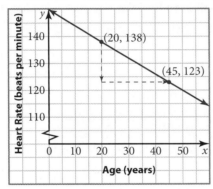

$$m = \frac{\text{rise}}{\text{run}}$$

$$= \frac{123 - 138}{45 - 20}$$

$$= -\frac{15}{25}$$

$$= -0.6$$

Substitute $m = -0.6$ and the coordinates of either one of the points into $y = mx + b$ to find the y-intercept.

$$y = mx + b$$
$$y = -0.6x + b$$
$$138 = -0.6(20) + b$$
$$138 = -12 + b$$
$$150 = b$$

It does not matter which of the points is substituted into $y = -0.6x + b$. Any point that lies on the line will give the same value for b.

The equation of the line that models this relation is $y = -0.6x + 150$, where y represents the heart rate and x represents the age of the person.

Math Connect

Sometimes it is not necessary to show all the values on the horizontal or vertical axis. If values are omitted, a scale break is shown.

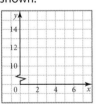

Key Concepts

- The equation of a line can be determined from a graph by finding the slope and identifying the *y*-intercept.

- The equation of a line can be determined if you know one point on the line and the slope (rate of change).

- If the slope and the coordinates of one point on the line are known, the *y*-intercept can be found either by patterning or by substituting known values into $y = mx + b$ and then solving for *b*.

Discuss the Concepts

D1. What information is needed to write the equation of any straight line?

D2. Describe two ways you could find the equation of the line with slope −3 that passes through (2, 1).

D3. Is it possible to find the equation of a line that joins two points if one of the points is an *x*-intercept and the second is a *y*-intercept? Explain.

Practise the Concepts **A**

For help with questions 1 and 2, refer to Example 1.

1. For each graph, determine the slope and *y*-intercept, then write the equation of the line in the form $y = mx + b$.

a)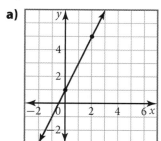

b)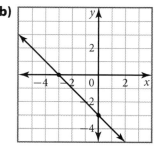

c)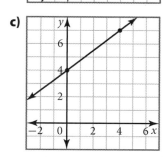

d)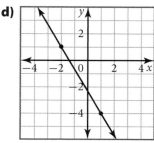

2. Given each slope and *y*-intercept, write the equation of the line, and then graph the line.

a) slope: 1, *y*-intercept: −1

b) slope: 3, *y*-intercept: 8

c) slope: $-\dfrac{2}{3}$, *y*-intercept: 0

d) slope: 0, *y*-intercept: −2

For help with questions 3 to 5, refer to Example 2.

3. For each linear relation, find the value of *y* when *x* = 0.

a)

x	y
0	
1	
2	
3	2
4	3

b)

x	y
0	
1	
2	
3	5
4	3

c)

x	y
−4	6.5
−3	5
−2	
−1	
0	

d)

x	y
−4	−11
−3	−7
−2	
−1	
0	

4. Matih plans to upgrade his car stereo and needs approximately $400. He currently has $50 in the bank, and plans to save $40 a week.

a) Determine the equation of the line that would model the amount, *y*, in Matih's bank account after *x* weeks.

b) After how many weeks will Matih have saved enough money?

5. Determine the equation of each line given the slope and the coordinates of one point on the line.

a) $m = 2$, A(4, 4)

b) $m = 1$, B(3, 7)

c) $m = -3$, C(2, −1)

d) $m = 0$, D(−2, −5)

e) $m = -2$, E(1, 1)

f) $m = 3$, F(−4, −5)

g) $m = 0.5$, G(0, 5)

h) $m = -\dfrac{3}{2}$, H(−3, 0)

For help with questions 6 and 7, refer to Example 3.

6. Solve each equation for *b*.

a) $8 = 3(2) + b$

b) $8 = 3(-3) + b$

c) $220 = 2.5(50) + b$

d) $0 = -3(-11) + b$

7. Determine the equation of the line passing through the given points.

a) C(2, 2) and D(3, 7) **b)** J(−1, 4) and K(5, 13)
c) L(0, 0) and M(100, −50) **d)** Q(−2, −3) and R(1, 6)
e) U(−9, 0) and V(3, −8) **f)** Y(−25, 16) and Z(15, 0)

Apply the Concepts **B**

8. Aimée wears a pedometer when she walks. Today, she walked 6.3 km in an hour and a half. If she walks at a constant speed, she can model her walking with a linear equation.

a) If the point (0, 0) represents Aimée's starting point, what is another point on this line?
b) On grid paper, graph these two points and draw a line connecting them.
c) Determine the slope and y-intercept of the line.
d) Write a linear equation to model Aimée's walks.
e) Use the equation. How far would Aimée walk in 2 h?

9. The graph is used to determine the cost of a service call for furnace repairs. Determine the equation of the line.

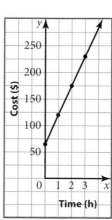

10. Jim has been in line for $3\frac{1}{2}$ h waiting to cross into the United States. He likes to relax doing puzzles. In a puzzle book, he reads the following brainteaser.

Four toothpicks are arranged to make a square.

a) What is the least number of toothpicks needed to build another square beside the first one? How many toothpicks are used in total?

b) Continue adding the least number of toothpicks possible until you have a row of 5 squares. How many toothpicks have you used?

c) What is the equation of the line that models this relationship?

11. Waneek spends a week at a winter resort. The cost of a 7-day snowboarding pass, including equipment rental, is $199. On the resort's web site, Waneek reads that a daily pass with no equipment rental is $25.

a) Calculate the cost of 7 daily passes without equipment rental.

b) How much is being charged for renting the equipment for the week?

c) What equation would model the cost of the week's pass, including equipment rental?

12. The total mass of a container with 30 bolts is 100 g, while the total mass of an identical container with 45 bolts is 130 g.

a) Determine an equation relating the total mass, y, to the number of bolts, x.

b) Find the mass of one bolt and the mass of the empty container.

13. Some salespeople are paid by a combination of a fixed weekly wage plus commission—variable earnings that are a percent of sales. Bor sells solar pool heating systems. He earns a weekly salary of $500 plus a commission on all sales. If Bor's sales were $10 000 in one week, his total earnings would be $1100. Determine the equation that represents Bor's weekly earnings.

14. Below is a distance–time graph of Jasmine's day at school. She left home at 7:30 (time = 0) and rode her bike to school, arriving at 7:45. After school, she found that her front tire was flat, so she walked her bike home.

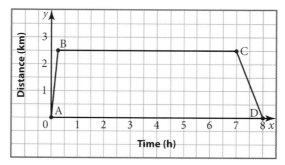

a) What time did Jasmine arrive back home?

b) How far is it from her home to her school?

c) Write the coordinates for points A, B, C, and D.

d) Use the end points to help you to determine the equation of each line segment.

e) What was Jasmine's speed, in kilometres per hour, on the way to school? On the way home?

Being able to graph linear relations and determine slopes by hand can often help you judge the reasonableness of answers to questions about data. One application of this occurs when people make scale drawings of items that are to be fixed, built, or remodelled. Some of these projects, like working with the roof of a house, involve slope.

Investigate

Tools

- grid paper
- ruler

Scale Drawings

The steepness of a roof is often referred to as its pitch. A 6–12 pitch, for example, has a 6 ft rise over a span of 12 ft.

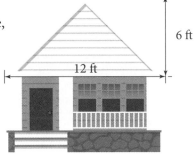

1. On grid paper, draw the roof of this house using a scale of 1 square represents 1 ft, so that the end points of the roof lie on the x-axis and the peak of the roof lies on the y-axis.

2. **a)** Calculate the slope of the left side of the roof.
   b) What is the y-intercept of this line segment?
   c) What is the equation of the line that represents the left side of the roof?

3. Follow the process described in step 2 to determine the equation of the right side of the roof.

Example   1

Graph a Line Using the *y*-Intercept and the Slope

For each line, identify the slope and *y*-intercept, then use them to graph the line.

a) $y = 2x - 3$

b) $y = -3x + 5$

Solution

a) The *y*-intercept is -3, so plot $(0, -3)$ first. In $y = mx + b$ form, the slope of the line is the coefficient of *x*, which is 2.

$$\text{slope} = \frac{\text{rise}}{\text{run}}$$
$$= \frac{2}{1}$$

From the *y*-intercept, other points on the line can be found by moving up 2 and right 1. Do this until three points have been plotted. These three points should all lie on the same line.

Draw the line and label the line with the equation.

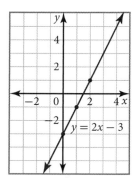

b) The *y*-intercept is 5, so plot $(0, 5)$ first. The slope of this line is -3. Draw the line and label the line with the equation.

$$\text{slope} = \frac{\text{rise}}{\text{run}}$$
$$= -\frac{3}{1}$$

From the *y*-intercept, other points on the line can be found by moving down 3 and right 1. Do this until three points have been plotted. These three points should all lie on the same line.

Draw the line and label the line with the equation.

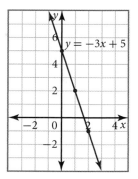

Example 2

Graph a Line When the Slope Is a Fraction

Graph each line.

a) $y = \dfrac{3}{4}x - 1$

b) $y = -\dfrac{1}{2}x + 4\dfrac{1}{2}$

Solution

a) The y-intercept is -1, so plot $(0, -1)$ first.

The slope of the line is $\dfrac{3}{4}$.

$$\text{slope} = \frac{\text{rise}}{\text{run}}$$

$$= \frac{3}{4}$$

From the y-intercept, other points on the line can be found by moving up 3 and right 4. Draw the line and label it with the equation.

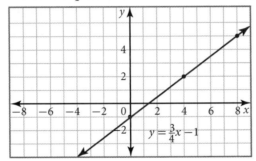

b) The y-intercept is $4\dfrac{1}{2}$, so plot $\left(0, 4\dfrac{1}{2}\right)$ first.

The slope of the line is $-\dfrac{1}{2}$.

$$\text{slope} = \frac{\text{rise}}{\text{run}}$$

$$= -\frac{1}{2}$$

From the y-intercept, other points on the line can be found by moving down 1 and right 2. Draw the line, and label it with the equation.

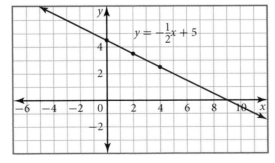

Example **3**

Model the Cost of a Pizza

A pizza at Monster Pizza costs $12.00 plus $1.75 per topping. Graph the linear relation that models the cost. Write an equation relating C, the cost in dollars, to t, the number of toppings.

Solution

Method 1: Use a Table of Values

Create a table of values for up to 4 toppings.

Number of Toppings	0	1	2	3	4
Cost ($)	12	13.75	15.15	17.25	19

Plot the points, then join them with a line.

The initial cost, with no toppings, is $12.00. The rate of change is 1.75. The equation is $C = 12 + 1.75t$.

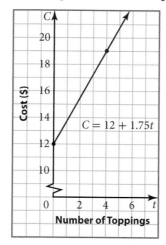

Method 2: Use the y-Intercept and the Slope

A pizza with no toppings cost $12.00. So, the initial value, or vertical-intercept, is 12. Plot (0, 12).

Each topping costs $1.75, so the rate of change is 1.75.
The slope of the line is 1.75. Use the slope to find the rise and the run.

$$1.75 = 1\frac{3}{4}$$

$$= \frac{7}{4}$$

The slope is $\frac{7}{4}$, so the rise is 7 and the run is 4.

From (0, 12), other points on the line can be found by moving up 7 and right 4. Draw and label the line.

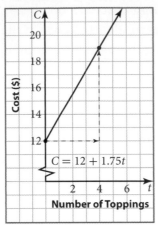

Key Concepts

- A linear relation can be graphed by plotting a series of points, or by plotting the *y*-intercept and then applying the slope to locate other points.

- Some situations can be represented by linear relations. If there is a constant rate of changes between two variables, this is the slope. The initial value is the y-intercept.

Discuss the Concepts

D1. In a word problem, such as Example 3, the equation $C = 12 + 1.75t$ occurs. How can you tell which number represents the *y*-intercept and which number represents the slope?

D2. A bowling alley charges $5 for shoe rental and $1 per game. Which linear relation models this situation? Explain your reasoning.

a) $y = 5x$

b) $y = 5x + 1$

c) $y = x + 5$

For help with questions 1 and 2, refer to Example 1.

1. For each equation, identify the slope and the *y*-intercept, then graph the line.

a) $y = 3x - 4$ **b)** $y = x + 3$

c) $y = -2x + 3$ **d)** $y = -x + 0.5$

e) $y = 7$

2. Use a graphing calculator with the standard window settings to check your graphs from question 1.

For help with questions 3 and 4, refer to Example 2.

3. Graph each line.

a) $y = \frac{1}{2}x + 2$ **b)** $y = \frac{2}{3}x - 4$

c) $y = -\frac{3}{4}x + 1$ **d)** $y = -1.25x$

4. Use a graphing calculator with the standard window settings to check your graphs from question 3.

For help with question 5, refer to Example 3.

5. A small pizza at Monster Pizza costs $3.50 plus $0.75 per topping. Create a graph of the linear relation that models the cost for up to 5 toppings.

6. Refer to the Investigate. Do the same activity for a roof with a 4–12 pitch.

7. A plane flying at an altitude of 1000 m begins to climb at a rate of 10 metres per second.

a) Graph the first 10 s of the plane's ascent. Plot time on the horizontal axis and altitude on the vertical axis.

b) What is the altitude of the plane after 7 s?

c) At what time did the plane have an altitude of 1040 m?

d) Write the equation that models the plane's altitude over time.

8. Since Jim is on the road a lot, he
has a PDA phone with Internet access
and a calling package that allows
him to phone anywhere in North
America. Jim paid $575 for the phone
and he pays $55 per month for his
Internet calling package.

a) Draw a graph of the total amount
that Jim has spent for this special
phone for one year.

b) What is the equation of the line that models the total cost?

9. A company's postage machine starts the week with a balance
of $40. Each time an envelope is stamped, $0.55 is deducted
from the balance.

a) Copy and complete the table
of values. Then graph the data.

b) Does the line have a positive slope
or a negative slope? Explain
your answer.

c) Calculate the slope of the line.

d) From the graph, estimate the
remaining balance in the machine
after 35 envelopes have been stamped.

e) Write the equation that models the
postage machine's remaining balance.

f) How many envelopes can be stamped
before the balance needs to be increased?
Explain your answer.

Envelopes Stamped	Remaining Balance ($)
10	
20	
30	
40	
50	

Achievement Check

10. Heidi plans to add a cedar deck to her house. She asked Robin and
Just Decks for estimates. Robin will charge $2000 for materials and
$50 per hour for labour. Just Decks will charge $1800 for materials
and $80 per hour for labour. Robin estimates the job will take
18 hours. Just Decks will send two workers. They estimate they
can complete the job in 9 hours. Who should Heidi choose to
build her deck? Explain your answer algebraically or graphically.

11. These equations are examples of equations of horizontal lines: $y = -3$ and $y = 7$.

   a) What is an example of an equation of a vertical line? [Hint: making a sketch or creating a table of values may help.]

   b) Select two points on the line in part a) and express the slope of this line using $m = \dfrac{\text{rise}}{\text{run}}$.

   c) Solve for m using a calculator. What does the calculator display indicate? Why?

12. The cost of providing bottled water at a high school basketball tournament is $25 for the rental of the coolers and $0.65 per bottle. The school plans to sell water for $1.25 per bottle.

   a) Graph the linear relation that represents the school's cost for up to 200 bottles of water.

   b) On the same set of axes, graph the linear relation that represents the school's income from selling up to 200 bottles of water.

   c) Write the equation representing each line.

   d) What are the coordinates of the point where the lines cross?

   e) What is the significance of this point?

Review of Key Terms

In your own words, define each of the Key Terms from this chapter.

1. **a)** rate of change   **b)** slope
   c) linear relation   **d)** y-intercept
   e) rise   **f)** run
   g) coefficient

Check your definitions with those provided in the chapter.

3.1 Slope as a Rate of Change,
pages 100 to 110

2. **a)** Copy and complete the table of values to find the rate of change.

x	y	Rate of Change
0	−2	
1	1	
2	4	
3	7	
4	10	
5	13	

   b) What is the relationship between the rate of change and the slope?
   c) What is the slope?
   d) What is the y-intercept?
   e) Write the equation of the line that models this linear relation.

3. A downtown parking meter allows 15 min of parking time for $0.25.

   a) Create a table of values, in increments of 15 min, for the cost of parking up to 2 h.
   b) Use a graphing calculator to create a scatter plot.

   c) Explain why this relationship can be modelled with a linear equation.

4. Use $m = \dfrac{\text{rise}}{\text{run}}$ to calculate the slope of each line segment.

a)
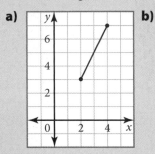

b)
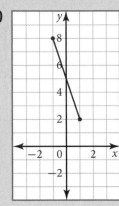

c)
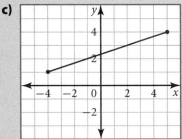

3.2 Investigate Slope and y-Intercept Using Technology, pages 111 to 117

5. Use a graphing calculator. Press [2nd] [TBLSET]. Set the table to start at 0 and go up in increments of 1. Use **G-T** mode and standard window settings. Graph the following linear relations. Sketch the calculator display in your notes.

   a) $y = 3x - 5$
   b) $y = -x + 2$
   c) $y = -0.25x + 7$
   d) $y = \dfrac{3}{4}x - \dfrac{3}{2}$

3.3 Properties of Slopes of Lines, pages 118 to 127

6. Refer to your graphs from question 5.

a) Which lines have a positive slope?

b) Which lines have a negative slope?

c) What is the *y*-intercept of each line?

d) Write an equation of a line that is parallel to each of the lines.

e) Write an equation of a line that is perpendicular to each of the lines.

f) List the equations in order from most steep to least steep.

7. Each table of values represents a linear relation. State whether the lines in each pair are parallel. Explain your answer.

a)

x	0	1	2	3	4
y	0	3	6	9	12

x	0	1	2	3	4
y	−12	−9	−6	−3	0

b)

x	0	1	2	3	4
y	10	7	4	1	−2

x	−1	−0.5	0	0.5	1
y	−10	−8.5	−7	−5.5	−4

3.4 Determine the Equation of a Line, pages 128 to 137

8. Determine the equation for each line in question 7.

9. Determine the equation of each line.
a) slope is 4, *y*-intercept is −3
b) slope is −2.7, *y*-intercept is 6.3
c) slope is 0, *y*-intercept is 2.5
d) slope is 2.5, *y*-intercept is 0

10. Determine the equation of each line.

a) slope is 2 and passes through (3, 8)

b) slope is −3 and passes through (2, 5)

c) slope is −2.5, passing through the origin

d) slope is $\frac{3}{4}$, passing through (2, 2)

e) slope is −1.4, passing through (−7, 7.5)

11. Determine the equation of each line.

a) passing through (−3, 6) and (9, 0)

b) passing through (1, −1) and (5, 5)

c) passing through (2, 500) and (10, 500)

d) passing through (−4.5, 8) and (2.5, −6)

3.5 Graph Linear Relations by Hand, pages 138 to 145

12. A $200 bond earns simple interest at a rate of 3% per year for 5 years.

a) How much interest does the bond earn each year? (Hint: Interest per year = amount invested multiplied by the interest rate expressed as a decimal.)

b) Create a table of values for the value of the bond at the end of each of the 5 years.

c) Graph the data from the table in part b).

d) Write the equation that models the value of the bond.

13. On the same set of axes, graph the pair of lines in question 7a).

1. State the slope, m, and the y-intercept, b, for each linear relation.

   a) $y = 2x + 5$

   b) $y = -\dfrac{1}{2}x + 3$

   c) $y = x - 7$

   d) $y = -3x - 2.5$

   e) $y = 32 + 1.8x$

   f) $y = 6$

2. Use $m = \dfrac{\text{rise}}{\text{run}}$ to determine the slope of each line segment.

   a)
   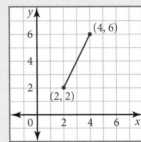

   b)
   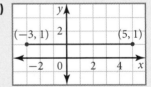

   c)
   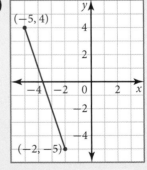

3. Determine the equation of each line.

   a) $m = 3, b = 1$

   b) slope is -2, y-intercept is 4

   c) a horizontal line passing through $(0, -9)$

4. On grid paper, graph each linear relation.

   a) $y = 2x - 1$

   b) $y = -3x + 5$

   c) $y = 3$

5. Surfing lessons cost $40 per half hour with a maximum lesson time of 2 h. There is a $5 surfboard rental fee for each lesson, regardless of the length of the lesson.

   a) Create a table of values comparing the total cost to the length of the lesson.

   b) Use a graphing calculator to create a scatter plot of the data from the table in part a).

   c) Write an equation relating C, the cost in dollars of a surfing lesson, to t, the length of the lesson in hours. Enter this equation into Y1, then press [GRAPH].

   d) While on vacation, Jesse had half-hour lessons on Monday and Tuesday, an hour-long lesson on Wednesday, and 90-min lessons on Thursday and Friday. How much were the surfing lessons?

6. Determine the equation of each line.

   a) $m = 2$, passing through $(-3, -5)$

   b) passing through $(-6, 3)$ and $(4, 1)$

   c) a horizontal line passing through $(2, 5)$

Chapter Problem Wrap-Up

Jim has used linear relations to calculate earnings, costs, distances, and the steepness of a hill. Now, he will use linear relations to interpret a map.

Jim is travelling a new route today. He checks the map to plan his route and determine where he will stop for meals. The scale on the map is 1 cm represents 5 km.

a) Is the relationship between the distance on the map and the actual distance linear? Explain.

b) Write an equation to model the relationship between the distance on the map and the actual distance. Let x represent the distance on the map and y represent the actual distance.

c) Graph the relation.

d) Interpret the meaning of the slope and the y-intercept in this situation.

---

7. Determine the equation of each line.

  a) $m = -\dfrac{3}{4}$, passing through (8, 8)

  b) passing through (−4, 3) and (6, 5)

8. A salesperson earns $200 per week plus 5% of total sales for sales up to $10 000. Let x represent total sales in dollars and y represent weekly earnings.

  a) Write an equation to represent this relation.

  b) What is the y-intercept? What does this value represent?

  c) What is the slope of this relation? What does it represent in this scenario?

  d) How much has to be sold to ensure an income of at least $550 per week?

9. While driving to Barrie, one of the tires on Moh's car picked up a nail. When he left his home, his tire was inflated to 240 kPa (kilopascals). The nail caused air to leak out of the tire at a rate of 0.8 kPa per minute.

  a) Write an equation that models P, tire pressure, related to t, the time in minutes since the nail entered the tire.

  b) Use a graphing calculator to display the graph and the table of values for the equation from part a). Adjust the window settings to view a graph for 2 hours from the time of picking up the nail. Sketch the calculator display.

  c) What will the tire pressure be 1 hour after picking up the nail?

  d) If the air continues to leak at the same rate, how long would it take for the tire to become completely flat, that is, have no air left in it?

4 Linear Equations

Paul is a meteorologist. He uses scientific methods to observe, understand, explain, and forecast the weather and how the atmosphere affects the world around us. Paul uses linear equations in his work studying the weather. In Chapter 3, you worked with graphs of linear relations. In this chapter, you will develop the algebraic skills needed to solve linear equations.

In this chapter, you will

- solve first-degree equations involving one variable, including equations with fractional coefficients
- determine the value of a variable in the first degree, using a formula (i.e., by isolating the variable and then substituting known values; by substituting known values then solving for the variable)
- express the equation of a line in the form $y = mx + b$ given the form $Ax + By + C = 0$

Reasoning and Proving

Representing · Selecting Tools

Problem Solving

Connecting · Reflecting

Communicating

Key Terms

constant term	standard form
formula	variable term
opposite operations	

Literacy Link

Use a Concept Circle to demonstrate the steps you would follow to solve equations.

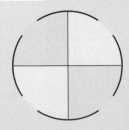

A market researcher studies the target market for a product. He or she determines the characteristics of the people most likely to buy the product. This information is used to develop marketing tools that will best reach the target population. Analyzing the data collected often involves the development and use of linear equations.

Get Ready!

Working With Fractions

1. Find the least common denominator for the fractions in each set. The first part has been done for you.

   a) $\dfrac{1}{4}, \dfrac{5}{6}$

   The least common denominator is the least common multiple of the denominators. List the multiples of each denominator:

   4: 4, 8, (12) 16, 20, 24, ...

   6: 6, (12) 18, 24, 30, 36, ...

   The least number that appears in both lists is 12. So, 12 is the least common denominator.

   b) $\dfrac{1}{5}, \dfrac{3}{10}$

   c) $\dfrac{2}{3}, \dfrac{1}{2}$

   d) $\dfrac{5}{6}, \dfrac{7}{18}$

   e) $\dfrac{1}{10}, \dfrac{1}{6}$

   f) $\dfrac{3}{4}, \dfrac{5}{8}, \dfrac{1}{16}$

   g) $\dfrac{1}{3}, \dfrac{4}{5}, \dfrac{7}{12}$

   h) $\dfrac{5}{6}, \dfrac{1}{2}, \dfrac{2}{9}$

Operations With Integers

2. Simplify. Use integer tiles when they help. The first part has been done for you.

   a) $4 + (-3) - (-5) + (+3) - 6$

   $4 \boxed{+ (-3)} \boxed{- (-5}) + (+3) - 6$

   $= 4 - 3 + 5 + 3 - 6$

   $= 1 + 5 + 3 - 6$

   $= 6 + 3 - 6$

   $= 9 - 6$

   $= 3$

   b) $1 - (-2) + (-2) - 4 + 2$

   c) $-3 - (-1) + (-4) + 5 + 3 - 4$

   d) $-3 + 5 + (-1) + 2 - 4 - 2$

   e) $2(3 + 4) - 3(7 + 2) + (-2 + 5)$

   f) $-4(1 - 4 + 5) - (4 + 3 - 1)$

Simplifying Algebraic Expressions

3. Simplify. The first part has been done for you.

   a) $4 + 4r - z + 3r + 5z - 2$

   $= 4 - 2 + 4r + 3r - z + 5z$

   $= 2 + 7r + 4z$

   b) $7y - 3 + 2y$

   c) $2 + 3r - 5 + r$

   d) $3x + 3y - 2x + 4$

   e) $k - 5t - 6k + 2t$

   f) $4t - (-2t) + (4 - 7t) + 7 - 7t + 11$

   g) $3x - y + z - 2y + 3x - 7y - 7z + 2y$

   h) $3q - 2p + 4 - 5 + 6p - 2q - (-3q)$

Chapter Problem

Angela is in charge of finding a location for her school's athletic banquet. She talks to friends at two other schools that held their banquets at the same hall that Angela would like to use. Cory's school was charged $6100 for 160 guests, and Anne's school was charged $4000 for 100 guests. Angela does not yet know how many people plan to attend the athletic banquet. How can she use the information her friends gave her to develop an equation comparing the total cost to the number of guests? In this chapter, you will learn the skills needed to answer this question.

4. Expand and simplify. The first part has been done for you.

a) $3(x + 2)$

$$3(x + 2)$$
$$= 3(x) + 3(2)$$
$$= 3x + 6$$

b) $2(q + 3) + 11q$
c) $8(4 - p) - 3(p + 5)$
d) $5(k - 1) + 3(2k - 2)$
e) $-2(e - 7) - 4(-3e + 5)$
f) $4(3k + 7) - 2(2 - 4k)$
g) $2(x + 4) - 3(3x - 4)$
h) $3(5r - 3) - 4(2r - 5)$

Evaluating Expressions

5. Evaluate each expression for $x = 2$ and $y = -1$. The first part has been done for you.

a) $4x + 3y$

$$= 4(2) + 3(-1)$$
$$= 8 - 3$$
$$= 5$$

b) $-7y$
c) $2x + 3y$
d) $2xy + 3yx - y$
e) $xy - xy + 2x - 2y + 3xy$
f) $\dfrac{3x + y}{5} + \dfrac{2x + y}{2}$

Modelling Equations With Algebra Tiles

6. Use algebra tiles to model each equation. The first part has been done for you.

a) $3x - 4 = 8$

b) $x - 1 = 5$
c) $12 = 4 + k$
d) $11 = 3r - 4$
e) $3z + 11 = 17$
f) $6 - 2a = -2$

4.1 Solve One- and Two-Step Linear Equations

Bungee jumping is popular among thrill seekers. Jumpers leap from bridges, dams, or cranes with elastic cords tied to their ankles or to a chest harness. How does the bungee operator determine the length of bungee cord to use for each jumper?

Investigate

Bungee Jumping

Ali is a bungee jump operator. For safety, he weighs each jumper before the jump. The relationship between the maximum bungee length, y, and the weight, x, of the jumper is linear. The graph shows the relationship for the bungee Ali uses.

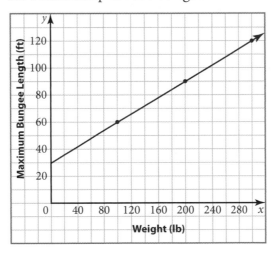

Work with a partner.
1. Write the equation of this relation in the form $y = mx + b$.
   a) In this situation, what does the value of b represent?
   b) What does the value of m represent?

Math **Connect**

The word algebra is derived from the Arabic *al-jabar*. Western Europeans learned their algebra from the works of Persian mathematician Muhammed ibn Musa al-Khowarizmi.

2. Suppose you were going to bungee jump from Ali's platform. Calculate the maximum bungee length for your jump.

3. Ali's platform is 150 ft above the ground.
   a) Write an equation you can use to find the maximum allowable weight of a jumper using Ali's bungee.
   b) Solve the equation from part a). Describe the steps you followed to solve this equation.
   c) Refer to your answer from part b). Should Ali allow a jumper with this weight to jump? Explain.

To solve a linear equation means to find the value of the variable that makes the equation true. This is the value of the variable that makes the left side of the equation equal to the right side. When solving a linear equation, you can use **opposite operations** to undo each operation.

When more than one mathematical operation is applied in an equation, the order in which the operations are *undone* is important. When undoing operations, think about the order of operations—division, multiplication, addition, and subtraction—in the reverse order.

opposite operations
- operations that "undo" one another
- addition and subtraction are opposite operations
- multiplication and division are opposite operations

Example **1** | **Solve a Two-Step Linear Equation**

For the equation $2x - 3 = 1$
  a) use algebra tiles to solve the equation
  b) use a flow chart to describe the steps needed to solve the equation
  c) check your solution

Solution

a) $2x - 3 = 1$

To isolate the variable term, 2x, add 3 to the left side.
To keep the equation balanced, add 3 to the right side.

$2x - 3 + 3 = 1 + 3$

Remove zero pairs.

$$2x = 4$$
$$x = 2$$

Since each x-tile pairs with 2 unit tiles, the solution is $x = 2$.

b) To solve the equation, undo the subtraction by adding 3 to both sides, then undo the multiplication by dividing both sides by 2.

$$2x - 3 = 1$$

start with x → multiply by 2 → subtract 3 → result is 1

$$2x - 3 + 3 = 1 + 3$$
$$2x = 4$$
$$\frac{2x}{2} = \frac{4}{2}$$
$$x = 2$$

result is 2 ← divide by 2 ← add 3 ← start with 1

c) One way to check your solution is to substitute it into the equation, then check that the left side (LS) and right side (RS) are equal.

$$LS = 2x - 3 \quad RS = 1$$
$$= 2(2) - 3$$
$$= 4 - 3$$
$$= 1$$

Since LS = RS, the solution is correct.

Math Connect

It is a good practice to always check your solution to make sure your answer is correct.

Example **2**

Solve a Linear Equation Involving a Fraction

Solve the equation $\frac{3k}{4} = 9$, and check your solution.

Solution

Method 1: Use Benchmarks to Convert the Fraction to a Decimal

$$\frac{3k}{4} = 9$$

Remember, $\frac{3}{4}$ is equivalent to 0.75.

$$0.75k = 9$$

Now this is a one-step equation.

$$\frac{0.75k}{0.75} = \frac{9}{0.75}$$
$$k = 12$$

Method 2: Use a Flow Chart

$$\frac{3k}{4} = 9$$

start with k → multiply by 3 → divide by 4 → result is 9

$$4 \times \frac{3k}{4} = 4 \times 9$$
$$3k = 36$$
$$\frac{3k}{3} = \frac{36}{3}$$
$$k = 12$$

result is 12 ← divide by 3 ← multiply by 4 ← start with 9

Check: Substitute $k = 12$ in the original equation.

$$LS = \frac{3k}{4} \qquad RS = 9$$

$$= \frac{3(12)}{4}$$

$$= 9$$

Since LS = RS, the solution $k = 12$ is correct.

Example **3** **Volume of a Gas**

The graph shows the relationship between the volume of a gas in cubic centimetres, y, and the temperature in degrees Celsius, x.

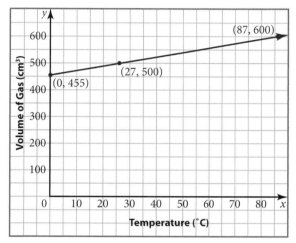

a) Write an equation in the form $y = mx + b$ for this relation. What do the values of m and b represent?

b) Find the temperature at which the volume of gas is 725 cm³.

Solution

a) Using the points (27, 500) and (87, 600), the rise is 100 and the run is 60.

$$m = \frac{\text{rise}}{\text{run}}$$

$$= \frac{100}{60}$$

$$= \frac{5}{3}$$

The y-intercept is 455.

The equation of the line is $y = \frac{5}{3}x + 455$.

The y-intercept, 455, represents the volume of the gas when the temperature is 0°C. The slope, $\frac{5}{3}$, represents the change in volume for each 1°C change in temperature.

b) Substitute $y = 725$ into the equation.

$$725 = \frac{5x}{3} + 455$$

$$725 - 455 = \frac{5x}{3} + 455 - 455$$

$$270 = \frac{5x}{3}$$

$$3(270) = 3\left(\frac{5x}{3}\right)$$

start with x → multiply by 5 → divide by 3 → add 455 → result is 725

$$810 = 5x$$

$$\frac{810}{5} = \frac{5x}{5}$$

result is 162 ← divide by 5 ← multiply by 3 ← subtract 455 ← start with 725

$$162 = x$$

Another way to check the solution is to use a graphing calculator.

- Press $\boxed{Y=}$ and type 725 in Y1.
- Press $\boxed{\blacktriangledown}$.

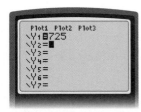

- Enter the right side in Y2.
- Press $\boxed{(}$ 5 $\boxed{\div}$ 3 $\boxed{)}$ $\boxed{X,T,\theta,n}$ $\boxed{+}$ 455.

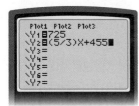

- Press $\boxed{WINDOW}$. Use the window settings shown:

- Press $\boxed{2nd}$ [CALC] 5 $\boxed{ENTER}$ $\boxed{ENTER}$ $\boxed{ENTER}$ to find the point where the two lines intersect.

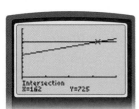

The coordinates of the point of intersection of the two lines are $x = 162$ and $y = 725$. That is, when $x = 162$, the y-coordinates of Y1 = 725 and Y2 = $\left(\frac{5}{3}\right)x + 455$ are both 725. Therefore, the solution $x = 162$ is correct.

Key Concepts

- Equations can be solved in different ways, including flow charts, algebra tiles, and opposite operations.

- One way to check the solution to a linear equation is to substitute the solution into the original equation. If the left side and the right side of the equation have the same value, the answer is correct.

- When a graphing calculator is used to check the solution, the left and right sides of the equation are graphed as Y1 and Y2 respectively. The value of x when the y-values are equal is the solution.

Discuss the Concepts

D1. Explain the steps you would follow to solve each equation.

    a) $3x - 5 = 7$ **b)** $5 - \dfrac{f}{4} = -15$

D2. Which two of these linear equations have the solution $k = 5$? How did you find out?

    a) $\dfrac{k}{5} = 6$ **b)** $k + 5 = 10$

    c) $5k = 25$ **d)** $k - 5 = 10$

Practise the Concepts   Ⓐ

For help with questions 1 to 6, refer to Example 1.

1. Which operation, addition, subtraction, multiplication, or division, is needed to undo the operation in each linear equation?

    a) $3x = 24$ **b)** $11 = r + 5$

    c) $k - 4 = 8$ **d)** $7u = 21$

    e) $\dfrac{s}{11} = 13$ **f)** $4 = y - 9$

2. Solve each equation in question 1.

3. Solve each linear equation.

    a) $12 = 3x$ **b)** $s + 5 = 11$

    c) $y - 3 = 14$ **d)** $\dfrac{x}{11} = 3$

    e) $x + 3 = 5$ **f)** $21 = 3t$

4. Solve each linear equation.

    a) $x - 4 = -5$ **b)** $\dfrac{x}{6} = 3$

    c) $16 = -4x$ **d)** $4 = x - 1$

    e) $-6 = \dfrac{x}{5}$ **f)** $\dfrac{x}{-3} = -3$

5. List, in order, the steps required to solve each linear equation.

a) $9 = 7 - 2y$ **b)** $\dfrac{w}{5} - 5 = 5$

c) $\dfrac{a}{8} - 3 = 7$ **d)** $4k - 3 = 13$

6. Solve each equation, then check your solution.

a) $3 = 3x - 3$ **b)** $2x - 6 = 12$

c) $11 = 5x + 6$ **d)** $2w - 3 = 11$

Achievement Check

7. Drake is going snowboarding today. The weather is sunny and very cold. He will wear snow pants, a jacket, a helmet, goggles, and gloves. Think of the steps involved in putting on his snowboarding equipment.

a) Illustrate these steps using a flow chart.

b) At the end of the day, Drake comes into the lodge and takes off his equipment. Is there only one way to undo the dressing steps? Explain.

c) Explain why the order of operations for simplifying expressions can also be used to create a flow chart when solving an equation.

For help with question 8, refer to Example 2.

8. Solve each equation, then check your solution.

a) $\dfrac{2r}{7} = -4$ **b)** $\dfrac{3x}{4} = 15$

c) $14 = \dfrac{7k}{5}$ **d)** $9 = -\dfrac{3y}{11}$

e) $\dfrac{5r}{9} = 10$ **f)** $\dfrac{4t}{3} = -8$

g) $-6 = -\dfrac{2g}{5}$ **h)** $\dfrac{2w}{9} = -10$

9. Solve each equation, then check your solution.

a) $\dfrac{y}{6} + 4 = 7$ **b)** $\dfrac{t}{12} - 1 = 1$

c) $\dfrac{x}{3} - 1 = -2$ **d)** $0.5r + 11 = 5$

e) $1.6 = 0.4k - 3.2$ **f)** $\dfrac{t}{3} - 6 = -1$

For help with question 10, refer to Example 3.

10. The graph shows how the total cost, in dollars, to ship workbooks is related to the number of workbooks.

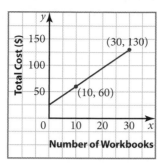

a) Write an equation in the form $y = mx + b$ for this relation.

b) What do the values of m and b represent?

c) Jee-Yun has a budget of $200 for workbooks. How many can she buy?

Literacy Connect

11. Write the order of operations you would use to put on hockey equipment for a practice, followed by the opposite operations you would use to remove them after the practice. Or, choose another sport and write the order of operations for putting on and removing the appropriate equipment.

12. When treating a sick child, a doctor may need to estimate the child's body surface area (BSA). This information helps the doctor determine appropriate doses of medicine. The BSA, in square centimetres, for a child can be estimated using the formula $BSA = 1321 + 0.3433m$, where m represents the child's mass in kilograms.

a) Find the BSA for a child with mass 12 kg.

b) Suppose that to receive a certain treatment, a child must have a BSA greater than 1333 cm². What is the minimum mass a child must have, to receive this treatment?

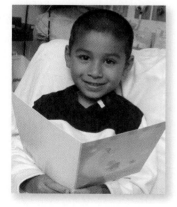

Chapter Problem

13. A banquet hall charges according to the equation $C = 25n + 250$, where C represents the total cost in dollars to rent the hall, and n represents the number of people attending the event. If the total cost to rent the hall for a particular event was $3375, how many people attended the event?

14. Dawson knows that the formula for the perimeter of a rectangle is $P = 2l + 2w$. He has 180 m of fencing to enclose a rectangular play area with a maximum width of 32 m. What is the minimum length of the play area? Explain.

15. Sap from sugar maple trees is boiled down to create maple syrup. The relationship between the mass of sugar in 100 g of sap, y, and the boiling temperature (in degrees Fahrenheit) above that for water, x, can be approximated by the linear relation
$y = 7.4x + 20.5$.

Find the number of degrees Fahrenheit above the temperature at which water boils that sap becomes maple syrup.

There are approximately 66 g of sugar in 100 g of maple syrup.

16. Kwan coaches baseball. She has $450 to buy uniforms for the team. Each uniform costs $30.
    a) Write an equation showing the relationship between the total cost in dollars, C, and the number of uniforms, n.
    b) There are 16 players on the team. Will there be enough uniforms? Explain.

17. The average of two numbers is 43. If one number is 38, what is the other number? How did you find the number?

Extend the Concepts C

18. Use opposite operations to rearrange, or "solve," each formula to isolate the indicated variable.
    a) $P = 2(l + w)$, for l
    b) $P = \dfrac{E}{t}$, for E
    c) $A = \dfrac{1}{2}(b \times h)$, for b
    d) $V = \pi r^2 h$, for h

19. These equations represent the total cost to charter buses from three different bus companies. In each equation, C represents the total cost in dollars, and n represents the number of passengers.

    Company X: $C = 35n + 500$
    Company Y: $C = 25n + 2000$
    Company Z: $C = 37.50n$

    Layton spends $10 150 to charter buses to transport 326 passengers to a reunion.

    a) Which bus company did Layton use?
    b) Did Layton choose the best company if he wanted to spend as little as possible to charter the buses? Explain your answer.

4.2 Solve Multi-Step Linear Equations

Patrice is an air traffic controller. She ensures that planes in the airspace surrounding the airport are a safe distance apart. Omar is a biologist studying the bird population in a region. How might Patrice and Omar use linear equations at work?

Investigate Order the Operations

Part A: Make Tea

A series of steps is listed below, but the steps are not in the correct order. Write the steps in order so that the desired outcome will be reached.

You are making tea for your parents.
- Let the tea steep for four minutes.
- Fill the kettle with cold water.
- Put two teabags into the teapot.
- Warm the teapot by filling it with hot water.
- Pour the hot water out of the teapot.
- Serve the tea.
- Plug in the kettle.
- Remove the teabags.
- When the kettle boils, pour boiling water over the teabags.

Part B: Pack Up a Drill

The steps listed below are out of order. Arrange them in the correct order to allow the outcome to be reached.

You have just helped to build a doghouse, and it is time to put away the cordless drill. Write these steps in the reverse order to that which you would have followed to get the drill out of its case.

- Put the drill bit back into the case.
- Remove the battery from the cordless drill.
- Remove the drill bit from the drill.
- Put the battery into the battery charger.
- Put the drill back into the case.

Which part of the investigation did you find easier to do? Why?

The process of undoing steps is much easier when the order in which they would initially be done is clearly understood.

Example **1** **Identify the Steps Required to Solve a Multi-Step Linear Equation**

For the linear equation $\dfrac{2x + 10}{3} = 20$

a) write the equation in words.

b) list, in order, the steps required to solve the equation.

Solution

a) Multiply x by 2.
Add 10 to the product.
Divide by 3.
The result is 20.

b) To solve the equation, perform the opposite operations in the reverse order:

Multiply 20 by 3, $\qquad\qquad\qquad\quad 20 \times 3 = 60$
Subtract 10 from the product. $\qquad 60 - 10 = 50$
Divide by 2 to find the value of x. $\qquad \dfrac{50}{2} = 25$
The solution is $x = 25$.

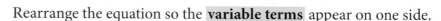

Example 2 — Solve a Linear Equation With a Variable Term on Each Side

Solve the equation $6x + 5 = 4x - 7$.

variable term
- a term that includes a letter or symbol to represent an unknown value
- in the equation $7x + 3 = -5$, the variable term is $7x$

constant term
- a numerical term which cannot change; that is, it remains constant
- does not include a variable
- in the equation $7x + 3 = -5$, the constant terms are 3 and -5

Solution

Model the equation using algebra tiles.

$$6x + 5 = 4x - 7$$

Rearrange the equation so the **variable terms** appear on one side.

$$6x + 5 - 4x = 4x - 4x - 7$$

Simplify each side by removing zero pairs.

$$2x + 5 = -7$$

Rearrange the equation so the **constant terms** appear on the other side.

$$2x + 5 - 5 = -7 - 5$$

$$2x = -12$$

The algebra tiles can be arranged so that each x-tile pairs with 6 negative unit tiles.

Therefore, $x = -6$.

Example 3 — Solve a Linear Equation With Brackets and a Variable Term on Each Side

Solve the equation $3(x - 1) + 1 = 5(x - 2)$.

Solution

Model $3(x - 1) + 1 = 5(x - 2)$ with algebra tiles.
There are 3 groups of $(x - 1)$, or ▬▬▭ , plus 1 on the left side, and 5 groups of $(x - 2)$, or ▬▬▭▭ on the right side.

$$3(x + 1) + 1 = 5(x - 2)$$

Muliply to eliminate the brackets.

$$3x - 3 + 1 = 5x - 10$$

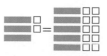

Simplify by removing the zero pair.

$$3x - 2 = 5x - 10$$

Move the variable terms to the right side.

$3x - 3x - 2 = 5x - 3x - 10$

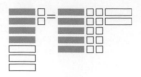

Simplify by removing zero pairs.

$-2 = 2x - 10$

Move the constant terms to the left side.

$-2 + 10 = 2x - 10 + 10$

$8 = 2x$

The algebra tiles can be arranged so that each x-tile pairs with 4 unit tiles.

Therefore, $x = 4$.

<table><tr><td>**Example**</td><td>**4**</td></tr></table>

Solve a Multi-Step Linear Equation Involving Fractions

Solve the equation $\dfrac{x + 3}{8} + \dfrac{x + 1}{3} = 3$.

Solution

Method 1: Multiply to Eliminate the Fraction

Find the least common multiple of the denominators.

8: 8, 16, $\boxed{24}$ 32, 40

3: 3, 6, 9, 12, 15, 18, 21, $\boxed{24}$ 27

Multiply each term in the equation by 24.

$$24\left(\frac{x + 3}{8}\right) + 24\left(\frac{x + 1}{3}\right) = 24(3)$$

$$\overset{3}{24}\left(\frac{x + 3}{8}\right) + \overset{8}{24}\left(\frac{x + 1}{3}\right) = 24(3)$$

$3(x + 3) + 8(x + 1) = 72$ *Multiply to eliminate the brackets.*

$3x + 9 + 8x + 8 = 72$

$3x + 8x + 9 + 8 = 72$ *Collect like terms.*

$11x + 17 = 72$

$11x + 17 - 17 = 72 - 17$ *Subtract 17 from both sides.*

$11x = 55$

$\dfrac{11x}{11} = \dfrac{55}{11}$

$x = 5$

Method 2: Use a Computer Algebra System (CAS)

1. Press CATALOG to access list of calculator commands.

2. Press 4 ▼ ENTER to paste "lcm(" on the command prompt line.

3. Press 8 , 3) ENTER.

4. Press F2 3 for **expand**.
(24 (x +
3) ÷ 8) ENTER.

Notice that 24 divided by 8 is 3 and that $3(x + 3)$ is $3x + 9$ using the distributive property. Check this using a CAS.

5. Press F2 3 for **expand**.
• Press 3 (x +
3)) ENTER.

• Press F2 3 for expand.
• Press 24, (x +
1) ÷ 3)
ENTER.

Notice that 24 divided by 3 is 8 and that $8(x + 1)$ is $8x + 8$ using the distributive property. Check this using a CAS.

- Press $\boxed{\text{F2}}$ 3 for **expand**.
- Press 8 $\boxed{(}$ $\boxed{X}$ $\boxed{+}$ $\boxed{1}$ $\boxed{)}$ $\boxed{)}$ $\boxed{\text{ENTER}}$.

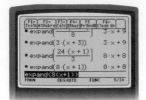

6. Press 3 $\boxed{\times}$ 24, $\boxed{\text{ENTER}}$ to multiply the right side of the equation by the LCD.

7. Combine the results from steps 4, 5, and 6.
- Press 3 $\boxed{X}$ $\boxed{+}$ 9 $\boxed{+}$ 8 $\boxed{X}$ $\boxed{+}$ 8 $\boxed{=}$ 72 $\boxed{\text{ENTER}}$.

8. Press 11 $\boxed{X}$ $\boxed{+}$ 17 $\boxed{-}$ 17 $\boxed{=}$ 72 $\boxed{-}$ 17 $\boxed{\text{ENTER}}$.

9. Press 11 $\boxed{X}$ $\boxed{\div}$ 11, $\boxed{=}$ 55 $\boxed{\div}$ 11 $\boxed{\text{ENTER}}$.

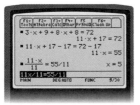

The solution is $x = 5$.   *Notice that both methods produce the same solution to the equation.*

Key Concepts

- Multi-step linear equations can be solved using opposite operations, algebra tiles, or a computer algebra system.
- When a linear equation involves fractions, it is useful to multiply each term by the least common multiple of the denominators.

Discuss the Concepts

D1. Describe the steps you would follow to solve each equation to obtain the solution below.

a) $5(x - 3) + 4 = 2(+ 3) + 1$
$x = 6$

b) $\dfrac{3m + 1}{5} = -4$
$m = -7$

D2. When a linear equation has variable terms on both sides, how do you decide whether to move the variable terms to the left side or to the right side? Explain.

Practise the Concepts

For help with questions 1 and 2, refer to Example 1.

1. List, in order, the steps required to solve each equation.

a) $3(z + 5) = 12$

b) $\dfrac{3x - 5}{2} = 5$

c) $\dfrac{2(t - 4)}{3} = 8$

d) $12 = 3(k + 4)$

e) $\dfrac{3}{4}(d + 2) = -3$

f) $\dfrac{4}{5}a - 3 = 5$

2. Solve each equation in question 1.

For help with question 3, refer to Example 2.

3. Solve each equation.

a) $3w - 2 = 2w + 3$

b) $5q + 6 = 4q - 9$

c) $6t - 7 = 2t + 5$

d) $-2x + 4 = 3x - 2$

e) $5c = 6c + 7$

f) $6 - 5k = 4 + 3k$

For help with question 4, refer to Example 3.

4. Solve each equation.

  a) $3(x + 6) = 2(x - 1)$ **b)** $2y - 3(-1) = 6 - 4y$
  c) $1 - (2 + w) = w + 5$ **d)** $3(2 - k) = 10 + k$
  e) $3(j + 1) = 5(j - 3)$ **f)** $4(3g - 5) = -2(46 + 3g)$

For help with question 5, refer to Example 4.

5. Solve each equation.

  a) $\dfrac{4a - 1}{3} = 5$ **b)** $0.4w + 0.6 = -3$

  c) $\dfrac{2(k - 3)}{3} = 12$ **d)** $0.2v = 0.6v + 1.7$

  e) $\dfrac{k}{4} - 2 = -\dfrac{4}{3}$ **f)** $\dfrac{2}{3}(x + 1) = -8$

  g) $\dfrac{1}{3}(2h + 3) = 5$ **h)** $2.5(3j - 1) = -25$

  i) $\dfrac{r + 5}{3} + 5 = -r$ **j)** $\dfrac{q - 2}{3} - \dfrac{q + 4}{4} = 5$

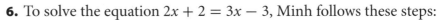

Apply the Concepts B

6. To solve the equation $2x + 2 = 3x - 3$, Minh follows these steps:
   - Choose any number for x.
   - Substitute the number into the left and right sides of the equation and simplify.
   - Compare the results.
   - If the left and right sides have the same value, the number chosen is the solution.
   - If the left and right sides do not have the same value, Minh chooses a different number and tries again.

   Would you recommend using this approach to solve a linear equation? Why or why not?

Literacy Connect

7. Think of something you do every day, and write the steps you would have to do to undo it.

8. Mr. Singh has $300 in a savings account that pays 0.5% per year simple interest. In the equation $A = 300 + (0.005 \times 300)n$, A represents the total amount in Mr. Singh's account in dollars, and n represents the number of years. At this rate, how long will it take for the balance in Mr. Singh's account to reach $375?

9. Flight 47 leaves Toronto Pearson International Airport en route to Vancouver. It travels at an average speed of 500 km/h. One hour later, a cargo flight leaves Pearson for Vancouver, travelling at an average speed of 750 km/h. Let t represent the time in hours that Flight 47 has flown. Solve the equation $500t = 750(t - 1)$ to find out when the cargo plane catches up with Flight 47.

10. Dave's cottage is on a river. He goes to visit a friend at his cottage upstream. It takes $\frac{3}{4}$ h to travel to his friend's cottage and $\frac{1}{2}$ h to return home. The speed of the boat in still water is 20 km/h. Let x represent the speed of the current in kilometres per hour.

   a) As Dave travels upstream, the speed of the current reduces the speed of the boat. Write an expression to represent the speed at which Dave travels upstream.

   b) When Dave returns home, he is travelling with the current, so the speed of the current increases the total speed. Write an expression to represent the speed at which Dave travels home.

   c) Solve the equation $\frac{3}{4}(20 - x) = \frac{1}{2}(20 + x)$ to find the speed of the current.

11. Jack and Diane are bus drivers who drive the same route. Jack drives the regular bus, which travels at an average speed of 35 km/h. Diane drives the express bus, which travels at an average speed of 60 km/h. Diane completes her route in $\frac{3}{4}$ h less time than Jack does. Solve the equation $60(t - 0.75) = 35t$ to find the length of time Jack takes to complete the route. How long does Diane take?

12. An inlet pipe can fill a storage tank in 6 h. An outlet pipe will empty the same tank in 8 h. By accident, both pipes are left open. Use the equation $\frac{1}{6}x - \frac{1}{8}x = 1$ to find the number of hours it will take to fill the tank.

13. Omar is studying two species of birds on an island with area 150 000 m^2. Each nesting pair of species A requires 75 m^2 of territory, and each nesting pair of species B requires 100 m^2. Omar believes the population of species A is double that of species B. Let n represent the number of nesting pairs of species A.

a) Write an expression that represents the number of nesting pairs of species B.

b) Write an equation using the information presented in the question. Use the equation to find the number of nesting pairs of each species the island can support.

Chapter Problem **14.** These equations show how the total costs in dollars, C, to rent three different banquet halls are related to the number of people, n, attending the event.

| Hall X: $C = 35n + 500$ |
| Hall Y: $C = 25n + 2000$ |
| Hall Z: $C = 37.50n$ |

Solve each equation to find the number of guests for which the total cost at each hall would be the same.
a) $35n + 500 = 25n + 2000$ for Hall X and Hall Y
b) $25n + 2000 = 37.5n$ for Hall Y and Z
c) $35n + 500 = 37.5n$ for Hall X and Hall Z

15. Dwight is a racecar driver. He knows the distance an object travels can be found using the formula $d = vt + \frac{1}{2}at^2$, where d represents the distance travelled in metres, v represents the starting speed in metres per second, t represents the time interval of the trip in seconds, and a represents the acceleration in metres per second squared during the interval.

a) Dwight travels 53 000 m by accelerating at 24 m/s² for 30 s from a fixed starting speed. What is Dwight's starting speed?

b) Suppose Dwight had accelerated for 60 s from the same starting speed. How far would he travel?

c) Is the distance travelled in part b) double the distance in part a)? Explain why or why not.

16. A person's index of cardiorespiratory fitness can be found by taking three 30-s pulse measurements over the course of one workout. The index is determined by the formula

$$I = \frac{50d}{a + b + c}$$

where I represents the fitness index, d represents the duration of the physical activity in seconds, and a, b, and c are the three 30-s pulse measurements. If a fitness index of 73.5 is found over a 5-min high-impact physical activity with two pulse measurements of 70 and 60 being recorded, what is the third pulse measurement?

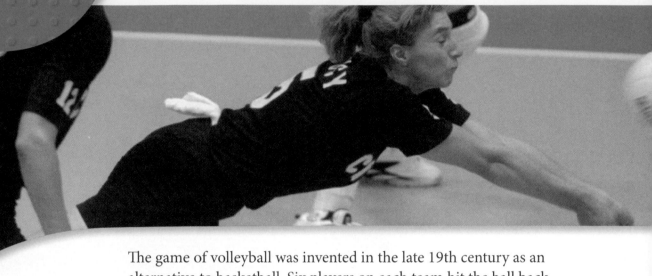

4.3 Model With Formulas

The game of volleyball was invented in the late 19th century as an alternative to basketball. Six players on each team hit the ball back and forth over the net. The players try to hit the ball to the floor in the opposing team's court. In volleyball, an *attack* is any offensive hit of the ball and a *kill* is an attack that results in an immediate point.

formula
• describes an algebraic relationship between two or more variables

Use Formulas to Solve Problems

The attack percent, *Pct*, in volleyball is calculated using this **formula**: $Pct = \dfrac{K - E}{TA}$, where K is the number of kills, E is the number of attack errors, and TA is the total number of attacks.

1. Calculate the attack percent for each player.
   a) Kristi has 7 kills, 3 errors, and 25 attacks.
   b) Jessica has 11 kills, 2 errors, and 22 attacks.

2. Jade's attack percent is 0.571. She has 1 error in 7 attacks. Find the number of kills Jade has made. Describe the steps you used to solve this problem.

3. Merella's attack percent is −0.333. She has 1 kill and 2 errors. Find the total number of attacks Merella has made. How did you calculate the answer?

4. Use your answer to question 3 as a guide.
   a) Rewrite the formula to isolate total attacks.
   b) **Reflect** How are the steps you followed in part a) similar to the steps you followed in question 3?

Example 1

Rearrange Formulas

Rearrange each formula to solve for the indicated variable.

a) $y = mx + b$, solve for x

b) $A = P(1 + rt)$, solve for t

c) $w = u + at^2$, solve for a

Solution

In each formula, follow the same steps you would to solve an equation.

a)
$$y = mx + b \qquad \text{Subtract b from both sides of the equation.}$$
$$y - b = mx + b - b$$
$$y - b = mx \qquad \text{Divide both sides of the equation by m to isolate x.}$$
$$\frac{y - b}{m} = \frac{mx}{m}$$
$$\frac{y - b}{m} = x$$

b)
$$A = P(1 + rt) \qquad \text{Multiply to remove the brackets.}$$
$$A = P + Prt \qquad \text{Subtract P from both sides.}$$
$$A - P = P + Prt - P$$
$$A - P = Prt \qquad \text{Divide both sides by Pr to isolate t.}$$
$$\frac{A - P}{Pr} = \frac{Prt}{Pr}$$
$$\frac{A - P}{Pr} = t$$

c)
$$w = u + at^2 \qquad \text{Subtract u from both sides.}$$
$$w - u = u + at^2 - u$$
$$w = at^2 \qquad \text{Divide both sides by } t^2 \text{ to isolate a.}$$
$$\frac{w - u}{t^2} = \frac{at^2}{t^2}$$
$$\frac{w - u}{t^2} = a$$

Example | 2

Distance, Speed, and Time With One Object

At a constant speed, the distance, (d), an object travels when it moves at a constant speed depends on how long it travels, (t), and its speed (s). The formula relating distance, speed, and time is $d = st$.

Depending on their positions in orbit, the distance from Earth to Mars varies from a minimum of 56 000 000 km to a maximum of 402 000 000 km. A space probe travels 26 000 km/h. The mean distance between Earth and Mars is 150 000 000 km. How long does it take the probe to travel from Earth to Mars, on average?

Solution

Method 1: Substitute Then Solve

Substitute $d = 150\ 000\ 000$, $s = 26\ 000$. Then, solve for t.

$$d = st$$

$$150\ 000\ 000 = 26\ 000t \qquad \textit{Divide both sides by 26 000 to isolate t.}$$

$$\frac{150\ 000\ 000}{26\ 000} = \frac{26\ 000t}{26\ 000}$$

$$5769.23 \doteq t \qquad \textit{Since the values of d and s are known, isolate t.}$$

It would take the space probe approximately 5769 hours, or about 240 days to reach Mars.

Method 2: Rearrange the Formula First

$$d = st$$

$$\frac{d}{s} = \frac{st}{s}$$

$$\frac{d}{s} = t$$

Substitute $d = 150\ 000\ 000$ and $s = 26\ 000$.

$$\frac{150\ 000\ 000}{26\ 000} = t$$

$$t \doteq 5769.23$$

It would take the space probe about 5769 hours, or approximately 240 days to reach Mars.

Some formulas contain many variables. You must be sure what each variable represents as you solve the equation that results once values are substituted into the formula.

<table>
<tr><td>

Example **3**

</td><td>

Simple Interest

This formula shows how the amount of simple interest, I, earned on an investment is related to the amount invested (also called the principal) in dollars, P, the interest rate, r, (expressed as a decimal) and the time, t, of the investment in years.

$I = Prt$

Damon deposits $500 into a savings account that pays simple interest at a rate of 0.65% per year. How long will it take Damon to earn $130 in interest?

</td></tr>
</table>

Math Connect

A savings account is the easiest way to earn interest on your money.
To learn more about how to earn interest with your money, go to www.mcgrawhill.ca/links/foundations10 and follow the links.

Solution

Method 1: Substitute Then Solve

$I = 130$, $P = 500$, and $r = 0.65\%$ or 0.0065
Substitute these values into the equation.

$$130 = 500(0.0065)t$$
$$130 = 3.25t$$
$$\frac{130}{3.25} = \frac{3.25t}{3.25}$$
$$40 = t$$

It will take Damon 40 years to earn $130 in interest.

Method 2: Rearrange First

$I = Prt$ *Since the values of I, P and r are known, isolate t.*

$$\frac{I}{Pr} = \frac{Prt}{Pr}$$
$$\frac{I}{Pr} = t$$

Substitute $I = 130$, $P = 500$, and $r = 0.0065$.

$$\frac{130}{500 \times 0.0065} = t$$
$$t = 40$$

It will take Damon 40 years to earn $130 in interest.

Example 4

Taxes on a Meal

A local restaurant features a live band. The bill for food and beverages has 6% GST, 8% PST, and a 12% service charge added. The restaurant also adds a cover charge of $25. If x represents the cost for food and beverages, the total cost in dollars, C, can be calculated using this equation:

$$C = x + 0.06x + 0.08x + 0.12x + 25$$

Rana's total bill was $310.75. How much was the bill for Rana's food and beverages?

Solution

Method 1: Use Paper and Pencil

Collect like terms to simplify the equation.

$$C = x + 0.06x + 0.08x + 0.12x + 25$$
$$C = 1.26x + 25$$

Substitute $C = 310.75$ into the equation.

$$310.75 = 1.26x + 25$$
$$310.75 - 25 = 1.26x + 25 - 25$$
$$285.75 = 1.26x$$
$$\frac{285.75}{1.26} = \frac{1.26x}{1.26}$$
$$226.79 \doteq x$$

The bill for Rana's food and beverages was $226.79.

Method 2: Use a Computer Algebra System

1. Press [2nd] [F1] 1, [ENTER] to clear 1-character variables.

2. Press [F1], 8, to clear the home screen and the command prompt line.

3. Type 310.75 [=] [x] [+] .06[x] [+] .08[x] [+] .12[x] [+] 25 and press [ENTER].

4. Type 310.75 [−] 25 [=] 1.26[x] [+] 25 [−] 25 and press [ENTER].

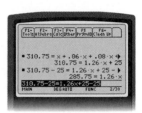

5. Type 285.75 [÷] 1.26 [=] 1.26[x] [÷] 1.26 and press [ENTER].

6. Press [2nd], 5 for **Number**. Then Right Arrow, 3 to paste "round(" to the command prompt line.

7. Type 226.7857143.
- Press [,] 2 [ )], [ENTER].

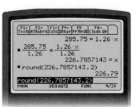

The bill for Rana's food and beverages was $226.79.

Key Concepts

- By reversing the order of operations, formulas can be rearranged in the same way as equations are solved.
- When values for variables are given, the values can be substituted first and then the resulting equation solved, or the formula can be rearranged and then the values substituted.
- There is more than one way to solve most problems. Choose the method you are most comfortable with.

Discuss the Concepts

D1. Describe the steps required to rearrange each formula to obtain the form shown below.

a) $V = adt$

$$w = \frac{V}{gh}$$

b) $E = mc^2$

$$\frac{E}{c^2} = m$$

c) $s = \dfrac{w - 10e}{t}$

$$e = \frac{st - w}{-10}$$

D2. Mina and Francesco are solving this problem:

An airplane travels 990 km in 4.5 h. How fast is the plane flying?

Mina's solution started

$$d = st$$
$$990 = 4.5t$$

Francesco's solution started

$$d = st$$
$$\frac{d}{t} = s$$
$$\frac{990}{4.5} = s$$

Who is correct? Explain.

Practise the Concepts **A**

For help with question 1, refer to Example 1.

1. Rearrange each formula to solve for the indicated variable.

a) $A = lw$, solve for w

b) $P = 2l + 2w$, solve for l

c) $y = mx + b$, solve for b

d) $C = 2\pi r$, solve for r

e) $V = lwh$, solve for h

f) $A = \dfrac{bh}{2}$, solve for h

For help with question 2, refer to Example 2.

2. a) A car travels at 45 km/h for 2.5 h. How far does the car travel?

b) Rearrange the formula $d = st$ to solve for s. Use this formula to find the speed of a truck that travels 262.5 km in 3.5 h.

c) Rearrange the formula $d = st$ to solve for t. Use this formula to find how long it would take a boat to travel 59.5 km at a speed of 34 km/h.

Reasoning and Proving

Representing | Selecting Tools

Problem Solving

Connecting | Reflecting

Communicating

For help with questions 3 to 5, refer to Example 3.

3. The formula for the amount of simple interest earned on an investment is $I = Prt$, where I is the interest earned, P is the principal, or amount invested, r is the interest rate as a decimal, and t is the time the investment is left in the bank (in years). Find the amount of interest earned on an investment of \$4000 at 0.85% interest after 4 years.

4. Use the simple interest formula $I = Prt$. Find the amount that needs to be invested at 8% per year for 10 years in order to earn \$2000 in interest.

5. a) Rearrange the formula $I = Prt$ to solve for t.

b) Rearrange the formula $I = Prt$ to solve for r.

c) Rearrange the formula $I = Prt$ to solve for P.

d) Copy and complete the table.

I	P	r	t
	2200	0.15	6
240	800		3
625		0.25	4
3300	2000		11
450	1800	0.05	
4400		0.04	22
	600	0.025	30
522	725	0.08	

For help with question 6, refer to Example 4.

6. An all-inclusive resort vacation charges an airport tax of \$150 plus 8% tax and 10% gratuity. If the total cost for a vacation is \$3926, what is the cost of the vacation before the extra fees and taxes?

Apply the Concepts B

7. Graham and Colin leave the same place at the same time and drive in opposite directions. Colin drives 10 km/h faster than Graham does. After 2 h, they are 200 km apart. How fast is each man driving?

8. Jenna and Maya have walkie-talkies with a range of 5 km. They leave the park on their bicycles, at the same time. Jenna rides east at 14 km/h and Maya rides west at 12 km/h. After half an hour, will they be able to use their walkie-talkies? How do you know?

9. a) Describe a situation in which you would rearrange a formula before substituting the known values and solving.

b) Describe a situation in which you would substitute known values into a formula before rearranging and solving.

10. The equation $s = \dfrac{w - 10e}{t}$ models the speed in words per minute, s, at which someone types. The speed, s, is related to the number of words typed, w, the number of errors, e, and the time spent typing in minutes, t.

Alex types 525 words in 5 min, with 10 errors. What is Alex's typing speed?

11. Use the equation for typing speed from question 10. Melanie's typing speed is 100 word/min. She types 800 words in 7 min. How many errors did Melanie make?

12. The formula $F = \dfrac{9}{5}C + 32$ relates temperature measured in degrees Fahrenheit, F, to temperature measured in degrees Celsius, C. Nalini's air conditioner is broken. Her thermostat, which is calibrated in degrees Fahrenheit, reads 88°F.

a) Rearrange the formula to isolate C.

b) Use the formula from part a) to find the temperature inside Nalini's house in degrees Celsius.

c) A quick way to approximate the conversion from degrees Celsius to degrees Fahrenheit is to double the temperature in degrees Celsius and add 30. This can be expressed using the formula $F = 2C + 30$. Rearrange this formula to isolate C.

d) Use your answer to part c) to find the approximate temperature inside Nalini's house in degrees Celsius.

e) Use a graphing calculator. Graph your equations from parts a) and c). Use the graph to explain why the short-cut formula gives a good approximation to the actual temperature.

Reasoning and Proving

Representing | Selecting Tools

Problem Solving

Connecting | Reflecting

Communicating

13. Underwater pressure in the ocean increases by about 51 kPa for every 5 m of depth. The Serafina submersible is designed to descend to 3000 m. How much pressure will the Serafina need to withstand at that depth?

14. a) A banquet hall charged $12 000 for an event that 250 people attended. If the hall has a flat fee of $4000 for an event plus a charge per person attending, what is the charge per person?

b) A second hall charged $12 600 for an event that 300 people attended. If this hall does not have a flat fee, how much does it charge per person?

c) Which hall would be a better deal for an event where 400 people are expected to attend? Explain your answer.

Achievement Check

15. With every increase in altitude of 1000 m, the temperature decreases by about 6°C. At the base of a mountain the temperature is 10°C.

a) Write an equation to model the temperature on the mountain.

b) The temperature outside the tents at the first camp for climbers is −10°C. How high up the mountain is the camp?

c) An airplane flies over the mountain at a height of 7.5 km. What is the temperature outside the plane?

Extend the Concepts C

16. One measure of a baseball pitcher's performance is WHIP, walks and hits per inning pitched. This statistic relates the number of runners who get on base per inning, r, to the total number of walks, w, the total number of hits, h, and the total number of innings pitched, i, according to the formula $r = \dfrac{w + h}{i}$.

The value of r is calculated to two decimal places.

A high school coach is trying to decide which pitcher to use in the final game. Copy and complete the table. Which pitcher should the coach choose? Why?

Pitcher	Total Walks (w)	Total Hits (h)	Total Innings (i)	WHIP (r)
Raymond	34	53	82	
Jesse	16	22	31	
Tran	55	72	101	
Harvinder	41	66	96	
Igor	27	38	53	

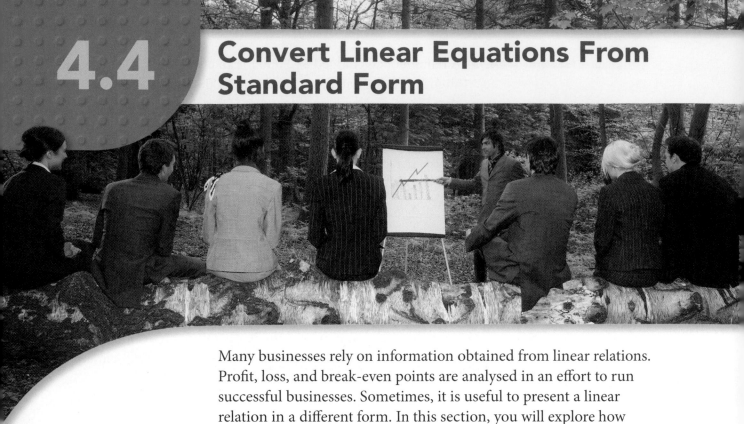

4.4 Convert Linear Equations From Standard Form

Many businesses rely on information obtained from linear relations. Profit, loss, and break-even points are analysed in an effort to run successful businesses. Sometimes, it is useful to present a linear relation in a different form. In this section, you will explore how different representations of linear equations are related.

Investigate

standard form
- a linear equation of the form $Ax + By + C = 0$
- A is a whole number
- B and C are integers
- A and B cannot both equal zero

Find the Initial Value and the Rate of Change

The equation $13x - 2y + 24 = 0$ is written in **standard form**. In this equation, y represents the total cost of a school field trip and x represents the total number of students going on the trip.

1. Use the graph.
   a) Find the slope of the line. What does the slope represent in this situation?
   b) What is the y-intercept? What does this value represent?
   c) Write the equation of the line in the form $y = mx + b$.

2. Rearrange the equation $13x - 2y + 24 = 0$ to isolate y. How does the result compare to your answer to part c)?

3. **Reflect** Explain why it is sometimes useful to rearrange an equation into slope y-intercept form.

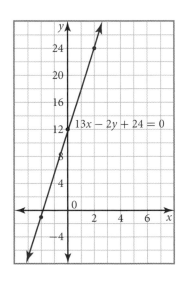

Rewrite a Linear Equation in Slope y-Intercept Form

Rearrange the equation $3x + y - 5 = 0$ into slope y-intercept form, then identify the slope and the y-intercept.

Solution

To write the equation in slope y-intercept form, rearrange the equation to isolate y.

$$3x + y - 5 = 0$$
$$3x + y - 5 + 5 = 0$$
$$3x + y = 5$$
$$3x + y - 3x = 5 - 3x$$
$$y = 5 - 3x \text{ or } y = -3x + 5$$

The slope of this linear relation is -3 and the y-intercept is 5.

Rearrange a Linear Equation Involving Fractions

Rewrite the equation $2x + 3y - 9 = 0$ in slope y-intercept form, then state the slope and y-intercept.

Solution

$$2x + 3y - 9 = 0$$
$$2x + 3y - 9 - 2x = 0 - 2x$$
$$3y - 9 + 9 = -2x + 9$$
$$3y = -2x + 9 \qquad \textit{Divide each term in the equation by 3.}$$
$$\frac{3y}{3} = -\frac{2x}{3} + \frac{9}{3}$$
$$y = -\frac{2x}{3} + 3$$

The slope is $-\dfrac{2}{3}$, and the y-intercept is 3.

Example **3** **Find the Number of Tickets Needed to Be Sold**

Tickets for a local theatre production are $2 per adult and $1 per child. The total revenue, the amount of money the theatre made, R, is $2x + y = R$ where x represents the number of adult tickets sold, and y represents the number of children's tickets sold.

The theatre company wants to bring in revenue of $750 for each of the next three shows. The number of adult tickets sold for these shows is 200, 225, and 175 respectively.

a) Write the revenue equation in slope y-intercept form.

b) How many children's tickets must be sold for each show to achieve the revenue target?

c) What is the advantage of rearranging the equation first?

Solution

a)
$$2x + y = R \qquad \textit{The total revenue wanted is \$750.}$$
$$2x + y = 750$$
$$2x + y - 2x = 750 - 2x$$
$$y = -2x + 750$$

b) First show: Second show: Third show:

Substitute $x = 200$.   Substitute $x = 225$.   Substitute $x = 175$.

$y = -2(200) + 750$ $y = -2(225) + 750$ $y = -2(175) + 750$

$\quad = -400 + 750 \qquad\quad = -450 + 750 \qquad\quad = -350 + 750$

$\quad = 350 \qquad\qquad\qquad = 300 \qquad\qquad\qquad = 400$

To meet the revenue target, 350 children's tickets must be sold for the first show, 300 for the second show, and 400 for the third show.

c) You could substitute each x-value into $2x + y = 750$, but each time, you would have to rearrange the equation to find the answer. Rearranging the equation into slope y-intercept form allows you to substitute and evaluate without rearranging.

Practise the Concepts **A**

1. Find the slope and y-intercept of each linear relation, then write the equation for the relation in slope y-intercept form.

a)
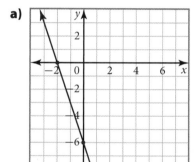

$3x + y + 6 = 0$

b)
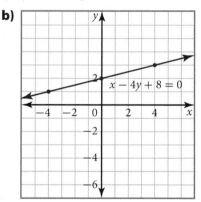

$x - 4y + 8 = 0$

c)
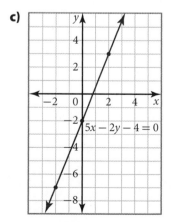

$5x - 2y - 4 = 0$

d)
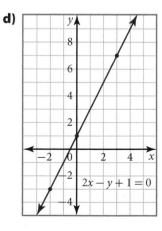

$2x - y + 1 = 0$

For help with question 2, refer to Example 1.

2. Rewrite each equation in slope y-intercept form.
- **a)** $2x + y - 1 = 0$
- **b)** $3x - y - 5 = 0$
- **c)** $2x + y - 4 = 0$
- **d)** $5x + y + 8 = 0$
- **e)** $x - y + 1 = 0$
- **f)** $2x - y - 3 = 0$

For help with question 3, refer to Example 2.

3. Rewrite each equation in slope y-intercept form, then state the slope and the y-intercept.
- **a)** $2x - y + 4 = 0$
- **b)** $3x + y - 2 = 0$
- **c)** $x - y + 4 = 0$
- **d)** $3x + y + 11 = 0$
- **e)** $8x - y - 5 = 0$
- **f)** $2x + y + 7 = 0$

4. Rewrite each equation in slope y-intercept form. State the slope and the y-intercept of each.
- **a)** $5x - 5y - 15 = 0$
- **b)** $2x - 3y + 12 = 0$
- **c)** $8x + 4y - 20 = 0$
- **d)** $x - 2y + 10 = 0$
- **e)** $x - 5y + 15 = 0$
- **f)** $3x - 4y + 12 = 0$
- **g)** $8x - 6y - 36 = 0$
- **h)** $3x + 6y + 18 = 0$

Apply the Concepts **B**

Math **Connect**

A 5-star sightseeing train will soon be running on the new Qinghai-Tibet railway in China. The transparent cars will allow views on all sides. Passengers will be able to shower on the train and enjoy dance performances and karaoke. A sightseeing holiday on this train will cost over $1000 per day.

For help with question 5, refer to Example 3.

5. A sightseeing train runs tours at four different times on Saturdays. An adult ticket is $3 and a child's ticket is $1. One Saturday, the total ticket revenue was $750. On this day, 150 tickets were sold for the first tour, 95 for the second, 125 for the third, and 96 for the fourth.
- **a)** Write an equation to model the total revenue for this Saturday.
- **b)** Rearrange the equation to isolate the variable representing children's tickets.
- **c)** Find the total number of children's tickets sold on this Saturday.

6. Describe the steps you would follow to rewrite the equation $3x + 2y - 3 = 0$ in slope y-intercept form.

7. a) Make a table of values and graph the equation $2x + 3y = 0$.
b) Find the slope and the y-intercept.
c) Rewrite the equation in slope y-intercept form.
d) Compared to standard form, $Ax + By + C = 0$, the equation $2x + 3y = 0$ has $C = 0$. Interpret what this means.

8. The line $3x + 4y + C = 0$ passes through $(1, 2)$. Find the value of C.

9. The line $Ax + 2y - 5 = 0$ passes through $(1, 0)$. Find the value of A.

10. The line $y = 4x + b$ passes through $(8, -3)$. Find the value of b.

Chapter Problem

Math Connect

Many event planners are graduates in business administration, marketing, or leisure and tourism management.

11. a) A banquet hall charges $6675 for an event with 175 guests. If the cost per person is $29, find the flat fee charged for the use of the hall.
b) The same hall charges another organization $11 875 for an event with 325 guests. If the cost for this event is $31 per person, how much is the flat fee for this organization?
c) What are some reasons why the same hall would have a different per-person charge and a different flat fee?

Extend the Concepts C

12. a) Rearrange the general case of the standard form of a linear equation, $Ax + By + C = 0$, into slope y-intercept form.
b) Use your result from part a) to find an expression for the slope and the y-intercept in terms of A, B, and C.

13. Describe the graph of the standard form of a linear equation, $Ax + By + C = 0$, in each case. Include an example and a sketch of your example.
a) $A \neq 0, B = 0, C = 0$ **b)** $A \neq 0, B \neq 0, C = 0$
c) $A \neq 0, B = 0, C \neq 0$ **d)** $A \neq 0, B \neq 0, C \neq 0$

Review of Key Terms

1. In your own words, define each of the key terms from this chapter.
   a) opposite operations
   b) variable term
   c) constant term
   d) formula
   e) standard form

Check your definitions against those provided in the chapter.

4.1 Solve One- and Two-Step Linear Equations, pages 154 to 162

2. For each linear equation,
   i) list the steps required to undo the operations
   ii) solve the equation

   a) $4x = 36$
   b) $x + 5 = 9$
   c) $\dfrac{x}{6} = 10$
   d) $6 - x = 16$

3. Solve each equation and check your solution.

   a) $2x + 4 = 10$
   b) $\dfrac{a}{5} + 6 = 10$
   c) $-\dfrac{y}{4} - 6 = 2$
   d) $\dfrac{w + 4}{6} = 3$

4. Alan takes a taxi from his house to his friend Drew's home. Their homes are 6 km apart. The taxi driver charges a flat fee of $10 plus $0.25/km. This can be modelled using the equation $C = 0.25x + 10$, where x represents the distance travelled in kilometres, and C represents the cost in dollars. How much will the taxi ride cost?

4.2 Solve Multi-Step Linear Equations, pages 163 to 173

5. Solve each linear equation.

   a) $-1.5x + 2 = -1$
   b) $\dfrac{1}{3}(k + 4) = 7$
   c) $\dfrac{2x - 4}{6} = 2$
   d) $\dfrac{4a}{5} - 6 = 2$
   e) $\dfrac{3x + 5}{10} = \dfrac{2x - 3}{7}$

6. At a dairy, milk containing 3% butterfat is mixed with cream containing 10% butterfat to make 200 L of reduced-fat cream containing 5% butterfat. Let x represent the number of litres of 3% milk. Use the equation $0.03x + 0.1(200 - x) = 0.05(200)$ to find the volume of milk and of cream used in the mixture.

4.3 Model With Formulas, pages 174 to 183

7. Describe the steps that could have been used to rearrange each formula.

a) $P = 2l + 2w$

$$\frac{P - 2w}{2} = l$$

b) $C = 2\pi r$

$$\frac{C}{2\pi} = r$$

8. Rearrange each formula to isolate the indicated variable.

a) $C = \pi d$, for d

b) $y = mx + b$, for m

c) $P = 2(l + w)$, for w

d) $S = \pi r^2 h$, for h

9. Use the simple interest formula $I = Prt$ to find the length of time $3000 would have to be invested at 0.5% to earn $180 in interest.

10. Jennifer pays $45 for a haircut. She wants to know how much the haircut costs before 6% GST, 8% PST, and 10% tip are added to the price. In the equation $C = x + 0.06x + 0.08x + 0.1x$, C represents the total cost and x represents the price of the haircut, both in dollars. Find the price of the haircut to the nearest cent.

11. Ari leaves the local community centre on his bike. He travels north. At the same time, Lisa leaves the community centre by car. She travels south. After 30 min, Ari and Lisa are 35 km apart. Suppose x represents Ari's speed and $(2x + 10)$ represents Lisa's speed, both in kilometres per hour. Find the speeds at which Ari and Lisa travel.

4.4 Convert Linear Equations From Standard Form, pages 184 to 189

12. Rearrange each equation into slope y-intercept form, then state the slope and the y-intercept.

a) $3x + y - 7 = 0$

b) $5x - y - 4 = 0$

c) $3x - 3y + 9 = 0$

d) $\frac{x}{2} + 7y - 14 = 0$

e) $y - 6 = 0$

f) $\frac{x}{2} - \frac{4y}{3} + 8 = 0$

13. The line $2x + y - C = 0$ passes through $(1, 5)$. Find the value of C.

14. The line $3x + By + 6 = 0$ passes through $(2, 1)$. Find the value of B.

1. Solve each equation and check your solution.
  a) $x + 4 = 12$
  b) $2x + 5 = 7$
  c) $-7k = 28$
  d) $8 - t = 10$
  e) $3d - 1 = 8$

2. Solve each equation.
  a) $\dfrac{3t + 4}{2} = 5$
  b) $1.25k + 0.75 = 0.5k$
  c) $6(x - 2) = 3x$
  d) $3(y + 1) = 2(y - 3)$
  e) $\dfrac{x + 6}{3} = 2 + \dfrac{x - 2}{5}$

3. Masani is testing 25 g of fertilizer. She plans to give each test plant 0.4 g of the fertilizer and have 8 g left over for future tests. Solve the equation $0.4n + 8 = 25$ to find the number of plants Masani can use in her test.

4. Rearrange the equation $A = P(1 + rt)$ to isolate r.

5. Mitchell works in a lab. He plans to mix a 35% solution of acid with an 80% solution to make 70 mL of a 50% solution. Let x represent the number of millilitres of 35% solution. Use the equation $0.35x + 0.8(70 - x) = 0.5(70)$ to find the volume of each type of acid used in the mixture.

6. Find the slope and the y-intercept of each linear relation, then write the equation for the relation in slope y-intercept form.

  a)
  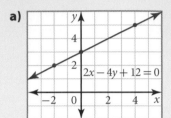

  b)
  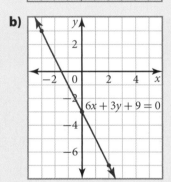

7. Rearrange each equation in the $y = mx + b$ form. Then, state the slope and y-intercept.
  a) $2x + y - 3 = 0$
  b) $6x - y - 1 = 0$
  c) $2x + 3y - 12 = 0$
  d) $4x - 5y + 10 = 0$
  e) $3x + 2y - 8 = 0$

8. Rearrange each formula to solve for the indicated variable.
  a) $P = 2a + b$, solve for a
  b) $A = P + Prt$, solve for r
  c) $A = \dfrac{(a + b)h}{2}$, solve for b

Chapter Problem Wrap-Up

In the chapter problem, Angela collects this information:

Cory's school was charged $6100 for 160 guests and Anne's school was charged $4000 for 100 guests at the same hall.

a) Plot the data points (160, 6100) and (100, 4000) on a coordinate grid. Join the points with a line segment.

b) Find the slope of the line.

c) Extend the line to find the *y*-intercept of the relation.

d) Interpret the meaning of the slope and the *y*-intercept.

e) What assumptions do you need to make for this relation to accurately describe the properties of the fees at the hall?

---

9. When a polygon is constructed on a geoboard, the enclosed area can be found by counting the number of pegs on the perimeter of the polygon and the number of pegs in the interior of the polygon. The formula for the area is $A = \frac{1}{2}(P - 2) + I$, where *A* represents the area, *P* represents the number of pegs on the perimeter, and *I* represents the number of pegs in the interior.

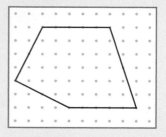

a) Find the area of a polygon with 22 pegs in the interior and 14 pegs on the perimeter.

b) Rearrange the formula to solve for the number of interior pegs.

c) Use your answer to part b) to find the number of interior pegs for a polygon that has area 32 and 30 pegs on the perimeter.

10. The total cost of a meal at a banquet hall is $20 per person, plus a $500 charge for renting the hall.

a) If there is a $500 charge for renting the hall itself, write an equation for the cost of booking the hall.

b) Find the total cost for 60 guests.

c) Suppose the total cost was $2160. Find the number of guests.

5 Linear Systems

Many amusement parks offer two kinds of daily admission. You can buy an all-inclusive pass for unlimited use of the rides and attractions, or you can pay a lower price for entry and then buy tickets for the rides and attractions. How can you decide which is the better value? In this chapter you will use systems of linear equations to solve problems like this one.

In this chapter, you will

- determine graphically the point of intersection of two linear relations
- solve systems of two linear equations involving two variables with integral coefficients, using the algebraic method of substitution or elimination
- solve problems that arise from realistic situations described in words or represented by given linear systems of two equations involving two variables, by choosing an appropriate algebraic or graphical method

Reasoning and Proving

Representing | Selecting Tools

Problem Solving

Connecting | Reflecting

Communicating

Key Terms

elimination method

linear system

point of intersection

substitution method

Literacy Link

Use a Venn diagram to help you choose which method to use to solve a linear system. How would you draw the Venn diagram?

Gordana owns her own aesthetics business. She has to set the prices for the services she provides so that her business will be profitable. How might Gordana use linear systems to help set prices?

Get Ready!

Algebraic Expressions

1. Simplify by collecting like terms. The first part has been done for you.

   a) $2d + 5 - 4d - 9$
   $= 2d - 4d + 5 - 9$
   $= -2d - 4$

   b) $3x + 4 + 2x - 1$
   c) $11y - 5 + 2y + 8$
   d) $7m - 3m + 5 + 11$
   e) $3c + 5 - 2c - 10$
   f) $5v + 3 - 4v + 7$

Manipulate and Solve Equations

2. Rearrange each equation to isolate y. The first part has been done for you.

   a) $-3x + 8y = 11$
   $-3x + 8y + 3x = 3x + 11$
   $8y = 3x + 11$
   $\dfrac{8y}{8} = \dfrac{3x}{8} + \dfrac{11}{8}$
   $y = \dfrac{3x}{8} + \dfrac{11}{8}$

   b) $3x - y = 4$
   c) $4x + y = 9$
   d) $4x - 2y = 14$
   e) $5x - 2y = 6$
   f) $2x + 3y - 1 = 0$
   g) $4x + 6y - 9 = 0$

3. For each equation, find the value of y when $x = 3$. The first part has been done for you.

   a) $2x + y = 8$
   $2(3) + y = 8$
   $6 + y = 8$
   $6 + y - 6 = 8 - 6$
   $y = 2$

   b) $y = 3x + 1$
   c) $y = 4x - 3$
   d) $y = 8x + 1$
   e) $x - y = 9$
   f) $3x - 2y = 8$
   g) $12x + 5y = 17$

4. For each equation, find the value of x when $y = 4$.

   a) $3y + 3x = 1$
   b) $4y = 2x + 7$
   c) $x - 2y = 9$
   d) $y = 6x + 1$
   e) $3x - 2y = 16$
   f) $y = 3x + 1$
   g) $2x - 2y = 9$
   h) $y = 13x - 19$

Graph Linear Relations

5. Graph each linear relation. The first part has been done for you.

   a) $y = 2x - 1$

   The y-intercept is −1 and the slope is 2.

   Plot the point (0, −1), then move up 2 units and right 1 unit to find two other points on the line.

   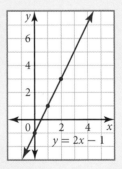

   b) $y = 4x + 6$
   c) $y = -x - 3$
   d) $y = -3x + 2$
   e) $y = -5x + 1$
   f) $y = 4x + 7$
   g) $y = -2x + 6$

Chapter Problem

Logan volunteers for a dog rescue organization. He is planning a series of events to raise money for the organization. In this chapter, you will learn how to calculate the break-even point, and the amount Logan should charge for each event to make sure that he covers his costs.

6. Graph each linear relation. The first part has been done for you.

a) $2x + y = 4$

Rewrite the equation in slope y-intercept form.

$2x + y - 2x = -2x + 4$

$y = -2x + 4$

The y-intercept is 4 and the slope is −2.

Plot the point (0, 4), then move down 2 units and right 1 unit to find two other points on the line.

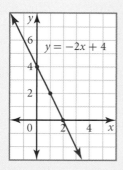

b) $4x - y = 8$

c) $-x + y = -3$

d) $-3x - y = 3$

e) $-5x + y - 10 = 0$

f) $-3x - y = 9$

g) $y = 4x + 6$

Translate Words to Algebra

7. Write an equation to represent each situation. The first part has been done for you.

a) The cost to have flyers delivered is $50 plus $0.10 per flyer. Callum spends a total of $400 to have flyers delivered. *Let n represent the number of flyers Callum has delivered.*
$400 = 0.1n + 50$

b) Ron earns $8.50/h. Last week, he earned $52.00.

c) The total mass of a metal storage drum is 90 kg. The mass of an empty drum is 18 kg and the mass of the liquid stored in the drum is 2.3 kg/L.

d) Bohdan pays $300 to rent a car. He pays a flat fee of $125 plus $0.35/km.

e) Linnea earns $270 for the first 30 h she works in a week. After that, she earns $12/h. Last week, Linnea earned $450.

5.1 Solve Linear Systems by Graphing

Eirlys is planning to join a gym. She is trying to decide between two different payment plans. How can Eirlys use linear equations to help her decide?

Investigate

Tools

- graphing calculator

Compare Taxi Fares

Trip Taxi charges $2.50 plus $0.20/km. Comfort Taxi charges $0.50/km.

1. Let x represent the distance travelled in kilometres and y represent the total cost of a trip. Write an equation to represent the total cost for each taxi company.

2. Suppose you plan to travel 12 km. Which taxi company should you choose? Why?

3. Suppose you plan to travel 35 km. Which taxi company should you choose? Why?

4. Use a graphing calculator.

- Press [WINDOW].
  Enter the window settings shown.
- Press [Y=]. Enter the equation for Trip Taxi as Y1 and the equation for Comfort Taxi as Y2.

- Press [2nd] [CALC] 5 [ENTER] [ENTER] [ENTER]. Record the coordinates of the point of intersection. What do these coordinates mean in terms of this situation?

5. Check that the coordinates from question 4 lie on the line representing the total cost of a trip with Trip Taxi and on the line representing the total cost of a trip with Comfort Taxi. How did you check?

6. Are there any other points that lie on both lines? How do you know?

7. Reflect What is the significance of the point of intersection of two linear equations?

A **linear system** is a set of two or more linear relations considered at the same time. Graphically, the solution to a linear system is the **point of intersection** of the relations.

Example 1

Solve a Linear System by Graphing

Solve this linear system, then check.

$$y + 2x = -5 \; \text{①} \qquad\qquad y = \frac{2}{3}x + 3 \; \text{②}$$

Solution

Rearrange equation ① into slope y-intercept form.

$$y + 2x = -5$$
$$y + 2x - 2x = -5 - 2x$$
$$y = -5 - 2x$$
$$y = -2x - 5$$

The slope is -2 and the y-intercept is -5.

Equation ② is in slope y-intercept form. The slope is $\frac{2}{3}$ and the y-intercept is 3.

Use the slope and y-intercept to graph each line on the same coordinate grid. Label each line with its equation.

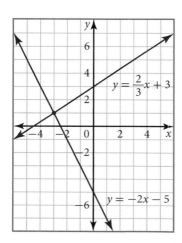

From the graph, the point of intersection is $(-3, 1)$. Check these coordinates in each of the original equations.

Equation ①

$$LS = y + 2x \qquad RS = -5$$
$$= 1 + 2(-3)$$
$$= 1 - 6$$
$$= -5$$
$$= RS$$

Equation ②

$$LS = y \qquad RS = \frac{2}{3}x + 3$$
$$= 1$$
$$\qquad\qquad = \frac{2}{3}(-3) + 3$$
$$\qquad\qquad = -2 + 3$$
$$\qquad\qquad = 1$$
$$\qquad\qquad = LS$$

The solution to this linear system is $(-3, 1)$.

Example 2

Choose a Fitness Club

KC Fitness Club charges a flat fee of $25 per month plus $5 per visit. Workout Zone charges a flat fee of $35 per month plus $3 per visit. For how many visits per month is the total cost the same for both fitness clubs?

Solution

Let x represent the number of visits per month.
Let y represent the total cost for the month in dollars.

KC Fitness Club

$$y = 5x + 25$$

The total cost for the month is $25 plus $5 for each visit.

Workout Zone

$$y = 3x + 35$$

The total cost for the month is $35 plus $3 for each visit.

Use a graphing calculator. Graph both equations in the same window.
- Press [2nd] [CALC] 5 [ENTER] [ENTER] [ENTER].

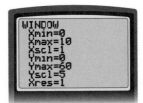

The point of intersection is $(5, 50)$. This means that the total cost for both fitness clubs is $50 when 5 visits are made in one month.

Key Concepts

- The solution to a linear system is the point of intersection of the lines.
- A linear system can be solved by graphing the lines, then reading the point of intersection from the graph.
- To check the solution to a linear system, substitute the coordinates of the point of intersection into the original equations.

Discuss the Concepts

D1. a) Explain, in your own words, what it means to solve a system of equations.

   b) Compare your answer from part a) with that of one of your classmates.

D2. Is it possible for a linear system to have no solution? Explain your reasoning.

D3. Describe in words how you would solve the linear system $y = 3x + 1$ and $y = -2x + 3$.

Practise the Concepts A

For help with questions 1 to 4, refer to Example 1 or Example 2.

1. Find the point of intersection of each linear system. Check your answers.

   a) $y = 2x + 3$
   $y = 4x - 1$

   b) $y = -x - 7$
   $y = 3x + 5$

   c) $y = -x + 5$
   $y = x + 1$

   d) $y = x + 4$
   $y = -x - 2$

2. Solve each linear system by graphing.

   a) $y = 2x$
   $y = 4x + 1$

   b) $y = \frac{1}{2}x - 2$
   $y = \frac{3}{4}x + 4$

   c) $y = 2x - 3$
   $y = \frac{5}{2}x + 1$

   d) $y = 4x - 5$
   $y = \frac{9}{5}x - 10$

3. Solve each linear system by graphing. Check your answers.

a) $3x + y = 7$
$-x + 2y = 7$

b) $y = 7x + 3$
$x - y = 3$

c) $2x + 3y = 8$
$x - 2y = -3$

d) $5x - y = -4$
$2x - 3y = 1$

4. Find the point of intersection by graphing. Check your answers.

a) $-2x - y = -8$
$x + y = 9$

b) $x + 2y = -5$
$3x - y = -1$

c) $y = 2x + 1$
$2x + y = 1$

d) $x + y = 7$
$x - y = -1$

Apply the Concepts B

For help with questions 5 to 7, refer to Example 2.

5. Sherwood Tennis Club charges a
$150 initial fee to join the club, and
then a $20 monthly fee. Coronation
Tennis Club charges an initial fee of
$100 and $30 per month.

a) Write an equation to represent the
cost to be a member of the Sherwood
Tennis Club.

b) Write an equation to represent the cost to be a member of
Coronation Tennis Club.

c) Graph the equations from parts a) and b).

d) Find the point of intersection of the lines. What does this
point represent?

e) If you were planning to join for a year, which club should
you join? Why?

6. FunNGames Video rents game machines for $10 and video games
for $3 each. Big Vid rents game machines for $7 and video games
for $4 each. Let y be the total rental cost and x the number of
games rented.

a) Write an equation to represent the total cost for a rental
from FunNGames Video.

b) Write an equation to represent the total cost for a rental
from Big Vid.

c) Find the point of intersection.

d) What does this point of intersection represent?

7. Katrin is looking at banquet halls for her parents' anniversary party. Moonlight Hall charges a fixed cost of $1000 plus $75 per guest. Riverside Hall charges $1500 plus $50 per guest. Let C represent the total cost, and n represent the number of guests.

    a) Write an equation to represent the total cost for Moonlight Hall.

    b) Write an equation to represent the total cost for Riverside Hall.

    c) Find the number of guests for which the total cost is the same at both halls.

8. Solve this linear system by graphing.

$$4x - y - 7 = 0 \ \text{①} \qquad\qquad -2x - y - 1 = 0 \ \text{②}$$

9. During the winter months, Don uses his pickup truck to clear snow from driveways. Don charges $15 per driveway. Morgan's Snow Removal charges $150 for the season.

    a) Write an equation to represent the total cost for Don to clear your driveway for the season.

    b) Write an equation to represent the total cost for Morgan's Snow Removal to clear your driveway for the season.

Literacy Connect

    c) Explain how you would decide who to hire to clear your driveway this winter.

....

Achievement Check

10. This graph shows the costs of fitness programs at three different facilities. Describe the meaning of the intersections of the lines. What advice would you give to someone based on the graph?

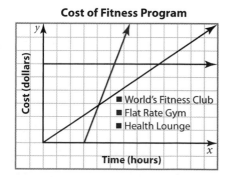

Cost of Fitness Program

■ World's Fitness Club
■ Flat Rate Gym
■ Health Lounge

y — Cost (dollars)

x — Time (hours)

11. Gabriella works in a leather clothing factory. She is paid $80 per day plus $10 for each jacket she makes. Chan also works in the factory. He makes a flat fee of $110 per day.

a) Write an equation to represent the total amount Gabriella earns in one day.

b) Write an equation to represent the total amount Chan earns in one day.

c) How many jackets must Gabriella make in order to make as much in a day as Chan? Show your work.

12. Find the point of intersection of $3x - 2y = 14$ and $4x + y = 15$ by graphing.

Chapter Problem

Math **Connect**

The break-even point is the point at which the cost is exactly equal to the revenue.

13. Logan is renting a theatre for a fundraising screening of *Best in Show*. The theatre rental is $675 plus $2 per person for operating the snack bar. Let C represent the cost for the event if it is held at this theatre. Let n represent the number of tickets sold by the students.

a) Write an equation to show the cost for the theatre.

b) Write an equation to show the revenue (the total amount from ticket sales) if Logan charges $8.50 per ticket.

c) How many tickets must Logan sell in order to break even?

Extend the Concepts **C**

14. Use a graphing calculator. Graph $y = 2x + 4$ and $y = 2x - 5$ in the same window.

a) From the graph, does it appear that these lines will intersect?

b) What is the result when you use the Intersect feature to find the point of intersection? Explain.

15. a) Find the slope and y-intercept for each equation.

$y = 3x - 4$ ①
$6x - 2y = 8$ ②

What do you notice?

b) On grid paper, graph the linear system from part a). What do you notice about the lines?

c) How many solutions does this linear system have? Explain.

16. When two equations represent the same line, the lines are coincidental. How many points of intersection does a system of coincidental lines have? Explain.

17. Is it possible for a linear system to have exactly two solutions? Explain.

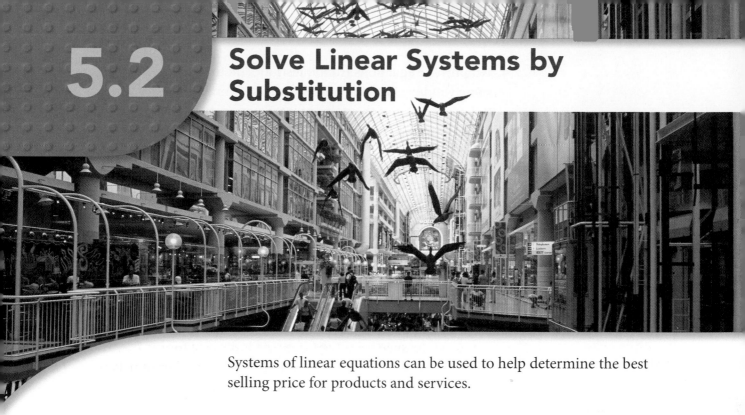

5.2 Solve Linear Systems by Substitution

Systems of linear equations can be used to help determine the best selling price for products and services.

Investigate

Tools
- graphing calculator or grid paper

A Class Problem

Each morning at the beginning of class, Ms. Edwards gives her math students a puzzle to solve. Here is today's puzzle:

The sum of Jane's age and her mother's age is 60. Jane's mother is 3 times as old as Jane. How old is Jane? How old is her mother?

Work with a partner.

1. Let x represent Jane's age in years and y represent her mother's age in years.
   a) Write an equation to represent the sum of their ages.
   b) Write an equation to represent the statement "Jane's mother is three times as old as Jane."

2. Use your equations from question 1 to write a single equation in terms of the variable x.
   a) Substitute the expression for y from the second equation into the first equation. This is called the **substitution method**.
   b) Solve the equation that results. Interpret the meaning of the solution in terms of this situation.

substitution method
- an algebraic method of solving a system of linear equations
- one equation is solved for one variable, then that value is substituted into the other equation

3. Use your result from question 2. Find the value of y. What does this value represent?

4. Graph your equations from question 1 on the same grid or in the same window. Find the point of intersection of the lines. How do the coordinates of the point of intersection compare to your results for questions 2 and 3? Explain.

Example 1

Solve by Substitution

Use the substitution method to solve this linear system.

$$4x - 7y = 20 \quad ① \qquad\qquad x - 3y = 10 \quad ②$$

Solution

The solution to a linear system is the point of intersection of the lines. At the point of intersection, the value of x and the value of y are the same for both equations.

$$4x - 7y = 20 \qquad ①$$
$$x - 3y = 10 \qquad ② \qquad \textit{Solve equation ② for x.}$$
$$4x - 7y = 20 \qquad ①$$
$$x = 3y + 10 \qquad ②$$

$$4(3y + 10) - 7y = 20 \qquad \textit{Substitute x = 3y + 10 from}$$
$$12y + 40 - 7y = 20 \qquad \textit{equation ② into equation ①.}$$
$$5y + 40 = 20$$
$$5y + 40 - 40 = 20 - 40$$
$$5y = -20$$
$$\frac{5y}{5} = \frac{-20}{5}$$
$$y = -4$$

$$x - 3y = 10 \qquad \textit{Substitute the value y = −4}$$
$$x - 3(-4) = 10 \qquad \textit{into equation ② to find the}$$
$$x + 12 = 10 \qquad \textit{value of x.}$$
$$x + 12 - 12 = 10 - 12$$
$$x = -2$$

Check the solution $(-2, -4)$ in equation ①.
$$\text{LS} = 4x - 7y \qquad\qquad \text{RS} = 20$$
$$= 4(-2) - 7(-4)$$
$$= -8 + 28$$
$$= 20$$
$$= \text{RS}$$

The solution to the linear system is $(-2, -4)$.

Example **2**

Supply and Demand

Rachelle is an economist. She evaluates the effect of changing the price on the supply and the demand for a product. The selling price in dollars, y, of a product is related to the number of units sold, x, according to these equations:

Demand: $y + 0.4x = 10$ Supply: $y = 0.6x + 2$

Solve this system algebraically. What does the solution represent?

Solution

The solution to a linear system is the point of intersection of the lines.

Demand: $y + 0.4x = 10$ ①
Supply: $y = 0.6x + 2$ ②   *Substitute $y = 0.6x + 2$ from equation ② into equation ①.*

$$(0.6x + 2) + 0.4x = 10$$
$$x + 2 = 10$$
$$x + 2 - 2 = 10 - 2$$
$$x = 8$$

$y = 0.6x + 2$ *Substitute the value $x = 8$ into*
$y = 0.6(8) + 2$ *equation ② to find the value of y.*
$y = 4.8 + 2$
$y = 6.8$

Check the solution $(8, 6.8)$ in equation ①.

$$\begin{aligned} \text{LS} &= y + 0.4x & \text{RS} &= 10 \\ &= 6.8 + 0.4(8) \\ &= 6.8 + 3.2 \\ &= 10 \\ &= \text{RS} \end{aligned}$$

The solution to the linear system is $(8, 6.8)$. When the price of the product is $6.80, 8 units are sold.

Example **3**

Find the Break-Even Point

Katherine is selling T-shirts to raise money for diabetes research. The supplier charges a $210 design fee plus $3 per T-shirt. Katherine plans to sell the T-shirts for $10 each. How many T-shirts does Katherine need to sell in order to break even?

Solution

Let C represent the total cost of the T-shirts, in dollars, and n represent the number of T-shirts. Use the information to write a system of equations.

$C = 3n + 210$ ①

$C = 10n$ ②

The total cost of the T-shirts is $210 plus $3 per T-shirt.

Katherine will break even when the total sales of T-shirts is equal to the total cost to produce the T-shirts.

$$C = 3n + 210 \quad ①$$
$$C = 10n \qquad ②$$
$$10n = 3n + 210$$
$$10n - 3n = 3n + 210 - 3n$$
$$7n = 210$$
$$\frac{7n}{7} = \frac{210}{7}$$
$$n = 30$$

Substitute C = 10n from equation ② into equation ①.

$C = 10n$

$C = 10(30)$

$C = 300$

Substitute the value n = 30 into equation ② to find the value of C.

Check the solution (30, 300) in equation ①.

LS $= C$ RS $= 3n + 210$

    $= 300$ $= 3(30) + 210$

                                   $= 90 + 210$

                                     $= 300$

                                     $=$ LS

Katherine needs to sell 30 T-shirts to break even.

Key Concepts

- A system of linear equations can be solved algebraically using the substitution method.
- To solve a linear system by substitution, one equation is solved for one variable, then that value is substituted into the other equation.
- The break-even point is the point at which the cost to produce an item is equal to its selling price.

Discuss the Concepts

D1. Explain why you can solve the system of equations $y = 3x + 1$ and $x + y = 3$ by substituting $3x + 1$ for y in the second equation.

D2. Describe how to use the substitution method to solve the system $2x + y = 8$ and $4x + 3y = 12$.

D3. How is solving a linear system by substitution the same as solving by graphing? How is it different?

Practise the Concepts A

For help with questions 1 to 3, refer to Example 1.

1. Use the substitution method to solve each linear system.

a) $3x + 2y - 1 = 0$
$y = -x + 3$

b) $3x - y = 4$
$x + y = 8$

c) $x + 4y = 5$
$x + 2y = 7$

d) $2x + y = 3$
$4x - 3y = 1$

e) $2x + 3y = -1$
$x + y = 1$

f) $x - 3y = -2$
$2x + 5y = 7$

g) $6x + 5y = 7$
$x - y = 3$

h) $x - 3y = 5$
$7x + 2y = 12$

2. Solve each linear system.

a) $2x - y = 5$
$3x + y = -9$

b) $4x + 2y = 7$
$-x - y = 6$

c) $6x + 3y = 5$
$x - 2y = 0$

d) $8x - y = 10$
$3x - y = 9$

3. Solve each linear system using the substitution method.

a) $x + y = -2$
$x - y = 6$

b) $x - y = 9$
$x + y = 3$

c) $2x + y = 2$
$3x + 2y = 5$

d) $2x - 3y = 6$
$2x - y = 7$

4. Malcolm is twice as old as Sundeep. The sum of their ages is 39.
   a) Write an equation to represent the information in the first sentence.
   b) Write an equation to represent the information in the second sentence.
   c) Use the method of substitution to find the ages of the boys.

For help with question 5, refer to Example 2.

5. For Nina's retirement party, her family decides to rent a hall for a dinner. Regal Hall costs $500 for the hall rental and $15 per guest, and Party Place charges $410 for the hall and $18 per guest.
   a) Write a system of linear equations to represent the situation.
   b) How many guests must attend for the charges to be the same? Solve by substitution.

For help with question 6, refer to Example 3.

6. Carly rents a theatre for a spring concert. The theatre charges $825 plus $2 per person. Carly plans to charge $7 per person. Let C represent the cost for the event. Let n represent the number of people attending.
   a) Write a system of linear equations to represent the situation.
   b) How many tickets must Carly sell in order to break even?
   c) What is the price per ticket?

Literacy Connect

7. When solving a linear system by substitution, how do you decide which variable to solve for first?

8. Dmitri plays hockey. He earns 1 point for every goal he scores and 1 point for every assist. This season he earned 63 points. He scored 17 fewer goals than assists.
   a) Write a system of linear equations to represent this information.
   b) How many goals did Dmitri score this season? How many assists did he have?

9. Sam makes two types of quilts. The first type costs $25 for fabric and $40 per hour for hand quilting. The second type costs $50 for fabric and $22 per hour for machine quilting. For what number of hours are the costs the same?

10. Solve the linear system $3x - y = 19$ and $4x + 3y = 12$ by substitution.

11. A band held a concert in its hometown. A total of 15 000 people attended. The tickets cost $8.50 per student and $12.50 per adult. The concert took in a total of $162 500. How many adults came to the concert?

12. Vito wants to hire a truck to do some moving. Athena's Garage charges $80 for the day plus $0.22/km. City Truck Rental charges $100 per day and $0.12/km.
   a) Write a linear system to represent this problem.
   b) Solve the system of equations. Interpret the solution in terms of the problem.
   c) Which company should Vito hire? Explain.

13. Minden Karate Club has a competition for the students. If you win a grappling match you are awarded 5 points. If you tie, you are awarded 2 points. Rebecca grappled 15 times with 3 losses and her score was 42 points. How many grapples did Rebecca win?

Chapter Problem **14.** Logan is selling dog tags to raise money for the dog rescue organization. The company that makes the tags charges a flat fee of $348 plus $2 per tag. Logan plans to sell the tags for $5 each.
   a) Write an equation to show the total cost for the dog tags.
   b) Write an equation to show the revenue.
   c) How many dog tags must Logan sell in order to break even?

Extend the Concepts C

15. Is $(3, -5)$ a solution to the linear system $2x + 5y = 19$ and $6y - 8x = -54$? Explain.

Math Connect

Remember, parallel lines have the same slope.

16. a) Try to use the substitution method to solve the system $y = 3x$ and $y = 3x - 7$. What do you notice?
   b) Graph the system. What do you notice?
   c) Explain why there is no solution for this linear system.

17. a) Try to use the substitution method to solve the system $3y - 6x = 15$ and $y = 2x + 5$. What do you notice?
   b) Graph the system. What do you notice?
   c) Explain why there is more than one solution for this linear system.

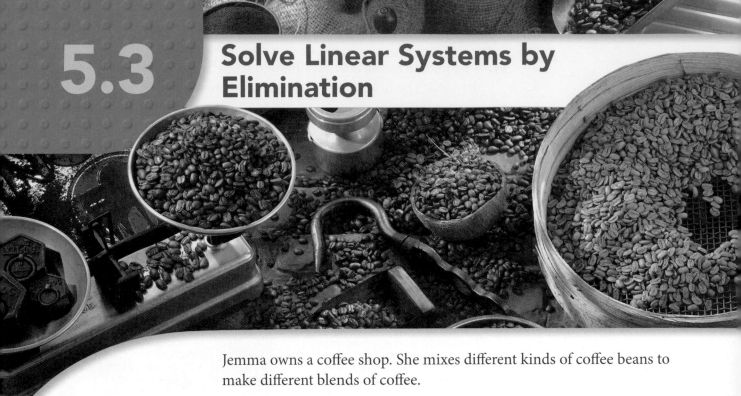

5.3 Solve Linear Systems by Elimination

Jemma owns a coffee shop. She mixes different kinds of coffee beans to make different blends of coffee.

Investigate A Add or Subtract Linear Equations

Tools

- grid paper

Work in a group of four.

1. a) Each person chooses a different linear system.

System A	
$x - y = 1$	①
$2x + 5y = 16$	②

System B	
$x - 3y = 6$	①
$3x + 4y = -21$	②

System C	
$x - y = 2$	①
$2x + 3y = 14$	②

System D	
$x + y = 5$	①
$2x - 5y = 17$	②

b) On grid paper, graph the linear system. Label each equation. What is the point of intersection?

2. a) Add the equations in your linear system. Label the resulting equation ③.

b) Graph equation ③ on the same set of axes as you used in question 1. What do you notice?

3. a) Subtract one equation from the other. Label the resulting equation ④.

b) Graph equation ④ on the same set of axes as you used in questions 1 and 2. What do you notice?

4. Compare your results with students in other groups who graphed the same linear system.

5. Compare your results with other members of your group.

6. Reflect Make a statement about the equation that results from adding or subtracting the equations in a linear system.

Investigate **B** **Multiply a Linear Equation by a Constant**

Tools
- grid paper

Work in a group of four.

1. a) Each person chooses a different linear equation.

Equation A	**Equation B**
$y = 4x + 3$	$2x + y = 5$

Equation C	**Equation D**
$y = -x - 2$	$3x - y = 1$

b) Use grid paper. Graph the line and label it with its equation.

2. a) Choose a number between -5 and 5. Multiply each term in your equation by the number you chose.

b) Graph the resulting equation on the same set of axes. What do you notice?

c) Choose a different number. Multiply each term in your original equation by the number and graph the result on the same set of axes.

4. Compare your results with students in other groups who graphed the same line.

5. Compare your results with other members of your group.

6. Reflect Make a statement about the equation that results from multiplying each term in an equation by a constant.

elimination method
- an algebraic method of solving a system of linear equations
- the equations are added or subtracted to eliminate one variable

When two linear equations are added or subtracted, the resulting equation passes through the same point of intersection. When each term in a linear equation is multiplied by a constant, the resulting equation gives the same line. In this section, you will apply these principles to use another algebraic method to solve linear systems, the **elimination method**.

Example 1

Solve by Elimination

Use the elimination method to solve the linear system
$3x + y = 19$ and $4x - y = 2$.

Solution

Write the equations so like terms appear in a column.

$$\begin{array}{ll} 3x + y = 19 & ① \\ + \underline{4x - y = 2} & ② \\ 7x = 21 & ③ \end{array}$$

Add the equations to eliminate y.
Solve equation ③ for x.

$$\frac{7x}{7} = \frac{21}{7}$$
$$x = 3$$

$$3x + y = 19$$
$$3(3) + y = 19$$
$$9 + y = 19$$
$$9 + y - 9 = 19 - 9$$
$$y = 10$$

Substitute the value x = 3 into
equation ① to find the value of y.

Check the solution (3, 10) in equation ②.

$$\begin{array}{ll} \text{LS} = 4x - y & \text{RS} = 2 \\ = 4(3) - (10) \\ = 12 - 10 \\ = 2 \\ = \text{RS} \end{array}$$

The solution is (3, 10).

Example 2

Solve a Linear System

Solve the linear system $4x - 2y = 6$ and $x + y = 6$.

Solution

$$\begin{array}{ll} 4x - 2y = 6 & ① \\ x + y = 6 & ② \end{array}$$

$$\begin{array}{ll} 4x - 2y = 6 & ① \\ + \underline{2x + 2y = 12} & ③ \\ 6x = 18 \end{array}$$

Multiply each term in equation ② by 2.
Label the new equation ③.
Add ① + ③.

$$\frac{6x}{6} = \frac{18}{6}$$
$$x = 3$$

$$x + y = 6$$
$$3 + y = 6$$
$$3 + y - 3 = 6 - 3$$
$$y = 3$$

Substitute the value x = 3 into equation ② to find the value of y.

Check the solution (3, 3) in equation ①.

$$\begin{aligned} \text{LS} &= 4x - 2y \\ &= 4(3) - 2(3) \\ &= 12 - 6 \\ &= 6 \\ &= \text{RS} \end{aligned} \qquad \text{RS} = 6$$

The solution is (3, 3).

Example **3** **Make a Coffee Blend**

Jemma is making 120 kg of a new blend of coffee that will sell for $15/kg. The blend is made from two kinds of coffee: one that sells for $18/kg, and another that sells for $10/kg. How much of each type of coffee should Jemma use to make the new blend?

Solution

Let x represent the mass, in kilograms, of the coffee that sells for $18/kg.
Let y represent the mass, in kilograms, of the coffee that sells for $10/kg.

$$\begin{aligned} x + y &= 120 \qquad ① \\ 18x + 10y &= 1800 \qquad ② \\ \underline{10x + 10y} &= \underline{1200} \qquad ③ \\ 8x &= 600 \\ \frac{8x}{8} &= \frac{600}{8} \\ x &= 75 \end{aligned}$$

Jemma will make 120 kg of the blend.

The blend will sell for $15/kg, so the cost for 120 kg is $1800.

Multiply each term in equation ① by 10. Label the new equation ③. Subtract ② − ③.

$$\begin{aligned} x + y &= 120 \\ 75 + y &= 120 \\ 75 + y - 75 &= 120 - 75 \\ y &= 45 \end{aligned}$$

Substitute the value x = 75 into equation ① to find the value of y.

Check the solution (75, 45) in equation ②.

$$LS = 18x - 10y \qquad\qquad RS = 1800$$
$$= 18(75) - 10(45)$$
$$= 1350 - 450$$
$$= 1800$$
$$= RS$$

Jemma should use 75 kg of the coffee that sells for $18/kg and 45 kg of the coffee (that sells for $10/kg) to make the blend.

Key Concepts

- A system of linear equations can be solved algebraically using the elimination method.
- To solve a linear system by elimination, the equations are added or subtracted to eliminate one variable.
- When each term in an equation is multiplied by a constant, the resulting equation produces the same line when graphed.

Discuss the Concepts

D1. Consider the linear system $x + y = 5$ and $x - y = 7$.

    a) To eliminate the x terms, would you add or subtract the two equations? Explain.

    b) To eliminate the y terms, would you add or subtract the two equations? Explain.

    c) Will you end up with the same point of intersection if you add or subtract the two equations? Explain.

D2. What is the main difference between the method of substitution and the method of elimination?

Practise the Concepts ▸ A

For help with question 1, refer to Example 1.

1. Use the elimination method to solve each linear system.

    a) $x + y = 2$
        $3x - y = 2$

    b) $x - y = -1$
        $3x + y = -7$

    c) $2x + y = 8$
        $4x - y = 4$

    d) $2x - y = -6$
        $4x + y = -6$

    e) $2x + y = -5$
        $-2x + y = -1$

    f) $4x - y = -1$
        $-4x - 3y = -19$

For help with question 2, refer to Example 2.

2. Solve each linear system by elimination. Check your answer.

    a) $2x + y = 7$
        $x - y = -1$

    b) $3x + 2y = -1$
        $-3x + 4y = 7$

    c) $x - y = 3$
        $2x + y = 3$

    d) $3x + 2y = 5$
        $x - 2y = -1$

    e) $2x + 5y = 3$
        $2x - y = -3$

    f) $2x - y = 3$
        $4x - y = -1$

3. Solve each linear system.

    a) $x + 2y = 2$
        $3x + 5y = 4$

    b) $3x + 5y = 12$
        $2x - y = -5$

    c) $2x - 3y = -12$
        $6x + 5y = -8$

    d) $4x - 7y = 19$
        $3x - 2y = 11$

4. Solve each linear system.

    a) $4x + 3y = 4$
        $8x - y = 1$

    b) $5x - 3y = 2$
        $10x + 3y = 5$

    c) $5x + 2y = 48$
        $x + y = 15$

    d) $2x + 3y = 8$
        $x - 2y = -3$

Apply the Concepts **B**

Math Connect

Spice mixes are blends of spices or herbs. Many are pre-mixed and packaged for sale. For example, lemon pepper, chili powder, curry powder, Chinese five-spice powder, and garlic salt.

Literacy Connect

For help with question 5, refer to Example 3.

5. Abby mixes cinnamon and nutmeg to make 25 g of a spice mix. Cinnamon costs 9¢/g and nutmeg costs 12.5¢/g. The spice mix costs 9.7¢/g. How much of each spice does Abby need to use?

6. Tickets for a play cost $5 for adults and $3 for children. A total of 800 tickets are sold and total sales are $3600.

    a) Write a system of linear equations to represent the situation.

    b) How many adult tickets are sold?

7. When flying into the wind, an airplane travels at an average speed of 540 km/h. When flying with the wind, the airplane travels at an average speed of 680 km/h. Let *s* represent the speed of the airplane with no wind and *w* represent the wind speed.

    a) Write a system of linear equations to represent the situation.

    b) Describe how you would calculate the wind speed.

8. Eleni rents a car on two separate occasions. The first time, she pays $180 for 3 days and 150 km. The next time, she pays $180 for 2 days and 400 km.

a) What is the average cost per day?

b) What is the average cost per kilometre?

Chapter Problem

9. Logan's next fundraising event is dog grooming. A local dog groomer will charge a flat fee of $120 plus $8 per dog. Logan plans to charge customers $16 per dog.

a) Write a linear system to represent this situation.

b) What is the minimum number of customers Logan needs to make money from this event?

Extend the Concepts **C**

10. An inlet pipe on a storage tank will fill the tank in 9 h. An outlet pipe will empty the same tank in 12 h. Suppose both pipes are open. How long will it take to fill the tank?

11. Sarah can paint a fence in 5 h. Wesley can paint the fence in 6 h. They decide to work together. How long will it take Sarah and Wesley to paint the fence?

12. Songi's car's radiator has a capacity of 25 L. It is currently full of water mixed with antifreeze. One-fifth of the volume of the solution is antifreeze. The weather is getting colder and Songi wants to change the mixture so that the solution will be three-fifths antifreeze. How much of the solution in her radiator does Songi need to drain and replace with antifreeze?

5.4 Solve Problems Involving Linear Systems

The Snowbirds Demonstration Team is a group of pilots and technicians from the Canadian Forces. They fly more than 50 different formations and manoeuvers at air shows all over North America. Linear equations can be used to model the flight paths of the Snowbirds for some of their manoeuvres.

Investigate

Tools

- grid paper or graphing calculator

Choose a Method to Solve a Linear System

1. Use a graph to solve the linear system $y = 3x + 1$ and $y = 4x - 3$.

2. Use a graph to solve the linear system $x + y = 101$ and $300x - y = 200$.

3. Compare your results from questions 1 and 2.
   a) Why was it difficult to solve the linear system in question 2 by graphing?
   b) Which method might have been easier to use? Why?

4. **a)** Use the substitution method to solve the linear system from question 1.
   b) Use the elimination method to solve the linear system from question 1.
   c) Compare your answers from questions 1, 4a), and 4b). What do you notice?
   d) Which method did you find easiest to use in solving the linear system $y = 3x + 1$ and $y = 4x - 3$? Why?

5. a) Use the substitution method to solve the linear system from question 2.

b) Use the elimination method to solve the linear system from question 2.

c) Compare your answers from questions 2, 5a), and 5b). What do you notice?

d) Which method did you find easiest to use in solving the linear system $x + y = 101$ and $300x - y = 200$? Why?

6. Reflect When might you choose to solve a system of equations each way?

a) by graphing

b) by substitution

c) by elimination

<table>
<tr><td>Example</td><td>1</td></tr>
</table>

Find the Number of Cars and Trucks

Neil's little brother has a total of 8 cars and trucks to play with. For his birthday, he wants to double the number of cars he has. If he does, he will have a total of 11 cars and trucks. How many cars does Neil's brother have now? How many trucks?

Solution

Let x represent the number of cars Neil's brother has now and y the number of trucks he has now.

$2x + y = 11$ ①
$x + y = 8$ ②

The values of x and y that solve this system must be whole numbers. It is not possible to have part of a car or truck.

Method 1: Solve by Substitution

Rearrange one equation to isolate y.

$$2x + y = 11 \quad\quad ①$$
$$y = 8 - x \quad ②$$

$$2x + (8 - x) = 11$$
$$2x + 8 - x = 11$$
$$x + 8 = 11$$
$$x + 8 - 8 = 11 - 8$$
$$x = 3$$

Substitute 8 − x for y into equation ①.

$$y = 8 - x$$
$$y = 8 - 3$$
$$y = 5$$

Substitute x = 3 into equation ② and solve for y.

Check the solution $(3, 5)$ in equation ①.

$$\begin{aligned} LS &= 2x + y \\ &= 2(3) + 5 \\ &= 6 + 5 \\ &= 11 \\ &= RS \end{aligned} \qquad RS = 11$$

The solution is $(3, 5)$. Neil's brother has 3 cars and 5 trucks now.

Method 2: Solve by Graphing Using Technology

Rearrange each equation to isolate y.

$$2x + y = 11 \qquad\qquad x + y = 8$$
$$2x + y - 2x = 11 - 2x \qquad x + y - x = 8 - x$$
$$y = 11 - 2x \qquad\qquad y = 8 - x$$

- Use a graphing calculator. Press $\boxed{\text{Y=}}$. Enter the equations $Y1 = 11 - 2x$ and $Y2 = 8 - x$.

- Use standard window settings. Press $\boxed{\text{GRAPH}}$.

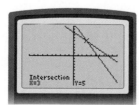

- Press $\boxed{\text{2nd}}$ [CALC] 5 $\boxed{\text{ENTER}}$ $\boxed{\text{ENTER}}$ $\boxed{\text{ENTER}}$.

The solution is $(3, 5)$. Neil's brother has 3 cars and 5 trucks now.

In Example 1, the problem can be solved by graphing, or algebraically using the substitution method or the elimination method. Choose the method you find easiest to work with.

Investing

Mari invests $3000 in two funds. The education savings plan pays interest at a rate of 7% per year and the guaranteed investment certificate (GIC) pays interest at 5% per year. At the end of the year, she has earned $190 in interest. How much did Mari invest at each rate?

Solution

Let e represent the amount invested in the education savings plan. Let g represent the amount invested in the GIC.

$e + g = 3000$ ①   *Mari invests a total of $3000.*

$0.07e + 0.05g = 190$ ②   *Express each percent as a decimal.*

This system of equations would be difficult to solve by graphing. Solve by elimination.

$$0.07e - 0.05g = 190 \quad ②$$
$$\underline{0.05e + 0.05g = 150 \quad ③}$$
$$0.02e \qquad\qquad = 40$$
$$\frac{0.02e}{0.02} = \frac{40}{0.02}$$
$$e = 2000$$

Multiply each term in equation ① by 0.05 to get equation ③, then subtract ② − ③.

$$e + g = 3000$$
$$2000 + g = 3000$$
$$2000 + g - 2000 = 3000 - 2000$$
$$g = 1000$$

Substitute e = 2000 into equation ① and solve for g.

Check the solution (2000, 1000) in equation ②.

$\text{LS} = 0.07e + 0.05g$ $\text{RS} = 190$
$\quad = 0.07(2000) + 0.05(1000)$
$\quad = 140 + 50$
$\quad = 190$
$\quad = \text{RS}$

Mari invested $2000 in the education savings plan at 7% and $1000 in the GIC at 5%.

Key Concepts

- A linear system can be solved by graphing or algebraically.
- Different methods of solving a linear system should give the same solution.

Discuss the Concepts

D1. Describe a situation in which you would solve a linear system by graphing. Give an example.

D2. Give an example of a linear system you would solve using the substitution method. Explain why you would use substitution to solve the system.

D3. Give an example of a linear system you would solve using the elimination method. Explain why you would use elimination to solve the system.

Practise the Concepts Ⓐ

Reasoning and Proving

Representing   Selecting Tools

Problem Solving

Connecting   Reflecting

Communicating

For help with question 1, refer to Example 1.

1. Julia's annual salary in dollars, S, can be represented by the equation $S = 30\,500 + 500n$ where n is the number of years she has worked for the company. Aysha works for another company. Her annual salary can be represented by the equation $S = 26\,000 + 1000n$ where n represents the number of years Aysha has been working there. After how many years will the two women have the same salary? What will that salary be?

For help with questions 2 and 3, refer to Example 2.

2. Silvio invests $8000 for his children's education. He invests part of the money in a high-risk bond that pays 5% interest per year, and the rest in a lower-risk bond that pays 3.25% per year. After one year, he has a total of $312.50 in interest. How much did Silvio invest at each rate?

3. Gareth plans to go to college in a year and needs to save for tuition. He invests his summer earnings of $3050, part at 8% interest per year, and part at 7.5% per year. After one year, Gareth has earned a total of $234 in interest. How much did he invest at each rate?

4. To join Jungle Gymnastics Club, Sonja will pay a monthly fee of $25 and an initiation fee of $200. If she chooses to join Brant Gymnastics Club, she will pay an initial fee of only $100 but $35 per month.
   a) After how many months are the costs the same?
   b) If Sonja plans to do gymnastics for 6 months, which club should she join? Why?
   c) If Sonja plans to do gymnastics for more than a year, which club should she join? Why?

5. Solve the linear system $y = 2x - 1$ and $3x - y = 5$. Which method did you use? Why?

6. For a basketball tournament, Marcus orders T-shirts for all the participants. The medium-sized shirts cost $4 per shirt, and the large-sized shirts cost $5 per shirt. Marcus orders a total of 70 shirts. He spends $320. How many of the shirts are medium-sized?

7. Students hold a car wash to raise money for a school trip to the west coast. They charge $7 per car and $10 per van. If they washed a total of 52 cars and vans and earned $457, how many cars did they wash? How many vans did they wash?

Achievement Check

8. Meredith drove 255 km from Kingston to Toronto in $2\frac{3}{4}$ h. She drove part of the way at 100 km/h and the rest of the way at 60 km/h.
   a) Suppose the equation for time is $\dfrac{x}{100} + \dfrac{y}{60} = 2.75$. What do the variables represent?
   b) Write an equation for the total distance.
   c) Solve the linear system to find the distance Meredith drove at each speed.

9. Which method would you use to solve the system $3x - y = 8$ and $4x - y = -15$? Why?

10. For a contest, students have to solve this problem:
The length of a rectangle is 6 cm more than its width. The perimeter of the rectangle is 84 cm. What are the dimensions of the rectangle?

a) One student says the dimensions of the rectangle are 39 cm by 45 cm. Is the student correct? How do you know?

b) What is the answer to the contest problem?

Extend the Concepts C

11. The ordered pairs $(1, 3)$ and $(-2, -9)$ are both solutions to the linear system $y = 4x - 1$ and $8x - 2y = 2$. Explain how this is possible.

Math Connect

The 48 000 m^2 Kempinski Hotel Mall in Dubai, opened in 2006. The hotel is attached to the world's third-largest indoor ski resort. It offers a unique chance to ski in the middle of the desert.

12. Students are planning a ski trip. They have a choice between two packages. The first package costs $630 per student. It includes 2 meals a day and accommodation for 9 days. The second package costs $720 per student. It includes 3 meals a day and accommodation for 9 days.

a) What is the cost per meal?
b) What is the cost per day for accommodation?

13. Harvinder drives 400 km in 5.5 h. For the first part of his trip, his average speed is 80 km/h. For the second part of his trip, his average speed is 60 km/h.

a) Let x represent the distance Harvinder travels at 80 km/h. Let y represent the distance he drove at 60 km/h. Write a system of equations to represent this situation.

b) How far does Harvinder drive at each speed?

Review of Key Terms

1. Explain the meaning of each term in your own words.

   a) linear system
   b) point of intersection
   c) substitution method
   d) elimination method

5.1 Solve Linear Systems by Graphing, pages 198 to 204

2. Solve each linear system by graphing.

   a) $y = 2x + 3$
   $y = x + 4$

   b) $2x - y = -13$
   $x - y = -10$

   c) $x + y = 7$
   $3x - y = 5$

   d) $2x - y = 2$
   $4x + y = 10$

3. Use a graphing calculator to solve each linear system. Round answers to two decimal places where necessary.

   a) $y = -3x + 4$
   $y = 4x + 13$

   b) $y = 5x - 6$
   $y = \frac{2}{5}x - \frac{3}{5}$

   c) $y = -4x + \frac{2}{3}$
   $y = 2x + \frac{8}{3}$

   d) $y = 6x - 13$
   $y = -\frac{3}{4}x - \frac{5}{2}$

5.2 Solve Linear Systems by Substitution, pages 205 to 211

4. Solve each linear system by substitution.

   a) $y = 7x + 1$
   $2x + y = 10$

   b) $2x + y = 4$
   $4x - y = -1$

   c) $x - y = 7$
   $3x + y = 5$

   d) $x + y = 5$
   $x - y = -1$

5. On his farm, Maddock plants a total of 20 ha. He plants both corn and canola. If he plants three times as much corn as canola, how many hectares of each type of plant does he plant?

6. A teacher plans to buy books for her class. She has 28 students and wants to buy a book for each one of them. The books cost $5 each for softcovers and $8 each for hardcovers. The teacher has $173 to spend. How many of each type of book can she buy?

5.3 Solve Linear Systems by Elimination, pages 212 to 218

7. Solve each linear system by elimination.

a) $x + 2y = 3$
$x - 4y = 0$

b) $3x + 2y = 18$
$x - 3y = -5$

c) $2x - 3y = -19$
$4x + 6y = 28$

d) $3x + y = 4$
$6x - y = -1$

8. Isabella rode her motorcycle at constant speed. It took her 2 hours to travel 216 km with the wind behind her. The return trip took her 3 hours riding into the wind.

a) Let s represent the speed of the motorcycle and w represent the speed of the wind. Write a linear system to represent this situation.

b) Find the speed of the motorcycle and the speed of the wind.

9. The Athletic Council wants to buy a total of 45 volleyballs and basketballs. The council has $435 to spend. Each volleyball costs $8 and each basketball costs $11. How many of each type of ball can be purchased?

5.4 Solve Problems Involving Linear Systems, pages 219 to 225

10. Solve each linear system. Which method did you use each time? Why?

a) $x + 3y = 7$
$2x + 4y = 11$

b) $2x - y = 27$
$x + y = 12$

c) $y = -x + 8$
$y = 6x + 1$

d) $y = 2x - 8$
$x - y = 4$

11. Anna has a total of $6000 to invest. She puts part of it in an investment paying 8% per year, and the rest in an investment paying 6% per year. At the end of one year, Anna earned $440 in interest. How much did she invest at each rate?

12. Doug is buying a new cell phone. He has narrowed his choices down to two plans. The first plan costs $40 per month with unlimited calling. The second plan costs $10 per month plus $0.10 per minute. Which plan should Doug choose? Explain your choice.

13. Carlie has a jar of coins. She tells her sister that the jar has 45 quarters and dimes altogether and the value of the coins is $6.30. Find the number of each type of coin in the jar.

1. Solve by graphing.

   a) $y = 2x + 3$
   $y = x + 4$

   b) $y = 3x - 4$
   $y = \frac{1}{2}x + 1$

   c) $y = -5x + 2$
   $y = x + 8$

2. Solve by substitution.

   a) $2x - y = 3$
   $x - y = 4$

   b) $x = 4y - 3$
   $2x + y = 6$

   c) $x - 2y = 7$
   $2x = 3y + 13$

3. Solve by elimination.

   a) $2x - y = -13$
   $x - y = -10$

   b) $2x - y = -2$
   $x + 2y = 9$

   c) $4x - 3y = 11$
   $2x + 3y = -1$

4. Solve the linear system. Which method did you use? Why?
   $4x + 5y = 3$
   $2x - 3y = 7$

5. a) Explain how you would solve this linear system.
   $y = 7x + 1$
   $2x + y = 10$

   b) What is the solution?

6. Nathan and Vivek have part-time jobs at the same company. Nathan is paid $10 per shift and $4 for each item he makes in his shift. Vivek is paid $40 per shift and $1 per item he makes.

   a) Write a system of linear equations to represent this situation.

   b) How many items must each person make in one shift to earn the same amount of money?

   c) How much will they each earn for that shift?

7. Ramona is planning to have graduation shirts made. Company A charges a $40 set-up fee plus $5 per shirt for printing. Company B charges a $100 set-up fee plus $2 per shirt for printing.

   a) Write a system of linear equations to represent this situation.

   b) Find the number of shirts for which the cost is the same for both companies.

   c) Under what circumstances should Ramona choose company A? Company B? Explain.

Chapter Problem Wrap-Up

To wrap-up his fundraising campaign, Logan organized a dog show. The cost to rent the park was $1300 plus $2.50 per person for the snack bar fee. Logan charged $5 for each student ticket and $8 for each adult ticket. His total ticket sales were $3585 and the total attendance was 525 people.

a) How many students attended the dog show?

b) How many adults attended the dog show?

c) How much money did Logan raise with this event for the dog rescue organization?

8. Snowbound Adventures charges a $5 flat fee plus $1/h to rent snowboarding equipment. Shred-Zone charges a $7 flat fee plus $0.50/h to rent snowboarding equipment.

   a) Write a linear equation to represent the total cost for each company.

   b) What is the point of intersection of the linear system? What do the coordinates of the point of intersection mean in terms of this situation?

   c) Describe a situation in which it was cheaper to rent equipment from Snowbound Adventures.

9. The school sold 108 tickets for the spring concert. Student tickets cost $2 each and adult tickets cost $5 each.

   a) The concert proceeds were $351. How many students attended?

   b) If each of the 108 concert attendees paid an average of $3 for refreshments, find the total revenue from the concert.

10. Barbara and her daughter Linda are choosing a new cell phone plan. CellularPlus charges $10 per month and $0.35 per minute for any minutes used during the month. CheapCell charges $20 per month and $0.15 per minute for every minute used in the month. For what number of minutes per month will the plans cost the same amount?

Task

Charity Fundraising

The Student Council at your school plans to raise money for a local charity. The fundraising committee has two options and needs to determine which option will raise the greater amount of money.

Option A

60/40 Raffle

Raffle tickets are sold for $4 each. The person whose ticket is drawn wins 40% of the total amount collected from ticket sales. The remaining 60% goes to the charity.

Option B

Battle of the Bands

The committee rents the local community theatre to hold a battle of the bands contest. The theatre always charges the same fixed rental fee. Two other schools ran similar fundraisers earlier in the year. One school sold 100 tickets and raised $50 for charity. The second school sold 300 tickets and raised $1050 for charity. Each of the schools charged the same price for tickets.

1. For Option A, let x represent the number of raffle tickets sold and y represent the amount that goes to the charity. Write an algebraic equation to model the amount raised for charity by Option A.

2. a) For Option B, let p represent the price of one ticket and r represent the fixed rental fee at the community theatre. Use the information about the fundraisers held by the other two schools to determine the fixed rental fee and the ticket price.

   b) Use your answer from part a). Let x represent the number of tickets sold for the battle of the bands and y represent the amount raised for charity. Write an algebraic equation to model the amount raised for charity by Option B.

3. a) Write and then solve a system of linear equations to determine the number of tickets that must be sold for Options A and B to raise the same amount of money.

   b) Under what conditions would you recommend using Option A? Option B?

4. a) Suppose 200 tickets are sold. Which option would raise more money? How much more?

   b) Without calculating the difference, will the difference between the amount raised using each option increase or decrease if only 100 tickets are sold? Explain your reasoning.

Chapter 3:
Linear Relations

1. Find the slope of each line segment.

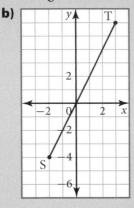

a)

b)

2. A taxi driver charges a $2 flat fee plus $0.35/km. The cost can be modelled by the equation $C = 0.35d + 2$, where C is the cost in dollars and d is the distance in kilometres.
   a) Make a table of values showing the cost for trips from 0 to 10 km.
   b) Graph the costs from part a).
   c) Find the slope of the line. What does the slope represent?

3. a) Graph the relation $y = -3x + 1$.
   b) Calculate the rate of change.
   c) Determine the value of y when $x = 0$.

4. Write an equation for each line given the slope and y-intercept.
   a) slope: 2, y-intercept: 4
   b) slope: $\frac{3}{2}$, y-intercept: $-\frac{1}{4}$
   c) slope: -3, y-intercept: 0
   d) slope: 0, y-intercept: $\frac{1}{2}$

5. Determine the equation of each line.
   a) passing through $(5, 8)$ and $(-2, 1)$
   b) passing through $(0, 4)$ and $(3, 13)$
   c) passing through $(0, 75)$ and $(25, 0)$
   d) passing through $(-8, 4)$ and $(6, \frac{1}{2})$

6. Determine the equation of each line.
   a) slope of -4, through $(-1, -6)$
   b) through $(3, 4)$ and $(1, -6)$
   c) a vertical line through $(1, -6)$

Chapter 4:   Linear Equations

7. Solve each linear equation.
   a) $3x - 8 = 7$
   b) $\frac{x}{3} + 2 = 6$
   c) $6 - 4x = 2x + 12$
   d) $2(x + 1) = 3x + 6$
   e) $\frac{2(t + 3)}{4} = t - 2$
   f) $\frac{x + 2}{3} = \frac{2x + 1}{4}$

8. Ji Hwan joined the local wellness centre. He paid an initial fee of $100 and will pay $5 per visit. The relation can be modelled using the equation $C = 100 + 5x$, where C is the total cost in dollars and x is the number of visits.

  a) What will be the total cost if Ji Hwan uses the centre 26 times?

  b) How many times can he use the centre for $400?

9. Rearrange each formula to solve for the indicated variable.

  a) $P = 2l + 2w$, for l

  b) $A = \pi r^2$, for r

  c) $S = 2\pi rh$, for h

10. Use the simple interest formula $I = Prt$ to find the principal amount that was invested to earn $600 in interest after 6 years at 2%.

11. Rearrange each equation into slope y-intercept form, then state the slope and y-intercept.

  a) $2x + y - 6 = 0$

  b) $3x - y + 4 = 0$

  c) $4x - 3y - 6 = 0$

12. The line $2x + By - 8 = 0$ passes through the point $(1, 3)$. Find the value of B.

Chapter 5: Linear Systems

13. Graph to solve each system of equations.

  a) $y = 2x - 2$
  $y = 3x - 3$

  b) $2x + y = -4$
  $-x - 2y = 5$

14. Solve each system of linear equations by substitution. Check your solution.

  a) $y = 3x + 2$
  $x + 2y = 11$

  b) $3x + y = -9$
  $x - 2y = 4$

15. Solve each system of linear equations by elimination. Check your solution.

  a) $x + 3y = 2$
  $3x + 2y = -1$

  b) $2x - y = -3$
  $6x + 4y = 12$

16. Angela is seeking a venue for her school's athletic council banquet. Primo Banquet Hall charges $2000 plus $50 per person. The Lookout Banquet Hall charges $1500 plus $75 per person.

  a) Write an equation to represent the total cost for each banquet hall.

  b) Find the point of intersection for the linear system.

  c) What does this point represent?

17. Joan needs to rent a theatre for a concert. The theatre charges $700 plus $3 per person. Joan plans to sell tickets for $10 per person. Let C represent the cost of the event and n represent the number of people attending the concert.

  a) Write a linear system to represent the situation.

  b) How many tickets must be sold to break even?

  c) What will be the total cost?

6 Quadratic Relations

An important factor in aircraft design is the shape of the aircraft's nose. The speed at which an aircraft will fly dictates the ideal aerodynamic nose shape. A commercial aircraft that travels at speeds less than the speed of sound has a rounded nose that is parabolic in shape.

In this chapter, you will

- collect data that can be represented as a quadratic relation, from experiments using appropriate equipment and technology, or from secondary sources; graph the data and draw a curve of best fit, if appropriate, with or without the use of technology
- determine, through investigation using technology, that a quadratic relation of the form $y = ax^2 + bx + c$ $(a \neq 0)$ can be graphically represented as a parabola, and determine that the table of values yields a constant second difference
- identify the key features of a graph of a parabola (i.e., the equation of the axis of symmetry, the coordinates of the vertex, the y-intercept, the x-intercepts, and the maximum or minimum value), using a given graph or a graph generated with technology from its equation, and use the appropriate terminology to describe the features

Reasoning and Proving

Representing — Selecting Tools

Problem Solving

Connecting — Reflecting

Communicating

Key Terms

axis of symmetry	minimum	second differences
first differences	parabola	vertex
maximum	quadratic relation	x-intercepts

Literacy Link

Use Circle, Wheel, and Spoke diagrams to activate prior knowledge and to reflect on questions you may have about concepts in this chapter.

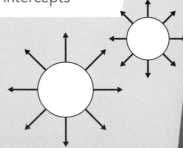

Many people have careers in the aerospace industry. Their education, knowledge, skills, and experience are essential to the development of the sophisticated products used in this industry. Aerospace manufacturing technologists design and manufacture such products.

Get Ready!

Evaluating Expressions

1. Substitute the given x-value to find the value of each expression. The first part has been done for you.

a) $3x^2 + 2, x = -1$

$= 3(-1)^2 + 2$

$= 3(1) + 2$

$= 3 + 2$

$= 5$

b) $x^2 - 3, x = 1$

c) $-2x^2 + 3x - 1, x = -2$

d) $0.5x^2 + 0.25, x = 5$

e) $-0.02x^2 - 3.12, x = 3$

Linear Relations

2. For each relation, make a table of values for $x = -3$ to $x = 3$, then graph the relation. The first part has been done for you.

a) $y = 3x + 2$

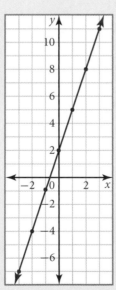

x	y
−3	−7
−2	−4
−1	−1
0	2
1	5
2	8
3	11

b) $y = -x + 6$

c) $y = 2x - 1$

d) $y = -2x + 3$

e) $y = 0.5x - 3$

3. Use a graphing calculator. Graph each relation from question 2.

4. State the x- and y-intercepts for each relation.

a)

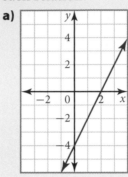

b)

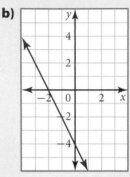

c)

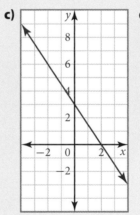

d)

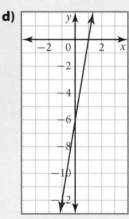

Chapter Problem

Archeologists discovered a 1.8 million-year-old fossilized jawbone (A) of an early human in Tanzania's Olduvai Gorge. Another fossilized early human jawbone (B), dated to 2.5 million years ago, was found at the Makapansgat Valley archaeological site in South Africa. These discoveries give scientists a unique opportunity to learn more about the evolution of early humans. Describe the shape of the fossils. Which mathematical relation would best model the shape of the jawbones?

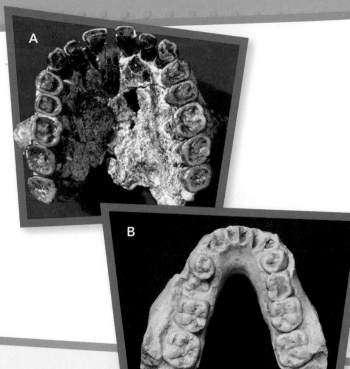

A

B

Lines of Symmetry

5. How many lines of symmetry does each figure have? Copy or trace each figure. Draw the lines of symmetry for each figure. The first one has been done for you.

a)

The hexagon has two lines of symmetry.

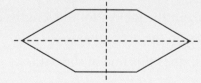

b)

c)

d)

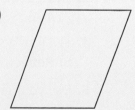

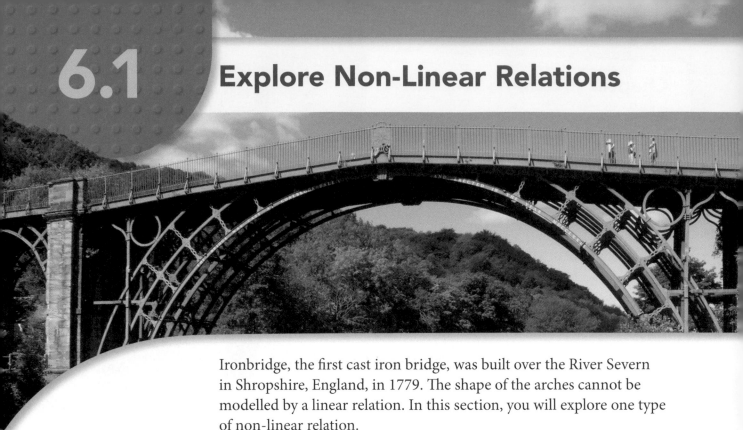

6.1 Explore Non-Linear Relations

Ironbridge, the first cast iron bridge, was built over the River Severn in Shropshire, England, in 1779. The shape of the arches cannot be modelled by a linear relation. In this section, you will explore one type of non-linear relation.

Investigate

Area of a Rectangle

Tools

- grid paper

1. On grid paper, draw different rectangles with perimeter 26 units. Copy and complete the table for rectangles with lengths from 1 unit to 12 units.

Length (units)	Width (units)	Area (square units)
1	12	12
2		

2. On grid paper, graph the data from the table. Plot the lengths on the horizontal axis and the areas on the vertical axis.

3. Draw a line of best fit. How well does this line fit the data? Explain.

4. **a)** Draw a smooth curve through the points.
   b) Reflect Describe the shape of the graph.

5. Use your graph. Estimate the area of a rectangle with length 2.5 units.

quadratic relation
- an equation that describes a parabola
- an equation of the form $y = ax^2 + bx + c$, where $a \neq 0$

parabola
- a symmetrical U-shaped graph
- the graph of a quadratic relation

The relationship between the length of a rectangle with fixed perimeter and the area of the rectangle is not linear. It is an example of a **quadratic relation**. The graph of a quadratic relation is called a **parabola**.

Example **1**

Draw a Line or Curve of Best Fit

Graph the data in each table. Draw a line or a curve of best fit through the points. Explain your choice.

a)

x	y
0	1
1	3
2	5
3	7
4	9
5	11
6	13
7	15
8	17

b)

x	y
0	16
1	9
2	4
3	1
4	0
5	1
6	4
7	9
8	16

Solution

a)

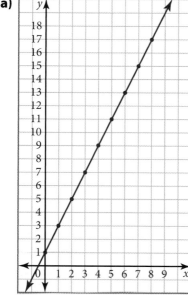

The points lie in a line, so I drew a line of best fit.

b)

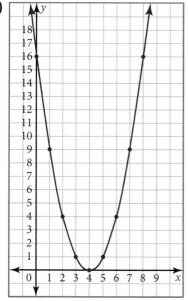

The points do not lie in a line, so I drew a curve of best fit.

Example 2

Area of a Triangle

The formula for the area of a triangle is
$A = \frac{1}{2}bh$, where b represents the length
of the base and h represents the height.
In a right isosceles triangle, the length of
the base equals the height.

a) Find the area of a right isosceles triangle
   with each base length from 1 cm to 6 cm.
   Record the base lengths and areas in a table.

b) Graph the data. Draw a smooth curve through the points.

Solution

a)

Base Length (cm)	Area (cm²)
1	0.5
2	2
3	4.5
4	8
5	12.5
6	18

b)

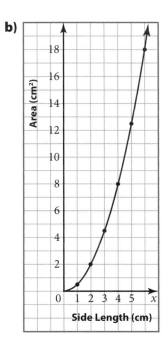

Key Concepts

- A quadratic relation is one type of non-linear relation.
- The graph of a quadratic relation is called a parabola.

Discuss the Concepts

D1. Describe how the graph of a quadratic relation differs from the graph of a linear relation.

D2. Refer to the tables of values in Example 1. Describe how the data in the tables compare.

For help with question 1, refer to Example 1.

1. Graph each set of data. Draw a line or a curve of best fit through the points. Explain your choice.

a)

x	y
3	12
4	7
5	4
6	3
7	4
8	7
9	12

b)

x	y
0	4
2	5
4	6
6	7
8	8
10	9
12	10

c)

x	y
1	0
2	7
3	12
4	15
5	16
6	15
7	12
8	7

d)

x	y
0	8
1	6.5
2	6
3	6.5
4	8
5	10.5
6	14
7	18.5

For help with questions 2 and 3, refer to Example 2.

2. The first five figures in a pattern are shown.

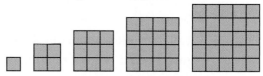

a) Copy and complete the table for five figures.

Side Length (units)	Area (square units)
1	1
2	

b) Graph the data comparing the side lengths and areas of the squares. Draw a curve of best fit through the points.

3. The formula for the area of a circle is $A = \pi r^2$, where r is the radius of the circle.

a) Find the area of five circles with radii 1 cm to 5 cm. Record the radii and the areas in a table.

b) Graph the data in the table. Join the points with a smooth curve.

4. a) List all the possible whole number dimensions of a rectangle with perimeter 18 cm. Find the area of each rectangle. Record the dimensions and the areas in a table.

b) Graph the data for length and area. Show length on the horizontal axis and area on the vertical axis.

c) Use the graph from part b). Estimate the area of a rectangle with length 4.5 cm.

5. The first four figures in a pattern are shown.

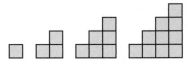

a) Copy and complete the table for the first eight figures in the pattern.

Base	Height	Perimeter	Area
1	1	4	1
2	2	8	3
3			6
			10

b) Draw a graph comparing the bases and perimeters of the figures. What type of relationship exists between the base of a figure and its perimeter? Why?

c) Draw a graph comparing the bases and areas of the figures. What type of relationship exists between the base of a figure and its area? Why?

d) Find the perimeter and the area of the figure whose base is 15 units.

6. The first four figures in a pattern are shown.

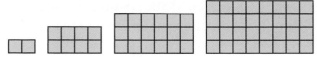

a) Copy and complete the table for the first eight figures in the pattern.

Width	Length	Area
1	2	2
2	4	8
3	6	

b) What type of relationship exists between the width and the length of these figures? Why?

c) What type of relationship exists between the width and the area of these figures? Why?

d) Find the width and the area of the figure whose length is 16 units.

e) Vito plans to use square patio stones to cover an area that has the same shape as the figures in this pattern. If the perimeter is 60 units, what is the area?

7. Lucien has a secret, which he tells to two friends. These friends each tell two friends, and so on. Suppose there are 257 students in the school.

Number of People	Number of Conversations

a) Draw a diagram to model Lucien's situation. You need only to draw the first four steps.

b) Copy and complete the table.

c) Graph the data.

d) Does the relation appear to be linear, quadratic, or neither? How do you know?

8. Sandy has 50 m of edging to create a garden. Use grid paper. Draw all the possible rectangles with perimeter 50 units. Change the length and the width by 1 m each time. Make a table of your findings.

   a) Create a table of values that represents the area as the width increases by 1 m, from 1 m to 10 m and the length decreases by 1 m.

   b) On grid paper, draw a graph comparing the widths and areas.

   c) Draw a curve of best fit.

   d) Use the graph to determine the length and width Sandy should use to have the greatest area for the garden.

Extend the Concepts **C**

Math Connect

The time it takes to complete one full swing of a pendulum, back and forth, is called the *period* of the pendulum.

9. Pendulums of different lengths are compared. The weight at the end is the same for all pendulums. The data represent the time it takes a pendulum to complete one swing.

   a) Use grid paper to plot the data.

   b) Draw a line or curve that best fits the data.

   c) Is the relation linear or quadratic?

   d) Use the graph to predict the time it will take a 90-cm pendulum to make one complete swing.

   e) Use the graph to predict the time it will take a 50-cm pendulum to make one complete swing.

   f) What can you conclude about the length of a pendulum and the length of time it takes to make one complete swing?

   g) Predict how the data would change if you placed a heavy weight at the end of each pendulum.

Length (cm)	Times (s)
5	0.46
10	0.64
20	0.90
40	1.27
60	1.55
80	1.80
100	2.00
120	2.20

6.2

Model Quadratic Relations

Sundials have been used for thousands of years to tell time. The part of the sundial that casts a shadow is called a gnomon. Each day, as the sun moves across the sky, the shadow cast by the upper tip of the gnomon traces a path from west to east. At certain times of the year, this path can be modelled by a quadratic relation.

Investigate A

Use Technology to Collect Data

Start the Ranger program in the CBL/CBR APP.

- Press 3.

Set up and start the sample.

- Press [ENTER] [▼] [1] [▼] [▼] [ENTER]
  [▲] [▲] [▲] [▲] [ENTER].

Tools

- Calculator-Based Ranger (CBR™)
- graphing calculator

Math Connect

The word "quadratic" comes from the Latin *quadrare* meaning "to square."

- Detach the cable from the CBR. Bend your knees and place your feet shoulder width apart. Hold the CBR in front of you with both hands so that its circular face and trigger button are down. Press the Trigger button on the CBR and then jump. Attach the cable to the CBR. To transfer the data to the calculator press ENTER.

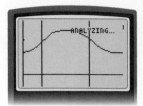

- To select the region of the graph, press ENTER 4 1. Use the arrow keys to move the cursor to a point where the quadratic curve begins. Press ENTER.

- Use the arrow keys to move the cursor to the right of the maximum and press ENTER. The window will be automatically resized to accommodate the domain selected.

- To quit the CBL/CBR APP, press ENTER 7.

- To construct the quadratic fit:

- Press STAT ▶ 5 VARS ▶ 1 1 ENTER.

- Press GRAPH to graph the quadratic.

The last screen tells you where your time and distance data are located.

1. What was the maximum height of your jump? How do you know?

2. What was the maximum height reached by the CBR? How do you know?

3. **Reflect** Refer to the equation that models the quadratic portion of the jump. Describe the characteristics of the equation. How is this equation different from a linear equation?

A quadratic relation can be modelled by an equation of the form $y = ax^2 + bx + c$. The coefficient on the squared term cannot be 0. Here are three examples of quadratic relations:

$$y = x^2 \qquad\qquad y = 5x^2 - 4 \qquad\qquad y = 2x^2 + 3x + 1$$

Tools

- graphing calculator

1. Copy and complete the table.

Width (mm)	Depth (mm)
0	
5	
10	
15	
20	
25	
30	
35	
40	
45	
50	
55	

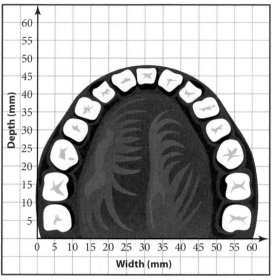

2. Use a graphing calculator. Press [STAT] 1 [ENTER].
Enter the width data in L1 and the depth data in L2.

- Press [WINDOW]. Use the window settings shown.

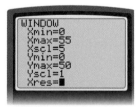

- Press [2nd] [STAT PLOT] [ENTER]. Use the settings shown.
- Press [GRAPH].

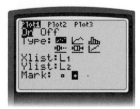

3. Press [STAT] [▶] 5 [2nd] [L1] [,] [2nd] [L2] [,] [VARS] [▶] 1 1 [ENTER]. Record the equation of the curve of best fit.

- Press [GRAPH].
- Press [Y=]. Record the equation in Y1.

4. Reflect What type of relation fits the data?

The Path of a Basketball

The graph shows the path of a basketball shot. The basketball must not touch the gymnasium ceiling, which is 5.5 m high. On this shot, will the basketball touch the ceiling? Show your work.

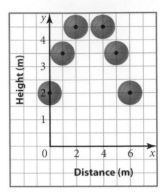

Solution

These points can be read from the graph.

Distance (m)	Height (m)
0	2.0
1	3.5
2	4.5
4	4.5
5	3.5
6	2.0

Enter the distance data in L1 and the height data in L2. Draw a scatter plot of the data.

- Press [STAT] [▶] 5 [2nd] [L1] [,] [2nd] [L2] [,] [VARS] [▶] 1 1 [ENTER].
- Press [GRAPH].
- Press [2nd] [CALC] 4.

  Use the arrow keys to move the cursor to the left of the highest point on the graph. Press [ENTER].

  Use the arrow keys to move the cursor to the right of the highest point on the graph.

- Press [ENTER] [ENTER].

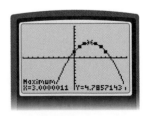

The maximum height of the ball is just under 4.8 m, so the ball will not touch the ceiling.

Key Concepts

- A quadratic relation can be represented by an equation of the form $y = ax^2 + bx + c$, where $a \neq 0$.
- A graphing calculator can be used to find the equation of the parabola of best fit.

Discuss the Concepts

D1. Describe how the equation representing a quadratic relation is different from the equation representing a linear relation.

Practise the Concepts **A**

1. Is each relation linear or quadratic? How do you know?

   a) $y = x^2 + 1$ **b)** $y = 2x + 1$ **c)** $y = 3x^2$

   d) $y = x^2 - 7x + 4$ **e)** $y = 6x$ **f)** $y = \frac{1}{2}x^2$

For help with question 2, refer to Example 1.

2. Use a graphing calculator to graph each set of data. Describe the type of relation that best represents the data.

a)

x	y
−4	57
−3	34
−2	17
−1	6
0	1
1	2
2	9
3	22
4	41

b)

x	y
−3	−18
−2	−13
−1	−8
0	−3
1	2
2	7
3	12

c)

x	y
0	0.25
0.5	1.875
1	3.25
1.5	4.375
2	5.25
2.5	5.875
3	6.25
3.5	6.375

3. The table shows the temperature of an outdoor swimming pool recorded each hour, starting at 10 a.m. Use a graphing calculator. Plot the data and draw the curve of best fit.

Elapsed Time (h)	Temperature (°C)
1	20.0
2	23.5
3	25.0
4	25.0
5	23.5
6	20.0

4. The table shows the height and horizontal distance of a golf ball after it is hit.

Horizontal Distance (m)	Height (m)
0	0
20	7.2
40	12.8
60	16.8
80	19.2
100	20.0
120	19.2
140	16.8
160	12.8

a) Draw a scatter plot of the data.
b) Find the equation of the curve of best fit.
c) Describe the relationship between the horizontal distance the ball travels and the height of the ball.

5. Matt and Jordan measured the time it took for a ball to roll down a ramp. They repeated the experiment several times, each time they changed the height of the end of the ramp. Their results are shown in the table.

Height Above Ground (cm)	Time (s)
2	3.0
3	2.2
4	1.9
5	1.6
6	1.4
7	1.2
8	1.1
9	1.0
10	0.88
11	0.83

a) Draw a scatter plot of the data.

b) Find the equation of the line or curve of best fit.

6. For a science project Thalia and Lee tracked the growth of a bacterial culture over several days and collected the following data.

a) Draw a scatter plot of the data.

b) Find the equation of the curve of best fit.

c) What type of graph is it?

d) What type of relationship is it?

Day	Number of Bacteria (1000s)
1	25
2	100
3	200
4	400
5	600
6	900
7	1200
8	1600
9	2000
10	2500
11	3000
12	3600

7. The data shown were collected by the depth finder on a fishing boat as it passed over an underwater formation.

a) Using a graphing calculator, plot the points and draw the line or curve of best fit.

b) What is the shape of the formation the fishers passed over?

c) Does the graph properly represent a picture of the formation the boat passed over? Why or why not?

d) What do you need to do to properly interpret the data?

Time (s)	Depth (m)
0	100.124
0.5	153.345
1.0	202.457
1.5	237.763
2.0	265.675
2.5	306.67
3.0	275.56
3.5	244.342
4.0	206.45
4.5	154.67
5.0	105.34

Reasoning and Proving

Representing | Selecting Tools

Problem Solving

Connecting | Reflecting

Communicating

8. Christine measured the distances required to stop a car from different initial speeds.

Speed (km/h)	Reaction Distance (m)	Braking Distance (m)	Total Stopping Distance (m)
50	18	40	58
60	22	72	94
70	26	98	124
80	29	128	157
90	33	162	195
100	37	200	237

a) Draw a graph comparing the initial speed to the reaction distance.

b) Draw another graph comparing the initial speed to the braking distance.

c) Draw a third graph comparing the initial speed to the total stopping distance.

d) What type of relation best models each graph? Why?

e) Describe how the police can use similar data and the length of a skid mark to estimate the speed a car was travelling.

Chapter Problem **9.** The picture is of a lower jawbone found by a hiker. Examine the photo to determine the data.

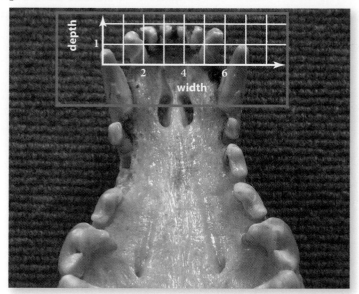

a) Working with a partner, use the grid overlay to find data points from the photo. Create a table of values.

b) Enter the data into a graphing calculator. Determine the equation that best represents the relation.

Literacy Connect **10.** A *parable* is a story designed to mirror a life lesson, often through comparison or allegory. Explain why the mathematical term *parabola* and the literary term *parable* have similar names.

Extend the Concepts

11. Use grid paper. For each relation, make a table of values and graph the relation.

a) $y = -2x^2 + 3x + 5$

b) $y = x^2 + 2x - 1$

c) $y = -x^2 - 5x - 1$

6.3 Key Features of Quadratic Relations

Astronauts simulate microgravity, once called weightlessness, by flying an airplane through a parabolic curve. The plane climbs, levels off, and then as it proceeds down the drop, astronauts experience microgravity. The plane levels off and then begins to climb again for another session. Each cycle lasts about one minute.

Investigate A   The Shape of Quadratic Relations

Tools

- graphing calculator

1. a) Press [WINDOW]. Use the window settings shown.

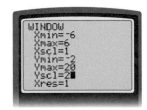

b) Press [Y=]. Enter $Y1 = x^2$. Press [GRAPH].
  - Press [Y=]. Leave the equation in Y1.
    Enter $Y2 = 2x^2$.
  - Press [GRAPH].
  - Press [Y=]. Leave the equations in Y1 and Y2.
    Enter $Y3 = 4x^2$. Press [GRAPH].
  - Press [Y=]. Leave the previous equations.
    Enter $Y4 = 7x^2$.
  - Press [GRAPH].

c) How did each parabola compare to the previous parabola?

d) Sketch the four parabolas, on one set of axes, in your notebook. Label each parabola with its equation.

2. a) Press WINDOW. Use the window settings shown.

b) Press Y=. Clear all the equations from question 1.

Enter $Y1 = x^2$. Press GRAPH.

- Press Y=. Leave the equation in Y1.

  Enter $Y2 = \left(\dfrac{1}{2}\right)x^2$. Press GRAPH.

- Press Y=. Leave the equations in Y1 and Y2.

  Enter $Y3 = \left(\dfrac{1}{4}\right)x^2$. Press GRAPH.

- Press Y=. Leave the previous equations.

  Enter $Y4 = \left(\dfrac{1}{5}\right)x^2$. Press GRAPH.

c) How did each parabola compare to the previous parabola?

d) Sketch the four parabolas, on one set of axes, in your notebook. Label each parabola with its equation.

3. a) Press WINDOW. Use the window settings shown.

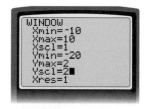

b) Press Y=. Clear all the equations from question 1.

Enter $Y1 = -x^2$. Press GRAPH.

- Press Y=. Leave the equation in Y1.

  Enter $Y2 = -2x^2$. Press GRAPH.

- Press Y=. Leave the equations in Y1 and Y2.

  Enter $Y3 = -4x^2$. Press GRAPH.

- Press Y=. Leave the previous equations.

  Enter $Y4 = -\left(\dfrac{1}{2}\right)x^2$. Press GRAPH.

- Press Y=. Leave the previous equations.

  Enter $Y5 = -\left(\dfrac{1}{3}\right)x^2$. Press GRAPH.

c) How do these parabolas compare to the parabolas you graphed in questions 1 and 2?

4. Reflect Given a quadratic equation of the form $y = ax^2$, describe the effect on the graph of changing the value of a.

Investigate **B** **Features of a Parabola**

Tools

- grid paper

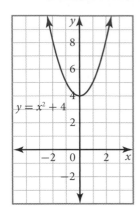 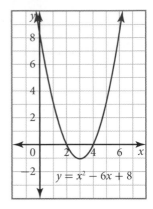 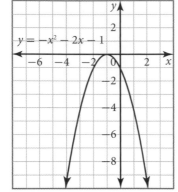

For each graph:

1. Copy the graph onto grid paper. Does the parabola open upward or downward? What does this tell you about the sign of the coefficient of x^2?

2. What is the ordered pair at the point where the parabola changes direction from decreasing to increasing (for a parabola that opens upward) or from increasing to decreasing (for a parabola that opens downward)? This point is the **vertex** of the parabola.

3. If the parabola opens upward, what is the least y-value? This is the **minimum**. If the parabola opens downward, what is the greatest y-value? This is the **maximum**.

4. Draw the line of symmetry. This is the **axis of symmetry**. What is the x-value of every point on the axis of symmetry? How does this compare to the x-value at the vertex?

5. What are the x-coordinates of the points where the parabola crosses the x-axis? These are the **x-intercepts**.

6. **Reflect** Describe how to identify the vertex, the maximum or minimum value, the axis of symmetry, and the x-intercepts of a parabola.

vertex

- the point at which the parabola changes from decreasing to increasing or from increasing to decreasing

maximum/minimum

- the greatest/least y-value on the graph
- the y-value at the vertex

axis of symmetry

- the vertical line that passes through the vertex
- the line of symmetry
- the equation of the axis of symmetry is $x = p$, where p is the x-coordinate of the vertex

x-intercepts

- the x-coordinate(s) of the point(s) at which the parabola crosses the x-axis

The axis of symmetry of a quadratic relation is a vertical line that passes through the vertex. Every point on the axis of symmetry has the same x-coordinate, so the equation of the axis of symmetry is $x = a$, where a is the x-coordinate of the vertex.

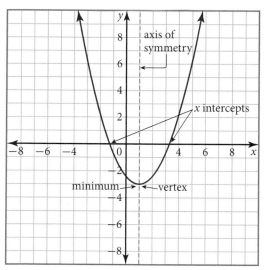

Example	1

Key Features of a Quadratic Relation Given a Graph

Identify the following for the quadratic relation shown:

a) the coordinates of the vertex
b) the equation of the axis of symmetry
c) the y-intercept
d) the maximum or minimum value
e) the x-intercepts

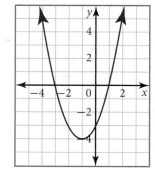

Math Connect

Every point on a vertical line has the same x-coordinate, so the equation for a vertical line is $x = a$, where a represents the x-coordinate of each point on the line.

Solution

a) The vertex of this parabola is $(-1, -4)$.
b) The axis of symmetry is the vertical line that passes through the vertex. The equation of the axis of symmetry is $x = -1$.
c) The y-intercept is -3.
d) The minimum value is -4, the y-coordinate of the vertex.
e) There are two x-intercepts, -3 and 1.

Example 2

Key Features of a Quadratic Relation Given an Equation

A quadratic relation is given by the equation $y = 2x^2 - 4x + 6$.

a) Use a graphing calculator to graph the relation.

b) Identify the maximum or minimum value and the coordinates of the vertex.

c) Write the equation of the axis of symmetry.

d) Identify the y-intercept.

e) Identify the x-intercepts.

Solution

a) Press $\boxed{\text{Y=}}$.

Enter Y1 = $2x^2 - 4x + 6$.

• Press $\boxed{\text{WINDOW}}$.

Use the window settings shown.

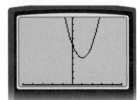

• Press $\boxed{\text{GRAPH}}$.

b) Press $\boxed{\text{2nd}}$ [CALC] 3.

Use the arrow keys to move the cursor to the left of the minimum point, press $\boxed{\text{ENTER}}$. Use the arrow keys to move the cursor to the right of the minimum point, press $\boxed{\text{ENTER}}$ $\boxed{\text{ENTER}}$.

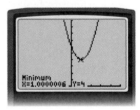

The minimum value is 4. The coordinates of the vertex are (1, 4).

c) The equation of the axis of symmetry is $x = 1$.

d) Press $\boxed{\text{2nd}}$ [CALC] 1.

Type 0, then press $\boxed{\text{ENTER}}$.

The y-intercept is 6.

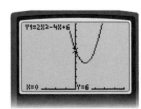

e) The vertex is above the x-axis and the graph opens upward, so there are no x-intercepts.

Example **3**

Key Features of a Quadratic Relation in Design

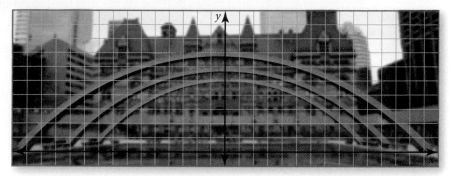

Nathan Phillips Square, a Toronto landmark, incorporates several concrete parabolas as design elements in its central fountain/skating rink. In the photograph, the arches are overlaid with a grid.

a) Identify the maximum value of the front arch. In this photograph, suppose each grid square represents 1 m. How high is the arch at its tallest point?

b) What are the *x*-intercepts? Find the horizontal width of the opening at the base of the arch.

Solution

a) From the photograph, the maximum value is 7. At the tallest point, the arch is 7 m high.

b) The *x*-intercepts are −14 and 14. The horizontal distance between the intercepts is 28. The horizontal width at the base of the arch is 28 m.

Key Concepts

- If the coefficient of the squared term is positive, the parabola opens upward and has a minimum value. If the coefficient of the squared term is negative, the parabola opens downward and has a maximum value.

- The vertex of a parabola is the point at which the parabola changes from decreasing to increasing or from increasing to decreasing.

- The maximum or minimum value is the *y*-coordinate of the vertex.

- The axis of symmetry is the vertical line that passes through the vertex.

- The *x*-intercepts are the *x*-coordinates of the points at which the parabola crosses the *x*-axis. A parabola may have zero, one, or two *x*-intercepts.

Discuss the Concepts

D1. Amir states that the vertex and the maximum or minimum value are the same thing. Is Amir correct? Why or why not?

D2. How do you know whether a quadratic relation has a maximum or a minimum value?

D3. A student says that a parabola has one y-intercept but could have two x-intercepts. Is the student correct? Why or why not?

Practise the Concepts A

For help with question 1, refer to Example 1.

1. For each graph, identify
   a) the coordinates of the vertex
   b) the equation of the axis of symmetry
   c) the y-intercept
   d) the maximum or minimum value
   e) the x-intercepts

A
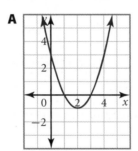

B
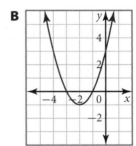

C
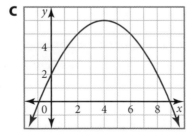

D
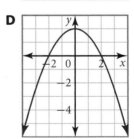

E
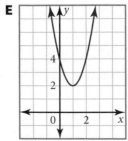

F
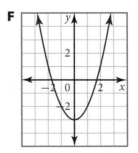

For help with questions 2 and 3, refer to Example 2.

2. Large satellite dishes are used to receive broadcast signals transmitted by orbiting satellites.

   This satellite dish uses a parabolic curve to reflect signals. Its shape can be modelled by the quadratic relation $y = \frac{1}{2}x^2 + 2x + 3$.

   a) Use a graphing calculator to graph the relation.
   b) Identify the coordinates of the vertex.
   c) Write the equation of the axis of symmetry.
   d) Identify the y-intercept.
   e) Identify the maximum or minimum value.
   f) Identify the x-intercepts.

3. A homemade solar oven makes use of a parabola to reflect the sun's rays through its vertex. The solar oven can actually cook food. Its shape can be modelled by the equation $y = -2x^2 - 4x - 3$.
   a) Use a graphing calculator to graph the relation.
   b) Identify the coordinates of the vertex .
   c) Write the equation of the axis of symmetry.
   d) Identify the y-intercept.
   e) Identify the maximum or minimum value.
   f) Identify the x-intercepts.

For help with question 4, refer to Example 3.

4. Parabolas often appear in the architecture of Antonio Gaudi, such as this doorway to Guell Palace in Spain. The graph models the shape of a similar doorway.

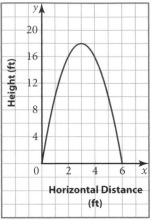

   a) What are the coordinates of the vertex?
   b) What does the vertex tell you about the height of the doorway?
   c) What is the y-intercept?
   d) What are the x-intercepts?
   e) What do these x-intercepts tell you about the base of the doorway?
   f) Why might an architect use a parabola in a building?

Literacy Connect

5. Find pictures of arches in architecture. Use a grid overlay to decide whether each arch can be modelled by a quadratic relation. How can you find out?

Chapter Problem

6. The photograph shows a lower jawbone that was discovered in 1964. The jawbone is estimated to be 1.5 million years old. Suppose 1 grid square represents 1 cm.

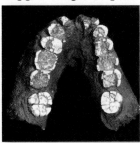
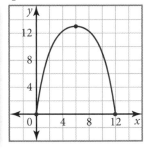

   a) Find the approximate coordinates of the vertex.
   b) Find the equation of the axis of symmetry.
   c) Find the maximum value (depth) of the jawbone.
   d) Find the x-intercepts.
   e) Find the width of the jawbone.

Reasoning and Proving

Representing   Selecting Tools

Problem Solving

Connecting   Reflecting

Communicating

Achievement Check

7. A natural stone bridge forms over a river. Water erodes the rock surface making a hole for water to pass through, which enlarges gradually over time. The largest natural stone bridge is the Rainbow Bridge in Utah. It has an approximately parabolic shape.

The curve can be modelled by the equation $h = -0.0159d^2 + 290$, where h is the height and d is the width, both in feet.

a) Graph the equation using a graphing calculator.

b) Find the vertex.

c) What does the vertex tell you about the bridge?

d) What is the span of the Rainbow Bridge?

Extend the Concepts   C

8. During a field goal attempt in a football game, the height (h) in feet of a football is given by $h = -0.02d^2 + 0.9d$, where d is the distance from the kicker to the ball in yards.

a) Use the equation to graph the path of the ball.

b) How far is the ball from the kicker when it hits the ground?

c) Graph the relation on grid paper. Include an appropriate scale.

d) The kick is headed straight between the goal posts. If the posts are 10 yd away from the kicker and 13.2 ft high, will this field goal be successful? Why or why not?

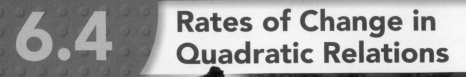

6.4 Rates of Change in Quadratic Relations

For a linear relation, the rate of change of *y* with respect to *x* is constant. In this section, you will use rates of change, also called **first differences** to identify quadratic relations.

Investigate

first differences
- the differences between the *y*-values that correspond to consecutive *x*-values
- the rate of change of *y*-values with respect to the *x*-values

First and Second Differences in Quadratic Relations

A snowboarder makes two runs.

Part A: Snowboarder Travels Down a Ramp

In the first run, the snowboarder travels down a ramp to the bottom of the slope.

For this run, the graph comparing height to the horizontal distance from the starting point is linear.

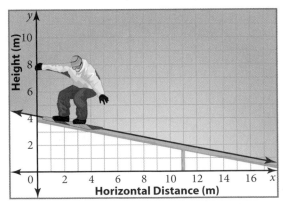

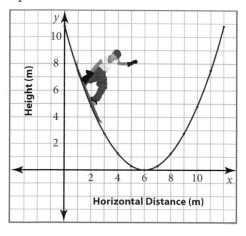

Math Connect

In Chapter 3, you connected the rate of change of a linear equation with the slope of the line. Rates of change can also be called first differences. For a linear relation, first differences are constant; they represent the slope of the line.

1. Copy and complete the table. What pattern do you notice in the first differences?

Horizontal Distance (m)	Height (m)	First Differences
1	4.0	
2	3.8	$3.8 - 4.0 = -0.2$
3	3.6	
4	3.4	
5	3.2	
6	3.0	

2. What do the first differences mean in terms of the snowboarder's motion?

Part B: Snowboarder Rides the Curve

In the second run, the snowboarder travels down one side of a parabolic curve and up the other. For this run, graphing height against horizontal distance from the starting point produces a parabola.

3. Copy the table. Calculate the rates of change or first differences. What do you notice about the first differences? How is this different from your response to question 1?

Horizontal Distance (m)	Height (m)	First Differences	Second Differences
0	10.8		
1	7.5	$7.5 - 10.8 = -3.3$	
2	4.8	$4.8 - 7.5 = -2.7$	$-2.7 - (-3.3) = 0.6$
3	2.7		
4	1.2		
5	0.3		
6	0		
7	0.3		
8	1.2		
9	2.7		
10	4.8		
11	7.5		
12	10.8		

4. The rate of change, or first differences, shows how quickly the height is changing compared to the horizontal distance. When first differences are not constant, it is useful to calculate **second differences**. Second differences are calculated by subtracting consecutive first differences.

a) Calculate the second differences.

b) What pattern do you notice in the second differences? What does this mean in terms of this situation?

5. Reflect Draw conclusions based on your observations for both snowboard runs. Can you estimate the shape of the graph from the table of values, without graphing? Explain.

When first differences are constant, the relation is linear and the graph is a line. A linear relation can be represented by an equation of the form $y = mx + b$.

When second differences are constant, the relation is quadratic and the graph is a parabola. A quadratic relation can be represented by an equation of the form $y = ax^2 + bx + c$, where $a \neq 0$.

second differences
- the difference between consecutive first differences
- for a quadratic relation, second differences are constant

Quadratic Relations in Architecture

Jivan centred the grid on the cross section of the stadium. Distances to the left of centre are recorded as negative values and distances to the right of centre are recorded as positive values.

A tennis stadium is designed for optimum viewing of tennis matches. The cross section of a tennis stadium is a parabolic curve. The lower level seats rise in a shallow curve from the floor. The upper level seats are steeper. This ensures that everyone can see the court properly. Jivan takes a photograph of the interior of the stadium, and superimposes a grid. He makes this table of values.

Horizontal Distance (m)	Height (m)
−8	3.0
−6	1.8
−4	1.0
−2	0.5
0	0
2	0.5
4	1.0
6	1.8
8	3.0

a) Would a linear or a quadratic model better represent the data? How do you know?

b) Use a graphing calculator to find the equation of the line or curve of best fit.

Solution

a) Use first and second differences to decide if a linear or a quadratic model is better.

Horizontal Distance (m)	Height (m)	First Differences	Second Differences
−8	3.0		
−6	1.8	$1.8 - 3.0 = -1.2$	
−4	1.0	$1.0 - 1.8 = -0.8$	$-0.8 - (-1.2) = 0.4$
−2	0.6	$0.6 - 1.0 = -0.4$	$-0.4 - (-0.8) = 0.4$
0	0.6	$0.6 - 0.6 = 0$	$0 - (-0.4) = 0.4$
2	1.0	$1.0 - 0.6 = 0.4$	$0.4 - 0 = 0.4$
4	1.8	$1.8 - 1.0 = 0.8$	$0.8 - 0.4 = 0.4$
6	3.0	$3.0 - 1.8 = 1.2$	$1.2 - 0.8 = 0.4$
8	4.6	$4.6 - 3.0 = 1.6$	$1.6 - 1.2 = 0.4$

From the table, first differences are not constant, but second differences are constant. A quadratic model would fit the data better.

b) Press STAT ENTER. Enter the distances in list L1 and the heights in list L2.

- Press 2nd [STAT PLOT] 1. Use the window settings shown.

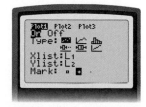

- Press STAT ▶ 5 2nd [L1] , 2nd [L2] , VARS ▶ 1 1 ENTER.

- Press GRAPH to display the data and the curve of best fit.

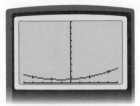

- Press Y= to display the equation.

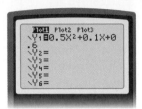

The equation of the curve of best fit is $y = 0.05x^2 + 0.1x + 0.6$.

Key Concepts

- A quadratic relation can be represented by an equation of the form $y = ax^2 + bx + c$, where $a \neq 0$.
- The graph of a quadratic equation has the shape of a parabola.
- A quadratic relation has constant second differences.

Discuss the Concepts

D1. Explain how you can determine, without graphing, if data in a table of values represent a quadratic relation.

D2. At its centre, the edge of the roof of the Rogers Centre in Toronto forms a parabola. Refer to the photograph. Explain how you could find the equation of the quadratic relation that models the shape of the roof.

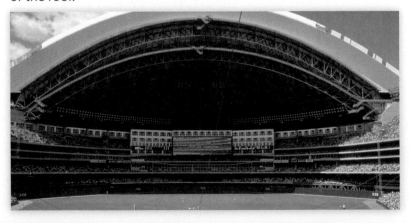

For help with questions 1 and 2, refer to the Investigate.

1. Make a table of values for each relation. Use the table to determine if the relation is quadratic.

   a) $y = x^2 - 6x + 8$ for x-values from 0 to 6
   b) $y = x^2 + 7x + 12$ for x-values from -7 to 0
   c) $y = x^2 - 3x + 10$ for x-values from -2 to 5
   d) $y = x^2 + 3x - 18$ for x-values from -6 to 3

2. Determine if each relation is linear, quadratic, or neither.

a)

x	y
1	1
2	2
3	3
4	4
5	3
6	2
7	1

b)

x	y
1	5.916
2	5.657
3	5.196
4	4.472
5	3.317
6	0

c)

p	q
0	3.25
1	2.75
2	2.25
3	1.75
4	1.25
5	0.75
6	0.25

For help with question 3, refer to the Example.

3. A foam-core raft is left in a lake for several months. Over the summer, the foam takes on water. In the fall, the raft is removed from the lake and placed on shore, and the water drains away.

   The amount of water held in the foam core can be represented by the equation $y = -0.04x^2 + x$, where x represents time in months and y is the amount of water in litres held in the raft.

   a) Enter the equation into a graphing calculator and make a table of values.
   b) Graph the relation.
   c) Calculate the first differences. Are they constant? Why or why not?
   d) Calculate the second differences. Are they constant? Explain.
   e) Suppose water weighs 1 kg/L and the wood and foam weigh 75 kg. How much does the raft weigh when it is put into the lake at the beginning of May? How much does it weigh when it comes out at the end of October?

4. This graph shows a quadratic relation.

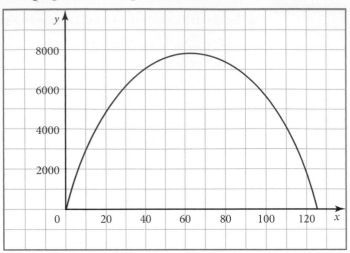

a) Make a table of values for the graph.

b) Use a graphing calculator to find the equation for this quadratic relation.

Literacy Connect

5. Explain how you can use first and second differences to determine if a relation is quadratic.

Achievement Check

6. Use grid paper. Follow these steps to draw a parabola.

a) Draw the axis of symmetry at $x = 3$.

b) Plot the vertex $(3, 3)$ and the x-intercepts $(0, 0)$ and $(6, 0)$.

c) Sketch the parabola.

d) Place your pencil at the vertex. Draw two diagonal lines (at approximately 45° on either side of the line of symmetry) from the vertex to the parabolic curve.

e) When your pencil meets the curve, change direction and draw a vertical line down to the bottom of the graph (parallel to the y-axis).

f) Draw an arrow on the end of the line. This is the path radio waves follow when received and transmitted by a parabolic dish.

7. For any 4-sided polygon, two diagonals can be drawn. Copy these figures into your notebook.

i)

ii)

iii)

iv)

a) Draw the diagonals. Copy and complete the table.

b) Use the pattern between the number of diagonals and the number of sides. Add data for an eight-sided and a nine-sided figure.

Number of Sides	Number of Diagonals
4	2
5	5
6	
7	

c) Use a graphing calculator to find the equation of the relation.

d) Use your equation to predict the number of diagonals for a 20-sided figure.

8. Place your hand flat on a piece of grid paper with your fingers close together and your thumb close to your hand.

With your pencil, place a dot at the tip of each finger and thumb. Remove your hand and join the points with a smooth curve.

a) Draw a set of axes so the origin coincides with the dot for your little finger. Estimate the coordinates of each point. Enter the data in lists on a graphing calculator. Find the equation of the parabola of best fit. Press [2nd] [TABLE]. Record five rows of the table of values. Find the second differences.

b) Move the axes so the origin coincides with the dot for the tip of a different finger. Estimate the coordinates of each point. Plot the data and find the equation of the parabola of best fit. Press [2nd] [TABLE]. Record five rows of the table of values. Find the second differences.

c) Compare the equations and second differences from parts a) and b).

Review of Key Terms

axis of symmetry	quadratic relation
first differences	second differences
maximum	vertex
mininum	x-intercepts
parabola	

1. Copy each statement. Use one of the key terms to complete the statement.

a) The graph of a quadratic relation is a _____.

b) A parabola that opens upward has a _____ value.

c) The _____ of a parabola is the point at which the parabola changes from increasing to decreasing or vice versa.

d) The _____ passes through the vertex of a parabola.

6.1 Explore Non-Linear Relations, pages 238 to 244

2. The figures in the pattern represent the first four triangular numbers.

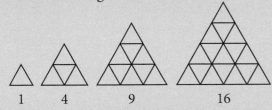

1   4   9   16

a) Copy and complete the table of values for the first eight triangular numbers.

Figure	Triangular Number
1	1
2	

b) Graph the data. Sketch a line or curve of best fit.

6.2 Model Quadratic Relations, pages 245 to 253

3. The table shows the temperature in degrees Fahrenheit measured inside a greenhouse each hour.

Elapsed Time (h)	Temperature (°F)
0	57
1	66
2	75
3	88
4	98
5	101
6	100
7	98
8	90
9	84
10	77
11	72
12	65

a) Graph the data.

b) Find the equation of the curve of best fit.

6.3 Key Features of Quadratic Relations, pages 254 to 263

4. Graph the quadratic relation $y = 2x^2 + 4x - 1$ using a graphing calculator. Sketch the graph in your notebook.

a) Identify the coordinates of the vertex.

b) Write the equation of the axis of symmetry.

c) Identify the y-intercept.

d) Identify the maximum or minimum value.

e) Identify the x-intercepts.

5. An archer shoots an arrow at a target 20 m away. The following data show the height of the arrow above the ground at various times after it was shot.

Time (s)	Height (m)
0.5	1.527
1.0	2.578
1.5	3.242
2.0	3.519
2.5	3.401
3.0	2.915
3.5	2.033

a) Plot the data on grid paper, placing time on the x-axis and height on the y-axis.

b) Draw a line or curve of best fit.

c) What is the shape of the graph?

d) If the arrow hit the target at 3.5 s, how far had it gone after 2 s? How far had it travelled after 3 s? How did you find out?

6. In the cross-section of a large tree, concentric circles form around the centre. Each ring represents one year of growth. One particular tree increased in radius by approximately 0.5 cm with each new ring.

a) Draw a graph comparing the age of the tree to the number of rings.

b) Name the type of relationship between age and number of rings.

c) Do you think the graph comparing the number of rings to the age of the tree would be linear, quadratic, or neither? Why?

d) If the radius increased by 0.5 cm each year, by how much did the circumference increase each year?

e) Can you tell how old a tree is by measuring the circumference of the trunk? Explain.

6.4 Rates of Change in Quadratic Relations, pages 264 to 271

7. The shape of the roof of a movie theatre is represented by the equation $h = -0.08d^2 + 3.15$, where h is the height, in metres, of the roof from the top of the walls, and d is the width, in metres, from the centre of the roof to the walls.

a) Create a table of values for x-values from −5 to 5.

b) Find the first and second differences.

c) Based on second differences, what shape is the roof?

d) Verify your conclusion by graphing the equation using a graphing calculator.

1. Graph each set of data. Then, draw the line or curve of best fit.

   Which data sets appear to be quadratic?

   a)

x	y
−3	6
−2	1
−1	−2
0	−3
1	−2
2	1
3	6

   b)

x	y
−3	−6
−2	−5
−1	−4
0	−3
1	−2
2	−1
3	0

   c)

x	y
−3	−2
−2	6
−1	9
0	3
1	8
2	11
3	13

2. Which of these relations appear to be quadratic? Explain.

   a)
   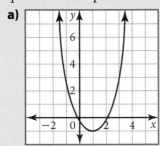

   b)
   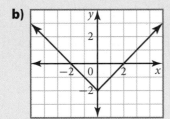

   c)
   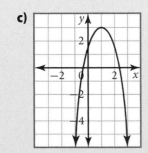

   d)
   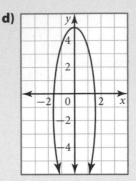

3. This table shows the times taken for a ball to roll down a ramp at different angles. The length of the ramp is constant.

Angle (°)	Time (s)
15	2.6
20	1.5
25	1.2
30	0.95
35	0.8
40	0.6

   a) Use a graphing calculator. Draw a scatter plot of the data.

   b) Find the equation of the line or curve that best fits the data.

   c) Is the relationship between angle and speed best modelled by a linear or quadratic relation? Why?

4. A quarterback passes the football. The equation $h = -0.01d^2 + 0.4d + 10$ represents the path of the ball, where h is the height of the ball in metres and d is the horizontal distance, in metres, that the ball travels.

   a) Use a graphing calculator to graph the path of the ball.

   b) Make a table of values and use it to find second differences.

Chapter Problem Wrap-Up

The archeologist needs to determine the mathematical relation that best fits the shape of these jawbones. Collect the data, determine the type of relation, and describe some key features based on that relation.

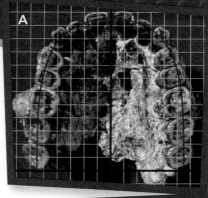

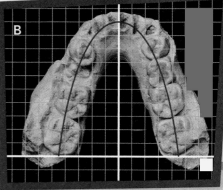

a) Create a table of values for each jawbone.
b) Find the first and second differences.
c) What type of relation best models the shape of each jawbone? Why?
d) Identify the vertex for each jawbone.
e) Write the equation of the axis of symmetry for each jawbone.
f) Identify the x-intercepts.

---

5. The graph shows a quadratic relation.

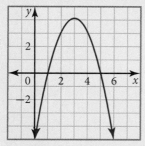

a) Identify the coordinates of the vertex.
b) Find the equation of the axis of symmetry.
c) Identify the y-intercept.
d) Does the parabola have a maximum or a minimum value? What is the maximum or minimum value?
e) Identify the x-intercepts.

6. The photograph shows the Harbour Bridge in Sydney, Australia. A grid has been placed over the photo to help you collect the data for the bottom arch. One grid space represents 50 ft.

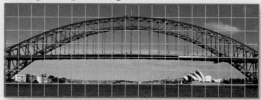

a) Examine the photograph. Make a table of values comparing the horizontal distance with the height from the roadway.
b) Use the table of values to calculate first and second differences.
c) Enter the horizontal distances in list L1 and the heights in list L2. Find and record the equation of the curve of best fit.
d) Graph the relation.

7 Quadratic Expressions

Science North is an interactive science museum in Sudbury, Ontario. The complex consists of two snowflake-shaped buildings, which are connected by a rock tunnel. Visitors can explore many fascinating exhibits on the environment, space, the human body, robotics, projectile motion, and more. Some of the exhibits can be modelled using quadratic expressions. In this chapter, you will learn the skills needed to work with quadratic expressions.

In this chapter, you will

- expand and simplify second-degree polynomial expressions involving one variable that consist of the product of two binomials or the square of a binomial, using a variety of tools and strategies
- factor binomials and trinomials involving one variable up to degree two, by determining a common factor, using a variety of tools
- factor simple trinomials of the form $x^2 + bx + c$, using a variety of tools
- factor the difference of squares of the form $x^2 - a^2$

Reasoning and Proving

Representing | Selecting Tools

Problem Solving

Connecting | Reflecting

Communicating

Key Terms

difference of squares	perfect square trinomial
factor	quadratic expression

Literacy Link

Make connections between mathematical concepts by creating a web. Write the big ideas in large circles and the examples and details in smaller circles. Connect the ideas by drawing lines between the circles.

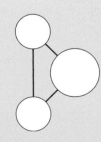

Interior design is an art and a science. Designers plan space, help select colours, and design effective lighting. They develop detailed budgets and computer models of the proposed changes to homes, public buildings, commercial buildings, and hospitals. Designers consider environmental concerns, any special needs of users, and changing technology.

Get Ready!

Polynomials

1. Identify the **numerical coefficient** in each term. The first part has been done for you.

a) $-5x$
    -5

b) $6x^2$

c) $2x$

d) $-7x^2$

2. Identify each expression as a monomial, binomial, trinomial, or polynomial. Choose the name that best describes the expression. The first part has been done for you.

a) $2x^2 + 3x$

   This expression has two terms. It is a binomial.

b) $-15x$

c) $x^2 + 4x - 6$

d) $-7x + 1 + (x^2 - 4x - 38)$

Algebraic Expressions

3. Multiply or divide. The first part has been done for you.

a) $2(-3p)$
    $-6p$

b) $-4(-5q)$

c) $(6r)(3r)$

d) $-14x \div 7$

e) $\dfrac{-24x^2}{-4x}$

f) $\dfrac{18x^2}{-9x^2}$

4. Simplify each expression. The first part has been done for you.

a) $2x + 6 - 4x + 8$
    $= 2x - 4x + 6 + 8$
    $= -2x + 14$

b) $x^2 + 5x + 3x + 15$

c) $3x^2 - 12x + 5x^2 + 15x$

d) $3x + 5 + (x^2 - 6x - 10)$

5. Expand each expression. The first part has been done for you.

a) $2(x - 3)$

   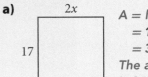

   $= 2x - 2(3)$
   $= 2x - 6$

b) $-4(x^2 + 3x - 5)$

c) $5x(2x + 3)$

d) $-3(x^2 - 2x - 1)$

6. Evaluate each expression in question 5 when $x = -2$. The first part has been done for you.

   $2(x - 3)$
   $= 2(-2 - 3)$
   $= -10$

7. Calculate the area of each rectangle. The first part has been done for you.

a)

   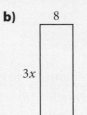

   $A = lw$
   $= 17(2x)$
   $= 34x$

   The area of the rectangle is 34x square units.

b)

   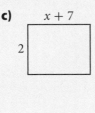

c)

Number Operations

8. Square each term. The first part has been done for you.

a) -4
    $(-4)^2$
    $= (-4) \times (-4)$
    $= 16$

b) $7x$

c) $-3x$

d) $9x$

Chapter Problem

Rheena's backyard has a square vegetable garden that measures 7 m by 7 m. There is a tool shed in one corner of the garden that measures 3 m by 3 m at the base. Rheena plans to change the layout of the garden without changing the total area that is cultivated. She will lay sod over the area in front of the shed.

a) Using Rheena's plan for the new garden, calculate all the dimensions of the new vegetable garden using the information provided.

b) Rheena wants to enclose her new garden with a fence to keep deer out. She will use the side of the shed (3 m) so she can reduce the amount of fencing she will need. The installed cost of the fencing is $8.95/m. Use the formula for perimeter to calculate the cost of the fencing.

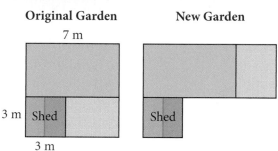

Original Garden   New Garden

9. Evaluate each expression. The first part has been done for you.

a) $7^2 - 5^2$
$= 49 - 25$
$= 24$

b) $(-2)^2 - (-1)^2$

c) $9^2 - 4^2$

d) $8^2 - (-3)^2$

Measurement

10. Devon is designing a web page. She needs to calculate the area of the shaded region. The small square is reserved for an advertisement. The large square has side length 20 cm and the small square has side length 9 cm. Find the area of the shaded part.

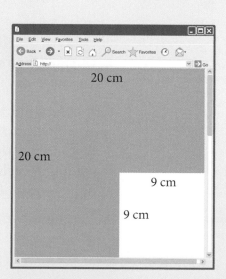

Multiply Two Binomials

A Canadian Football League football field is 110 yd long by 65 yd wide, goal line to goal line. Its playing area is 7150 sq yd. Sometimes, it is useful to divide a large rectangle into smaller rectangles, then to find the area of each of the smaller rectangles. In this section, you will use this method to find the product of two binomials.

Investigate A

Use Algebra Tiles to Find the Area of a Rectangle

Tools

- algebra tiles

Work with a partner.

1. What is the length of this rectangle? The width?

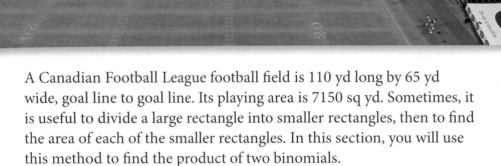

2. Use the area formula to write an expression for the area of the rectangle.

3. Draw a frame like the one shown. Use algebra tiles to model the length along the top, and the width along the left side. Inside the frame, build a rectangle with the dimensions $x + 3$ by $x + 2$.

quadratic expression

- an algebraic expression that can be written in the form $ax^2 + bx + c$, where $a \neq 0$.

4. Use the algebra tiles to find a **quadratic expression** for the area of the rectangle.

Investigate B — Use an Area Model to Find the Area of a Rectangle

Work with a partner.

Math Connect

A two-digit number can be represented in binomial form, for example 38 is $(30 + 8)$. There are two terms inside the brackets, so this is the binomial representation of the number 38.

1. A lot for a custom home is 26 m by 35 m. Find the area of each smaller rectangle. Add the areas to find the area of the lot.

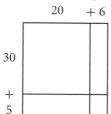

2. The plans for a new campground include an area with electrical services. The diagram shows the dimensions of the area with electrical service. Use the same process as in question 1. Write an expression to represent the area with electrical service.

Investigate C — Use Technology to Multiply Binomials

Work with a partner.

Tools

- Computer Algebra System (CAS)

1. Use a CAS to find the product and simplify each. Use the "expand" command.

   a) $(x + 3)(x + 4)$ **b)** $(y + 8)(y + 7)$

   c) $(a - 2)(a + 7)$ **d)** $(-b - 3)(b - 6)$

2. Refer to your answers to question 1.

   a) Compare the products. How are the products the same? How are they different?

   b) How is the coefficient on the x-term in each product related to the constant terms in its binomial factors?

   c) How is the constant term in each product related to the constant terms in its binomial factors?

3. Reflect Compare the methods used to multiply binomials in each Investigate. How are the methods the same? How are they different?

| Example | 1 |

Find the Product of Two Binomials

Find the product $(2x + 3)(x + 1)$.

Solution

Method 1: Use Algebra Tiles

Draw a multiplication frame. Model each binomial using algebra tiles.

Use algebra tiles to fill in the rectangle.

The rectangle contains 2 x^2-tiles, 5 x-tiles, and 3 unit tiles.
So, $(2x + 3)(x + 1) = 2x^2 + 5x + 3$.

Method 2: Use an Area Model

Draw an area model to find the product. Draw a rectangle with length $2x + 3$ and width $x + 1$. Divide the rectangle into smaller rectangles. Find the area of each smaller rectangle, then find the sum.

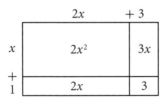

You were first introduced to area models when you learned multiplication. This is the same concept.

$$(2x + 3)(x + 1)$$
$$= 2x^2 + 2x + 3x + 3$$
$$= 2x^2 + 5x + 3$$

Math Connect

In this text, a large green square

represents x^2, a green rectangle

represents x, and a small green square ■ represents $+1$.

Method 3: Use a Multiplication Pattern

The product can be calculated by multiplying pairs in the order shown by the arrows.

$$(2x + 3)(x + 1) = 2x^2 + 2x + 3x + 3$$
$$= 2x^2 + 5x + 3$$

Multiply the first terms, the outside terms, the inside terms, then the last terms.

Method 4: Use the Distributive Property of Multiplication

$$(2x + 3)(x + 1) = (2x + 3)(x) + (2x + 3)(1)$$

2x + 3 multiplies x and it multiplies +1.

$$= (2x + 3)(x) + (2x + 3)(1)$$
$$= 2x^2 + 3x + 2x + 3$$
$$= 2x^2 + 5x + 3$$

Method 5: Use a CAS

- Press $\boxed{\text{F2}}$ 3: expand. Enter $(2x + 3)(x + 1)$.
- Press $\boxed{\text{ENTER}}$.

So, $(2x + 3)(x + 1) = 2x^2 + 5x + 3$.

Example **2** **Multiply Two Binomials**

Expand and simplify $(x - 4)(2x + 1)$.

Solution

$$(x - 4)(2x + 1) = 2x^2 + x - 8x - 4$$
$$= 2x^2 - 7x - 4$$

Remember, the product of a negative and a positive is negative; the product of two negatives is positive.

Example **3** **Square a Binomial**

Expand and simplify.

$(3x + 2)^2$

Solution

Method 1: Use Algebra Tiles

$(3x + 2)^2 = (3x + 2)(3x + 2)$

Draw a multiplication frame. Model each binomial using algebra tiles.

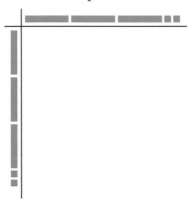

Use algebra tiles to fill in the rectangle.

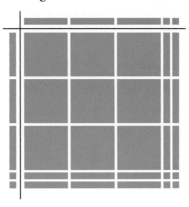

What do you notice about the shape made by the tiles when you fill in the frame?

The rectangle contains 9 x^2-tiles, 12 x-tiles, and 4 unit tiles.

$(3x + 2)^2 = (3x + 2)(3x + 2)$
$\qquad\qquad = 9x^2 + 12x + 4$

Method 2: Use a Multiplication Pattern

$$(3x + 2)^2 = (3x + 2)(3x + 2)$$

$$= 9x^2 + 6x + 6x + 4$$
$$= 9x^2 + 12x + 4$$

Method 3: Use the Distributive Property

$$(3x + 2)^2 = (3x + 2)(3x + 2)$$

$$= 3x(3x + 2) + 2(3x + 2)$$
$$= 9x^2 + 6x + 6x + 4$$
$$= 9x^2 + 12x + 4$$

Even though the two binomials are identical, one is still being distributed over the other.

perfect square trinomial
• the result of squaring a binomial

The square of a binomial results in a **perfect square trinomial**; that is, the first term is a perfect square and the last term is a perfect square.

Example **4** **Calculate the Area of a Rectangle**

A rectangular ski area has a width equal to $x + 1$ and a length equal to $x + 3$. Both measures are in kilometres.

a) Find the quadratic expression that represents the ski area.
b) Verify your answer using algebra tiles.
c) Calculate the actual area if $x = 2$ km.

Solution

a) Area = length × width

$$A = (x + 3)(x + 1)$$

$$= x^2 + 3x + x + 3$$
$$= x^2 + 4x + 3$$

b) $(x + 1)(x + 3)$

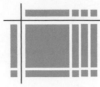

$= x^2 + 4x + 3$

c) Substitute $x = 2$ into either of the expressions above and evaluate.

$$A = x^2 + 4x + 3 \qquad \text{or} \qquad A = (x + 1)(x + 3)$$
$$= (2)^2 + 4(2) + 3 \qquad\qquad = (2 + 1)(2 + 3)$$
$$= 4 + 8 + 3 \qquad\qquad\qquad = 3 \times 5$$
$$= 15 \qquad\qquad\qquad\qquad = 15$$

The actual area is 15 km^2.

Math Connect

When working with algebraic expressions, the instructions *multiply*, *find the product*, and *expand* all mean to multiply each term in the first expression by each term in the second expression, then to simplify.

Key Concepts

- The product of two binomials, each with a variable term and a constant term, is a quadratic expression of the form $ax^2 + bx + c$.
- The square of a binomial is a perfect square trinomial.
- The product of two binomials can be found by multiplying each term in one binomial by each term in the other binomial using a variety of methods.

Discuss the Concepts

D1. When two binomials are multiplied, describe how the constant term in the resulting trinomial is related to the constant terms in the binomials. How is the coefficient of x in the trinomial related to the constant terms in the binomials?

D2. Which method do you prefer when multiplying binomials? Explain your reasons to a partner.

D3. Describe the process you would use to expand $(x + 7)(x + 4)$.

Practise the Concepts Ⓐ

For help with question 1, refer to Example 1.

1. Find each product.

a) $(x + 3)(x + 2)$ **b)** $(x + 5)(x + 4)$

c) $(x + 8)(x + 1)$ **d)** $(x + 3)(x + 2)$

e) $(x + 9)(x + 3)$ **f)** $(x + 5)(x + 6)$

For help with question 2, refer to Example 2.

2. Expand and simplify.

 a) $(2x + 1)(3x + 7)$ **b)** $(3x - 4)(3x + 5)$

 c) $(5x + 3)(x - 2)$ **d)** $(2x - 3)(3x - 2)$

For help with questions 3 and 4, refer to Example 3.

3. Expand and simplify.

 a) $(x + 5)^2$ **b)** $(x + 7)^2$

 c) $(x + 3)^2$ **d)** $(x + 6)^2$

 e) $(x + 8)^2$ **f)** $(x + 4)^2$

4. Expand and simplify.

 a) $(2x + 1)^2$ **b)** $(4x - 1)^2$

 c) $(3x + 2)^2$ **d)** $(5x - 2)^2$

For help with question 5, refer to Example 4.

5. A two-lane bridge has width $x + 3$ and length $4x + 5$.

 a) Sketch a rectangle with these dimensions.

 b) Find a quadratic expression that represents the area of the bridge.

6. Find each product.

 a) $(x + 5)(x + 2)$

 b) $(x + 5)(x - 2)$

 c) $(x - 5)(x + 2)$

 d) $(x - 5)(x - 2)$

7. Refer to your answers to question 6.

 a) Did the products result in the same quadratic expression?

 b) What difference do you notice among the resulting expressions?

Apply the Concepts **B**

For help with question 8, refer to Example 4.

8. The cottage dock in the diagram is square. Find the quadratic expression for the area of the dock.

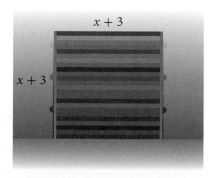

9. Write a quadratic expression for the area of the yard shown.

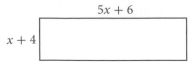

$5x + 6$

$x + 4$

10. A tennis club is redesigning its court area. They want to add several new courts and some benches for waiting players.

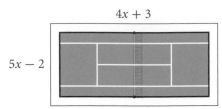

$4x + 3$

$5x - 2$

a) Write a quadratic expression to represent the total court area.

b) The club plans to place a fence around the court area. Write an expression for the perimeter of the court area to determine how much fencing will be required.

11. A builder is developing a site for a new subdivision with extra-long lots. Dmitri plans to buy lot 18.

a) Find an expression to represent the area of lot 18.

b) If $x = 35$ ft, find the actual area of lot 18.

c) According to city by-laws, houses are only permitted to occupy 40% of their lots. What is the maximum area that Dmitri's house can occupy? Check with your local by-law department to see if the 40% rule applies in your area.

| 1 | 3 | 5 | 7 | 9 | 11 | 13 | 15 |
| 16 |
| 17 |

| 2 | 4 | 6 | 8 | 10 | 12 | | 14 |
| 18 |

| 33 | 31 | 29 | 27 | 25 | 23 | | 19 |
| 20 |

| 21 |

| 35 | 34 | 32 | 30 | 28 | 26 | 24 | 22 |

$x + 5$

lot 18 $4x + 10$

12. A public skateboard park is $x + 3$ units wide and $2x - 6$ units long.

a) Write a quadratic expression to represent the area of the skateboard park.

b) If $x = 11$ m, calculate the actual area of the skateboard park in square metres.

c) If concrete resurfacing costs $\$4.99/m^2$, calculate the cost of resurfacing the skateboard park.

13. Explain to a classmate how to multiply two binomials. Try to establish a general rule. Record your explanation.

14. Rheena decides to have a smaller shed with a walkway around it.

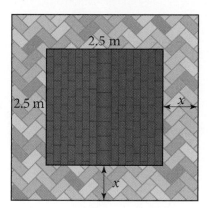

2.5 m

2.5 m

x

x

a) Write a quadratic expression for the total area covered by the shed and walkway.

b) Suppose the walkway is 0.75 m wide. What is the total area covered by the shed and the walkway?

Extend the Concepts C

15. Expand and simplify the expression $(x + 3)(x + 7) - (x + 5)^2$.

16. A photography student wishes to place a photograph on a mat background before framing. The student will need to calculate both the area of the photograph and the area of the mat.

$3x - 5$

$2x + 3$

$4x + 10$

$7x - 13$

a) Find an expression to represent each area:

   i) the area of the photograph

  ii) the total area of the mat

 iii) the visible area of the mat after the photograph is placed on top

b) Calculate all three areas if $x = 15$ cm. The guideline for design is that no more than 75% of the mat area should be covered by the photograph. Does this photograph follow that guideline?

7.2 Common Factoring

The goal area of a regulation soccer field is 120 sq yd. The dimensions of this rectangular area can be determined by finding pairs of factors of 120. **Factoring** is the opposite of expanding.

factor
- to express a number as the product of two or more numbers
- to express an algebraic expression as the product of two or more algebraic expressions

$$5(x + 7) \xrightarrow{\text{expanding}} \xleftarrow{\text{factoring}} 5x + 35$$

In the same way that addition is the opposite of subtraction, and multiplication is the opposite of division, factoring is the opposite of expanding.

The expression $5(x + 7)$ is the factored form.
The expression $5x + 35$ is the expanded form.

The greatest common factor (GCF) is 5.
Sometimes the GCF contains a variable.

$$2x^2 + 6x = 2x(x + 3)$$

In this case, the greatest common factor is $2x$.

Investigate A   Use Algebra Tiles to Find the Greatest Common Factor

Tools
- algebra tiles

Work with a partner.

1. Use algebra tiles to model a rectangle with area $4x + 8$.
   a) How many different rectangles can you make? Sketch each rectangle.
   b) Record the dimensions of each rectangle.
   c) Which of the rectangles has one side that represents the greatest common factor of the area of the rectangle?

2. Use your answer to question 1. Write the expression $4x + 8$ in factored form.

3. Repeat question 1 for a rectangle with area $3x^2 + 9x$.

4. Use your answer to question 3. Write the expression $3x^2 + 9x$ in factored form.

5. Reflect Explain how you can use rectangles to help factor an expression.

Use a CAS to Find the Greatest Common Factor

Work in groups.

1. Use a CAS to factor each trinomial. Use the "factor" command.
  a) $3x^2 + 6x + 9$
  b) $5x^2 + 10x + 15$
  c) $7x^2 + 14x + 21$
  d) $9x^2 + 18x + 27$

2. Reflect Refer to your answers to question 1.
  a) Which factor appears in all four expressions?
  b) Does the greatest common factor contain a variable?
  c) What type of expression is the other factor?
  d) Describe the pattern in these four expressions.

Example 1   Find the Greatest Common Factor

Find the greatest common factor (GCF) of each set of terms.
  a) $6x$, 24
  b) $10x^2$, $15x$
  c) $6x^3$, $-12x^2$, $18x$

Solution

  a) $\text{GCF} = 6$ *The GCF for 6x and 24 is 6.*

  b) $\text{GCF} = 5x$ *Here, the GCF contains a variable.*

  c) $\text{GCF} = 6x$ *All three terms have 6 as a factor.*
                           They also all have x as a factor.

Example **2**

Factor Binomials by Finding the Greatest Common Factor

Find the greatest common factor. Then, write the binomial in factored form. Check your answer by expanding.

a) Factor $10x - 15$ completely.   *To factor completely means to find the GCF*
b) Factor $20x - 12x^2$ completely. *and write the binomial in factored form.*
c) Factor $-3x^2 + 12x$ completely. Write your answer so the first term inside the brackets has a positive coefficient.

Solution

a) $10x - 15$

$$10x - 15 = 5\left(\frac{10x}{5} - \frac{15}{5}\right)$$

The GCF of 10 and 15 is 5. Divide 5 into each term to find the other factor.

$$= 5(2x - 3)$$ *The other factor is a binomial.*

$5(2x - 3)$ is the factored form of $10x - 15$.

Check: $5(2x - 3)$
            $= 10x - 15$

$5(2x - 3)$

The expanded form is $10x - 15$.

b) $20x - 12x^2 = 4x(5 - 3x)$

The GCF is 4x.
What must we multiply 4x by to get 20x?
What must we multiply 4x by to get $12x^2$?

Check: $4x(5 - 3x)$
            $= 20x - 12x^2$

$4x(5 - 3x)$

c) $-3x^2 + 12x = -3x(x - 4)$

Sometimes, the negative is factored from the expression first. In this case, since the first term is negative, the GCF for $-3x^2$ and 12x is $-3x$. Check your answer by expanding.

Check: $-3x(x - 4)$
            $= -3x^2 + 12x$

$-3x(x - 4)$

Example **3**

Factor a Trinomial by Finding the Greatest Common Factor

Factor $3x^2 - 9x + 12$ completely.

Solution

$3x^2 - 9x + 12$
$= 3(x^2 - 3x + 4)$

The GCF for 3, 9, and 12 is 3. Divide 3 into each term to write in factored form.

Example 4

Find the Dimensions of a Rectangle

The liner notes for a CD form an area represented by the binomial $12x + 3x^2$.

a) Write an expression for the dimensions of the liner notes by factoring its area.

b) Find the actual dimensions if $x = 6$ cm.

c) Determine an algebraic expression for the perimeter.

d) Find the perimeter using the actual dimensions from part b).

e) Check your answer by substituting $x = 6$ cm into your expression from part c). Does your answer match the one you got in part d)?

Solution

a) $A = 12x + 3x^2$

   $\quad = 3x(4 + x)$

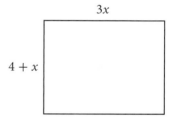

Once the expression is factored, the GCF represents the measure of one of the sides of the rectangle, in this case $3x$. The other side is $4 + x$.

b) Substitute $x = 6$.

Length:	$3x$	Width:	$4 + x$
	$= 3(6)$		$= 4 + 6$
	$= 18$		$= 10$

The actual dimensions of the rectangle are 18 cm by 10 cm.

c) Perimeter is $2 \times$ length $+ 2 \times$ width. Substitute the expressions for the length and the width.

$P = 2l + 2w$

$\quad = 2(3x) + 2(4 + x)$

$\quad = 6x + 8 + 2x$

$\quad = 8 + 8x$

d) From part b), $l = 18$, $w = 10$.

$P = 2l + 2w$

$\quad = 2(18) + 2(10)$

$\quad = 36 + 20$

$\quad = 56$

The perimeter is 56 cm.

e) Substitute $x = 6$ into the expression for perimeter found in part c).

$$P = 8 + 8x$$
$$= 8 + 8(6)$$
$$= 8 + 48$$
$$= 56$$

The perimeter is 56 cm.

The answer is the same as the answer found in part d).

Key Concepts

- Some polynomials can be factored by finding the GCF (greatest common factor).
- The GCF for a polynomial may be a constant, a variable, or both.
- If the area of a rectangle is given as a polynomial, factor the polynomial to find the possible side lengths of the rectangle.

Discuss the Concepts

D1. Describe the steps you would use to find the greatest common factor of any three numbers. What is the first thing you would do?

D2. Explain how factoring and expanding are related.

D3. If you know the polynomial that represents the area of a specific rectangle, describe how you can find the length and width of that rectangle.

Practise the Concepts **A**

For help with question 1, refer to Example 1.

1. Find the greatest common factor of each set of terms.

 a) 8, 18   **b)** $10x$, 25

 c) $4x^2$, $12x$ **d)** $4x^2$, $8x^2$, $12x$

For help with question 2, refer to Example 2.

2. Find the greatest common factor. Then, write the binomial in factored form.

 a) $3x + 15$ **b)** $4x^2 + 8x$

 c) $5x^2 - 10x$ **d)** $-7x + 21x$

For help with question 3, refer to Example 3.

3. Factor each polynomial.

   a) $3x^2 - 12x + 18$ **b)** $-10x^2 + 20x - 30$

   c) $-9x^2 - 3x + 9$ **d)** $4x^2 - 6x + 8$

4. Factor each polynomial completely.

   a) $6x^2 + 12x$ **b)** $9x^2 + 18x$

   c) $4x^2 + 24x$ **d)** $15x^2 + 30x$

5. Refer to your answers to question 4.

   a) Does each greatest common factor contain a variable?

   b) What type of expression is the other factor?

6. Factor each polynomial completely. Check your answer by expanding.

   a) $8x - 24$ **b)** $x^2 + 5x$

   c) $x^2 - 10x$ **d)** $4x^2 + 16x + 24$

For help with question 7, refer to Example 4.

7. A swimming pool has the area shown.

   a) Factor completely the expression representing the area to determine the length and the width of the swimming pool.

   b) Find the actual measures of its sides if $x = 2$ m.

   c) Find the perimeter of the pool.

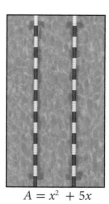

$A = x^2 + 5x$

Apply the Concepts **B**

For help with question 8, refer to Example 4.

8. Find the dimensions of each rectangle.

   a)

$$A = 21x^2 + 3x$$

   b)

$$A = 2x^2 + 18x$$

9. The area of a soccer field can be represented by the binomial $100x^2 + 4000$, where x is measured in metres. FIFA rules say that a standard soccer field is longer than it is wide. In most cases, the length of a soccer field is 100 m.

a) Factor the polynomial that represents the area to find an expression to represent the width of the soccer field.

b) Substitute values for $x = 0, 1, 2, 3, 4, 5, 6, 7,$ and 8 to find possible widths of the field.

c) Which value(s) of x will generate possible measurements for the width of a regulation FIFA soccer field?

d) Which value(s) of x will not generate possible measurements for the width of a regulation FIFA soccer field?

Achievement Check

10. A rectangular piece of tin has dimensions 20 cm by 30 cm. A square with side length x centimetres was removed from each corner, then the sides were folded up to make a tray.

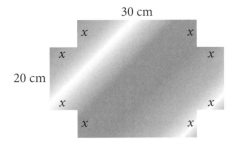

30 cm

20 cm

a) Use each method to find an expression for the area of tin used in the tray.
Method 1: Calculate the original area of tin and subtract the areas of the 4 squares that were removed.
Method 2: Find the sum of the areas of the bottom and each of the four sides of the tray.

b) Show that Methods 1 and 2 give equivalent areas.

c) Find the area of the tin used in the tray if x is 3 cm.

11. Two neighbouring lawns, the areas of which are represented by the binomials $2x^2 + 7x$ and $2x^2 + 9x$, are combined to form one large mowing contract. The shape of the combined lawns is rectangular.

    a) Find an expression to represent the area of the combined lawns.

    b) Factor the expression in part a) to determine possible dimensions of the combined lawns.

    c) What are the actual dimensions of the combined lawns if $x = 13$ m?

12. Write two trinomials whose GCF is 5.

13. Write two binomials whose GCF is $6x$.

14. Which of these binomials are factored completely? Factor completely any that are not.

    a) $14x^2 - 28x = 14(x^2 - 2x)$ **b)** $5x^2 + 30x = 5x(x + 6)$

    c) $7x^2 - 56 = 7(x^2 - 8)$ **d)** $3x^2 + 39x = 3(x^2 + 13x)$

Literacy Connect   **15.** Adding and subtracting are opposite operations, also called inverse operations. Expanding and factoring are also inverse operations. What other inverse operations do you know? Compare answers with others in the class.

Chapter Problem   **16.** Suppose the area of Rheena's original garden is represented by the expression $7x^2 + 42x$. Factor the expression to find the garden's dimensions. Then find the actual measurements if $x = 1$ m.

 Extend the Concepts **C**

17. Factor completely.

    a) $8xy - 4y$ **b)** $2x^3 - 4x^2$

    c) $-9x^3 + 15x^2 - 21x$ **d)** $5x^2y - 10xy + 15xy^2$

18. The diagram shows the area for a side of a DVD case. The actual perimeter is 66 cm. Find the dimensions of the DVD case in centimetres.

$$A = x^2 + 5x$$

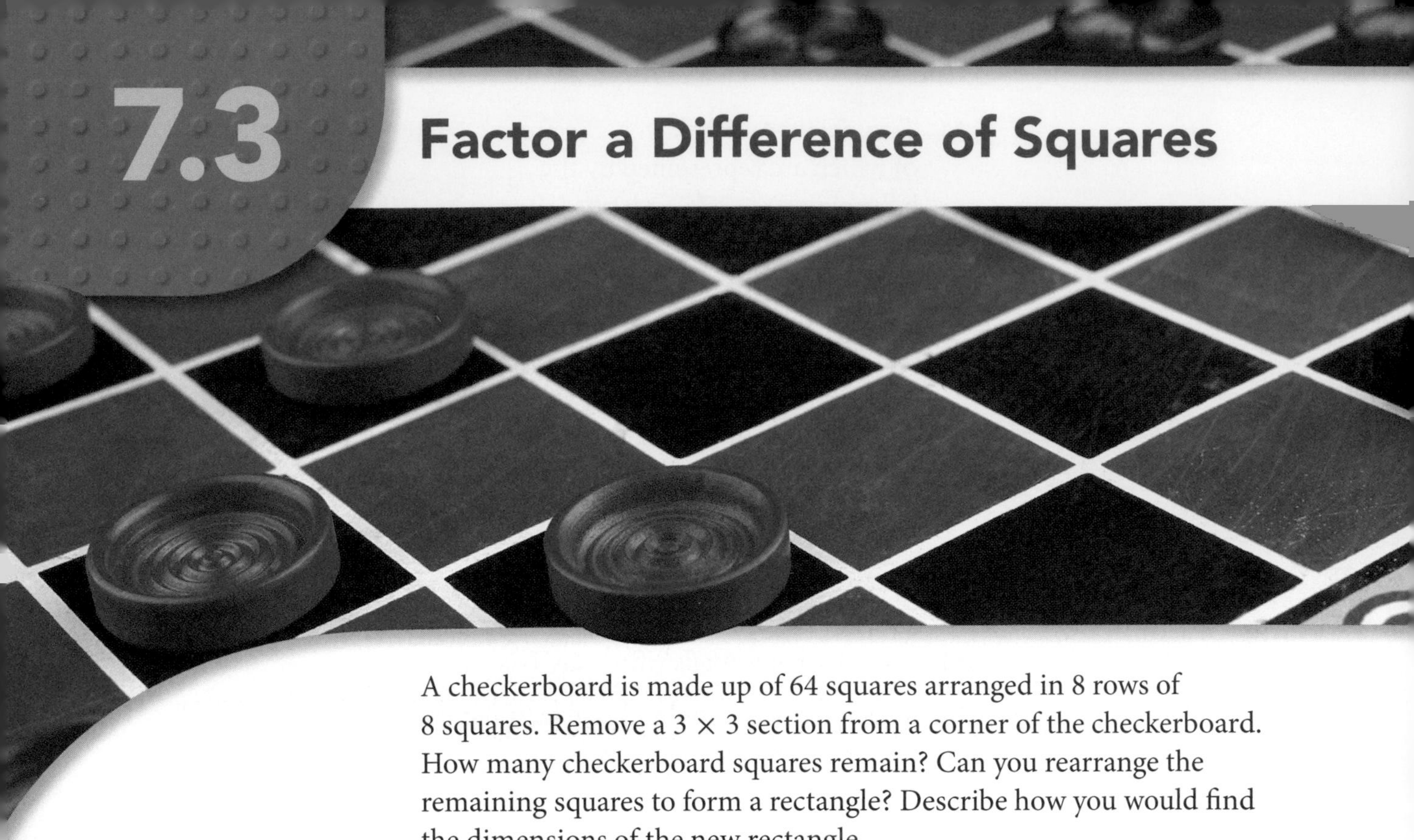

7.3 Factor a Difference of Squares

A checkerboard is made up of 64 squares arranged in 8 rows of 8 squares. Remove a 3 × 3 section from a corner of the checkerboard. How many checkerboard squares remain? Can you rearrange the remaining squares to form a rectangle? Describe how you would find the dimensions of the new rectangle.

Investigate A

Find the Difference Between the Areas of Two Squares

Tools
- grid paper
- ruler
- scissors

Work with a partner.

1. Draw a 5 cm × 5 cm square on grid paper.

2. Draw a 3 cm × 3 cm square inside the large square, in the bottom right-hand corner.

3. Cut the 3 cm × 3 cm square and calculate the remaining area.

4. Cut and rearrange the remaining area to form a rectangle.

5. What are the dimensions of this rectangle?

6. **Reflect** How did you find these dimensions? Describe how the dimensions of the rectangle are related to the dimensions of the large and small squares.

7. Rewrite the dimensions of the rectangle using the dimensions of the large square and the small square.

8. Copy the table.

Large Square Area	Small Square Area	Remaining Area Difference Between Squares	Dimensions of the Rectangle and Its Area
5^2	3^2	$5^2 - 3^2 = 16$	$(5 + 3) \times (5 - 3)$ $= 8 \times 2$ $= 16$

9. Repeat the above steps for each pair of squares. Record your results in the table.

a) $9 \times 9, 4 \times 4$ **b)** $10 \times 10, 5 \times 5$ **c)** $12 \times 12, 6 \times 6$

10. If the large square has side a and the small square has side b, extend the pattern to write two binomials to represent the dimensions of the rectangle.

<table><tr><td style="background:black;color:white">**Investigate**   **B**</td></tr></table>

Find a Pattern

Mark is sending envelopes overseas. The dimensions of the envelopes are shown. One binomial represents the width of the envelope, and the other, the length.

1. Expand each pair of binomials.

a) $(x + 1)(x - 1)$ **b)** $(x + 2)(x - 2)$ **c)** $(x + 3)(x - 3)$
d) $(x + 4)(x - 4)$ **e)** $(x + 5)(x - 5)$

2. Look at your answers to question 1. How many terms does each product have? What name do we give to this type of polynomial?

3. If the binomials represent length and width, what do the answers in question 1 represent?

4. a) Reflect Do you see a pattern between the first terms in the binomials and the first term in the answer? Explain.
b) Reflect Do you see a relationship between the second terms in the binomials and the second term in the answer? What rule can you determine from the pattern? Explain.

difference of squares
• a binomial in which a square term is subtracted from another square term
• the factors of a difference of squares are binomials with identical terms but opposite operations

The product of two binomials that share identical terms but have opposite operations of addition and subtraction is called a **difference of squares**.

Example 1

Find the Square Root of a Number

Write the positive square root of each.

a) 9   **b)** 25

c) x^2 **d)** $4x^2$

Math Connect

Go to www.
mcgrawhill.ca
/links/
foundations10 to
try some square
root calculators.

Solution

a) $\sqrt{9} = 3$ **b)** $\sqrt{25} = 5$

Think of a number that when multiplied by itself equals the number you are to find the square root of. For example, when you multiply 3 by 3, you get 9. So, 3 is the positive square root of 9.

c) $\sqrt{x^2} = x$ **d)** $\sqrt{4x^2} = 2x$

Example 2

Express a Number as a Power

Write each number as a power of its positive square root.

a) 16   **b)** 9

Solution

a) $16 = 4^2$ **b)** $9 = 3^2$

Find the positive square root of the number, and then express it as a power with 2 as the exponent.

Example 3

Recognize a Difference of Squares

Which expressions are difference of squares? How do you know?

a) $x^2 - 25$ **b)** $x^2 + 16$

c) $1 - 49x^2$ **d)** $4x^2 + 10$

Remember the difference of squares is a binomial. The first term is a square, the second term is a square, and the operation between them is subtraction.

Solution

a) Yes, x^2 is the square of x and 25 is the square of 5, and the operation between them is subtraction. This binomial is a difference of squares.

b) No, the operation between the two square terms is addition. The product of a positive number and a negative will not yield a positive, so $x^2 + 16$ cannot be factored as a difference of squares.

c) Yes, 1 is a square number and $49x^2$ is a square term, and the operation between the two terms is subtraction.

d) No, the operation between the two square terms is addition. The product of a positive number and a negative will not yield a positive, so $4x^2 + 10$ cannot be factored as a difference of squares.

Example 4

Factor a Difference of Squares

Factor each differences of squares.
Check your answer by expanding.

a) $x^2 - 36$ **b)** $9 - x^2$

Solution

a) $\begin{aligned} &x^2 - 36 \\ &= x^2 - 6^2 \\ &= (x + 6)(x - 6) \end{aligned}$ **b)** $\begin{aligned} &9 - x^2 \\ &= 3^2 - x^2 \\ &= (3 + x)(3 - x) \end{aligned}$

Check:

a) $\begin{aligned} &(x + 6)(x - 6) \\ &= x^2 - 6x + 6x - 36 \\ &= x^2 - 36 \end{aligned}$ **b)** $\begin{aligned} &(3 + x)(3 - x) \\ &= 9 - 3x + 3x - x^2 \\ &= 9 - x^2 \end{aligned}$

Notice that the x-terms have a zero sum due to their opposite signs.

Example 5

Find the Difference Between the Areas of Squares

a) Factor the binomial $x^2 - 2^2$.

b) Sketch a diagram to represent the situation.

Solution

a) $x^2 - (2)^2 = (x + 2)(x - 2)$

b)

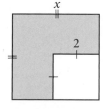

Key Concepts

- A difference of squares is a binomial with square terms as the first and second terms, separated by a subtraction sign.
- The factors of a difference of squares are two binomials. In one binomial factor the square roots of each term of a difference of squares are added, and in the other binomial factor the square roots of each term of a difference of squares are subtracted.

Discuss the Concepts

D1. Give three examples of a square constant term. Give another two examples of a square variable term. How can you tell when a constant or variable term is a square?

D2. What operation between the two terms do you expect to see in a difference of squares? Are any other operations possible? Compare answers with your classmates.

Practise the Concepts (A)

For help with question 1, refer to Example 1.

1. Find the positive square root of each number.

   a) 49   **b)** 81   **c)** 100

For help with question 2, refer to Example 2.

2. Write each number as a power of its positive square root.

   a) 25   **b)** 36   **c)** 16

For help with question 3, refer to Example 3.

3. Which expressions are differences of squares? Provide reasons for your decision.

   a) $x^2 - 9$ **b)** $49 + x^2$ **c)** $100 - 36x^2$

For help with question 4, refer to Example 4.

4. Factor each difference of squares. Check your answer.

   a) $x^2 - 81$ **b)** $x^2 - 121$ **c)** $x^2 - 144$

   d) $400 - x^2$ **e)** $25 - x^2$ **f)** $49 - x^2$

   g) $100 - x^2$ **h)** $225 - x^2$ **i)** $16x^2 - 121$

For help with question 5, refer to Example 5.

5. A square has area x^2 square centimetres. At one corner, a smaller square with sides 6 cm long has been removed.

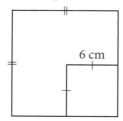

6 cm

a) Write the binomial to represent the difference between the two areas.

b) Factor the binomial to find expressions for the dimensions of a rectangle with area equal to the remaining area of the large square.

c) Find the actual dimensions of this rectangle if $x = 10$ cm.

Apply the Concepts B

6. A screen capture of a web page is measured by its area.
   a) Find two binomials that represent the dimensions of the web page.
   b) Calculate the area of the rectangle if $x = 25$ cm.

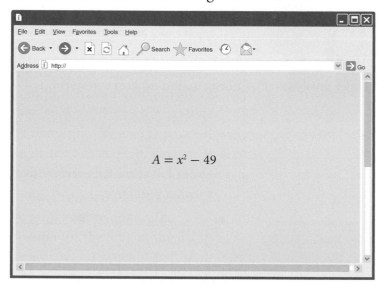

$$A = x^2 - 49$$

7. The area of the top of a classroom art table shown is represented by the expression $100 - x^2$.

a) If the length is represented by $10 + x$, find the expression to represent its width.

b) Find the actual dimensions if $x = 4$ ft.

c) Calculate the area.

$10 + x$

$A = 100 - x^2$

Literacy Connect

8. Is $x^2 - y^2$ a difference of squares? Explain.

9. The senior band is designing a brochure to raise money for their trip to Europe. They want to design their brochure to be visually pleasing and to make the best use of the paper supplies they have.

- Work with a partner.
- Use *The Geometer's Sketchpad®* or construction paper. Copy each diagram, which shows a large square with a smaller square inside.
- Remove the small square located inside the large square. Write the binomial that represents the remaining area after subtraction.
- Remove the remaining small rectangle along the dotted line.
- Rearrange the pieces to form a larger rectangle. Determine the expressions that represent the dimensions of the newly formed brochure.

a)

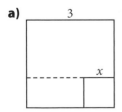

3

x

b)

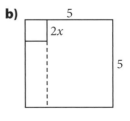

5

$2x$

5

c)

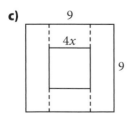

9

$4x$

9

10. Explain why $x^2 + 1$ is not a difference of squares and $x^2 - 1$ is.

11. Alexa decides to factor $x^2 + 25$ to find the length and width of her brochure. She finds it is $(x + 5)$ long and $(x + 5)$ wide. Explain Alexa's mistake.

12. Factor $2x^2 - 18$. Is it a difference of squares? Why or why not? Is it possible to factor this binomial? Explain your answer.

13. Factor completely.
   a) $8x^2 - 18$
   b) $48x^2 - 27$
   c) $5x^2 - 45y^2$

14. A playground is in the shape of a square. The play equipment is located in a square area inside the playground. The perimeter of the play equipment area is 32 m. If the difference between the area of the entire playground and area of the play equipment is 336 m^2, find the dimensions of the entire playground.

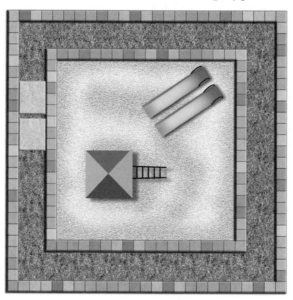

7.4 Factor Trinomials of the Form $x^2 + bx + c$

John bought a rectangular parcel of land in a popular vacation region. He plans to fence the property. John must determine the perimeter of the property to determine how much fencing he will need.

Investigate A   Find the Dimensions of a Rectangle

Tools
- algebra tiles

The area of John's property can be represented by the trinomial $x^2 + 7x + 10$.

Work with a partner.

1. Draw a frame like the one shown.

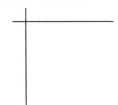

2. Inside the frame, build a rectangle that has area $x^2 + 7x + 10$. How many different rectangles can you build?

3. Which algebra tiles represent the length of the rectangle? The width? Write expressions for the dimensions of the rectangle.

4. Write the factors and the area in equation form.

5. Expand the factors to check.

6. **Reflect** How many different expressions can you write for the dimensions of the rectangle? How is this related to the number of rectangles you can build? Explain.

Investigate B

Find the Dimensions of a Rectangle With Area Represented by a Trinomial of the Form $x^2 + bx + c$

Tools

- algebra tiles

Work with a partner.

1. Use algebra tiles to represent each trinomial. Each time, arrange the tiles to make a rectangle.

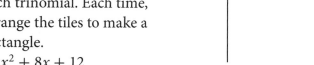

   a) $x^2 + 8x + 12$
   b) $x^2 + 9x + 14$
   c) $x^2 + 7x + 10$
   d) $x^2 + 6x + 8$

2. Factor each trinomial from question 1 to find the dimensions of the rectangle. Write expressions for the length and width of each rectangle.

3. Check that the dimensions of each rectangle are correct by multiplying the length and width.

4. What is the common binomial factor in each of the factored forms? Explain the pattern that results.

5. **Reflect** For each trinomial, compare the coefficient of x and the constant term to the constant terms in its binomial factors. How are the constant terms of the binomial factors related to the terms in the trinomial product?

Example 1

Find Integers With a Given Product and Sum

Find a pair of integers with each product and sum.

a) Product: 10   Sum: 7   **b)** Product: -18 Sum: -7

Solution

a) The product is positive, so both integers have the same sign. That is, both are positive, or both are negative. The sum is positive, so both integers are positive.

Find pairs of numbers whose product is 10. Check each pair to determine if its sum is 7.

Factors of 10	Sum of Factors
1, 10	11
2, 5	7

The integers 2 and 5 have product 10 and sum 7.

b) The product is negative so one of the integers is positive and the other is negative.

Factors of −18	Sum of Factors
−1, 18	17
−2, 9	7
2, −9	−7

The integers 2 and −9 have product −18 and sum −7.

Example 2   Factor Trinomials

Factor each trinomial. Check your answers by expanding.

a) $x^2 - 10x + 16$ **b)** $x^2 + 9x - 22$

Solution

a) The constant term, +16, is positive and the coefficient of x, −10, is negative. Find two negative numbers whose product is 16 and whose sum is −10.

$$x^2 - 10x + 16$$
$$= (x - 8)(x - 2)$$

$-8 \times (-2) = 16$

$-8 + (-2) = -10$

Check: $(x - 8)(x - 2)$
$$= x^2 - 2x - 8x + 16$$
$$= x^2 - 10x + 16$$

b) The constant term, −22, is negative and the coefficient of x, +9, is positive. Find two numbers with opposite signs whose product is −22 and whose sum is +9.

$$x^2 + 9x - 22$$
$$= (x + 11)(x - 2)$$

$11 \times (-2) = -22$

$11 + (-2) = 9$

Check: $(x + 11)(x - 2)$
$$= x^2 - 2x + 11x - 22$$
$$= x^2 + 9x - 22$$

Example 3   Find the Dimensions of a Rectangle

A rectangle has area represented by the trinomial $x^2 + 4x - 21$.

a) Factor the trinomial to find expressions for dimensions of the rectangle.

b) Calculate the actual dimensions if $x = 50$ cm.

$x^2 + 4x - 21$

Solution

a) The constant term, -21, is negative. Find two integers with opposite signs whose product is -21 and whose sum is $+4$.

$$x^2 + 4x - 21 \qquad\qquad +7 \times (-3) = -21$$
$$= (x + 7)(x - 3) \qquad\quad +7 + (-3) = 4$$

The dimensions of the rectangle are $(x + 7)$ by $(x - 3)$.

b) Substitute $x = 50$.

$$x + 7 \qquad\qquad\qquad x - 3$$
$$= 50 + 7 \qquad\qquad = 50 - 3$$
$$= 57 \qquad\qquad\quad = 47$$

If $x = 50$ cm, the actual dimensions are 57 cm by 47 cm.

Key Concepts

- To find the factors of a trinomial in the form $x^2 + bx + c$, look for the pair of numbers whose sum is b and whose product is c.
- Factoring is the opposite of expanding.

Discuss the Concepts

D1. Which two integers multiply to give -16 and have a sum of $+6$? Explain.

D2. Is $(x + 9)(x + 4)$ the factored form of $x^2 - 13x + 36$? Explain.

Practise the Concepts **A**

1. Find a pair of integers with each product and sum.
   a) Product: 20   Sum: 9
   b) Product: 18   Sum: 11
   c) Product: 12   Sum: -7
   d) Product: -14 Sum: -5

For help with question 2, refer to Example 2.

2. Factor each trinomial. Check your answers by expanding.
   a) $x^2 + 12x + 36$ **b)** $x^2 - 12x + 27$
   c) $x^2 + 7x - 30$ **d)** $x^2 - 16x - 36$

For help with questions 3 to 6, refer to Example 3.

3. For each rectangle, find binomials that represent the length and the width.

a)
$$A = x^2 + 4x + 4$$

b)
$$A = x^2 - 4x - 5$$

c)
$$A = x^2 + 9x - 22$$

d)
$$A = x^2 - 9x + 20$$

4. Find binomials that represent the dimensions of the rectangle with area $x^2 + 2x + 1$.

5. Use algebra tiles to construct a rectangle with each area.
   a) $A = x^2 + 12x + 20$
   b) $A = x^2 + 5x + 6$
   c) $A = x^2 + 9x + 14$

6. a) Factor each trinomial from question 5. Write the binomials that represent the dimensions of each rectangle.
   b) Write the area in factored form.

7. A rectangle has area $x^2 + 8x + 15$.
   a) Factor the trinomial.
   b) Calculate the actual dimensions if $x = 4$ cm.

$$A = x^2 + 8x + 15$$

Apply the Concepts **B**

8. Find binomials that represent the length and width of two rectangular driveways with areas represented by these trinomials.
   a) $x^2 - 3x - 10$
   b) $x^2 - 5x + 6$

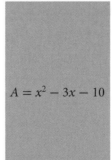
$A = x^2 - 3x - 10$

$A = x^2 - 5x + 6$

9. Leanne says the factors of the trinomial $x^2 - 10x - 24$ are $(x - 6)(x - 4)$. Is Leanne correct? Explain and make corrections if necessary.

Achievement Check

10. The area of an Olympic-sized pool is modelled by the quadratic equation $A = x^2 + 9x + 8$.
   a) Find expressions for the dimensions of the pool.
   b) Suppose the length of the pool is 33 m. Find the area of the pool.

11. If the two constant terms in a trinomial's binomial factors are -7 and $+4$, write the trinomial in the form $x^2 + bx + c$.

12. If the trinomial $x^2 + 5x + c$ can be factored, find as many positive and negative values for c as possible.

13. If the trinomial $x^2 + bx - 13$ can be factored, find possible values for b.

Literacy Connect **14.** Use algebra tiles. Explain why $x^2 + 3x + 2$ can be factored but $x^2 + 2x + 3$ cannot be factored. Record your work.

Chapter Problem **15.** The area of Rheena's original garden is represented by the trinomial $x^2 + 12x + 36$.
   a) Factor the trinomial to find the length and width of her original garden.
   b) What is the shape of Rheena's garden? How do you know?
   c) Calculate the actual dimensions if $x = 1$ m.

Extend the Concepts

16. Factor completely.
   a) $3x^2 + 21x + 30$ **b)** $4x^2 - 12x - 72$
   c) $-x^2 + 4x - 3$ **d)** $2x^2 + 4x + 2$

17. The perimeter of a rectangle is 32 cm. Its area is shown in the diagram. Find the actual dimensions of the rectangle.

$$A = x^2 + 5x - 14$$

Review of Key Terms

Copy the terms into your notebook. Match each term with its definition.

1. a) perfect square trinomial

i) a binomial where a square term is subtracted from another square term

b) factor

ii) a trinomial that can be written in the form $x^2 + bx + c$

c) difference of squares

iii) express as a product

d) quadratic expression

iv) the result of squaring a binomial

7.1 Multiply Two Binomials, pages 280 to 289

2. Expand and simplify.

a) $(x + 8)(x - 9)$ **b)** $(2x + 3)(x - 5)$

c) $(3x - 1)(2x - 3)$ **d)** $(x + 6)(x - 6)$

3. Expand each square.

a) $(x + 5)^2$ **b)** $(x - 7)^2$

c) $(2x + 3)^2$ **d)** $(3x - 2)^2$

4. Enrico multiplies two binomials as shown.
$(2x - 3)(x + 7) = 2x^2 - 11x + 21$
Is Enrico correct? If not, correct Enrico's mistake.

5. The dimensions of a rectangular poster are shown.

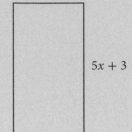

a) Find an expression to represent its area.

b) Calculate its actual area if $x = 20$ cm.

c) The writing on the poster covers approximately 880 cm^2. Will this comply with the design request that no more than 40% of the total poster will be covered with words?

6. The diagram shows the dimensions of a small rectangle inside a large one. Find the expression that will represent the difference between the areas.

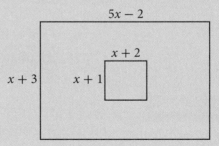

7.2 Common Factoring, pages 290 to 297

7. Find the greatest common factor of each expression. Then factor each expression.

a) $5x - 25$

b) $8x^2 + 20x$

c) $27 + 15x - 6x^2$

8. Factor completely.

a) $4x - 20$ **b)** $6x^2 + 15x$

c) $7x^2 - 14x - 21$

9. The area of the floor of a squash court is shown in the diagram.

a) Find the dimensions of the floor.

b) Find an expression that represents the perimeter of the squash court floor.

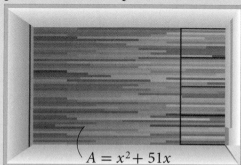

$A = x^2 + 51x$

10. Factor completely.

a) $14x^2 - 12x$

b) $-10y^2 + 15y^3$

c) $30x^3 - 24x^2 + 12x$

7.3 Factor a Difference of Squares, pages 298 to 305

11. State which expressions are differences of squares and express them as the product of two binomials.

a) $x^2 - 16$ **b)** $2x^2 + 9$

c) $49 - 9x^2$ **d)** $4 - 25x^2$

12. Factor, then check your answer by expanding.

a) $x^2 - 25$ **b)** $81x^2 - 100$

c) $64 - 121x^2$ **d)** $x^2 - 36$

13. a) Write an expression to represent the difference between the areas of the two squares.

b) Factor the expression.

14. Show that the difference between the two areas in the diagram can be expressed in the factored form $5(2x + 7)$.

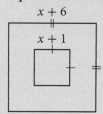

7.4 Factor Trinomials of the Form $x^2 + bx + c$, pages 306 to 311

15. For each trinomial, write the pair of integers whose sum equals b and whose product equals c.

a) $x^2 + 7x + 10$

b) $x^2 - 6x + 9$

c) $x^2 + 8x - 9$

d) $x^2 - 13x + 36$

16. Find expressions for the dimensions of each rectangle.

a)
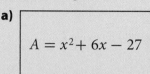

$A = x^2 + 6x - 27$

b)
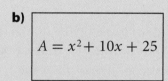

$A = x^2 + 10x + 25$

1. Expand and simplify.

  a) $(x + 3)(x + 9)$

  b) $(2x - 1)(x + 5)$

  c) $(x + 6)^2$

  d) $(x - 7)(x + 7)$

2. Find the area of each rectangle.

  a)

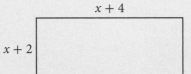

$x + 4$

$x + 2$

  b)

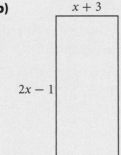

$x + 3$

$2x - 1$

3. Find the greatest common factor, then factor completely.

  a) $16x^2 - 24x$

  b) $15x^2 + 20x$

  c) $-14x^2 - 6x$

  d) $-7 - 14x + 21x^2$

4. Factor.

  a) $x^2 + 10x + 21$

  b) $x^2 - 3x - 4$

  c) $x^2 - 10x + 25$

  d) $x^2 - 100$

5. Find the actual perimeter of the large-screen television shown below, if $x = 100$ cm.

$A = x^2 + 13x - 30$

6. Explain why $x^2 + 14x + 49$ is called a perfect square trinomial.

7. The diagram shows two squares. The large square represents a concrete slab on which there is a storage shed, represented by the small square.

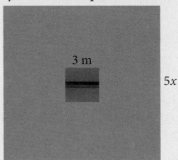

3 m

$5x$

  a) Write the binomial that represents the difference of the two areas.

  b) Suppose the remaining area is rearranged to make a rectangle with the same area. Find the dimensions of the rectangle.

  c) Calculate the actual dimensions of the rectangle in part b) if $x = 1$ m.

Chapter Problem Wrap-Up

Rheena plans to change the layout of her garden without changing the total area that is cultivated. Her backyard has a 7 m by 7 m vegetable garden. The tool shed in one corner of the garden measures 3 m by 3 m at the base.

a) Find the area of the original garden, including the shed.

b) Subtract the area of the shed from the total area to find the dimensions of the original garden.

c) Rheena plans to add a new layer of topsoil 10 cm thick over all of her garden. How much topsoil would she need to cover the surface of the old garden?

d) Will she need the same amount of topsoil for the new garden? Explain your answer.

e) Could Rheena have reconfigured the new garden area another way? Explain with the use of a scale diagram.

8. Examine the expression $9a^2 - 18a$.

   a) Factor the expression as many ways as possible.

   b) Which of these factored forms represents the completely factored form? Explain.

9. The diagram shows a pool surrounded by a wooden walkway. The dimensions are given as binomials.

   a) Find the expression to represent the area of the wooden deck.

   b) Calculate the actual area of the deck if $x = 1.2$ m.

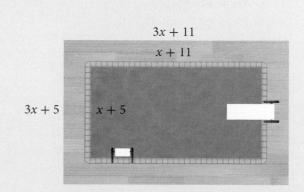

$3x + 11$

$x + 11$

$3x + 5$

$x + 5$

8 Represent Quadratic Relations

In this chapter, you will solve a variety of problems involving quadratic relations, including problems involving sports, engineering, business, motion, trajectory, and projectiles. You will solve problems by interpreting graphs of quadratic relations.

In this chapter, you will

- compare, through investigation using technology, the graphical representations of a quadratic relation in the form $y = x^2 + bx + c$ and the same relation in the factored form $y = (x - r)(x - s)$, and describe the connections between each algebraic representation and the graph
- solve problems involving a quadratic relation by interpreting a given graph or a graph generated with technology from its equation
- solve problems by interpreting the significance of the key features of graphs obtained by collecting experimental data involving quadratic relations

Reasoning and Proving

Representing | Selecting Tools

Problem Solving

Connecting | Reflecting

Communicating

Key Terms

zeros

Literacy Link

Use these diagrams to help you consider the properties of quadratic relations, and list examples and comparisons.

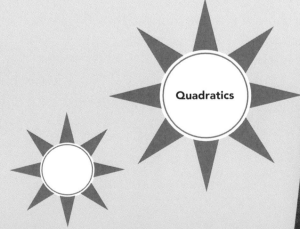

Quadratics

A civil engineering technician is involved in the planning and construction of building projects. He or she may use computer aided design (CAD) software to create drawings of buildings, highways, and other structures. Some technicians become building inspectors, draftspeople, or sales representatives for construction firms.

Get Ready!

Relations

1. Graph each relation.

a)

x	y
−2	7
−1	10
0	13
1	16
2	19
3	22

b)

x	y
−2	−2
−1	−5
0	−6
1	−5
2	−2
3	3

c)

x	y
−2	−8
−1	−7
0	−6
1	−5
2	−4
3	−3

d)

x	y
−2	9
−1	3
0	1
1	3
2	9
3	19

2. Refer to the relations in question 1. Is each relation linear, quadratic, or neither? How do you know?

Linear Systems

3. Find the solution to each linear system. The first part has been done for you.

a)

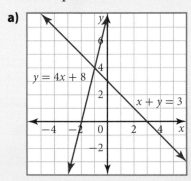

The solution is the point of intersection, (−1, 4).

b)

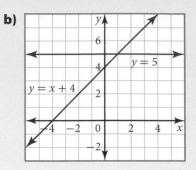

Key Features of Quadratic Relations

4. For each parabola, identify the coordinates of the vertex, the equation of the axis of symmetry, and the x- and y-intercepts. The first part has been done for you.

a)

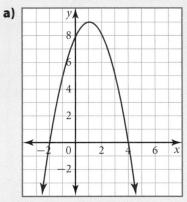

The coordinates of the vertex are (1, 9).

The equation of the axis of symmetry is x = 1.

The x-intercepts are −2 and 4, and the y-intercept is 8.

b)

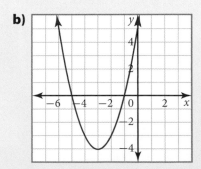

Chapter Problem

The municipal recreation and parks committee approved a motion at its last meeting to build a skateboard arena in a neighbourhood park. The arena will be enclosed by a chain-link fence 2 m high. The city budget allows for 80 m of fencing. The arena will be rectangular and will contain two skateboard ramps. One ramp will have the shape of a parabola that opens upward, and the other ramp will have the shape of a parabola that opens downward. How could you determine the dimensions of the skateboard arena so it has the greatest area possible?

c)

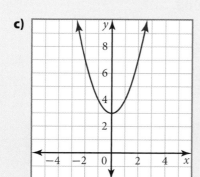

d)

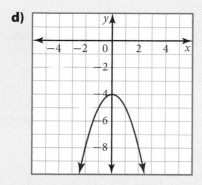

Algebraic Operations

5. Substitute the known value into the equation, then solve for the indicated variable. The first part has been done for you.

a) Find the value of x when $y = -2$.

$$y = -3x + 7$$
$$-2 = -3x + 7$$
$$-9 = -3x$$
$$x = 3$$

b) Find the value of y when $x = -1$.
$$y = x^2 - 3x + 6$$

c) Find the value of x when $y = 2$.
$$y = x^2 - 7$$

6. Expand and simplify each expression.

a) $-4x(x - 2)$ **b)** $(x + 5)(x + 3)$

c) $(x - 3)(x + 1)$

7. Factor each polynomial.

a) $-5x^2 + 10$ **b)** $3x^2 - 15x$

c) $x^2 + 7x - 18$

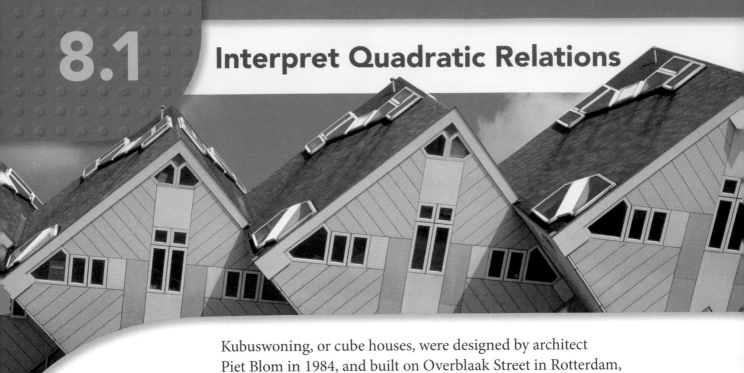

8.1 Interpret Quadratic Relations

Kubuswoning, or cube houses, were designed by architect Piet Blom in 1984, and built on Overblaak Street in Rotterdam, The Netherlands. The houses are on top of a pedestrian bridge over a major highway. The walkway below the cube houses has offices, shops, a school, and a playground.

Investigate

Tools

- graphing calculator

Surface Area of a Cube

1. Copy and complete the table for cubes with side lengths from 1 cm to 6 cm.

Side Length (cm)	Surface Area (cm²)
1	6
2	

2. a) Use a graphing calculator.

- Press [STAT] [ENTER]. Enter the side lengths in list L1 and the surface areas in list L2.
- Press [2nd] [STAT PLOT] [ENTER]. Choose the settings shown.

b) Do the data appear to be quadratic? Explain.

c) Press [STAT] [▶] 5:QuadReg [2nd] [L1] [,] [2nd] [L2] [,] [VARS] [▶] 1 1 [ENTER].

3. Use the equation from question 2 to find the surface area for a cube with each side length.

a) 10 cm **b)** 22 cm **c)** 8 cm

4. Reflect Explain why the relationship between the side length and the surface area of a cube is quadratic.

Example	1

Interpret the Graph of a Quadratic Relation

The path of a ball that was thrown in the air is modelled by the graph. The y-values represent the height of the ball in metres and the x-values represent the horizontal distance in metres that the ball has travelled.

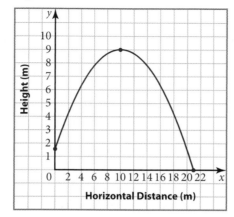

a) What was the maximum height the ball reached?
b) How far had the ball travelled horizontally to reach this maximum height?
c) What horizontal distance did the ball travel before it hit the ground?

Solution

a) From the graph, the vertex is (10, 9). The ball reached a maximum height of 9 m.
b) The maximum height was reached when the ball had travelled a horizontal distance of 10 m.
c) When the ball hits the ground, its height is zero. The x-intercept is (21, 0). The ball hit the ground 21 m from the point at which it was thrown.

Example 2

Find the Height of a Support Post

The arched support of a bridge can be modelled by the quadratic relation $y = -0.024x^2 + 2.4x$, where y represents the height in feet, and x represents the horizontal distance in feet. A vertical support post is to be installed 40' from the base of the arch. How tall should the support post be?

Solution

Method 1: Use the Equation

The support post is to be installed 40' from the base of the arch. This is the horizontal distance. Substitute $x = 40$ into the equation and solve for y.

$$y = -0.024x^2 + 2.4x$$
$$= -0.024(40)^2 + 2.4(40)$$
$$= -0.024(1600) + 96$$
$$= -38.4 + 96$$
$$= 57.6$$

The support post will be 57.6' tall.

Method 2: Use the Graph

Use a graphing calculator.

• Press [WINDOW]. Use the window settings shown.

• Press [Y=]. Enter Y1 = $-0.024x^2 + 2.4x$.

Press [GRAPH].

• Press [2nd] [CALC] 1. Enter 40 for x, and press [ENTER].

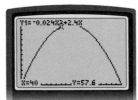

The support post will be 57.6' tall.

Key Concepts

- A quadratic relation can be represented by a graph, or by an equation of the form $y = ax^2 + bx + c \; (a \neq 0)$.
- The equation or the graph of a quadratic relation can be used to solve problems.

Discuss the Concepts

D1. What are some advantages to using a graph to solve a problem involving a quadratic relation? What are some disadvantages?

D2. Describe a situation in which you would use the equation of a quadratic relation, rather than the graph, to solve a problem.

Practise the Concepts

For help with questions 1 and 2, refer to Example 1.

1. A cascading fountain forms a stream of water that can be modelled by the quadratic relation shown in the graph.

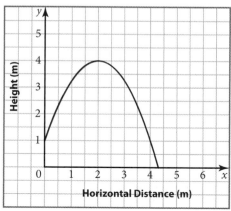

a) Use the graph to find the maximum height reached by the stream of water.

b) How far from the fountain did the stream of water reach this maximum height?

c) What horizontal distance from the centre of the fountain did the water reach?

d) Assume this stream of water does not leave any drops of water in its path. How far from the centre of the fountain could a person 1.8 m tall stand, under the water stream, and not get wet?

e) How tall is the base that the fountain rests upon?

2. The graph shown below models the path of a ball thrown up in the air. The height is in metres, and the time is in seconds.

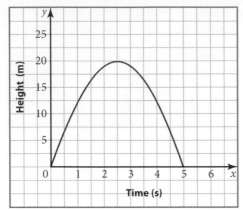

a) What is the maximum height reached by the ball?

b) When did the ball reach the maximum height?

c) How long was the ball in the air?

For help with question 3, refer to Example 2.

3. The quadratic relation $h = -5t^2 + 180$ models the path of a ball that was dropped from a height, where h represents the height of the ball in metres and t represents time in seconds.

a) Graph the relation.

b) From what height was the ball dropped?

c) Find the height of the ball after 3.5 s.

Apply the Concepts B

4. The table below shows the flight of a golf ball after it was hit from the tee toward the green.

Horizontal Distance (m)	Height of Golf Ball (m)
0	0
30	22.5
50	29.2
80	26.7
90	22.5
100	16.7

a) Use a graphing calculator. Graph the relation.

b) Find the equation of the curve of best fit.

c) Determine the horizontal distance the ball travelled with this hit.

d) If the green was roughly 120 m away, did the ball land on the green?

5. Data were collected for a ball being dropped from a platform to the floor.

a) Plot the data using a graphing calculator.

b) Find the equation that models this situation. What do the variables represent?

c) How long did it take the ball to reach the floor?

d) What was the height of the platform?

Time (s)	Height Above the Floor (m)
0	10.0
0.5	9.7
1.0	8.9
1.5	7.5
2.0	5.6
2.5	3.0
3.0	0

6. The table shows the areas of circles with different radii.

a) Use a graphing calculator. Graph the relation.

b) Do the points appear to form a parabola? Explain.

c) Find the quadratic equation that fits the data.

d) Find the area of a circle with radius 10 cm.

Radius of Circle (cm)	Area (cm^2)
0	0
1	3.14
2	12.56
3	28.26
4	50.24
5	78.50

Literacy Connect

7. The Capilano Bridge in Vancouver B.C. is suspended from heavy cables anchored to opposite sides of a gorge. The table shows the height of the bridge above the river at different horizontal distances from one end of the bridge.

a) Use a graphing calculator. Graph the data.

b) Do the data appear to be quadratic? Explain.

c) The bridge dips in the centre. At what horizontal distance from the end is the bridge 70 m above the water? How did you find out?

Height of Bridge Above River (m)	Horizontal Distance (m)
72.94	0
71.50	20
70.54	40
70.06	60
70.06	80
70.54	100
71.50	120
72.94	140

8. The table shows the height and the horizontal distance travelled by a football after it is kicked.

Horizontal Distance (yd)	Height of Football (ft)
0	0
10	42
20	68
30	68
40	42
50	0

a) Plot the data using a graphing calculator.

b) Find the quadratic equation that models this situation.

c) At what horizontal distance did the ball reach its maximum height?

9. A local concert promoter knows that she can sell concert tickets at $40 per person and can expect an attendance of 8000 people. She conducts a survey and finds that if she raises the price of the ticket by $1 the attendance at the concert drops by 150 people.

a) Copy and complete the table.

Price of Ticket ($)	Attendance	Revenue ($1000s)
40	8000	320
41		
42		
43		
44		
45		
46		
47		
48		
49		
50		
51		
52		

b) Plot revenue versus ticket price using a graphing calculator.

c) Estimate the price of the ticket that would generate the most revenue.

10. A rescue flare is fired into the air. The table shows the height of the flare at different times after being fired. The flare ignites once it reaches its maximum height.

Time (s)	Height of Flare (m)
0	0
0.5	82.5
0.75	118.1
1.0	150.0
1.4	193.2
1.8	226.8
2.0	240.0

a) How long after it is fired will the flare ignite?

b) At what height does the flare ignite?

Chapter Problem

11. The city plans to enclose a rectangular garden near the skateboard park. The budget allows for 28 m of edging to enclose the garden. Which dimensions will give the greatest area using the 28 m of edging?

a) Copy and complete the table.

Width (m)	Length (m)	Area of Garden (m²)
1	13	
2	12	
3	11	
4	10	
5	9	
6	8	
7	7	
8	6	
9	5	
10	4	
11	3	
12	2	
13	1	

b) Graph the data.

c) What dimensions give the greatest area?

Achievement Check

12. The table shows the height above the water of a person diving off a cliff.

Time (s)	Height (m)
0	70
0.5	68
1.0	63
1.5	56
2.0	46
2.5	34
3.0	20
3.5	2

a) Find the quadratic equation that models the path of the diver.

b) What was the diver's initial height?

c) When does the diver hit the water?

Extend the Concepts C

13. A cross-section of a satellite dish can be modelled by the quadratic relation $d = -0.0016w(w - 300)$, where w represents the horizontal distance across the dish in centimetres and d represents the depth of the dish in centimetres.

a) Copy and complete the table.

w (cm)	d (cm)
0	
25	
50	
75	
100	
125	
150	

b) Use a graphing calculator. Draw a scatter plot of the data. Find the quadratic equation that best fits the data.

c) Compare your answer from part b) to the equation given in the question. Show that the equations are the same.

8.2 Represent Quadratic Relations in Different Ways

Don is a landscaper. He works with the city designing, planting, and maintaining gardens, parks, and green spaces.

Investigate

Tools

- graphing calculator

Compare Graphs of Quadratic Relations

Use a graphing calculator with standard window settings.

1. a) Graph the relation $y = x^2 + x - 6$ in Y1.

b) Factor the trinomial on the right side of the equation.

c) Press [Y=] [▼] to move the cursor next to Y2.

- Press [◄] [◄] [ENTER] to change the line style to bold.
- Press [►] [►]. Enter the factored expression from part b) in Y2. Graph the relations in Y1 and Y2 on the same screen.

d) How do the graphs of the relations compare? Explain.

e) Press [2nd] [CALC] 3:minimum or 4:maximum. Check that the equation in Y1 is displayed in the top left corner of the screen. If it is not, press [▲] to toggle between Y1 and Y2.

- Press [◄] to move the cursor to the left of the maximum or minimum.
- Press [ENTER].
- Press [►] to move the cursor to the right of the maximum or minimum.
- Press [ENTER] [ENTER]. Record the maximum or minimum.

f) Find and record the maximum or minimum for the equation in Y2. How does this value compare to the maximum or minimum for the equation in Y1? Explain.

g) The *x*-intercepts of a quadratic relation are the **zeros**.

- Press [2nd] [CALC] 2:zero. Check that the equation in Y1 is displayed in the top left corner of the screen. If it is not, press [▲] to toggle between Y1 and Y2.
- Press [◀] to move the cursor to the left of the first *x*-intercept.
- Press [ENTER].
- Press [▶] to move the cursor to the right of the first *x*-intercept.
- Press [ENTER] [ENTER]. Record the zero. Repeat for the second *x*-intercept.

h) Find and record the zeros for the equation in Y2. How do these values compare to the zeros for the equation in Y1? Explain.

i) Compare each algebraic representation of the quadratic relation to its graph. What do you notice?

2. Repeat question 1 for each relation.

a) $y = x^2 + 5x + 4$ **b)** $y = x^2 - 8x + 15$

c) $y = -x^2 + 4x$ **d)** $y = x^2 - 12x + 36$

e) $y = -x^2 + 2x + 8$ **f)** $y = 3x^2 + 9x + 6$

3. a) Graph the relation $y = (x + 2)(x - 1)$ in Y1.

b) Expand and simplify the expression on the right side of the equation.

c) Enter the expanded expression from part b) in Y2. Change the line style for Y2 to bold. Graph the relations in Y1 and Y2 on the same screen.

d) How do the graphs of the relations compare? Explain.

e) Find and record the maximum or minimum for the equations in Y1 and Y2. How do these values compare? Explain.

f) Find and record the zeros for the equations in Y1 and Y2. How do these values compare? Explain.

g) Compare each algebraic representation of the quadratic relation to its graph. What do you notice?

4. Repeat question 3 for each relation.

a) $y = (x + 3)(x + 1)$ **b)** $y = -(x - 7)(x - 3)$

c) $y = x(x + 3)$ **d)** $y = (x + 1)(x - 5)$

e) $y = -(x + 4)^2$ **f)** $y = -2(x + 2)(x - 2)$

5. Reflect How does the graph of a quadratic relation in the form $y = x^2 + bx + c$ compare to the graph of the same relation in the factored form $y = (x - r)(x - s)$? Explain.

6. For a quadratic relation in the form $y = x^2 + bx + c$, explain what c represents in terms of the graph of the relation.

7. For the factored form of a quadratic relation $y = (x - r)(x - s)$, explain what r and s represent in terms of the graph of the relation.

Example 1

Analyze a Quadratic Relation

Given the quadratic relation $y = x^2 + 2x - 15$

a) Does the relation have a maximum or minimum value?
b) What is the y-intercept?
c) What are the zeros for the relation?

Solution

Method 1: Use Algebra

a) Since a is positive, the parabola opens upward. The parabola therefore has a minimum value.

b) The y-intercept is the value of y when $x = 0$.
$$y = x^2 + 2x - 15$$
$$= 0^2 + 2(0) - 15$$
$$= -15$$
The y-intercept is -15.

c) Factor the expression on the right side of the equation.

$y = x^2 + 2x - 15$ *Find two numbers whose product is −15 and whose sum is 2. The numbers are 5 and −3.*

$= (x + 5)(x - 3)$ *The zeros are the x-intercepts. When the product of two numbers is 0, at least one of the numbers is 0. Set each factor equal to zero and solve.*

$$\begin{aligned} \text{Either} \quad x + 5 &= 0 & \text{or} \quad x - 3 &= 0 \\ x &= 0 - 5 & x &= 0 + 3 \\ &= -5 & &= 3 \end{aligned}$$

The zeros are -5 and 3.

Method 2: Use a Graphing Calculator

a) Since a is positive, the parabola opens upward. The parabola has a minimum value.

b) Graph the relation $Y1 = x^2 + 2x - 15$.
- Press [2nd] [CALC] 1:value.
- Press 0 [ENTER].

The y-intercept is -15.

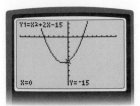

c) Press [2nd] [CALC] 2:zero.

Use the left arrow key to move the cursor to the left of the first point where the parabola crosses the x-axis. Press [ENTER]. Use the right arrow key to move the cursor to the right of the first point where the parabola crosses the x-axis.
- Press [ENTER] [ENTER].

Repeat the steps to find the other zero. The zeros are -5 and 3.

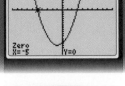

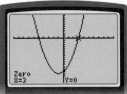

Example **2** **Interpret a Quadratic Equation**

The curve formed by a rope bridge can be modelled by the relation $y = x^2 - 11x + 10$, where x is the horizontal distance in metres and y is the height in metres.

a) Write the relation in factored form.

b) What are the zeros of the relation?

c) What is the horizontal distance from one end of the bridge to the other?

Solution

a) $y = x^2 - 11x + 10$ *The numbers -1 and -10 have a*
$\quad\ y = (x - 1)(x - 10)$ *sum of -11 and a product of 10.*

b) The zeros are the values of x when $y = 0$.

$0 = (x - 1)(x - 10)$

Either $x - 1 = 0$ or $x - 10 = 0$
$\qquad\qquad x = 1$ $x = 10$

The zeros are 1 and 10.

c) The horizontal distance from one end of the bridge to the other is $10 - 1$, or 9 m.

Key Concepts

- A quadratic relation can be expressed in the form $y = x^2 + bx + c$ or in the form $y = (x - r)(x - s)$.
- For a quadratic equation of the form $y = (x - r)(x - s)$, the x-intercepts are r and s.
- For a quadratic equation of the form $y = ax^2 + bx + c$, the y-intercept is c.
- The zeros of a quadratic relation are the x-intercepts.

Discuss the Concepts

D1. Describe how you could find the zeros of the quadratic relation $y = x^2 - 5x + 6$ without graphing the relation.

D2. How would you find the y-intercept of the relation $y = (x + 5)(4 - x)$ without graphing? Explain.

D3. The vertex of a quadratic relation is at $(2, -5)$. Does the relation have a maximum or a minimum value? Explain.

Practise the Concepts (A)

For help with questions 1 and 2, refer to Example 1.

1. Find the zeros of each quadratic relation, without graphing.
   a) $y = x^2 + 5x + 6$
   b) $y = x^2 + 7x - 18$
   c) $y = x^2 - 10x + 24$

2. Given the quadratic relation $y = x^2 + 3x - 4$
   a) Does the relation have a maximum or minimum value?
   b) What is the y-intercept?
   c) What are the zeros of the relation?

3. Find the maximum or minimum value of each quadratic relation.
   a) $y = x^2 + 8x + 15$
   b) $y = -x^2 - 2x$
   c) $y = -3x^2 - 21x - 18$

4. Which of these equations does the parabola represent?
   a) $y = (x + 2)(x - 3)$
   b) $y = (x - 2)(x + 3)$
   c) $y = x^2 + x - 6$

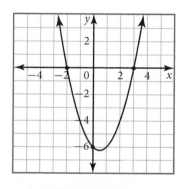

5. Find the maximum area, in square metres, of a rectangle whose area can be represented by the relation $A = x(15 - x)$.

15 − x

x

Apply the Concepts **B**

For help with question 6, refer to Example 2.

6. The curve formed by a cable on a suspension bridge can be modelled by the equation $y = x^2 - 10x + 16$.
   a) Write the equation in factored form.
   b) What are the zeros of the relation?
   c) All measures are in metres. What is the horizontal distance between the ends of the cable?

7. The minimum cost of maintaining an overhead crane depends on the number of hours the crane is in operation. The cost is given by the relation $C = 6t^2 - 36t + 154$, where C represents the cost in hundreds of dollars and t represents the time in hours that the crane has been operated.

   a) What is the minimum cost of maintaining the crane?
   b) Find the number of hours the crane operates for this minimum maintenance cost.
   c) Find the cost if the crane sits idle.

Math Connect

Profit is total revenue minus total cost.

8. A circuit board company earns a profit that can be represented by the relation $P = -3x^2 + 42x - 135$, where P represents the profit in tens of thousands of dollars and x represents the number of circuit boards in thousands manufactured per day.

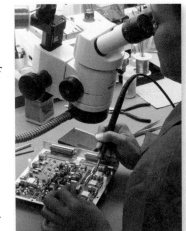

   a) Find the maximum profit the company can make each day.
   b) How many circuit boards should the company manufacture each day to earn this maximum profit?

Literacy Connect

9. Explain how companies whose profits can be modelled by a quadratic relation can use a parabola to determine the level of production that gives the maximum profit.

Chapter Problem **10.** The shape of one of the skateboard ramps to be built in the park can be modelled by the quadratic relation $d = 0.08l^2 - 0.8l$, where d represents the depth in metres and l represents the horizontal distance in metres.

a) Use a graphing calculator. Graph the relation $d = 0.08l^2 - 0.8l$.

b) Find the maximum depth of this skateboard ramp.

c) From the start of the ramp, what is the horizontal distance to the point with maximum depth?

d) What is the total horizontal distance across the ramp?

11. The path of a soccer ball can be represented by the relation $h = -0.05x^2 + 1.5x$, where h is the height of the soccer ball in yards and x is the horizontal distance the ball travels in yards. How far has the ball travelled horizontally when it reaches the ground?

Extend the Concepts

12. Without graphing, determine the zeros and the maximum or minimum value of the quadratic relation $y = -2x^2 + 12x - 10$.

13. Haley found the minimum of the quadratic relation $y = (x + 4)(x - 8)$ this way:

> The zeros of this relation are − 4 and 8.
>
> The x-coordinate of the vertex is halfway between − 4 and 8; it is 2.
>
> Substitute $x = 2$ into the equation and solve for y.
> $y = (2 + 4)(2 - 8)$
> $\quad = (6)(- 6)$
> $\quad = - 36$
> The minimum is −36.

Explain why Haley's method works.

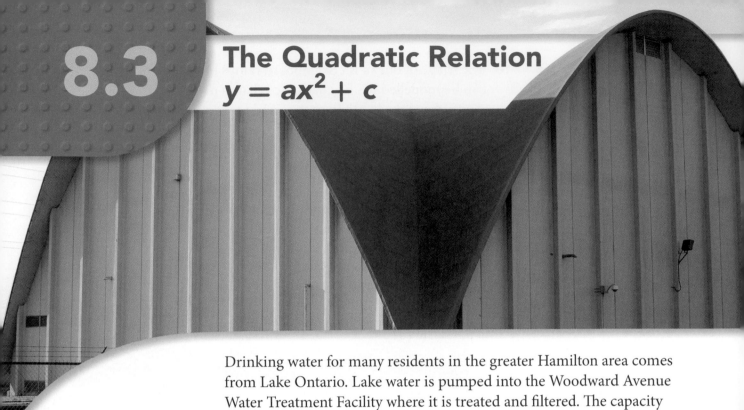

8.3 The Quadratic Relation $y = ax^2 + c$

Drinking water for many residents in the greater Hamilton area comes from Lake Ontario. Lake water is pumped into the Woodward Avenue Water Treatment Facility where it is treated and filtered. The capacity of this facility is 200 million gallons per day, although it usually operates at less than one half of its capacity.

Investigate A

The Significance of *a* and *c* in Quadratic Relations of the Form $y = ax^2 + c$

Tools

- Calculator-Based Ranger (CBR™)
- graphing calculator

1. Collect data from rolling a ball down a ramp inclined at different angles (for example, 15°, 30°, and 45°).

- Set up the ramp approximately 2 m long with an angle of inclination of 15°.
- Place the ball about 50 cm away from the CBR.

  Use these menu settings:

  Real Time: NO

  Time(s): 3

  Display: distance

  Begin On: [ENTER]

  Smoothing: Light

  Units: Centimetres

When the settings are correct, choose [START NOW].

• Press (ENTER).

When the clicking begins, release, but do not push the ball.
The graph will display automatically. Record the equation
associated with each ramp in the form $y = ax^2 + c$ and note
the direction of opening of the parabola.

Repeat the procedure with the ramp inclined at angles of
30° and 45°.

2. Predict what will happen if the angle of inclination is increased
to more than 45°.

3. Compare the values of a in each of the equations you found.

4. Compare the shapes of the parabolas obtained from the
experiments.

Investigate **B** **The Effect of Changing *c* in a Quadratic Relation
of the Form $y = ax^2 + c$**

Tools

- Calculator-Based Ranger
  (CBR™)
- graphing calculator

1. Conduct an experiment by dropping the same ball from different
heights (for example, 6 ft, 5 ft, and 4 ft).

2. Predict what will happen.

3. Compare the values of c in each of the equations
which are in the form $y = ax^2 + c$.

4. Compare the shape of each graph obtained.

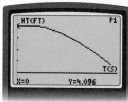

*Notice that the y-intercepts are different.
Compare the y-intercept with the c-value in
each equation. In this case the c-value is a
maximum. The a-value is negative and the
parabola opens downward.*

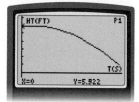

Example **1**

Find the Maximum or Minimum

Find the maximum or minimum of each relation.

   a) $y = 3x^2$ **b)** $y = x^2 - 9$ **c)** $y = -2x^2 + 32$

Solution

  a) In equation $y = 3x^2$, $b = 0$ and $c = 0$, so the y-intercept is 0. Since a is positive, 0 is the minimum.

  b) In equation $y = x^2 - 9$, a is positive and $b = 0$, so c represents the minimum. The minimum is -9.

  c) In equation $y = -2x^2 + 32$, a is negative and $b = 0$, so c represents the maximum. The maximum is 32.

Example **2**

Find the Zeros of a Quadratic Relation

Find the zeros of the relation $y = x^2 - 9$.

Solution

Method 1: Use Algebra

$y = x^2 - 9$

$y = (x + 3)(x - 3)$.

At the zeros, $y = 0$.

$0 = (x + 3)(x - 3)$

Either $x + 3 = 0$ or $x - 3 = 0$

                $x = 3$ $x = -3$

The zeros are -3 and 3.

> *Factor the expression $x^2 - 9$.*
> *It is a difference of squares so*
> $x^2 - 9 = (x + 3)(x - 3)$

Method 2: Use Technology

- Press ⌈ Y= ⌉. Enter the equation $Y1 = x^2 - 9$.
- Press ⌈GRAPH⌉. Press ⌈ 2nd ⌉ [CALC] 2:zero. Use the left arrow key to move the cursor to the left of the first x-intercept. Press ⌈ENTER⌉. Use the right arrow key to move the cursor to the right of the first x-intercept.
- Press ⌈ENTER⌉ ⌈ENTER⌉.

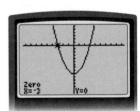

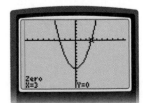

Repeat the steps to find the other zero.

So, the zeros for this relation are 3 and -3.

Example **3**

Interpret the Zeros of a Quadratic Relation

This building contains the equipment that pumps water from Lake Ontario to the Woodward Avenue Water Treatment Facility. A cross-section of the building is in the shape of a parabola. Its shape can be modelled by the quadratic relation $h = -0.045w^2 + 18$, where h represents the height in metres and w represents the horizontal distance in metres.

a) Graph the relation.
b) Find the height of the building.
c) Find the width of the building at ground level.

Solution

a) Press ⌈WINDOW⌉. Use the window settings shown.
  • Press ⌈ Y= ⌉. Enter Y1 = $-0.045x^2 + 18$.
  • Press ⌈GRAPH⌉.

b) Since the equation has the form $y = ax^2 + c$, the maximum is at c. In $h = -0.045w^2 + 18$, $c = 18$. The maximum is 18, so the height of the arch is 18 m. You can check this using a graphing calculator.
- Press [2nd] [CALC] 4:maximum.

c) The width of the arch is the distance from one x-intercept to the other.
- Press [2nd] [CALC] 2:zero. Use the left arrow key to move the cursor to the left of the first x-intercept.
- Press [ENTER]. Use the right arrow key to move the cursor to the right of the first x-intercept.
- Press [ENTER] [ENTER].
  Repeat the steps to find the other zero.

The zeros are -20 and 20. The distance between the zeros is 40, so the width of the building at ground level is 40 m.

Key Concept

- For a quadratic relation of the form $y = ax^2 + c$, the maximum or minimum value occurs at c, which is the y-intercept.

Discuss the Concept

D1. Consider the quadratic relations $y = -5x^2 + 45$ and $y = 2x^2 - 8$.

    a) Which relation has a maximum value? How do you know? What is the maximum?

    b) Which relation has a minimum value? How do you know? What is the minimum?

    c) How would you find the zeros for each relation?

D2. Explain why the relation $y = x^2 + 25$ has no zeros.

Practise the Concept A

1. Without graphing, order the parabolas in each set from narrowest to widest.

   a) $y = \frac{1}{3}x^2 - 7$
   $y = x^2 - 7$
   $y = 3x^2 - 7$

   b) $y = -4x^2 + 5$
   $y = -\frac{1}{2}x^2 + 5$
   $y = -0.75\,x^2 + 5$

For help with question 2, refer to Example 1.

2. For each relation, find the y-intercept and determine if it is a maximum, a minimum, or neither.

   a) $y = x^2 - 4$

   b) $y = 3x^2 + 7$

   c) $y = -5x^2 + 45$

   d) $y = -2x^2 - 8$

   e) $y = -\frac{1}{3}x^2 + 3$

   f) $y = -\frac{1}{2}x^2 + 5$

For help with question 3, refer to Example 2.

3. Graph each relation from question 2, then find the zeros.

Apply the Concept B

For help with question 4, refer to Example 3.

4. A ball is dropped from a platform. Its path can be represented by the relation $h = -5t^2 + 45$, where h represents the height of the ball in metres and t represents the time in seconds taken for the ball to fall to the ground.

   a) From what height was the ball dropped?

   b) How long did it take the ball to reach the ground?

5. A scuba diver starts her ascent to the surface of the water. The equation that models her ascent is $d = 2.5t^2 - 250$, where d is the depth in feet below the surface of the water and t the time in seconds taken to get to the surface.

a) How deep was the diver when she started to ascend?
b) How long did it take the diver to get to the surface of the water?
c) Suppose the diver had 20 s of air left in her scuba tank. Would she reach the surface safely?

6. Compare the relations $y = -3x^2 + 27$ and $y = -3(x + 3)(x - 3)$.
a) Graph the two relations.
b) What do you notice about the graphs? Explain.

Chapter Problem

7. The shape the other skateboard ramp to be built in the park can be modelled by the equation $h = -0.067d^2 + 1.5$, where h is the height of the ramp in metres and d is the horizontal distance in metres from the centre of the ramp.
a) What is the maximum height of this ramp?
b) What is the total horizontal distance across this ramp?

8. A large square with sides x m long contains a smaller square with sides 5 m long. The relation $A = x^2 - 25$ represents the difference between the areas.

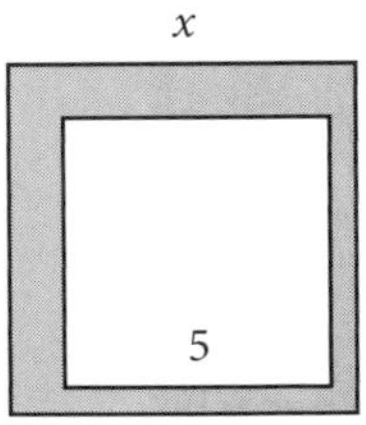

a) What is the minimum possible area of the larger square?
b) Graph this relation and find the dimensions of the large square if the difference between the areas is 75 m^2.

9. A footbridge has a parabolic arch. The equation $h = -0.0056d^2 + 20$ represents the shape, where h is the height in metres of the cable from the walkway and d the distance in metres from the centre of the arch to the end support.

a) What is the height of the arch at the centre of the bridge?
b) Find the distance between the two end supports.

10. The graph of the quadratic relation $y = ax^2 - 15$ passes through the point (2, 1). Find the value(s) of a.

11. The graph of the quadratic relation $y = -2x^2 + c$ passes through the point (5, 10). Find the value of c.

Literacy Connect **12.** The parabolic arch is used for its stability in architecture. Find some examples of the parabola in architecture. For what other reasons is the parabolic shape used?

Extend the Concept

13. The weight of an object in water is approximately one-sixth of its weight on land. If an object on land falls from a height of 100 m, its path can be represented by the equation $h = -5t^2 + 100$, where h represents the height of the object in metres, and t represents time in seconds.
a) Write an equation to represent the path of the same object falling the same distance in water.
b) How long will it take the object to fall 100 m on land?
c) How long will it take the object to fall 100 m in the water?

8.4 Solve Problems Involving Quadratic Relations

Many situations can be modelled using quadratic relations. Some examples are the path of a ball that is thrown in the air, the relationship between the number of units of a product sold and the price of the product, and the path of a diver. In this section, you will use quadratic relations to solve problems.

Example **1** **Find the Maximum Revenue**

A concert promoter knows that if she sells tickets to a concert for $30 each, she will sell all 8000 tickets. Market research indicates that, if she raises the price by $0.50, the number of tickets sold will drop by 100, but the revenue will increase. This situation can be modelled by the relation $R = -50x^2 + 1000x + 240\,000$, where R represents the revenue from ticket sales in dollars and x represents the number of times the ticket price is increased by $0.50.

a) Determine the maximum revenue. By how much does the concert promoter need to increase the ticket price to earn the maximum revenue?

b) Determine the ticket price at which she will earn the maximum revenue.

Solution

a) The maximum revenue is represented by the maximum of the parabola. Graph the relation.
Use the window settings shown.

- Press $\boxed{Y=}$. Enter the equation
$Y1 = -50x^2 + 1000x + 240\,000$.
Press $\boxed{GRAPH}$.
- Use $\boxed{2nd}$ [CALC] 4:maximum.
The maximum revenue is $245\,000.
The maximum occurs when $x = 10$, which means the ticket price is increased by $0.50 ten times, or by $5.

b) The ticket price that will generate the maximum revenue is $35.

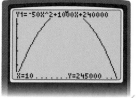

Example **2**

Model the Trajectory of a Model Rocket

A model rocket is launched from a platform. The trajectory of the rocket can be modelled by the relation $h = -5t^2 + 100t + 1$, where h is the height of the model rocket in metres and t is the time in seconds.

a) What is the height of the platform?
b) What is the height of the model rocket after 4 s?
c) What is the maximum height reached by the rocket? How long does the rocket take to reach this height?
d) How long is the model rocket above 300 m?
e) Approximately how long is the rocket in the air?

Solution

a) The height of the platform is the height of the rocket when $t = 0$. This is the y-intercept, which is the value of c in the equation. Since $c = 1$, the platform is 1 m above the ground.

b) To find the height of the rocket after 4 s, substitute $t = 4$ into the equation and solve for h.

$$h = -5t^2 + 100t + 1$$
$$= -5(4)^2 + 100(4) + 1$$
$$= -80 + 400 + 1$$
$$= 321$$

After 4 s, the rocket is 321 m above the ground.

c) Graph the relation and find the maximum. The maximum height reached by the rocket is 501 m. It takes the rocket 10 s to reach this height.

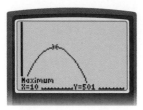

d) Graph the horizontal line $h = 300$. Enter Y2 = 300.

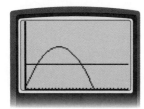

• Press $\boxed{\text{2nd}}$ [CALC] 5:intersect. Use the arrow keys to move the cursor close to the first point of intersection.

• Press $\boxed{\text{ENTER}}$ $\boxed{\text{ENTER}}$ $\boxed{\text{ENTER}}$. Record the coordinates of the point of intersection.

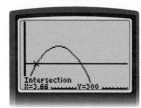

Repeat the steps to find the other point of intersection. The rocket is above 300 m from 3.66 s to 16.34 s.

$$16.34 - 3.66 = 12.86$$

The rocket is above 300 m for 12.86 s.

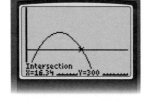

e) The rocket is in the air from the moment it takes off until it hits the ground again. When it hits the ground its height is 0. Find the zero for the relation. The rocket is in the air for 20.01 s.

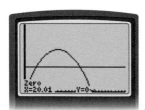

Key Concepts

- Many situations can be modelled using quadratic relations.

- Problems can be solved by finding the maximum or minimum, the y-intercept, or the zeros.

Discuss the Concepts

D1. Consider the following problem.

A golfer hits her tee shot into the rough and the ball stops approximately 120 yd from the green. There is a tree located 40 yd from the ball, directly in the path to the green. The golfer decides to try to hit the ball over the tree. The path of her shot can be represented by the relation $h = -0.018\,75x^2 + 2.25x$, where h is the height of the ball in yards and x is the horizontal distance in yards from where the second shot is taken.

a) Explain how you could determine whether the ball clears the tree.

b) How can you tell whether the ball lands near the centre of the green?

c) How could you determine the maximum height the golf ball reaches and how far it travels horizontally to reach this maximum height?

Practise the Concepts A

Use a graphing calculator.

For help with question 1, refer to Example 1.

1. A school council is planning a battle of the bands. They expect that 700 tickets will be sold if the ticket price is $5. A survey shows that if the ticket price is raised by $0.50, 50 fewer tickets will be sold. This situation can be modelled by the equation $R = -25p^2 + 100p + 3500$, where R represents the revenue from ticket sales in dollars and p represents the number of times the ticket price is increased by $0.50.

a) Find the maximum revenue the student council can make and the new ticket price it should charge in order to get the maximum revenue.

b) What is the original revenue before the ticket price is raised?

c) What part of the quadratic relation represents the original revenue?

For help with questions 2 to 4, refer to Example 2.

2. A model rocket is launched from a platform. Its flight path can be represented by the relation $h = -5t^2 + 100t + 15$, where h represents the height of the rocket in metres and t represents time in seconds.
   a) What is the height of the platform?
   b) What is the height of the model rocket after 4 s?
   c) What is the maximum height reached by the rocket?
   d) How long does the rocket take to reach this height?
   e) How long is the rocket above 300 m?
   f) Estimate how long the rocket stays in the air.

3. Two quarterbacks have a contest to see who can throw a football further. The first quarterback's throw has a trajectory represented by the equation $h = -0.021d^2 + 0.9d + 7$. The second quarterback's throw has a trajectory represented by the equation $h = -0.021d^2 + 0.8d + 7$, where h represents the height of the football in feet and d the horizontal distance in yards.
   a) Who threw the football further? By how many yards?
   b) Whose football reached the greater height?
   c) Explain why a football could be thrown further and lower at the same time.

4. A model rocket is launched from a platform. Its flight path can be modelled by the relation $h = -4.9t^2 + 100t + 13$, where h represents the height of the rocket in metres and t represents time in seconds.
   a) What is the height of the platform?
   b) What is the height of the model rocket after 7 s?
   c) What is the maximum height reached by the rocket?
   d) How long does the rocket take to reach this height?
   e) How long is the rocket above 400 m?
   f) Estimate how long the rocket stays in the air.

Apply the Concepts B

5. Two free kicks are taken in a soccer match. Each kick is directed at the goal, and the goalkeeper has no chance of making either save. The crossbar of the goal is 2.44 m high. The trajectory of each kick is modelled by a quadratic relation, where h represents the height of the ball in metres and d represents the horizontal distance in metres.
   Kick #1: $h = -0.007d^2 + 0.28d$
   Kick #2: $h = -0.007d^2 + 0.25d$

a) Could each kick score if the free kicks are taken from 25 m? Explain.

b) Could each kick score if they are taken from 20 m? Explain.

Achievement Check

6. A set of fireworks is designed to explode at the highest point. The equations that model the trajectories of the four different types of fireworks are $h = -5t^2 + 50t$, $h = -5t^2 + 60t$, $h = -5t^2 + 70t$, and $h = -5t^2 + 80t$, where h is the height in metres and t is the time in seconds.

a) Find the height and time at which each type of fireworks explodes.

b) Graph the relations. Describe how the graphs are similar and how they are different.

7. The Magdeburg Bus Company services about 240 000 riders per day at a fare of $2. The Magdeburg city council wants to raise the fare to cover some expenses. A survey indicates that for every $0.10 increase in the bus fare the ridership will drop by 10 000. The situation can be represented by the relation $R = -1000p^2 + 4000p + 480\,000$, where R represents the revenue from bus fares in dollars and p represents the number of times the bus fare is raised $0.10.

a) What is the maximum revenue Magdeburg will receive from the new bus fare?

b) How much is the increase in bus fare?

c) What is the new bus fare?

d) How many people will ride the bus if the fare increases $0.30?

8. The cost of extracting oil from a well can be modelled by the relation $C = 9x^2 - 144x + 608.50$, where C represents the cost per barrel, in dollars, for extracting x thousand barrels of oil.

a) Find the minimum cost per barrel extracted.
b) Find the number of barrels that should be extracted in order to meet this minimum cost.
c) Calculate the cost per barrel if 4000 barrels are extracted from the ground.

9. A football is punted and its path is modelled by the relation $h = -0.05d^2 + 2.5d + 0.75$, where h is the height of the ball in yards and d the horizontal distance in yards travelled by the ball.
a) From what height is the ball kicked?
b) What is the height of the ball when it has travelled a horizontal distance of 14 yd?
c) What was the maximum height reached by the ball?
d) How far down the field does the football reach this maximum height?
e) How far is the ball punted?

10. A ball is thrown and its path can be modelled by the relation $h = 7 + 40t - 5t^2$, where h is the height of the ball in feet and t is the time in seconds after the ball is thrown.
a) From what height is the ball thrown?
b) What is the height of the ball after 2 s?
c) What is the maximum height reached by the ball?
d) How long does it take the ball to reach this height?
e) How long is the ball above 70 ft?
f) Estimate how long the ball stays in the air.

11. The amount of gas a car uses to travel a fixed distance can be represented by the relation $F = 0.007\,78s^2 - 1.556s + 87$, where F is the number of litres of gasoline and s is the speed of the car in kilometres per hour.

a) What is the capacity of the gas tank of this car?

b) How many litres of gasoline are used if the car travels at 50 km/h?

c) What is the minimum fuel consumption? At what speed does this minimum fuel consumption occur?

Literacy Connect

d) Explain to a classmate or friend why it would be more efficient to travel at a steady speed of 100 km/h than at a steady speed of 120 km/h.

Extend the Concepts C

12. The Burlington Skyway bridge has two arched steel construction supports. Steel girders run vertically between them. The lower arch can be modelled by the relation $h = -0.004w^2 + 0.56w$ and the top arch can be modelled by the relation $h = -0.002w^2 + 0.28w + 13$. In each relation, h is the height in metres and d is the horizontal distance from one end of the bridge in metres. Find the height of two vertical steel girders that are situated 15 m from centre.

13. Wilbur is a lifeguard at a local conservation area. He has been told to enclose a swimming area at the beach with a total of 300 m of safety rope with floaters. Find the maximum swimming area Wilbur can enclose.

Review of Key Terms

Copy the statement. Use the key term to complete the statement.

1. The x-intercepts of a quadratic relation are sometimes called the _____.

8.1 Interpret Quadratic Relations, pages 320 to 328

2. Researchers studied photosynthesis in a species of grass. The table compares the efficiency of photosynthesis, y, as a percent, to the temperature, x, in degrees Celsius.
   a) Use a graphing calculator to plot the data.
   b) Find the equation of the curve of best fit.
   c) At what temperature is photosynthesis most efficient?

x (°C)	y (%)
−1.5	33
0	46
2.5	55
5	80
7	87
10	93
12	95
15	91
17	89
20	77
22	72
25	54
27	46
30	34

3. A walkway across a creek has the shape of a parabolic arch. The heights of the walkway at different horizontal distances are given in the table.

Height of Walkway (ft)	Horizontal Distance (yd)
0	0
3.2	5
4.8	10
4.8	15
3.2	20

a) Plot the data on a graphing calculator.
b) Find the equation of the curve of best fit.
c) What is the maximum height of the walkway? What is the horizontal distance at this point?

8.2 Represent Quadratic Relations in Different Ways, pages 329 to 335

4. a) Write an expression to represent the area of this rectangle.

20 − w

w

   b) Find the value of w that will produce the maximum area.

5. A rope was tied to trees at both ends. The curve of the rope can be modelled by the equation $y = x^2 - 12x$, where y is the height and x is the horizontal distance, both in feet. How far apart are the trees? How do you know?

8.3 The Quadratic Relation $y = ax^2 + c$, pages 336 to 343

6. A ball was dropped from a platform. Its path can be modelled by the quadratic relation $h = -4.9t^2 + 13$, where h represents the height of the ball in metres and t represents the time in seconds.
   a) What is the height of the platform?
   b) How long did it take the ball to land?
   c) Use a graphing calculator. How long did it take the ball to drop 8.1 m?

7. An archway was built for a wedding reception. The shape of the archway can be modelled by the quadratic relation $h = -0.15d^2 + 15$, where h represents the height of the archway in feet and d represents the horizontal distance in feet from the centre of the archway.

a) What is the maximum height of the archway?

b) What is the width of the archway at the base?

c) If the groom is 6 ft tall, how far from the centre can he walk safely under the archway?

8.4 Solving Problems Involving Quadratic Relations,
pages 344 to 351

Use a graphing calculator for questions 8 and 9.

8. A basketball jump shot was taken 24 ft from the basket. Its path can be modelled by the quadratic relation $h = -0.028d^2 + 0.672d + 10.5$, where h is the height of the ball in feet and d is the horizontal distance from the basket in feet.

a) What was the maximum height reached by the basketball?

b) Estimate the height that the jump shot was taken from.

c) The rim of the basket is 10 ft above the ground. Did the ball go in the basket? Explain.

9. Tickets for the Players Theatre sell for $5 each. A survey found that if the price increased by $0.50 there would be a drop in attendance of 25 people. Even though this might be the case, the Players Theatre would still have an increase in revenue. The quadratic relation that defines this situation is $R = -12.5p^2 + 125p + 2500$, where R represents the revenue from ticket sales in dollars and p the number of times the ticket price increases by $0.50.

a) Find the maximum revenue the Players Theatre could receive from a new ticket price.

b) Find the number of $0.50 increases needed to obtain this maximum revenue.

c) What will the new ticket price be?

Chapter 8 Practice Test

1. For each quadratic relation, find the *y*-intercept, the zeros, and the maximum or minimum value.

a) $y = -\dfrac{1}{2}x^2$ **b)** $y = x^2 + x - 2$

c) $y = x^2 - 49$ **d)** $y = x^2 + 4x$

2. During a practice, each time the quarterback threw the ball, the path of the ball was recorded. The table below shows the data for a pass to a receiver.

Height (ft)	Horizontal Distance (yd)
9.75	5
11.50	10
11.50	15
9.75	20

a) Use a graphing calculator. Create a scatter plot of the data.

b) Find the equation of the quadratic relation that best fits the data. Graph the equation.

c) Use the graph of the equation to find the maximum height of the ball.

d) How many yards downfield did the ball reach its maximum height?

e) Suppose the receiver who caught the ball was 27 yd downfield. At what height did he catch the ball?

3. Shaniqua dives off a cliff into the water below. Her path can be modelled by the relation $h = -4.9t^2 + 4.9t + 21.5$, where *h* is her height above the water in metres and *t* is the time in seconds.

a) What is the height of the cliff?

b) What is the maximum height Shaniqua reaches? When does she reach this height?

c) What height above the water is Shaniqua after 1.5 s?

d) How long will it take Shaniqua to hit the water?

4. The Golden Gate Bridge in San Francisco has cables for support. The cables extend from one support tower to another, a horizontal distance of about 4200 ft. The top of each tower is approximately 500 ft above the roadway. The suspension cable forms a parabolic arch that can be modelled by the equation $h = 0.000\,113(d - 2100)^2$, where *h* represents the height in feet of the cable above the roadway and *d* represents the horizontal distance in feet from one support tower.

a) Graph this relation on a graphing calculator.

b) What is the height of the cable above the roadway at a distance of 1000 ft from a support tower?

c) What is the horizontal distance from a support tower where the height of the cable is 90 ft?

Chapter Problem Wrap-Up

A rectangular skateboard arena will be enclosed by 80 m of chain-link fence that is 2 m high. The arena will contain two skateboard ramps. One ramp will have the shape of a parabola that opens upward, the other ramp with have the shape of a parabola that opens downward.

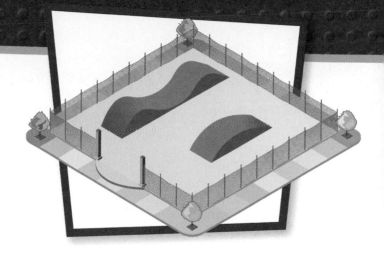

a) Calculate the dimensions of the skateboard arena so the arena has the greatest area possible.

b) The ramp that is in the shape of a parabola that opens downward spans a width of 6 m and has a maximum height of 1 m. Determine the equation that will model the shape of the ramp.

Height (m)	Horizontal Distance (m)
0	0
1	3
0	6

c) The ramp that is in the shape of a parabola that opens upward spans a width of 10 m and has a maximum height of 1.5 m. Determine the equation that will model the shape of the ramp.

Height (m)	Horizontal Distance (m)
1.5	0
0	5
1.5	10

---

5. The weekly profit for a manufacturer of picture frames can be modelled by the quadratic relation $P = -2x^2 + 24x - 54$, where P represents the profit in hundreds of thousands of dollars and x represents the number of picture frames in tens of thousands manufactured weekly.

a) Find the maximum weekly profit.

b) Find the number of picture frames needed to make this maximum weekly profit.

c) How many picture frames must be manufactured in order to make any weekly profit? Explain.

6. A field goal was attempted from 42 yd. Assume that the ball was travelling toward the middle of the goalposts. The path of the ball is modelled by the equation $h = -0.03d^2 + 1.50d$, where h is the height in feet and d is the horizontal distance in yards. The crossbar of the goalposts is 10 ft above the ground. Was the field goal good? Explain.

Home Run Derby

Data are shown below for three baseball players at a recent minor league home run hitting contest.

Juan
The ball followed a path modelled by the equation $h = -0.001d^2 + 0.5d + 2.5$ where h is the height of the ball in feet and d is the horizontal distance in feet.

Mark
The heights of the ball at different distances are given in the table below.

d (ft)	h (ft)
0	3
50	23
100	38
150	48
200	53
250	53
300	48
350	38
400	23

Barry
The path of the ball is shown on the graph below.

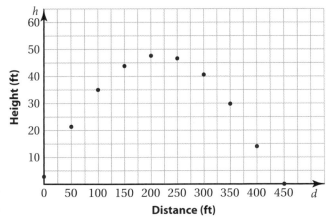

1. Represent the distance–height relationship for each player's ball as an equation, in a table, and on a graph. Record each representation.

2. Suppose there were no obstacles. Whose ball would travel the greatest distance before hitting the ground? The least distance? How did you find out?

3. Suppose the fence was 350 ft from home plate. At what height was each ball when it passed over the fence?

Chapter 6: Quadratic Relations

1. Create a scatter plot of each data set. Sketch a line or curve of best fit for the data.

a)

x	y
−3	−10
−2	−8
−1	−6
0	−4
1	−2
2	0
3	2

b)

x	y
−3	12
−2	6
−1	2
0	0
1	0
2	2
3	6

2. a) Use the graph shown, of a quadratic relation, to make a table of values.

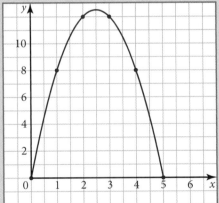

b) Enter the data into a graphing calculator. Find the equation of the quadratic relation.

c) Graph the relation.

d) Identify the coordinates of the vertex and the equation of the axis of symmetry.

3. a) Make a table of values for the quadratic relation $y = 4x^2 - 10x + 1$. Plot the points on a coordinate grid. Sketch a curve of best fit through the points.

b) Use the curve to approximate the x-intercepts and the coordinates of the vertex.

Chapter 7: Quadratic Expressions

4. Expand and simplify.

    a) $(x + 4)(x - 2)$

    b) $(x - 3)^2$

    c) $(2x + 3)(2x - 1)$

    d) $(3x - 1)^2$

5. Write an expression that represents the area of the shaded region.

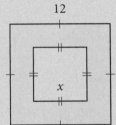

6. For each polynomial, find the greatest common factor (GCF), then factor the polynomial.

    a) $3x + 18$

    b) $5x^2 - 10x$

    c) $3x^2 + 9x - 18$

    d) $14x^3 + 28x$

7. A rectangular playing field has an area (in square metres) that can be represented by the relation $A = 10x^2 + 500x$.

   a) Factor the expression to find the dimensions of the field.

   b) Write an expression for the perimeter of the field.

   c) Find the area and the perimeter if $x = 10$ m.

8. Factor each expression.

   a) $x^2 - 9$ **b)** $25 - x^2$

9. Factor each expression.

   a) $x^2 - 3x - 18$ **b)** $x^2 - 11x + 18$

   c) $x^2 + 11x + 30$ **d)** $x^2 - 4x - 5$

Chapter 8:
Represent Quadratic Relations

10. The arched support of a bridge can be modelled by the quadratic relation $y = -0.018x^2 + 1.8x$, where y is the height in feet, and x is the horizontal distance in feet. A vertical support post is to be installed 36 ft from the base of the arch. How tall will the support post be?

11. The table shows Alyshia's heights after free falling out of a plane, before opening her parachute.

Time (s)	Height (m)
0	3100
5	2977.5
10	2610
15	1997.5
20	1140

a) Enter the data into a graphing calculator. Graph the data. Sketch the graph in your notebook.

b) Find the equation of the quadratic relation that represents the data.

c) Alyshia plans to open her parachute at an altitude of 730 m. How long after she jumps does she need to pull the rip cord?

12. The path of a ball after it is kicked can be modelled by the equation $h = 25t - 5t^2$, where h is the height in metres and t is the time in seconds.

   a) How long was the ball in the air?

   b) How long did it take the ball to reach its maximum height?

   c) What was the maximum height of the ball?

13. Francis has 500 ft of snow fencing to enclose a rectangular area for a skating rink. Find the maximum area that he can enclose.

14. The sale of televisions at a store has been steady at 18 televisions per week at a price of $440 per set. It is known that for every $20 decrease in price, 3 more televisions will be sold each week. The relation for revenue can be represented by the relation $R = 7920 + 960x - 60x^2$ where R is the total revenue in dollars and x is the number of times the price is decreased by $20.

   a) Find the maximum revenue.

   b) Find the price per television to maximize revenue.

Volume and Surface Area

Storage tanks are used in many industries. Frank works for a gravel quarry. He has to oversee the construction of new storage tanks for various grades of gravel and sand. Sheila is supervising the sandblasting and painting of the water tower in her city. What information do Frank and Sheila need in order to do their jobs?

In this chapter, you will calculate the surface area and volume of a variety of three-dimensional objects, using both metric and imperial units of measure.

In this chapter, you will

- use the imperial system when solving measurement problems
- perform everyday conversions between the imperial and metric systems and within these systems as necessary to solve problems involving measurement
- determine, through investigation, the formula for calculating the surface area of a pyramid
- solve problems involving the surface areas of prisms, pyramids, and cylinders, and the volumes of prisms, pyramids, cones, and spheres, including problems involving combinations of these figures, using the metric system or the imperial system, as appropriate

Reasoning and Proving

Representing   Selecting Tools

Problem Solving

Connecting   Reflecting

Communicating

Key Terms

cone	prism	sphere	volume
cylinder	pyramid	surface area	

Literacy Link

As you work through this chapter, create a Discussion Chart that summarizes the main ideas of each section. At the end of the chapter, review the main ideas by comparing your version with a partner.

Volume and Surface Area

A computer graphic artist has expertise in manipulating shapes on a computer to develop a design and layout. What skills do you think a computer graphic artist would use?

Get Ready!

Pythagorean Theorem

1. For each right triangle, find the length of the indicated side to the nearest tenth of a unit. The first part has been done for you.

a)

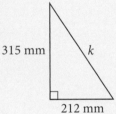

The length of one leg is 1 in. and the length of the hypotenuse is 6 in.

$1^2 + b^2 = 6^2$

$1 + b^2 = 36$

$b^2 = 36 - 1$

$b^2 = 35$

$b = \sqrt{35}$

$b \doteq 5.9$ in.

b)

315 mm
k
212 mm

c)

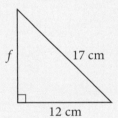

f
17 cm
12 cm

d)

d
7.2 m
3.5 m

e)

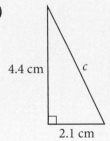

4.4 cm
c
2.1 cm

f)

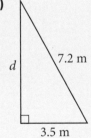

7.3 cm
x

g)

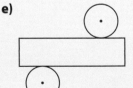

4.6 mm
p

Nets

2. For each net, identify the solid. The first part has been done for you.

a)

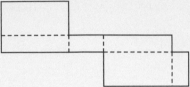

The net has three pairs of congruent rectangular faces. It is a net for a rectangular prism, or box.

b)

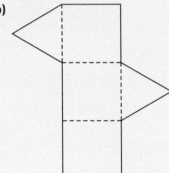

c)

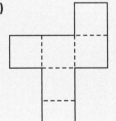

d)

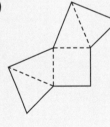

e)

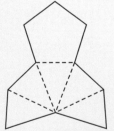

f)

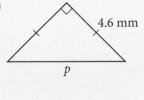

Chapter Problem

Consumers often decide whether to purchase an item based on the way it is packaged. Manufacturers devote a large number of resources to finding the best way to package their merchandise. Vanessa's new company manufactures and markets ski, skateboard, and snowboard accessories. She needs to design the packaging for her products. Vanessa plans to sell her products in both Canada and the United States. What does Vanessa need to consider as she designs packaging for her products?

Convert Measurements

3. Convert each measure to the unit indicated. The first part has been done for you.

a) 3.5 yd   feet

There are 3 ft in 1 yd.

So, 3.5 yd = 3.5 × 3, or 10.5 ft.

b) 241 cm   metres

c) 7.5 L   millilitres

d) 5.5 gallons   pints

e) 21 yd³   cubic feet

f) 1175.4 cm²   square metres

Area

4. Find the area of each figure.

a)

4 cm
8 cm

$A = l \times w$
$= 4 \times 8$
$= 32$

The area of the rectangle is 32 cm².

b)

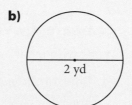

2 yd

c)

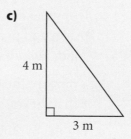

4 m
3 m

d)

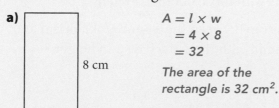

3 cm
3 cm
5 cm
11 cm

9.1 Volume of Prisms and Pyramids

When planning the heating and ventilation systems for a building, it is important to know the volume of air inside the building.

Tools

- nets of a prism and a pyramid with congruent bases and equal heights
- ruler
- sand
- scissors
- sheet of clear acetate
- tape

prism
- a solid with base and top faces that are congruent, parallel polygons
- all other faces are parallelograms

pyramid
- a solid with a polygon base
- all other faces are triangles

volume
- the amount of space occupied by an object
- measured in cubic units

Compare the Volume of a Prism and a Pyramid

Work with a partner.

1. Look at the nets for the **prism** and the **pyramid**. Identify and label the bases. How did you know which faces to label?

2. Copy the nets onto clear acetate. Then, cut out the nets for the prism and pyramid. Carefully fold and tape each net to form a solid. Do not tape the edges along the base.

3. Compare the bases and heights of the prism and the pyramid. What do you notice?

4. Fill the pyramid with sand. Pour the sand from the pyramid into the prism. Repeat until the prism is full. How many times did you have to do this?

5. Compare your results with those of other students.

6. Describe the relationship between the **volume** of a prism and the volume of a pyramid with the same base and height.

Example 1 Volume of a Square Prism

A candle is in the form of a square-based prism.

How much wax is needed to make the candle?

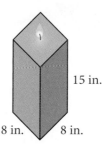

15 in.

8 in. 8 in.

Solution

To find the amount of wax needed, calculate the volume of the candle.

Find the area of the base. *Remember that the volume of a prism is found by multiplying the area of the base by the height.*

$A = s^2$
$\quad = 8^2$
$\quad = 64$

Find the volume.

$V = \text{area of base} \times \text{height}$
$\quad = 64 \times 15$
$\quad = 960$

The volume of wax needed to make the candle is 960 in.^{3}.

Example 2 Find the Volume of Air in a Greenhouse

Mohammed is planning to build a greenhouse in the shape of a rectangular pyramid. The dimensions of the floor are 12 ft by 18 ft and the height is 16 ft. The volume of air in the greenhouse will determine what type of ventilation system he should install. Find the volume of air in the greenhouse.

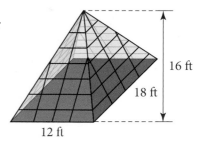

16 ft

18 ft

12 ft

Solution

The volume of a rectangular pyramid is one third the volume of a rectangular prism with the same base and height.

$V = \frac{1}{3}\,\text{area of base} \times \text{height}$
$\quad = \frac{1}{3} \times (12 \times 18) \times 16$
$\quad = 1152$

The volume of air in the greenhouse is 1152 ft^3.

Example **3**

Find the Volume of Space in a Tent

A tent is in the shape of an equilateral triangular prism.

How much space is there inside the tent?

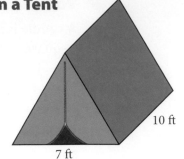

10 ft

7 ft

Solution

Volume is a measure of the amount of space. To find the volume, find the area of a triangular face (the base of the prism) and multiply by the length.

Find the height of the tent.
Each side of the triangle measures 7 ft.

Use the Pythagorean theorem to find the height of the triangle.

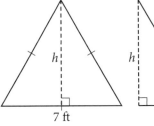

h h 7 ft

7 ft   3.5 ft

$$3.5^2 + h^2 = 7^2$$
$$h^2 = 7^2 - 3.5^2$$
$$h^2 = 36.75$$
$$h = \sqrt{36.75}$$
$$h \doteq 6$$

Find the area of the triangular face.
The base of the triangle is 7 ft and the height is approximately 6 ft.

$$A = \frac{1}{2}bh$$
$$= \frac{1}{2}(7)(6)$$
$$= 21$$

Find the volume of the tent.

$$V = \text{area of base} \times \text{height}$$
$$= 21 \times 10$$
$$= 210$$

There is approximately 210 ft^3 of space inside the tent.

Key Concepts

- The volume of an object is the amount of space occupied by the object.
- Volume is measured in cubic units.
- To find the volume of a prism, multiply the area of the base by the height of the prism.
- The volume of a pyramid is one third the volume of a prism with the same base and height.

Discuss the Concepts

D1. Gundeep calculates the volume of a rectangular prism with width 5 cm, height 4 cm, and length 8 cm to be 160 cm². What is his mistake?

D2. Isaac says that to find the volume of this triangular prism, he needs to use the Pythagorean theorem to find the height of the triangular face. Is Isaac correct? Explain why or why not.

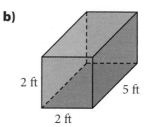

100 cm

35 cm

25 cm

Practise the Concepts **A**

For help with question 1, refer to Example 1.

1. Find the volume of each prism.

a)

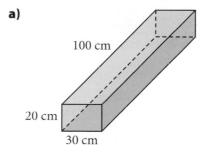

100 cm

20 cm

30 cm

b)

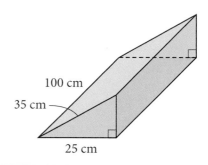

2 ft

5 ft

2 ft

c)

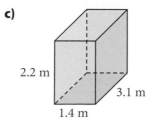

2.2 m

3.1 m

1.4 m

d)

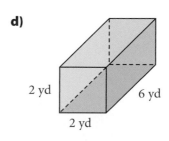

2 yd

6 yd

2 yd

2. Find the volume of each prism.

a)

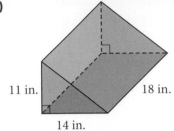

11 in.   18 in.

14 in.

b)

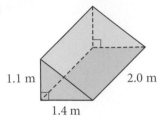

1.1 m   2.0 m

1.4 m

For help with question 3, refer to Example 2.

3. Find the volume of each pyramid.

a)

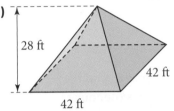

28 ft

42 ft

42 ft

b)

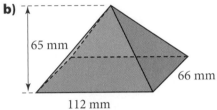

65 mm

66 mm

112 mm

c)

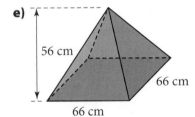

36 yd

30 yd

30 yd

d)

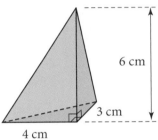

6 cm

3 cm

4 cm

e)

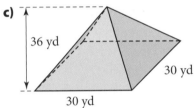

56 cm

66 cm

66 cm

f)

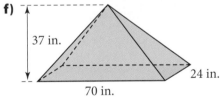

37 in.

24 in.

70 in.

For help with question 4, refer to Example 3.

4. Find the volume of each triangular prism.

a)

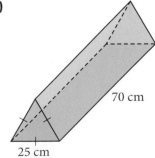

70 cm

25 cm

b)

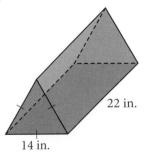

22 in.

14 in.

c)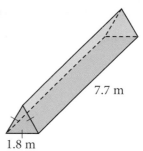

7 ft

2 ft

d)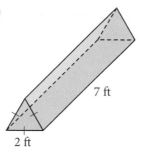

7.7 m

1.8 m

5. Find the volume of each prism.

a)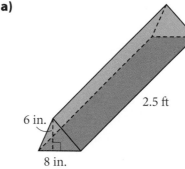

2.5 ft

6 in.

8 in.

b)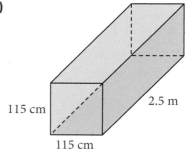

115 cm

2.5 m

115 cm

c)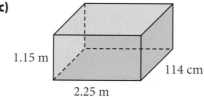

1.15 m

114 cm

2.25 m

6. Find the volume of each square-based pyramid.

a)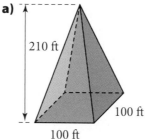

210 ft

100 ft

100 ft

b)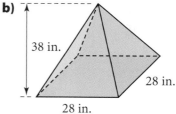

38 in.

28 in.

28 in.

Apply the Concepts B

7. Which has the greater volume, a rectangular prism with length 3", width 4" and height 5", or a cube with edges 4" long?

Literacy Connect

8. The most efficient way to package something is to leave very little space between the item and the package, so you can load the maximum number of items on a truck without a lot of wasted space. Think about buying a computer, television, or other piece of electronic equipment. Work with a partner to suggest some reasons for the way in which these items are packaged. Record your work.

Chapter Problem

9. Vanessa is deciding on packaging for her ski and snowboard goggles. She has narrowed the design of the box down to these possibilities:

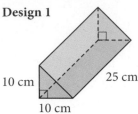

Design 1

10 cm
10 cm
25 cm

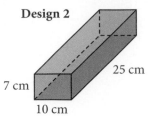

Design 2

7 cm
10 cm
25 cm

Reasoning and Proving

Representing | Selecting Tools

Problem Solving

Connecting | Reflecting

Communicating

a) Which package would be more efficient to ship and to store? Explain.
b) Which package would be more appealing to consumers? Why?
c) Which package should Vanessa use? Why?

10. Pharaoh Khufu's pyramid is one of the Pyramids of Giza in Egypt. It was built of limestone and granite in about 2566 B.C.E. Over time, some of the stone has worn away. The length of the square base was originally 754 ft, but is now 745 ft. The height of the pyramid was originally 481 ft, but is now 449 ft.

a) Find the volume of stone in the pyramid originally.
b) Find the volume of stone in the pyramid now.
c) What volume of stone has worn away?

11. A polymer resin is to be mixed in a rectangular container with length 100 cm, width 25 cm, and depth 20 cm. The resin will be poured into a rectangle-based pyramid mould with dimensions 15 cm by 20 cm at the base and height 300 cm.

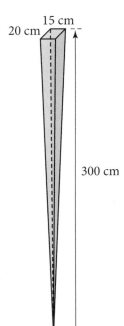

15 cm
20 cm
300 cm

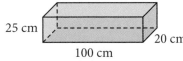

25 cm
100 cm
20 cm

a) Find the volume of the rectangular container.
b) Find the volume of the mould.
c) Is the rectangular container large enough to mix the resin for the mould? Explain.

12. Drew is buying groceries. He wants to buy some cheese, but he is not sure which size to get. The supermarket sells wedges of cheese in three sizes.

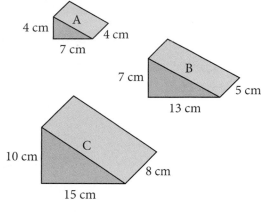

a) Find the volume of cheese in each wedge.

b) Suppose cheese wedge A costs $3.50, B costs $4.75, and C costs $6.50. Which is the best buy? Explain and justify your answer.

Extend the Concepts C

13. Three identical square-based pyramids are to be created by cutting a rectangular piece of foam that is 4 ft by 4 ft by 12 ft as shown. The base of each pyramid has side length 4 ft and height 4 ft.

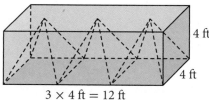

What volume of material is used in creating the three pyramids?

14. Discuss the effects that making the following changes would have on the volume of a rectangular prism with length l, width w, and height h.

a) The length and width are both doubled.

b) The height increases by a factor of three and the width decreases to one third of its original value.

c) All three measurements are doubled.

d) The length triples and the height and width decrease to half of their original values.

e) What would be the effect on the volume of a rectangular prism if its length were to triple in value? Explain your answer.

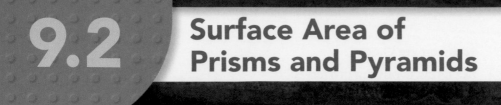

9.2

Surface Area of Prisms and Pyramids

A protective epoxy coating is being sprayed on the walls and floor of a new warehouse. How would you determine how much epoxy is required to complete the job?

Investigate

Tools

- grid paper
- ruler

How Much Wrapping Paper Is Needed?

Suppose you are wrapping a gift. The gift is packaged in a square-based pyramid. Each face is an equilateral triangle. Estimate the amount of wrapping paper needed to wrap the gift.

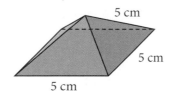

5 cm

5 cm

5 cm

1. On grid paper, draw a net of the pyramid. Label each face with its dimensions.

2. Find the area of each of the faces. Do you need to calculate the area of each triangular face? Why or why not?

surface area
- the total area of the surface of an object
- measured in square units

3. The **surface area** is the total area of the surface of an object. Find the surface area of the gift.

4. Is the amount of wrapping paper needed equal to the surface area of the gift? Why or why not?

5. Explain why it is also necessary to consider the dimensions of the wrapping paper.

Example **1** **Surface Area of a Rectangular Prism**

What is the least amount of wrapping paper needed to wrap this box?

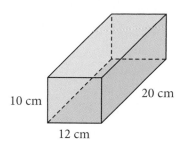

Solution

Sketch and label a net of the box.

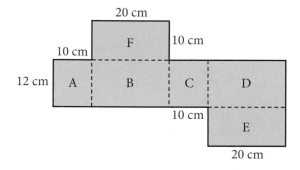

Faces A and C have dimensions 12 cm by 10 cm.
Area $= 12 \times 10$
     $= 120$

Faces B and D have dimensions 12 cm by 20 cm.
Area $= 12 \times 20$
     $= 240$

Faces E and F have dimensions 10 cm by 20 cm.
Area $= 10 \times 20$
     $= 200$

Add the areas of the faces.
Surface Area $= 2(120) + 2(240) + 2(200)$
            $= 1120$

To allow for overlap, more than 1120 cm^2 of wrapping paper is needed to wrap this box.

Example **2** **Surface Area of a Square-Based Pyramid**

The smallest of the three Pyramids of Giza in Egypt is the tomb of Pharaoh Menkaure, believed to be Pharaoh Khufu's grandson. The square base of this pyramid has length 344 ft and a slant height of 266 ft. What area of Menkaure's pyramid is exposed to the weather?

Solution

The base of the pyramid is not exposed to the weather.

Find the surface area of each triangular face. Each face has base 344 ft and height 266 ft.

$$A = \frac{1}{2}(344)(266)$$
$$= 45\ 752$$

There are four congruent triangular faces.

Exposed Surface Area $= 4(45\ 752)$
$$= 183\ 008$$

The exposed surface area of Menkaure's pyramid is 183 008 sq ft.

Example **3** **Surface Area of a Rectangular Pyramid**

The base of a rectangular prism has dimensions 8 cm by 6 cm. Its height is 5 cm. Find the surface area of this pyramid.

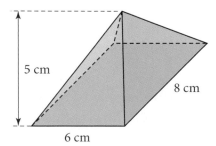

5 cm

8 cm

6 cm

Solution

Find the heights of the triangular
faces, which are the slant heights
of the pyramid.

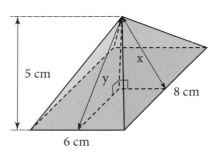

5 cm

6 cm

8 cm

$$x^2 = \left(\frac{6}{2}\right)^2 + 5^2 \qquad y^2 = \left(\frac{8}{2}\right)^2 + 5^2$$
$$x^2 = 9 + 25 \qquad y^2 = 16 + 25$$
$$x^2 = 34 \qquad y^2 = 41$$
$$x \doteq 5.8 \qquad y \doteq 6.4$$

Sketch a net of this pyramid.

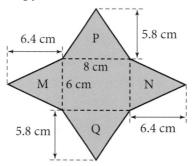

6.4 cm   P   5.8 cm

8 cm

M 6 cm N

5.8 cm   Q   6.4 cm

Find the areas of the pairs of congruent triangular faces.

Faces M and N are congruent.

$$A = 2\left(\frac{1}{2}\right)(6)(6.4)$$
$$= 38.4$$

Faces P and Q are congruent.

$$A = 2\left(\frac{1}{2}\right)(8)(5.8)$$
$$= 46.4$$

*Since there are two congruent faces,
the area of both faces together is
double the area of one of the faces.*

Find the area of the rectangular face.

$$A = 6 \times 8$$
$$= 48$$

Add the areas to find the surface area.

$$SA = 48 + 46.4 + 38.4$$
$$= 132.8$$

The surface area of this rectangular prism is 132.8 cm².

Key Concepts

- The surface area of an object is the total area of the surface of the object.
- Surface area is measured in square units.
- To find the surface area of a prism or pyramid, find the area of each face, then add the areas.

Discuss the Concepts

D1. Explain the difference between the height of a pyramid and its slant height.

D2. Suppose you know the side length of the base of a square-based pyramid and its height. Explain how you can find the slant height.

Practise the Concepts A

Where necessary, round your answers to one decimal place.

For help with question 1, refer to Example 1.

1. For each prism, draw and label a net, then find the surface area.

a)

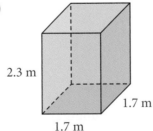

11 in. 26 in.
14 in.

b)

4 yd   8 yd
2 yd

c)

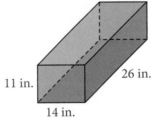

2.3 m
1.7 m
1.7 m

d)

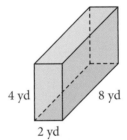

8 cm   22 cm
16 cm

e)

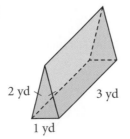

2 yd   3 yd
1 yd

f)

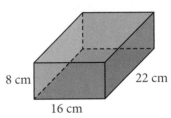

22 cm
22 cm   25 cm

For help with question 2, refer to Example 2.

2. For each square-based pyramid, draw and label a net, then find the surface area.

a)

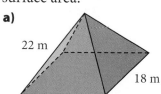

22 m

18 m

18 m

b)

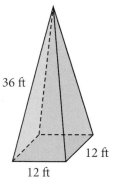

36 ft

12 ft

12 ft

c)

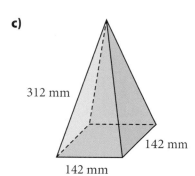

312 mm

142 mm

142 mm

d)

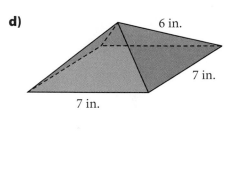

6 in.

7 in.

7 in.

For help with questions 3 and 4, refer to Example 3.

3. Find the surface area of each square-based pyramid.

a)

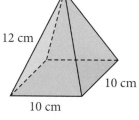

12 cm

10 cm

10 cm

b)

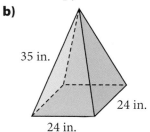

35 in.

24 in.

24 in.

c)

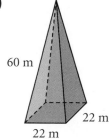

60 m

22 m

22 m

d)

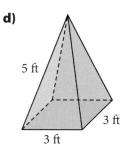

5 ft

3 ft

3 ft

4. Find the surface area of each rectangular-based pyramid.

a)

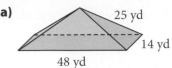

25 yd
14 yd
48 yd

b)

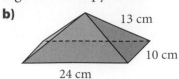

13 cm
10 cm
24 cm

c)

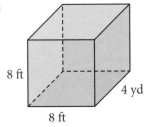

10 m
12 m
16 m

d)

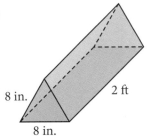

7 in.
5 in.
4 in.

5. Find the surface area of each prism.

a)

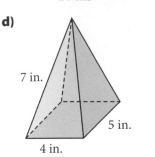

8 ft
4 yd
8 ft

b)

8 in.
2 ft
8 in.

6. Winnie is spraying a sealant on the concrete floor and walls in her basement. The basement floor is rectangular with dimensions 30' by 34' and the walls are 8' high. For what area does Winnie need to buy sealant?

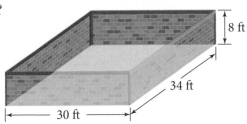

8 ft
34 ft
30 ft

Reasoning and Proving

Representing   Selecting Tools

Problem Solving

Connecting   Reflecting

Communicating

7. Which has greater surface area, a right triangular prism with a base and height of 5 cm and a length of 22 cm, or an isosceles triangular prism with a base of 6 cm, a side length of the triangle of 4 cm, and a length of 22 cm?

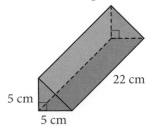

22 cm
5 cm
5 cm

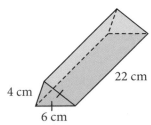

22 cm
4 cm
6 cm

8. The Louvre Museum in Paris, France, has a large square-based glass pyramid covering its main entrance. Each triangle on the slant surfaces has a base that measures 35.4 m and a slant height of 27.9 m.

   a) Calculate the amount of glass that was needed to cover the sides of this pyramid.

   b) A glass cleaner charges 32¢/m². How much will they charge to clean the outside of these windows?

Literacy Connect

9. Suppose a doghouse is constructed by placing a square-based pyramid on top of a cube with the same side length as the square base of the pyramid. Draw a diagram, and then explain how you would determine the total surface area of the doghouse that would need to be painted.

10. The cost to make the top of a rectangular container is 5¢/in.² and for all other sides is 4¢/in.² How much will it cost to make the rectangular box below?

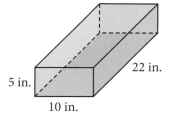

Chapter Problem

11. Vanessa has decided to package her winter toques for the United States in a package created using two square-based pyramids of side length 6 in. One of these pyramids will have height 5 in. while the second will have height 3 in. The toque will be placed between these two pyramids. The idea is to market the toque in a unique package that will also be stackable and easy to display on a shelf.

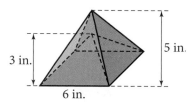

   a) Find the surface area of each pyramid. Each pyramid has an open base, so they will stack.

   b) The material used to make the outer pyramid costs 25¢/in.² and the material used to make the inner pyramid costs 21¢/in.² Find the total cost to produce each package.

12. A storage shed in the shape of an isosceles triangular prism is to be painted. The paint is sold in cans that each cover 40 m² and cost $16.50. How much will it cost to give the shed two coats of the paint?

You will not need to paint the bottom side of the prism.

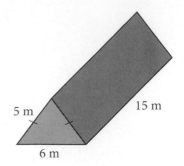

5 m

15 m

6 m

Extend the Concepts   C

13. Suppose someone wanted to cover the surface of Menkaure's pyramid with a 10 cm layer of plaster.

a) How many cubic metres of plaster would be needed? Ignore the slight change to the dimensions a 10 cm layer of plaster would create on the pyramid, and assume its surface to be relatively flat.

b) If the cost of plaster is $114/m³, what would the total cost of the plaster be?

c) If a worker can place 15 m³ of plaster per day, how many workers would be needed if the project were to be completed in 50 working days?

14. The height of a square-based pyramid is 6 cm and its slant height is 8 cm.

a) Calculate the dimensions of the base.

b) Find the volume of the pyramid.

c) Find the surface area of the pyramid.

15. Pyramids A, B, and C are each in the shape of square-based pyramids with height 12 cm. The base of pyramid A has side length 5 cm and the base of pyramid B has side length 9 cm. The volume of pyramid C is equal to the total volume of pyramids A and B. Find the side length of the base of pyramid C.

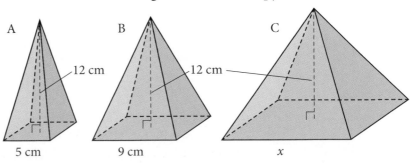

A

12 cm

5 cm

B

12 cm

9 cm

C

x

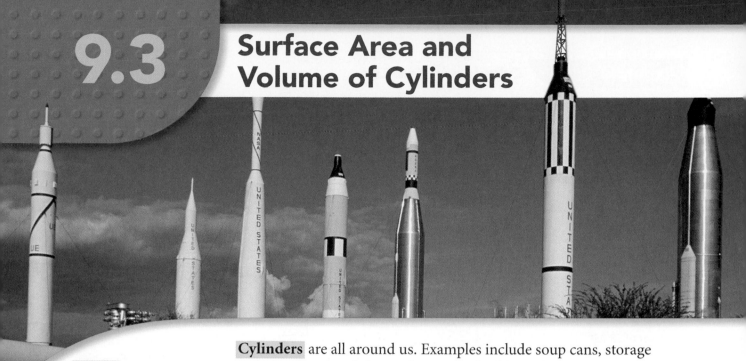

9.3

Surface Area and Volume of Cylinders

cylinder
- a three-dimensional object
- has two parallel circular bases

Cylinders are all around us. Examples include soup cans, storage tanks, architectural design features in buildings, large smoke stacks, and even rockets! Cylinders are relatively easy to manufacture, and they are efficient—a cylinder requires less material to make than a rectangular prism with the same height and volume.

Investigate

Tools
- paper tube
- scissors

Surface Area of a Cylinder

1. Trace one end of the paper tube on a sheet of paper.
   a) Measure the diameter of the circle.
   b) Measure and record the height of the tube.

2. Cut the tube lengthwise.
   Spread it out to form a rectangle.

3. Describe how the width of the rectangle is related to the height of the cylinder.

4. How is the length of the rectangle related to the cylinder? How could you use the diameter of the cylinder to determine the length of the rectangle?

5. Find the dimensions and the area of the rectangle.

6. Suppose the paper tube was closed at each end.
   a) What would the area of each circular face be?
   b) What would the surface area of the paper tube be?

7. **Reflect** How can you use circles and rectangles to find the surface area of a cylinder?

Example	1	**Cylinders in Real Life**

A soup can has radius 4.3 cm and height 11.5 cm.
  a) How much metal is needed to make the can?
  b) How much soup will the can hold?

Solution

  a) Find the surface area to determine the amount of metal
    needed to make the can.
    Sketch a net of the can.

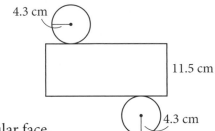

Find the area of a circular face.
$$A = \pi r^2$$
$$= \pi(4.3)^2$$
$$\doteq 58.088$$

Find the length of the rectangle.

$$l = C \qquad$$ *The length of the rectangle is equal to*
$$l = 2\pi r \qquad$$ *the circumference of the circular faces.*
$$= 2\pi(4.3)$$
$$\doteq 27.018$$

Find the area of the rectangle.
$$A = l \times w$$
$$= 27.018 \times 11.5$$
$$= 310.707$$

Find the surface area of the can.

$$SA = 2(58.088) + 310.707 \qquad$$ *The area of the two circular faces*
$$\doteq 321.883 \qquad$$ *together is double the area of*
one of the faces.

Approximately 321.9 cm² of metal will be used to make the
soup can.

  b) Find the volume to determine how much soup the
    can will hold.
$$V = \text{area of base} \times \text{height}$$
$$= 58.088 \times 11.5$$
$$\doteq 668.012$$

The soup can will hold approximately 668 cm³, or 668 mL of soup.

Example   2

Surface Area and Volume of a Cylinder

Find the surface area and volume of a cylinder with a radius of 18 in. and a height of 2 ft.

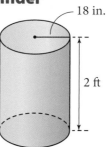

18 in.

2 ft

Solution

Convert all units to feet. Since there are 12 in., 1 ft, 18 in., is 1.5 ft.

$$SA = 2\pi r^2 + 2\pi rh$$
$$= 2\pi(1.5)^2 + 2\pi(1.5)(2)$$
$$\doteq 14.137 + 18.850$$
$$\doteq 32.987$$

The area of the circular faces is given by $2\pi r^2$, and the area of the rectangle is given by $2\pi rh$.

The surface area is approximately 33 ft^2.

$$V = \pi r^2 h$$
$$= \pi(1.5)^2(2)$$
$$\doteq 14.137$$

The volume is approximately 14 ft^3.

Example   3

Cylinder Within a Cylinder

The padding around the support posts of a mesh enclosure for a trampoline is in the shape of a cylinder that has been hollowed out by removing a smaller cylinder. The height of the padding is 6 ft. Each piece has an outer radius of 4 in. and an inner radius of 2 in. Find the volume of one piece of foam padding.

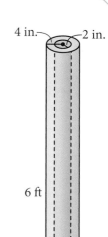

4 in.   2 in.

6 ft

Solution

Find the volume of a cylinder with radius 4 in. and height 6 ft (or 72 in.).

$$V = \pi r^2 h$$
$$= \pi(4)^2(72)$$
$$\doteq 3619.114$$

Volume is area of base multiplied by height. πr^2 represents the area of the base, and h represents the height.

Find the volume of a cylinder with radius 2 in. and height 6 ft (or 72 in.).

$$V = \pi r^2 h$$
$$= \pi(2)^2(72)$$
$$\doteq 904.779$$

Subtract the volume of the smaller cylinder from the volume of the larger cylinder to find the volume of foam.

$$= 3619.114 - 904.779$$
$$\doteq 2714.335$$

The volume of the foam padding is approximately 2714 in.^{3}

Example 4 Build Storage Tanks

A company that manufactures large volumes of liquid detergent needs a new cylindrical storage tank. The tank must hold 3320 m^3 of detergent.

a) If the tank is to have height 25 m, what diameter would be needed?

b) There must be a minimum of 3 m between tanks. How many storage tanks could be built on a rectangular field with dimensions 70 m by 140 m?

Solution

a) The volume of a cylinder is the area of the base times the height. The volume is 3320 m^3, and the height is 25 m. Find the area of the base.

$$V = \text{area of base} \times \text{height}$$
$$3320 = \text{area of base} \times 25$$
$$\text{area of base} = \frac{3320}{25}$$
$$\text{area of base} = 132.8$$

Find the radius of a circle with area 132.8 m^2.

$$A = \pi r^2$$
$$132.8 = \pi r^2$$
$$r^2 = \frac{132.8}{\pi}$$
$$r^2 \doteq 42.0169$$
$$r \doteq \sqrt{42.0169}$$
$$r \doteq 6.5$$

Therefore, the diameter of the tank is approximately 2 × 6.5 m, or 13 m.

Silos are structures for storing large quantities of grain or fermented feed, called silage. Silos are also sometimes used to store coal, cement, wood chips, or sawdust.

b) The diameter of each storage tank is 13 m. Since there must be 3 m between tanks, each storage tank can be thought of as needing a square area of land that is 16 m by 16 m.

Find the number of storage tanks that would fit along the width of the field.

$$\frac{70}{16} = 4.375$$

Therefore, 4 tanks could fit across the width of the field.

Find the number of storage tanks that would fit along the length of the field.

$$\frac{140}{16} = 8.75$$

Therefore, 8 tanks could fit across the length of the field.

This means that a total of 4×8, or 32 storage tanks could be built on the field.

Key Concepts

- The surface area of a cylinder is the sum of the areas of the two circular ends and the curved side.

- The surface area of a cylinder can be found using the formula $SA = 2\pi r^2 + 2\pi rh$.

- The volume of a cylinder is the area of the circular base times the height of the cylinder.

- The volume of a cylinder can be found using the formula $V = \pi r^2 h$.

- Surface area is measured in square units and volume is measured in cubic units.

Discuss the Concepts

D1. A cylinder has radius 30 in. and height 4 ft. Simone calculates the volume to be 135 716.8 in.^{3}, while her friend Nyomi calculates the volume to be 78.5 ft^3.

    a) Is it possible that both girls are correct? Explain.

    b) Who is correct? Justify your answer.

D2. a) Describe a situation in which using 3.14 to approximate the value of π is acceptable.

    b) Describe a situation in which it would be important to use the π key on a scientific calculator.

D3. A cylinder has radius 25 cm and height 150 cm. Suppose the height of the cylinder is doubled. How can you determine the effect on the volume of the cylinder?

For help with question 1, refer to Example 1.

1. Find the surface area and the volume of each cylinder.

a)

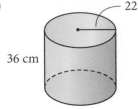
36 cm · 22 cm

b)

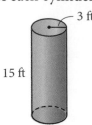
3 ft · 15 ft

c)

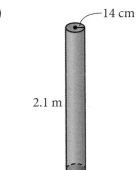
1.2 m · 2.2 m

d)

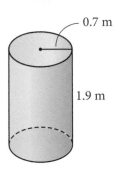
0.7 m · 1.9 m

For help with questions 2 and 3, refer to Example 2.

2. Find the surface area of each cylinder.

a)

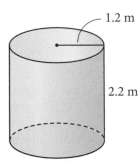
14 cm · 2.1 m

b)

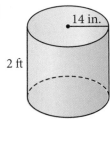
14 in. · 2 ft

c)

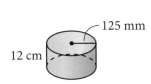
125 mm · 12 cm

d)

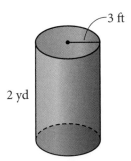
3 ft · 2 yd

3. Find the volume of each cylinder.

a)

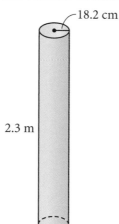

18.2 cm

2.3 m

b)

6.25 in.

3.5 ft

c)

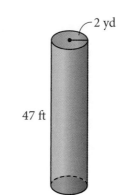

2 yd

47 ft

d)

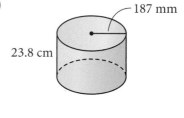

187 mm

23.8 cm

Apply the Concepts **B**

For help with question 4, refer to Example 3.

4. A cylindrical copper bolt sleeve is made
by drilling out the centre of a cylindrical
piece of copper. The diameter of the piece
of copper is 1.2 cm and the diameter of the
hole is 1 cm. The length of the piece of
copper is 14 cm.

a) Find the total volume of the copper bolt
sleeve and the hole.

b) Find the volume of the hole in the
bolt sleeve.

c) Find the amount of copper that is in
the sleeve.

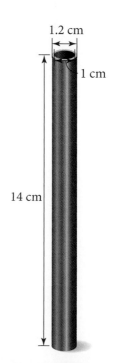

1.2 cm

1 cm

14 cm

5. Find the amount of material needed to make this hollow cylinder.

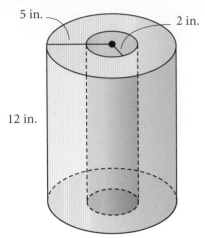

5 in.

2 in.

12 in.

For help with questions 6 to 8, refer to Example 4.

6. A cylinder has volume 425 cm^3 and height 22 cm. Find the radius of the cylinder to the nearest tenth of a centimetre.

7. A cylinder with radius 14 in. has volume 267.3 in.^{3}. Find the height of the cylinder to the nearest tenth of an inch.

8. A log with a uniform diameter of 26 cm is cut into 27 equal pieces, each with height 35 cm. The pieces are then to be painted on all surfaces.
a) Find the surface area of one piece.
b) What is the total area to be painted?

9. A building is in the shape of a cylinder with a radius of 30 m. The height of each floor is 3.4 m. The mechanical engineer needs to determine the volume of air the building will contain to help design the air exchange system. If there are 22 floors in the building, how much air is contained within the building?

10. A paint can is marked as containing 972 mL of paint. The can has a diameter of 10.6 cm and a height of 11.4 cm.
a) Find the volume of the can in cubic centimetres.
b) 1 cm^3 = 1 mL. Will 972 mL of paint fit in the can? How do you know?
c) Work with a partner. Why would the volume of the paint in the can not be 1000 mL or 1 L?

11. Vanessa plans to market replacement skateboard wheels in a tube by stacking four wheels inside a clear plastic cylinder that is slightly taller and wider than the wheels. Each wheel has diameter 5.4 cm and is 2.1 cm thick. The plastic to make the cylinder costs 35¢/cm². Suppose she designs the container so the radius of the cylinder is 0.8 mm greater than the radius of the wheel and the height is 0.1 cm greater than the height of a stack of four wheels.

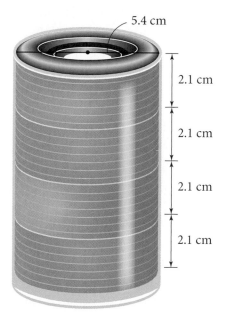

5.4 cm

2.1 cm

2.1 cm

2.1 cm

2.1 cm

a) What are the dimensions of the tube?

b) What is the surface area of one tube?

c) Find the cost to produce 10 000 tubes.

12. Work with a partner. You will each need a piece of paper with dimensions 8.5" by 11". Roll your piece of paper along the width to form a cylinder with the greatest possible diameter. Your partner rolls the other piece of paper along its length to form a cylinder with the greatest possible diameter. Which cylinder has greater volume? Justify your answer.

Literacy Connect

13. A cylinder will hold a maximum volume for a given surface area if the height of the cylinder is twice the radius. Suggest some reasons why manufacturers do not usually make cylindrical containers with these dimensions.

Extend the Concepts

14. A cylinder for storing refined gasoline has diameter 50 m and height 20 m. To save ground space, the company decides to redesign their storage tanks so that a tank will hold the same volume, but the height will be double its present value.

a) What will be the new diameter of a storage tank?

b) How much ground space is saved by using the new design?

Math Connect

Do you need more practice finding the surface area of cylinders? Go to www.mcgrawhill.ca /links/ foundations10 and follow the links.

15. Work in groups. A cylinder has radius r and height h. Describe how the volume would change in each case.

a) r remains unchanged and h doubles.

b) The radius increases by a factor of 3 while the height remains unchanged.

c) The radius remains unchanged and the height decreases to one third its original value.

d) Both r and h are doubled.

e) The radius increases by a factor of 4 while the height decreases to one quarter of its original value.

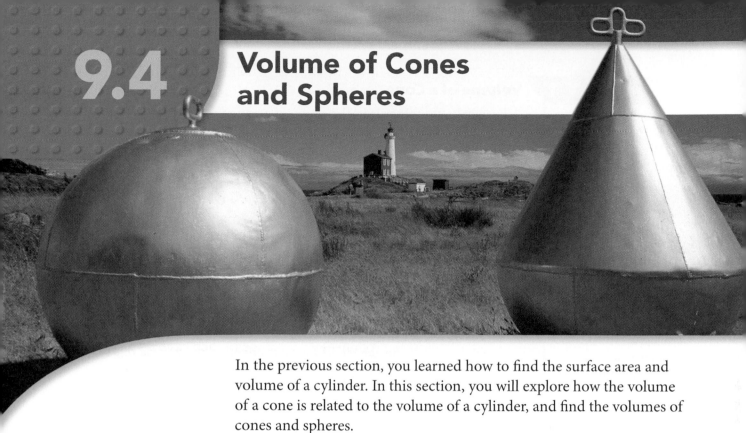

9.4 Volume of Cones and Spheres

In the previous section, you learned how to find the surface area and volume of a cylinder. In this section, you will explore how the volume of a cone is related to the volume of a cylinder, and find the volumes of cones and spheres.

Investigate

Tools

- nets of a cylinder and a cone
- ruler
- sand
- scissors
- sheet of clear acetate
- tape

cone

- a three-dimensional object with a circular base and a curved side surface that tapers to a point

Compare the Volume of a Cylinder and a Cone

Work with a partner.

1. Look at the nets for the cylinder and the **cone**. Identify and label the bases. How did you know which faces to label?

2. Copy the nets onto a sheet of clear acetate. Then, cut out the nets for the cone and the cylinder. Carefully tape each net to form a solid. Do not tape the bases in place.

3. Compare the bases and heights of the cylinder and the cone. What do you notice?

4. Fill the cone with sand. Pour the sand from the cone into the cylinder. Repeat until the cylinder is full. How many times did you have to do this?

5. Compare your results with those of other students.

6. Describe the relationship between the volume of a cylinder and the volume of a cone with the same base and height.

Example 1 — Volume of a Cone

A fireworks container is in the shape of a cone with height 14 cm and radius 4 cm. Find the volume of the container.

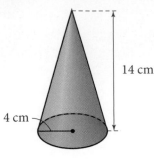

14 cm

4 cm

Solution

$$V = \frac{1}{3}\pi r^2 h$$

The volume of a cone is one-third the volume of a cylinder with the same base and height.

$$= \frac{1}{3}\pi(4)^2(14)$$

$$\doteq 234.572$$

The volume of the fireworks container is approximately 234.6 cm³.

---

sphere
- a three-dimensional ball-shaped object
- every point on the surface is an equal distance from a fixed point (the centre)

If you have ever taken a coin and spun it on its edge on a table, you have seen how a moving two-dimensional-like shape, such as the circle-shape of the coin, can create a three-dimensional image, such as a **sphere**. The diameter of the sphere would be the same as the diameter of the coin.

The formula for the volume of a sphere is $V = \frac{4}{3}\pi r^3$.

Example 2 — Volume of a Sphere

A beach ball has radius 0.25 m.
Find the volume of the beach ball.

Solution

$$V = \frac{4}{3}\pi r^3$$

$$= \frac{4}{3}\pi(0.25)^3$$

$$\doteq 0.065$$

The volume of the beach ball is approximately 0.07 m³.

Example **3** **Volume of a Cone and a Sphere**

An ice cream cone is made in the shape of a cone, and the scoop of ice cream is in the shape of a spherc (approximately). The radius of the scoop of ice cream is 4 cm and the radius of the cone is 3 cm. What cone height would be needed to hold half of the ice cream in one scoop?

Math Connect

Since $r = \dfrac{d}{2}$, you also can express the formula for volume of a sphere in terms of its diameter:

$$V = \frac{4}{3}\pi\left(\frac{d}{2}\right)^3$$

$$V = \frac{4}{3}\pi\frac{d^3}{8}$$

$$V = \frac{1}{6}\pi d^3$$

Solution

The volume of the cone must be one half the volume of the sphere. Find the volume of the sphere.

$$V = \frac{4}{3}\pi r^3$$

$$= \frac{4}{3}\pi(4)^3$$

$$\doteq 268.1$$

Half of this volume is $\dfrac{268.1}{2}$, or 134.05 cm^3.

The volume of the cone must be 134.05 cm^3.

Find the height of the cone.

$$V = \frac{1}{3}\pi r^2 h$$

$$134.05 = \frac{1}{3}\pi(3)^2 h$$

$$134.05 \doteq 9.425 \times h$$

$$\frac{134.05}{9.425} = h$$

$$14.2 \doteq h$$

The height of the cone would need to be approximately 14.2 cm.

Key Concepts

- The volume of a cone is one third the volume of a cylinder with the same base and height.
- The volume of a cone is given by the formula $V = \frac{1}{3}\pi r^2 h$.
- The volume of a sphere is given by the formula $V = \frac{4}{3}\pi r^3$ or $V = \frac{1}{6}\pi d^3$.

Discuss the Concepts

D1. The height of a cone is the vertical distance from the vertex to the base. The slant height is the distance from the vertex to the edge of the base. Suppose you know the slant height and radius of a cone. How would you calculate the height of the cone?

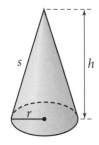

D2. Explain why two formulas were given for the volume of a sphere. How are the formulas the same? How are they different?

Practise the Concepts A

For help with question 1, refer to Example 1.

1. Find the volume of each cone. Round your answers to the nearest tenth of a unit.

a)

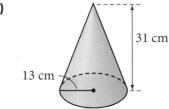

31 cm
13 cm

b)

8 in. 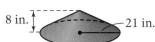 21 in.

c)

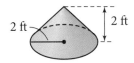

2 ft   2 ft

d)

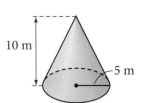

10 m
5 m

e)

35 mm   28 mm

f)

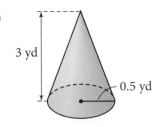

3 yd
0.5 yd

For help with question 2, refer to Example 2.

2. Find the volume of each sphere.

a)

3.2 m

b)

4 ft

c)

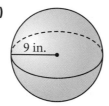

9 in.

d)

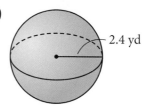

2.4 yd

e)

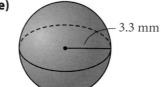

3.3 mm

f)

12.5 cm

For help with questions 3 and 4, refer to Example 3.

3. a) Find the volume of this cone.
 b) The volume of a sphere is one quarter the volume of this cone. Find the radius of the sphere.

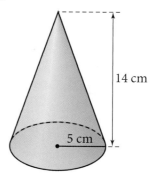

14 cm

5 cm

Apply the Concepts **B**

4. The radius of a sphere is 14 cm. The radius of a smaller sphere is 14 mm.
 a) Find the volume of each sphere.
 b) How many times larger is the volume of the larger sphere?

5. Find the volume of each ball.

a) 42 mm

b)  9 in.

c) 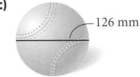 126 mm

d)  21 cm

6. A foam cube with side length 12" is to be shaped into the largest possible sphere.
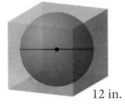
   a) Find the volume of the cube.
   b) What is the diameter of the largest possible sphere that can be made from this cube?
   c) Find the volume of the sphere.
   d) How much foam will be removed from the cube to form the sphere?

12 in.

Literacy Connect

7. Most round objects such as tennis balls and Ping-Pong balls are packaged in cylinders, rather than in spherical containers. Give some reasons as to why manufacturers do this.

Chapter Problem

8. Vanessa has decided to market her winter gloves in a plastic container that looks like a spherical snow globe. One tenth of the volume of the sphere will be removed to allow for flat upper and lower surfaces so the containers can be stacked on a shelf. The gloves have a volume of 860 cm³. Find the radius of the sphere.

Hint: 80% of $V = 860$

$$V = \frac{860}{0.80}$$

9. Measures for different cones are given in the table. Copy and complete the table. Show your work.

	Volume	Radius	Height
a)	227 cm³	27 mm	
b)	775 in.³		3 ft
c)	188 yd³	9 ft	
d)	56 m³		126 cm

10. A coffee scoop is in the shape of a cone with diameter 2.0 cm and height 2.5 cm. This scoop will be used to fill a coffee filter that is also in the shape of a cone. The filter has diameter 7.0 cm and height 12.2 cm. How many full scoops are needed to fill the coffee filter to 60% of its volume?

11. A glass jar in the shape of a cylinder with height 10 cm and radius 6 cm is to hold olives. Assuming that the olives are spheres with diameter 2 cm and that the jar is to hold 45 olives, how much liquid must be poured into each jar so that it is 95% full of olives and liquid?

12. Given each volume, find the radius of the sphere with this volume, to one decimal place.
  a) 125 cm³
  b) 2.2 yd³
  c) 2664 in.³
  d) 122 563 mm³

9.5 Solve Problems Involving Surface Area and Volume

Many objects are made up of combinations of prisms, pyramids, cylinders, cones, and/or spheres. In this section, you will find the surface area or volume of some everyday objects and some that are a little less common.

Investigate | **Surface Area and Volume of a Composite Solid**

To make a backyard hockey rink package, a company has developed a plastic bladder that can be filled with water. Once the water freezes, the top is removed to expose the ice. The bladder is made of high-strength plastic, and is filled with water to a depth of 4 in. The top and bottom surfaces are rectangular with rounded corners. The total length of the rink is 40 ft and the total width is 20 ft.

a) Describe the figures that form the surface of the ice. Find the area of the ice surface.

b) Which combination of objects make up the bladder? Find the surface area of plastic used in the bladder.

c) One cubic foot is equivalent to 7.48 gal. Suppose water pours out of a garden hose at a rate of 3 gal/min. How long will it take to fill the bladder?

d) The cost of the plastic material is 27¢/ft². Find the total cost of manufacturing the bladder.

Example **1** **Volume of a Pill Capsule**

A pill capsule is in the shape of a cylinder with half of a sphere (a hemisphere) on each end. The length of the cylindrical portion is 2 cm and the diameter is 3 mm. Find the volume of the capsule.

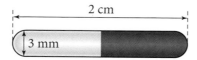

Solution

The pill capsule is a cylinder with two hemispheres, which are equivalent to a sphere.

$$V = V_{\text{cylinder}} + V_{\text{sphere}}$$

$$= \pi r^2 h + \frac{4}{3}\pi r^3$$

$$= \pi(0.15)^2(2) + \frac{4}{3}\pi(0.15)^3 \qquad \textit{Since } d = 0.3 \text{ cm}, r = 0.15 \text{ cm.}$$

$$\doteq 0.156$$

The volume of the pill capsule is approximately 0.16 cm³.

Example   **2**

Surface Area of a Barn

The exterior walls of a barn are to be painted. The barn is in the shape of a rectangular prism with an isosceles triangular prism for a roof.

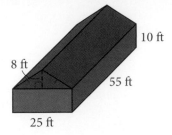

a) Find the total area to be painted.

b) The paint is sold in 1 gal cans. On the first coat of paint, a gallon of paint will cover an area of 400 ft². How many gallons of paint are needed for the first coat?

c) On the second coat of paint, a gallon will cover an area of 525 ft². How many gallons of paint are needed for both coats?

Solution

a) Sketch the walls that are to be painted.

Find the total area of the rectangular parts of the walls.
$$A = 2(55 \times 10) + 2(25 \times 10)$$
$$= 1600$$

Find the area of the triangular parts of the walls.
$$A = 2 \times \left(\frac{1}{2}\right)(25)(8)$$
$$= 200$$

Find the total area to be painted.
$$A = 1600 + 200$$
$$= 1800$$

An area of 1800 sq ft is to be painted.

b) Divide the total area by the area covered by each gallon of paint.
$$= \frac{1800}{400}$$
$$= 4.5$$

The barn will need 4.5 gal of paint for the first coat.

c) Find the amount of paint needed for the second coat.

$$= \frac{1800}{525}$$
$$= 3.4$$

Find the total amount of paint needed.

$$= 4.5 + 3.4$$
$$= 7.9$$

Five gallons of paint need to be purchased for the first coat, but there will be a half-gallon left over. Since 3.4 gallons are needed for the second coat, only 3 additional gallons need to be purchased.

Eight gallons of paint are needed.

Example **3** **Combination of a Rectangular Prism and a Cylinder**

A piece of wood is 8 in. wide, 2 ft long, and 1 in. high. Twelve holes, each with diameter 2 in. are drilled through the wood.
  a) Find the volume of the piece of wood before the holes are drilled.
  b) How much material is removed by the drill?

Solution

  a) Find the volume of the piece of wood.
$$V = l \times w \times h$$
$$= (24)(8)(1) \qquad \textit{Two feet is 24 in.}$$
$$= 192$$

The original volume of wood is 192 in³.

  b) Find the amount of wood removed for each hole.
Each hole is a cylinder with radius 1 in. and height 1 in.
For one hole,
$$V = \text{area of base} \times \text{height}$$
$$= \pi r^2 \times h$$
$$= \pi (1)^2 (1)$$
$$\doteq 3.14$$

Find the total amount of wood removed.

$$12 \times 3.14$$
$$= 37.68$$

The total amount of wood removed is approximately 37.68 in³.

Key Concepts

- When a figure is made up of a combination of shapes, use the appropriate formula for each shape to find the total required quantity.
- It is important to read questions carefully and to plan the steps of your solution.

Discuss the Concepts

D1. An inflatable toy has the shape of a small square-based pyramid on top of a rectangular prism. Suppose you are asked to find the surface area of the toy. Explain why you cannot add the surface area of the pyramid to the surface area of the prism.

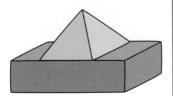

D2. To find the total volume of an object made up of more than one three-dimensional shape, Darnell found the volume of the individual shapes and added them together. Is Darnell correct? Explain your answer.

D3. The surface area of a cube with sides 2 cm long is 24 cm². The total surface area of two such cubes standing alone is 48 cm². But, the two cubes are stacked, the total exposed surface area is (48 — 8) or 40 cm². Extend this pattern to find the total exposed surface area for three cubes and for four cubes stacked.

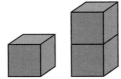

For help with questions 1 and 2, refer to Example 1.

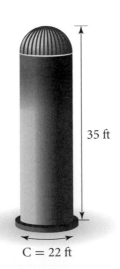

Math Connect

Silage is made by chopping and fermenting corn, alfalfa, or other grass or grain crops. It is stored in storage silos and fed to dairy cattle and sheep.

1. A storage silo is in the shape of a cylinder with a hemisphere at the top. The total height of the silo is 35 ft. The circumference of the cylinder is 22 ft.
   a) Find the radius of the silo.
   b) Find the height of the cylindrical portion of the silo.
   c) Find the volume of the cylindrical portion of the silo.
   d) Find the volume of the hemispherical portion of the silo.
   e) What is the total volume of the silo?

35 ft

C = 22 ft

2. The slate of a rectangular pool table has a width of 4 ft, a length of 8 ft, and a thickness of 2 in. Pockets are cut as shown in the diagram.

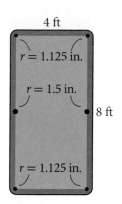

   a) Find the volume of slate removed for each pocket.
   b) Find the volume of the slate in cubic feet.
   c) If 1 ft^3 of slate weighs 166.6 lbs, what is the weight of the slate?

For help with question 3, refer to Example 2.

3. A doghouse in the shape of a square-based prism has a roof in the shape of a square-based pyramid. Find the total surface area that needs to be painted. Subtract 0.2 m^2 for the cut out doorway.

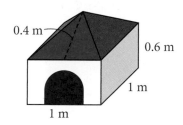

Apply the Concepts **B**

For help with question 4, refer to Example 3.

4. Ben is making a child's toy car from a rectangular block of wood. He drills two holes, each with diameter 1.4 cm, through the block for axles to support the wheels. The block of wood has length 15 cm, width 8 cm, and height 5 cm.

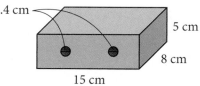

   a) What is the volume of the block of wood before the holes are drilled?
   b) What volume of wood remains after the holes are drilled?

5. Plans for a new theatre call for a hemispherical dome to be placed on top of a cube-shaped theatre. The side lengths of the cube are equal to the diameter of the dome. To adequately supply fresh air to the building, the engineers need to know the volume of air in the theatre. The radius of the dome is 155 ft.

   a) Find the volume of the cube-shaped portion of the theatre.
   b) Find the volume of the hemispherical portion of the theatre.
   c) Find the total volume of air in the theatre.

6. Vanessa has decided to package two items together for the holidays. She plans to market a combination of the toque in a pyramid attached on top of a square-based prism that will hold a pair of ski gloves.

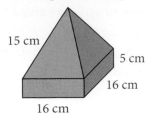

15 cm
5 cm
16 cm
16 cm

a) Find the surface area of this package.

b) What is the volume of the package? The height of the pyramid is 10.2 cm.

Achievement Check

7. Arthur is comparing two greenhouse designs, shown below. To allow for ventilation and irrigation systems, Arthur should choose the design that has more space in the peaked roof area. Which greenhouse design should Arthur choose? Why?

Greenhouse Plan A

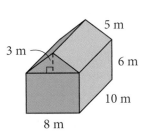

5 m
3 m
6 m
10 m
8 m

Greenhouse Plan B

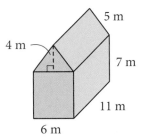

5 m
4 m
7 m
11 m
6 m

8. This set of stairs is positioned on a garage floor, against a wall.

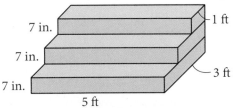

7 in.
7 in.
7 in.
1 ft
3 ft
5 ft

a) The stairs are to be painted. Find the area that needs to be painted.

b) If 1 L of paint covers 11.3 ft^2, how many litres of paint are needed to paint the stairs?

9. A trophy shop has a design for a plaque that needs to be silver-plated.

If the bottom side of the prism and the contact surface of the pyramid and the prism are the only surfaces that do not need to be silver-plated, find the surface area that needs to be silver-plated.

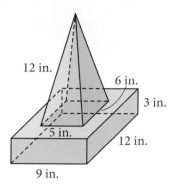

Literacy Connect **10.** A variety of materials and shapes are used in designing all structures.
   a) List some of the shapes commonly used in building homes.
   b) Give some reasons why architects design buildings and homes to include a variety of shapes.

Extend the Concepts C

11. Find the volume of this object.

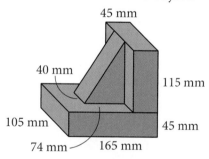

12. A designer is making a scale model of a garbage can to take to different manufacturers to get estimates of the cost to manufacture 10 000 units.

The shape of the garbage can is a cylinder with a hemisphere on the top. If the cylindrical portion is 1 m tall with radius 65 cm, and the designer has made a scale model of the object where she reduced all of the measurements by 40%, find
   a) the volume of the actual garbage can.
   b) the volume of the scale model.
   c) the percent decrease in the volume of the scale model compared to the actual object.

Review of Key Terms

1. Copy each definition, description, or example into your notebook, then match it with the best key term from the list below.

cone	sphere
cylinder	surface area
prism	volume
pyramid	

a) a three-dimensional object with length, width, and height

b) a Pyramid of Giza

c) a three-dimensional object with all points on its surface the same distance from the centre of the shape

d) a three-dimensional object with a circular base and a curved surface connecting the circle to a point called the vertex

e) the amount of space occupied by an object

f) a three-dimensional object with parallel circular faces

g) the total area of the surface of a three-dimensional object

9.1 Volume of Prisms and Pyramids, pages 364 to 371

2. Find the volume of each object.

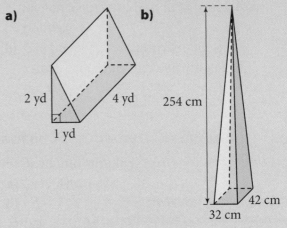

a) 2 yd, 4 yd, 1 yd

b) 254 cm, 42 cm, 32 cm

3. Suppose the length of a rectangular prism is doubled. What is the effect on the volume of the prism?

9.2 Surface Area of Prisms and Pyramids, pages 372 to 380

4. Find the surface area of each prism.

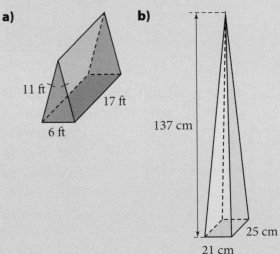

a) 11 ft, 17 ft, 6 ft

b) 137 cm, 25 cm, 21 cm

9.3 Surface Area and Volume of Cylinders, pages 381 to 390

5. Find the surface area and volume of each cylinder.

a)

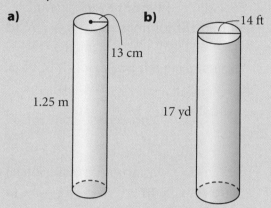

13 cm

1.25 m

b)

14 ft

17 yd

6. A log with a uniform diameter of 12" is cut into 8 equal pieces, each 22" long.
   a) Find the volume of wood in each piece.
   b) Find the total volume of the tree trunk.

9.4 Volume of Cones and Spheres, pages 391 to 397

7. Find the volume of each object.

a)

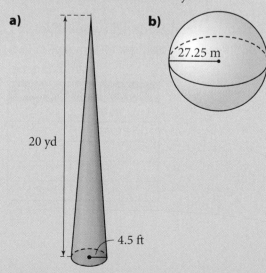

20 yd

4.5 ft

b)

27.25 m

8. A cubical container with sides 15 in. long is full of water. The water is poured into a rectangular prism with dimensions 20 in. by 18 in. by 54 in.
   a) Find the volume of each container.
   b) How much empty space is left in the rectangular prism?

9. If you were to pack a conical container with snow and melt it, the volume of meltwater would be about one-third the volume of the cone. The cone has radius 27 in. and height 77 in.
   a) Find the volume of the cone.
   b) Find the volume of meltwater in the cone.
   c) To what height would the water fill the cone?

9.5 Solve Problems Involving Surface Area and Volume, pages 398 to 405

10. Find the surface area of this composite shape, made of two square-based pyramids.

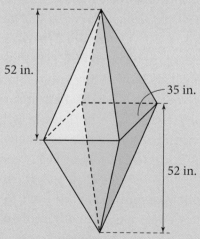

52 in.

35 in.

52 in.

1. Find the surface area and the volume of each object.

a)

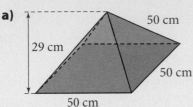

50 cm

29 cm

50 cm

50 cm

b)

8 yd

35 yd

2. Find the volume of each object.

a)

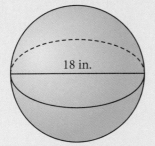

18 in.

b)

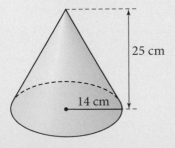

25 cm

14 cm

3. A cone has height 75 ft and radius 21 ft.
   a) Find the volume of the cone.
   b) A sphere with the same volume as the cone is to be constructed. Find the diameter of the sphere.

4. A cube has side length 18 in. A rectangular prism has length 12 in., width 8 in., and height 5 ft.
   a) Which object has the greater volume? How do you know?
   b) Which object has the greater surface area? Explain.

5. Erin is filling novelty balloons for her sister's cat-themed birthday party. When full, each balloon will be in the shape of a sphere with two cones. The sphere has radius 6". The cones each have radius 2" and height 6".

   a) Find the volume of helium needed to fill each balloon.
   b) Erin rents a helium tank to fill the balloons. The tank contains 14 ft³ of helium. How many balloons can Erin fill?

Chapter Problem Wrap-Up

For Canada, Vanessa packages skateboard wheels in a cylindrical container that is 8.5 cm tall with radius 2.78 cm. For the United States, however, she plans to use a container that is 3.5" tall with diameter 2.25".

a) Which container requires more material? How much more?

b) The wheels have diameter 5.4 cm and height 2.1 cm. Which container has more wasted space?

6. Owen is packing blocks into a box. Each block is in the shape of a right triangular prism, as shown. How many blocks can Owen fit in a box with volume 1000 cm^3? Justify your answer and state any assumptions you have made.

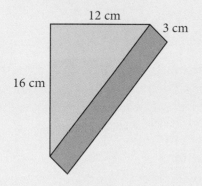

12 cm
3 cm
16 cm

7. A toy is made of a rectangular body, with a square-based pyramid on top, and four cylindrical wheels.

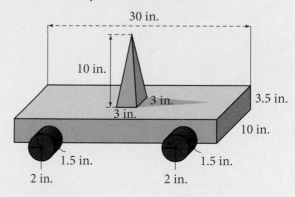

30 in.
10 in.
3 in.
3 in.
3.5 in.
10 in.
1.5 in.
1.5 in.
2 in.
2 in.

a) Find the total surface area of the toy.

b) If a container of model paint covers 300 in.^{2} on the first coat and 450 in.^{2} on the second coat, how many containers of paint will be needed to paint the toy with two coats?

Task

Design a Game

1. Work in groups of three to design a game. Each group's game must meet these criteria:

   - The game must include a game board.
   - There must be at least 30 numbered question cards, each with one question. There must be at least three original questions for each chapter of this textbook. Answers must be provided for all questions.
   - At least three different playing pieces must be included.
   - The game must include a number cube or cubes and a shaker, or a spinner.
   - Clear written rules and instructions describing how to play the game must be provided. The rules must indicate how points are awarded or lost and how to determine the winner.

2. Name your game, and design a box to package your game in. Ensure that the game board and all the playing pieces fit inside the box. Determine the surface area and volume of the box.

3. Trade games with another group. Play the other group's game.

4. Offer suggestions to the other group on how their game might be improved.

Chapter 1: Measurement Systems and Similar Triangles

1. The cost of porcelain tile flooring is $51.25/m². The Dhaliwal family is installing these tiles in the rectangular foyer of their home, which measures 15 ft by 12 ft. Find the cost of the flooring, before tax.

2. In the diagram, △JKL ~ △XYZ. Find the lengths of the indicated sides.

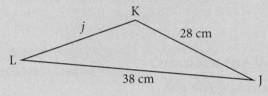

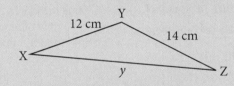

3. On a sunny day, Simon, who is 165 cm tall, casts a shadow that is 1.50 m long. At the same time, a nearby tree casts a shadow that is 425 cm long. How tall is the tree to the nearest hundredth of a metre?

Chapter 2: Right Triangle Trigonometry

4. Find each indicated length to the nearest tenth of a centimetre.

a)

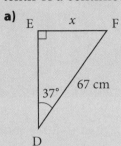

b)

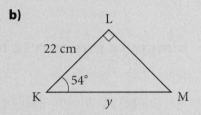

5. From a position 12.3 m from a light post, Melissa uses a transit that is 1.2 m above the ground to sight the top of the post. If the angle of elevation is 51.2°, find the height of the light post to the nearest tenth of a metre.

Chapter 3: Linear Relations

6. Find the slope of each line segment.

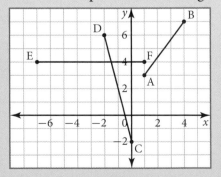

7. Determine the equation of each line.

   a) slope of $\frac{1}{2}$, y-intercept 4

   b) slope of $\frac{1}{2}$, through $(4, -4)$

   c) through $(3, -9)$ and $(-2, -4)$

8. On grid paper, graph each relation.

   a) $y = -\frac{1}{2}x + 5$ **b)** $y = -2x - 2$

9. Ski lessons cost $25 per hour, plus a $55 rental fee for the equipment.

   a) Create a table of values for 1 to 3 h of ski lessons.

   b) Graph the line that represents the data.

   c) Find the equation of the line.

   d) Find the cost of a 4-hour lesson.

   e) Find the cost of a 90-minute lesson.

Chapter 4: Linear Equations

10. Solve each linear equation.

   a) $3x - 5 = 4$ **b)** $\frac{k}{2} + 1 = 11$

   c) $\frac{2y + 3}{5} = 9$ **d)** $-2.5z + 4 = -1$

11. Rearrange each equation into slope y-intercept form.

   a) $4x - y + 5 = 0$

   b) $6x + y - 3 = 0$

   c) $4x - 15y + 36 = 0$

12. The line $3x - 2y + C = 0$ passes through $(5, -4)$. Find the value of C.

Chapter 5: Linear Systems

13. Solve the linear system $y = 4x + 2$ and $y = x - 4$ by graphing.

14. Solve each linear system by substitution.

   a) $x - y = 12$
      $y = 2x + 4$

   b) $y = -3x + 4$
      $y = 2x - 1$

15. Solve each linear system by elimination.

   a) $2x - 4y = -20$
      $x + y = 2$

   b) $3x - 4y = 11$
      $2x + y = 11$

16. Rick invested $15 000 in two investments: one that pays 8% interest and one that pays 5% interest. If he receives $1035 in interest at the end of the year, how much did he invest at each rate of interest?

Chapter 6: Quadratic Relations

17. Copy and complete the table. Determine if the relation is linear, quadratic, or neither.

x	y	First Differences	Second Differences
-3	31		
-2	18		
-1	9		
0	4		
1	3		
2	6		

18. For the graph, identify:
  a) the coordinates of the vertex
  b) the equation of the axis of symmetry
  c) the x- and y-intercepts
  d) the minimum or maximum value

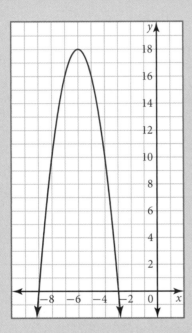

Chapter 7: Quadratic Expressions

19. Expand and simplify.
  a) $(x + 3)(x - 5)$
  b) $(2x + 1)(x - 1)$
  c) $(2x - 3)^2$

20. For each polynomial, find the GCF, then factor the polynomial.
  a) $18x - 27$
  b) $5x^2 + x$

21. The area of a rectangular parking lot can be represented by the equation: $A = 4x^2 + 200x$.
  a) Write expressions for the length and width of the parking lot.
  b) Find an expression for the perimeter of the lot.
  c) Find the area and the perimeter if $x = 50$ m.

22. Amrit factored the trinomial $x^2 + x - 42$ as $(x - 7)(x + 6)$. Is Amrit correct? Explain your answer and, if needed, made any corrections.

23. Factor each expression.
  a) $x^2 - 36$
  b) $x^2 + 6x - 7$
  c) $x^2 - 3x - 28$
  d) $x^2 + 4x - 5$

Chapter 8: Represent Quadratic Relations

24. The quadratic relation $h = -5t^2 + 20t + 100$ represents the path of a stone as it is thrown off a cliff, where h is the height in metres and t is the time in seconds.
  a) Graph the relation.
  b) From what height was the stone thrown?
  c) What was the maximum height reached by the stone? When did the stone reach the maximum height?

25. The cross section of a parabolic reflector can be modelled by the relation $y = 0.005x^2 - 0.08$, where x is the horizontal distance and y is the depth, both in metres.

a) Use a graphing calculator to graph the relation.

b) Identify the x-intercepts.

c) What is the diameter of the reflector?

Chapter 9: Volume and Surface Area

26. Find the surface area and the volume of each object.

a)

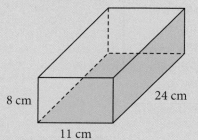

8 cm   24 cm

11 cm

b)

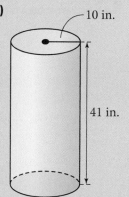

10 in.

41 in.

c)

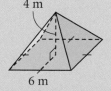

4 m

6 m

27. Find the volume of each object.

a) a cone with diameter 14 cm and height 23 cm

b) a sphere with radius 2 in.

28. The object shown is to be covered in gold leaf paper that costs 35¢ per square foot.

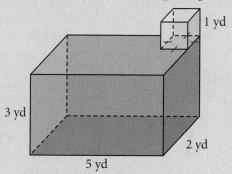

1 yd

3 yd

2 yd

5 yd

a) Find the total surface area of the shape that needs to be covered in the gold leaf paper.

b) How much will it cost to surface the shape with the gold leaf paper, excluding taxes?

Skills Appendix

Add and Subtract Integers

Main focus in Chapters 3 and 4

An integer is a number in the set …, $-3, -2, -1, 0, 1, 2, 3,$ ….
Integers can be added or subtracted.

Examples

1. $-4 + 5$
   $= 1$

2. $-5 - 2$
   $= -7$

3. $6 - (-9)$ *To subtract a negative integer add*
   $= 6 + 9$ *its opposite.*
   $= 15$

4. $-6 + (-5)$
   $= -11$

5. $5 + (-7) - (-8) + (-2)$ *Change subtract to add the opposite.*
   $= 5 + (-7) + 8 + (-2)$ *Then, add in order from left to right.*
   $= -2 + 8 + (-2)$
   $= 6 + (-2)$
   $= 4$

Practise

1. Find each difference.
   a) $7 - (-10)$
   b) $-5 - (-5)$
   c) $4 - (-4)$

2. Simplify.
   a) $8 + 9 - (-6)$
   b) $11 - 7 - (-7)$
   c) $-16 - (-5) + 8$

3. Simplify.
   a) $21 + 9 - (-12)$
   b) $1 - (-6) - (-7) + (-9)$
   c) $-1 + (-8) + (-3) - 5$
   d) $10 - (-3) - (-9) + (-12)$

Algebra Tiles

Main focus in Chapters 4 and 7

Algebra tiles can be used to model algebraic expressions and equations.

Example

Use algebra tiles to model the equation $2x - 5 = 3$.
Let ▬ represent the variable x.

The equation can be modeled as:

▬▬ ▬▬ □□□□□ = ■■■

Practice

1. Use algebra tiles to model each equation.

    a) $4 - 2x = 8$

    b) $x + 6 = 12$

    c) $-6 + x = 5$

Angle Properties

Main focus in Chapter 1

Opposite Angles and Supplementary Angles

When two lines intersect, the opposite angles are equal.
Angles are supplementary if their sum is 180°.

In the diagram, x is an opposite angle equal
to the angle marked 120°. So, $x = 120°$.

Angles x and y form a straight angle.
So $x + y = 180°$. Since $x = 120°$, $y = 60°$.
The angle y is a supplementary angle to x,
because their sum is to 180°.

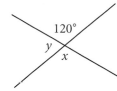

Angles of Parallel Lines

When transversal intersects a set of parallel lines, there are pairs
of angles that are related in the following way:

Alternate angles are equal.
They are represented by the
variable y in the diagram.

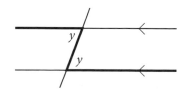

Corresponding angles are equal.
They are represented by the
variable x in the diagram.

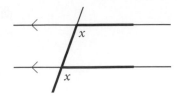

Co-interior angles are supplementary.
They are represented by variables
x and y in the diagram.

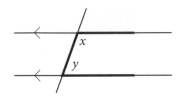

Example

Calculate the values for x, y, and z.

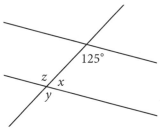

Using co-interior angles, $x + 125° = 180°$
$x + 125° - 125° = 180° - 125°$
$x = 55°$

Using corresponding angles, $y = 125°$
Using alternate angles, $z = 125°$

Practise

1. Identify the supplementary angle to each angle given.

   a) 65°   **b)** 130°

   c) 20°   **d)** 78°

   e) 90°   **f)** 8°

2. Solve for x, y, and z in each diagram.

   a)   **b)**   **c)**

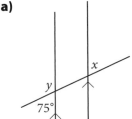
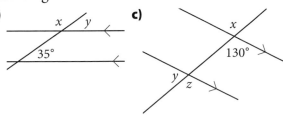

Area

Main focus in Chapters 5, 6, 7 and 9

The area of a figure refers to the number of square units needed to cover the surface.

Examples

1. Find the area.

Area of a circle is $A = \pi \times r^2$

$$\doteq 3.14 \times (4)^2$$
$$\doteq 3.14 \times 16$$
$$\doteq 50.24$$

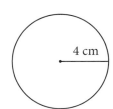

The area of the circle is approximately 50.24 cm^2.

2. Find the area.

Divide the figure into two sections:

A rectangle with dimensions 4 cm by 3 cm.

$A = 4 \times 3$
$\quad = 12$

A square with side length 1cm.

$A = 1^2$
$\quad = 1$

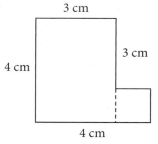

The area of the figure is $12 + 1$, or 13 cm^2.

Practise

1. Find the area of each figure.

a)

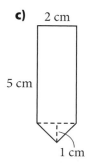

5 mm

3 mm

b)

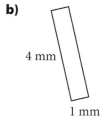

4 mm

1 mm

c)

2 cm

5 cm

1 cm

d)

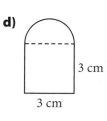

3 cm

3 cm

Common Factors

Main focus in Chapter 3 and 7

A common factor is a whole number that divides evenly into each number in a set of numbers. The greatest common factor is the greatest number that divides evenly into all the numbers in a set.

Example

Determine the greatest common factor of 36 and 120.

The factors of 36 are 1, 2, 3, 4, 6, 9, ⑫, 18, 36.
The factors of 120 are 1, 2, 3, 4, 5, 6, 10, ⑫, 30, 40, 60, 120.

So, the common factors are 1, 2, 3, 4, 6, and the greatest common factor is 12.

Practise

1. List the common factors, then determine the greatest common factors for each pair of numbers.
   a) 8, 12
   b) 16, 80
   c) 60, 150

2. List the common factors, and determine the greatest common factors for each set of numbers.
   a) 72, 81, 24
   b) 55, 60, 125
   c) 63, 77, 12
   d) 27, 99, 150

Convert Fractions to Decimals

Main focus in Chapter 3

A fraction can be converted to a decimal by dividing the numerator by the denominator. The decimal form is another way of representing the fraction.

Example

Express $\frac{3}{4}$ as a decimal.

$$
\begin{array}{r}
0.75 \\
4\overline{)3.00} \\
\underline{28} \\
20 \\
\underline{20} \\
0
\end{array}
$$

So, $\frac{3}{4}$ is 0.75.

1. Express each fraction as a decimal.

   a) $\frac{5}{25}$ b) $\frac{35}{100}$ c) $\frac{3}{8}$

   d) $\frac{7}{10}$ e) $\frac{13}{20}$ f) $\frac{1}{4}$

2. Express each fraction as a decimal rounded to one decimal place.

   a) $\frac{5}{7}$ b) $\frac{25}{150}$ c) $\frac{24}{56}$ d) $\frac{50}{60}$

Convert Measurements
Main focus in Chapter 1

Measurements can be converted from one unit to another.
Here are some conversion factors:
1 yd = 3 ft
1 c = 250 mL
1 gal = 4 qt
1 qt = 2 pt
$1 \text{ m}^2 = 10\ 000 \text{ cm}^2$

Examples

1. Convert 2.5 km to centimetres.
   There are 10 000 cm in 1 km.

   So, 2.5 km is 2.5 × 10 000 or 25 000 cm.

2. Convert 2 gal to pints.
   There are 8 pt in 1 gal.
   So, 2 gal is 2 × 8 or 16 pt.

3. Convert 1500 cm² to square metres.
   There are 10 000 cm² in 1 m².
   So, 1500 cm² is 1500 ÷ 10 000 or 0.15 m².

Practise

1. Convert each measure to the unit indicated.
   a) 138 L   millilitres
   b) 45 cm   kilometres
   c) 580 mL   litres
   d) 24 yd   feet
   e) 7000 cm²   square metres
   f) 7 yd³   cubic feet

Evaluate Expressions

Main focus in Chapters 3, 4, and 6

Expressions can be evaluated by substituting the given values for each variable.

1. Evaluate $3x + 1$, for $x = -2$.

$3x + 1 = 3(-2) + 1$ *Substitute −2 where you see the*
         $= -6 + 1$ *variable x.*
         $= -5$

2. Evaluate $5y - 10z$, when $y = 10$ and $z = 2$.

$5y - 10z = 5(10) - 10(2)$ *Substitute 10 where you see the*
           $= 50 - 20$ *variable y; substitute 2 for the variable z.*
           $= 30$

3. Evaluate $3x^2$, for $x = -1$.

$3x^2 = 3(-1)^2$
     $= 3(1)$
     $= 3$

1. Evaluate for $x = -3$.

a) $x + 1$ b) $-2x + 4$

c) $7 - x$ d) $\dfrac{1}{3}x$

2. Evaluate for $x = -2$ and $y = 3$.

a) $3y - 2x$ b) $y + 2x + 6$
c) $y - 6 + x$ d) $40 - 3x + 7y$

3. Evaluate for $x = 5$ and $y = -5$.

a) $y^2 - 1$ b) $x^2 + 3y$
c) $x + 6y + xy$ d) $8 - 3y + y + xy$

Fractions

Main focus in Chapter 1

Add and Subtract Fractions

Fractions can be added and subtracted by using a common denominator. A common denominator is a common multiple of the denominators of the set of fractions.

Multiply and Divide Fractions

Fractions can be multiplied by multiplying the numerator by the numerator, and denominator by the denominator.

Fractions can be divided by multiplying the first fraction by the reciprocal of the other fraction. The reciprocal of a fraction is found by transposing the numerator and the denominator.

1. Add $\frac{2}{5} + \frac{1}{2}$.

$$\frac{2}{5} + \frac{1}{2} = \frac{4}{10} + \frac{5}{10}$$

$$= \frac{9}{10}$$

The denominators 5 and 2 have a common multiple of 10.

Write each fraction with the common denominator of 10.

Add the numerators.

2. Subtract $\frac{3}{4} - \frac{2}{3}$.

$$\frac{3}{4} - \frac{2}{3} = \frac{9}{12} - \frac{8}{12}$$

$$= \frac{1}{12}$$

The denominators 4 and 3 have a common multiple of 12.

Write each fraction with the common denominator of 12.

Subtract the numerators.

3. Multiply $\frac{2}{7} \times \frac{3}{5}$.

$$\frac{2}{7} \times \frac{3}{5} = \frac{2 \times 3}{7 \times 5}$$

$$= \frac{6}{35}$$

Multiply the numerators.

Multiply the denominators.

4. Divide $\frac{3}{10} \div \frac{4}{5}$.

$$\frac{3}{10} \div \frac{4}{5} = \frac{3}{10} \times \frac{5}{4}$$

$$= \frac{3 \times 5}{10 \times 4}$$

$$= \frac{15}{40}$$

$$= \frac{3}{8}$$

The reciprocal of $\frac{4}{5}$ is $\frac{5}{4}$

Change the division sign to a multiplication sign and replace the second fraction with its reciprocal.

Reduce to lowest terms by dividing the numerator and the denominator by 5.

1. Add.

a) $\frac{2}{3} + \frac{1}{6}$

b) $\frac{3}{10} + \frac{1}{2}$

c) $\frac{1}{4} + \frac{2}{5} + \frac{1}{10}$

d) $\frac{5}{12} + \frac{1}{6} + \frac{1}{4}$

2. Subtract.

a) $\dfrac{3}{4} - \dfrac{3}{5}$

b) $\dfrac{5}{6} - \dfrac{1}{3}$

c) $\dfrac{11}{12} - \dfrac{3}{4}$

d) $\dfrac{8}{10} - \dfrac{2}{5} - \dfrac{1}{2}$

3. Multiply.

a) $\dfrac{5}{9} \times \dfrac{2}{7}$

b) $\dfrac{2}{15} \times \dfrac{3}{10}$

c) $\dfrac{9}{20} \times \dfrac{4}{5}$

d) $\dfrac{2}{5} \times \dfrac{3}{4} \times \dfrac{1}{2}$

4. Divide.

a) $\dfrac{2}{9} \div \dfrac{5}{6}$

b) $\dfrac{3}{10} \div \dfrac{2}{5}$

c) $\dfrac{5}{12} \div \dfrac{7}{10}$

d) $\dfrac{10}{9} \div \dfrac{6}{5}$

Graph Coordinates

Main Focus in Chapters 3, 5, 6, and 8

Ordered pairs can be plotted on a coordinate grid. The first coordinate in an ordered pair represents the horizontal distance from the y-axis. The second coordinate represents the vertical distance from the x-axis. An ordered pair is written (x, y).

Example

Plot the point A $(1, -2)$.

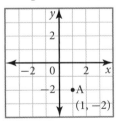

Point A is 1 unit to the right of the y-axis and 2 units down from the x-axis.

Practise

1. Identify the x-coordinate for each ordered pair.

a) $(2, 3)$

b) $(-1, -2)$

c) $(5, -6)$

d) $(0, 9)$

2. Identify the y-coordinate for each ordered pair.

a) $(1, 7)$

b) $(-8, -2)$

c) $(0, -3)$

d) $(-10, 20)$

3. Plot the points on a coordinate grid and label each point with its letter.
   a) A (3, 9)   **b)** B (−3, −4)
   c) C (0, 5)   **d)** D (6, 0)

4. Find the coordinates of points A, B, C, and D.

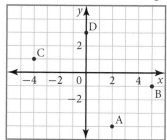

Graph Linear Relations

Main focus in Chapters 4 and 5

A linear relation, written in the form $y = mx + b$, has y-intercept b and slope m.

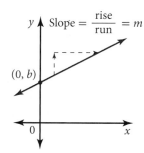

A table of values can also be used to graph a linear relation.

Examples

1. Graph the linear relation $y = 2x + 1$.

   The y-intercept is 1 and the slope is 2. Plot the point (0, 1).

   To find the next two points on the line, move up 2 units and right 1 unit; repeat from the second point.

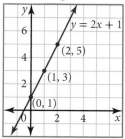

2. Graph the linear relation $3x + y = 3$.

$$3x + y = 3$$ *Rewrite the equation in slope*
$$3x - 3x + y = -3x + 3$$ *y-intercept form.*
$$y = -3x + 3$$ *Isolate y by subtracting 3x from both sides of the equation.*

The y-intercept is 3 and the slope is -3. Plot the point $(0, 3)$. To find the next two points on the line, move down 3 units and right 1 unit.

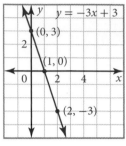

3. Make a table of values to graph the linear relation $2y + 5x = 4$.

x	y
−2	7
−1	4.5
0	2
1	−0.5
2	−3

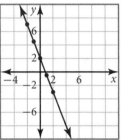

Practise

1. Graph each linear relation.
  a) $y = 2x - 3$ **b)** $y = -x + 2$ **c)** $y = \frac{3}{2}x - 1$

2. Graph each linear relation.
  a) $x + y = 5$ **b)** $2x - y = 1$ **c)** $2x + 2y = 6$

Intercepts
Main focus in Chapters 3 and 6

On a graph, the x-intercept is the x-value of the point at which the relation intersects the x-axis. The y-intercept is the y-coordinate of the point at which the relation intersects the y-axis.

Example

Identify the x- and y-intercepts for the relation.

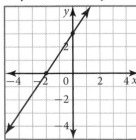

The x-intercept is -2.
The y-intercept is 3.

1. Identify the *x*- and *y*-intercepts for each relation.

a)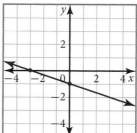

b)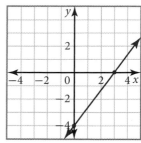

2. Draw a linear relation with the given *x*- and *y*-intercepts.
   a) *x*-intercept 4   *y*-intercept -1
   b) *x*-intercept -5 *y*-intercept -2.5

Isolate a Variable

Main focus in Chapter 4

Equations and formulas can be rearranged to isolate a variable.

Examples

1. Rearrange the equation to isolate *d*.

$$5d - 2e = 12 \qquad \textit{Add 2e to both sides of the equation.}$$
$$5d - 2e + 2e = 12 + 2e$$
$$5d = 2e + 12$$
$$\frac{5d}{5} = \frac{2e}{5} + \frac{12}{5} \qquad \textit{Divide all terms by 5.}$$
$$d = \frac{2e}{5} + \frac{12}{5}$$

2. Rearrange the equation to isolate *y*.

$$8 - 3y - 7x = 0 \qquad \textit{Subtract 8 and add 7x to both}$$
$$8 - 8 - 3y - 7x + 7x = 0 + 7x - 8 \quad \textit{sides of the equation.}$$
$$-3y = 7x - 8$$
$$\frac{-3y}{-3} = \frac{7x}{-3} - \frac{8}{-3} \qquad \textit{Divide all terms by -3.}$$
$$y = -\frac{7}{3}x + \frac{8}{3}$$

Practise

1. Rearrange each equation to isolate *y*.
   a) $8x + 3y = 2$ **b)** $6x - 4y = 7$
   c) $2x - y = 13$ **d)** $-5x + 6y = 11$

Least Common Denominator

Main focus in Chapter 4

To find the least common denominator of the fractions in a set, compare the denominators of the fractions.

Example

1. For the fractions $\frac{3}{8}$ and $\frac{7}{12}$:

   $\frac{3}{8}$ has denominator 8; the multiples of 8 are 8, 16, ⟨24⟩, 36, ...

   $\frac{7}{12}$ has denominator 12; the multiples of 12 are 12, ⟨24⟩, 36, 48...

   The least common multiple of 8 and 12 is 24. So, 24 is the least common denominator for $\frac{3}{8}$ and $\frac{7}{12}$.

2. For the set of fractions $\frac{1}{2}$, $\frac{3}{4}$ and $\frac{5}{6}$:

   $\frac{1}{2}$ has denominator 2; the multiples of 2 are 2, 4, 6, 8, 10, ⟨12⟩ ...

   $\frac{3}{4}$ has denominator 4; the multiples of 4 are 4, 8, ⟨12⟩ 16, ...

   $\frac{5}{6}$ has the denominator 6; the multiples of 6 are 6, ⟨12⟩ 18, 24, ...

   The least common multiple of 2, 4, and 6 is 12. So, 12 is the least common denominator for the set of fractions.

Practise

1. Determine the least common denominator for each pair of fractions.

   a) $\frac{1}{6}, \frac{2}{5}$

   b) $\frac{3}{7}, \frac{1}{4}$

   c) $\frac{4}{9}, \frac{5}{12}$

   d) $\frac{7}{10}, \frac{8}{15}$

2. Determine the least common denominator for each set of fractions.

   a) $\frac{3}{10}, \frac{4}{5}, \frac{1}{2}$

   b) $\frac{9}{4}, \frac{3}{8}, \frac{1}{3}$

   c) $\frac{24}{25}, \frac{49}{50}, \frac{37}{100}$

   d) $\frac{8}{9}, \frac{5}{8}, \frac{5}{12}$

Linear and Non-Linear Relations

Main focus in Chapter 8

A linear relation is a relation between two variables that forms a straight line when graphed. A non-linear relation does not produce a straight line when graphed.

Examples

1. Graph the equation $y = 2x + 3$. Is this relation linear or non-linear?

   Find at least three points to graph.

x	$y = 2x + 3$	Ordered pair
0	$2(0) + 3 = 3$	$(0, 3)$
1	$2(1) + 3 = 5$	$(1, 5)$
2	$2(2) + 3 = 7$	$(2, 7)$

   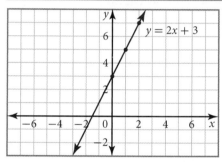

   This relation is linear since the points lie in a straight line.

2. Graph the equation $y = x^2 + 1$. Is this relation linear or non-linear

   Find at least three points to graph.

x	$y = x^2 + 1$	Ordered pair
−1	$(-1)^2 + 1 = 2$	$(-1, 2)$
0	$(0)^2 + 1 = 1$	$(0, 1)$
1	$(1)^2 + 1 = 2$	$(1, 2)$
2	$(2)^2 + 1 = 5$	$(2, 5)$

   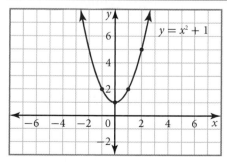

   This relation is non-linear since the points do not lie in a straight line.

1. Graph each relation to determine whether it is linear or non-linear.

a)

x	y
−1	1
0	−2
1	−3
2	−2
3	1

b)

x	y
−1	6
0	5
1	4
2	3
3	2

2. Graph each relation to determine if it is linear or non-linear.

a) $y = 4x + 3$

b) $y = 2x^2 - 1$

Lines of Symmetry

Main focus in Chapter 6

A line of symmetry divides a figure into two congruent parts that are reflections of each other. Some figures have more than one line of symmetry, while others may have no line of symmetry.

Examples

1. How many lines of symmetry does this pentagon have? Draw the line(s) of symmetry for the pentagon.

There are five lines of symmetry.

2. Complete the figure using the dashed line as the line of symmetry.

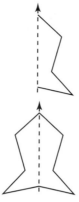

---

1. Copy or trace each figure. Draw the line(s) of symmetry for each figure.

a)

b)

2. Copy or trace each figure. Complete the figures using the dashed line as the line of symmetry.

a)

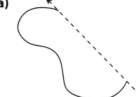

b)

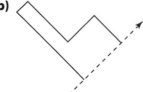

Lowest Terms
Main focus in Chapter 3

Fractions can be simplified by reducing them to lowest terms. Divide the numerator and denominator by the greatest common factor.

Example

Simplify the fraction $\dfrac{18}{20}$.

The factors of 18 are 1, ②, 3, 6, 9, 18.
The factors of 20 are 1, ②, 4, 5, 10, 20.
So, the greatest common factor is 2.

Divide the numerator and denominator by the greatest common factor to reduce the fraction to lowest terms.

$$\frac{18}{20} = \frac{18 \div 2}{20 \div 2}$$
$$= \frac{9}{10}$$

Practise

1. Simplify each fraction.

   a) $\dfrac{20}{40}$ b) $\dfrac{75}{125}$

   c) $\dfrac{33}{88}$ d) $\dfrac{36}{720}$

Multiply and Divide Expressions
Main focus in Chapters 4 and 7

Expressions can be multiplied or divided. Multiply or divide the numerical coefficients separate from the variables.

Examples

1. Multiply.

   $4r(-2r)$ *Multiply the numerical coefficients: $4 \times (-2) = -8$*
   $= -8r^2$ *Multiply the variables: $r \times r = r^2$.*

2. Divide

   $-36y^2 \div 4y$ *Divide the numerical coefficients $(-36) \div 4 = -9$*
   $= -9y$ *Divide the variables: $y^2 \div y = y$.*

3. Expand.

   $5y(2y - 1)$ *Multiply each term in the binomial by the monomial.*

   $= 5y(2y - 1)$
   $= 5y(2y) - 5y(1)$
   $= 10y^2 - 5y$

1. Multiply.
   a) $-5(-3y)$ b) $15(4p^2)$
   c) $2x(-x)$ d) $8(-2k)(3k)$

2. Divide.
   a) $16x \div (-4)$ b) $3k^2 \div k$
   c) $-27y^2 \div 9y$ d) $10b^2 \div (-2b^2)$

3. Expand.
   a) $-2(4x + 3)$ b) $3(-y^2 - 6y + 1)$
   c) $5a(7 - 2a)$ d) $-4(3p^2 - 7p + 5)$

Nets

Main Focus in Chapter 9

A net is a two-dimensional figure that can be folded to form a three-dimensional object.

Example

Identify the solid from the net.

This net has three isosceles triangles and one equilateral triangle. It is a net for a square-based pyramid.

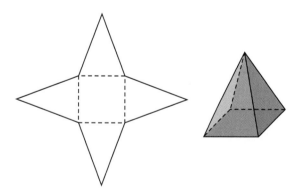

Practise

1. For each net, identify the solid.
   a)   b)   c)

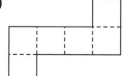

Polynomials

Main focus in Chapter 7

A polynomial is an algebraic expression made up of one or more terms, separated by addition or subtraction.

A polynomial with exactly *two* terms is a *bi*nomial.
A polynomial with exactly *three* terms is a *tri*nomial.
A polynomial with exactly *one* term is a *mono*mial.

The numerical coefficient is the numerical part of the term.

Examples

1. Identify each expression as a monomial, binomial, trinomial, or polynomial.
   a) $7x + 2y^2 - 3$
   This expression has three terms. It is a trinomial.

   b) $-4z$
   This expression has only one term. It is a monomial.

   c) $a^2 - 2b^2 + 1 - 3a$
   This expression has four terms. It is a polynomial.

2. Identify the numerical coefficient in each term.
   a) $5x$
   The numerical coefficient is 5.

   b) $-2y$
   The numerical coefficient is -2.

   c) $3y^2$
   The numerical coefficient is 3.

Practise

1. Identify each expression as a monomial, binomial, trinomial, or polynomial.
   a) $8p + 3q$
   b) $1 - y + 5z$
   c) $2r^2 - s + 4t - 2 + t^2$
   d) $a - b + a^2$

2. Identify the numerical coefficient in each term.
   a) $-5x$ **b)** $8y^2$
   c) $-p$ **d)** $24r$

Properties of Triangles

Main focus in Chapter 1

Sum of the Angles in a Triangle

The sum of the angles in any triangle is 180°.

Types of Triangles and Their Properties

A **right** triangle contains one angle that is 90°.

An **isosceles** triangle has two sides of equal length and contains two angles of equal size.

An **equilateral** triangle has three sides of equal length and contains three angles of equal size. Each angle measures 60°.

An **obtuse** triangle contains one angle that is greater than 90°.

An **acute** triangle contains angles that are all less than 90°.

Examples

1. Find the measure of x.

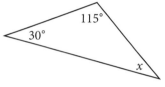

$$x + 30° + 115° = 180°$$
$$x = 180° - 30° - 115°$$
$$x = 35°$$

2. Identify each triangle as right, isosceles, equilateral, obtuse, or acute.

a) This triangle has one right angle and no equal sides. It is a right triangle

b) This triangle has two equal sides and two equal angles. The measure of the third angle is $180° - 2(40°)$ or 100°. This is an obtuse, isosceles triangle.

c) This triangle has no sides equal and one obtuse angle. It is an obtuse triangle.

d) This triangle has all sides equal. It is an equilateral triangle.

1. Determine the value of *x* in each triangle.

a)

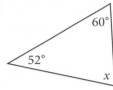

b)

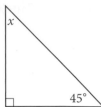

2. Find the measure of the third angle, given the measures of two angles of a triangle.

a) 20° and 40°

b) 60° and 60°

c) 45° and 90°

d) 30° and 55°

e) 12° and 86°

f) 66° and 77°

3. Draw a triangle with each set of properties.

a) An acute triangle with one angle that is 65°.

b) A right triangle with one angle that is 30°.

c) An isosceles triangle with two angles that are 20° each.

d) An obtuse triangle with one angle that is 140°.

Proportions

Main focus in Chapters 1 and 2

A proportion is a statement that two ratios are equal.

Variables in proportions can be solved for by cross-multiplying.

Example

Solve for *x*:

$$\frac{4}{x} \diagdown\!\!\!\!\nearrow \frac{20}{50}$$

$4 \times 50 = x \times 20$

$200 = 20x$ *Divide both sides of the equation by 20.*

$x = 10$

Practise

1. Solve.

a) $8 = \frac{x}{6}$

b) $10 = \frac{x}{2}$

c) $15 = \frac{30}{x}$

d) $\frac{x}{22} = 3$

2. Solve.

a) $\frac{x}{5} = \frac{3}{15}$

b) $\frac{80}{x} = \frac{4}{200}$

c) $\frac{85}{100} = \frac{5}{x}$

d) $\frac{6}{18} = \frac{x}{9}$

Pythagorean Theorem

Main focus in Chapter 9

The Pythagorean Theorem states that, in a right triangle, the square of the hypotenuse is equal to the sum of the squares of the other two sides.

This can be written $c^2 = a^2 + b^2$, where c is the length of the hypotenuse, and a and b are the lengths of the other two sides of the triangle.

Examples

1. Use the Pythagorean theorem to find the length of the indicated side to the nearest tenth of a centimetre.

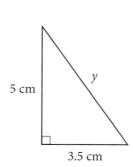

$$y^2 = 5^2 + 3.5^2$$
$$y^2 = 25 + 12.25$$
$$y^2 = 37.25$$
$$y^2 = \sqrt{37.25}$$
$$y \doteq 6.1$$

The length of the hypotenuse is needed. The lengths of the legs are 5 cm and 3.5 cm.

The hypotenuse is about 6.1 cm long.

2. Find the length of the indicated side to the nearest tenth of a millimetre.

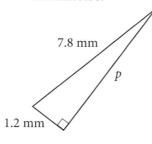

$$1.2^2 + p^2 = 7.8^2$$
$$1.44 + p^2 = 60.84$$
$$p^2 = 60.84 - 1.44$$
$$p^2 = 59.4$$
$$p = \sqrt{59.4}$$
$$p \doteq 7.7$$

The hypotenuse is 7.8 mm and one leg is 1.2 mm. The length of the other leg is needed.

The length of side p is about 7.7 mm.

Practise

1. Find the length of each indicated side.

a)

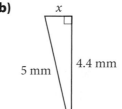

b)

c)

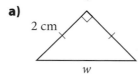

Ratios

Main focus in Chapter 2

Ratios are used to compare quantities measured in the same units.
Ratios can be simplified by dividing each term by a common factor.

Examples

1. The number of white hats sold in a store is 20, while the number of black hats is 10. Write the ratio comparing the number of white hats sold to the number of black hats sold.

   The ratio of white hats to black hats is 20 to 10 or 20 : 1 0.

2. Simplify the ratio 12 : 18.
   A common factor of 12 and 18 is the 6.

   $12 \div 6 = 2$
   $18 \div 6 = 3$
   So, 12:18 in simplest form is 2:3.

Practise

1. Simplify each ratio.
   a) 30 : 36   **b)** 4 : 14
   c) 25 : 100   **d)** 60 : 50

Rounding

Main focus in Chapter 2

Numbers can be rounded to help estimate answers to problems.

Examples

1. Round 87.81 to the nearest whole number.
   Look at the digits following the decimal point.
   0.81 is closer to 1 than to 0, so 87.81 rounded to the nearest whole number is 88.

2. Round 2.53 to one decimal place.
   Look at the digits following the tenths digit.
   0.03 is closer to 0.0 than to 0.1, so 2.53 rounded to one decimal place is 2.5.

Practise

1. Round to the nearest whole number.
   a) 4.4
   b) 9.92
   c) 8.674
   d) 2.299

2. Round to one decimal place.
   a) 7.92
   b) 8.419
   c) 10.766
   d) 100.9811

3. Round to two decimal places.
   a) 5.8910
   b) 0.138 99
   c) 11.7021
   e) 0.003 45

Simplify Expressions
Main focus in Chapters 4, 5, and 7

Terms in an expression are separated by plus or minus signs.
Like terms have the same variable raised to the same exponent.
Expressions can be simplified by collecting like terms.

Examples

1. Simplify $8a + 7 + 5a - 2 - 3a$.
   $= 8a + 5a - 3a + 7 - 2$ *Collect like terms.*
   $= 10a + 5$

2. Simplify $3 + 3y + 2z - 4y + z - 1$.
   $= 3y - 4y + 2z + z + 3 - 1$ *Collect like terms.*
   $= -y + 3z + 2$

Practise

1. Simplify.
   a) $3 + 6b - 2b + 10$
   b) $8k - 11 + 2k$
   c) $12 + 5f - 4 - 9f$
   d) $-5t + 17 + 7t - 15$

2. Simplify.
   a) $-6 + 5y + 2y + z + z + 2z$
   b) $7a + 2a + 6b + a + b$
   c) $12p + q - 1 - 3 - 2q + p$
   d) $3 + 2t + u + 5u + t - 3u$

Solve Equations

Main focus in Chapters 3 and 5

The solution to an equation is the value or values of the variable that make the equation true.

Examples

1. Solve
$$2x + 4 = 20$$
$$2x + 4 - 4 = 20 - 4 \quad \text{Subtract 4 from both sides of the equation.}$$
$$2x = 16 \quad \text{Divide both sides by 2.}$$
$$x = 8$$

2. Solve for x if $y = 2$.
$$x = 3y - 5$$
$$x = 3(2) - 5 \quad \text{Substitute 2 for y.}$$
$$x = 6 - 5$$
$$x = 1$$

3. Solve for y if $x = -3$.
$$2x - 3y = 12$$
$$2(-3) - 3y = 12 \quad \text{Substitute } -3 \text{ for x.}$$
$$-6 - 3y = 12$$
$$-6 - 3y + 6 = 12 + 6 \quad \text{Add 6 to both sides of the equation.}$$
$$-3y = 18$$
$$\frac{-3y}{-3} = \frac{18}{-3} \quad \text{Divide both sides of the equation by } -3.$$
$$y = -6$$

Practise

1. Solve for x.
   a) $-5x = 25$
   b) $2x + 2 = 12$
   c) $-10 + 3x = 30$
   d) $-x + 2 = 26$

2. For each equation, find the value of x when $y = 4$.
   a) $x = 7 - 2y$
   b) $x + 6y = -8$
   c) $3x - 2y = 12$
   d) $5y - x = 10$

Solve Linear Systems by Graphing

Main focus in Chapter 5

A linear system is a set of two or more linear equations considered at the same time. The solution to a linear system is the point of intersection of the lines.

Examples

1. Find the solution to the linear system.

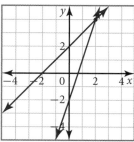

The solution to this linear system is the point of intersection of the lines. The solution is (2, 4).

Practise

1. Find the solution to each linear system.

a)

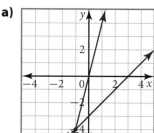

b)

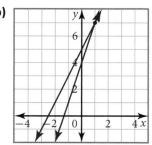

Squaring

Main focus in Chapters 2, 6, 7, and 9

When a number multiplies itself, the product is known as the square of the number.

Examples

1. $7 \times 7 = 49$

   This means that the square of 7 is 49.
   7×7 can also be written as 7^2.

   $$7 \times 7 = 7^2$$
   $$= 49$$

2. Find the square of 8.

$$8^2 = 8 \times 8$$
$$= 64$$

3. Evaluate.

$$8^2 + 7^2$$
$$= 8 \times 8 + 7 \times 7$$
$$= 64 + 49$$
$$= 113$$

4. Evaluate.

$$8^2 - 7^2$$
$$= 8 \times 8 - 7 \times 7$$
$$= 64 - 49$$
$$= 15$$

Practise

1. Find the value of each square.

a) 5^2 **b)** 3^2 **c)** 6^2

2. Evaluate.

a) $9^2 + 4^2$ **b)** $2^2 + 8^2$ **c)** $10^2 + 1^2$

3. Evaluate.

a) $8^2 - 2^2$ **b)** $9^2 - 6^2$ **c)** $20^2 - 10^2$

4. Evaluate.

a) $1^2 + 7^2 + 2^2$ **b)** $10^2 - 3^2 + 4^2$ **c)** $4^2 - 3^2 + 5^2$

Square Roots

Main Focus in Chapters 2 and 9

The square root of a number is a number that multiplies itself to give the original number.

The symbol $\sqrt{}$ represents the positive square root of a number.

Examples

1. The positive square root of 49 is 7 because $7 \times 7 = 49$.

2. Find $\sqrt{169}$.

$$\sqrt{169} = \sqrt{13 \times 13}$$
$$= 13$$

Practise

1. Find each square root.

a) $\sqrt{36}$ **b)** $\sqrt{64}$

c) $\sqrt{100}$ **d)** $\sqrt{9}$

2. Find each square root and round it to one decimal place.

    a) $\sqrt{20}$ **b)** $\sqrt{180}$

    c) $\sqrt{99}$ **d)** $\sqrt{129}$

Word Problems

Main focus in Chapter 5

An equation can be written to represent a situation described in a word problem.

Examples

1. Sally sells cups of lemonade for $0.50 each. Last Saturday, she made $26.50 selling lemonade.

Let x represent the number of cups of lemonade Sally sold. So, $26.50 = 0.5x$.

2. Marcus and his friends are forming a band. They rent music equipment to rehearse at a flat rate of $150 plus $75/h. Last weekend, they paid $375.

Let y represent the number of hours Marcus' band rehearsed. So, $375 = 150 + 75y$.

Practise

1. Write an equation to represent each situation.

    a) Damian spends approximately $45 for a pair of jeans. In one year, he spent $225 buying several pairs of jeans.

    b) Ming sold some of the CDs from his music collection at a garage sale. He sold them at a price of $8 each and made $136.

    c) Terry babysits for a flat rate of $25 plus $2 for each diaper change. Yesterday, she earned $31.

Technology Appendix

Contents

THE GEOMETER'S SKETCHPAD® BASICS

Menu Bar

1   **File** menu—open/save/print sketches

2   **Edit** menu—undo/redo/actions/
    set preferences

3   **Display** menu—control appearance
    of objects in sketch

4   **Construct** menu—construct new
    geometric objects based on objects
    in sketch

5   **Transform** menu—apply geometric
    transformations to selected objects

6   **Measure** menu—make various
    measurements on objects in sketch

7   **Graph** menu—create axes and plot measurements and points

8   **Window** menu—manipulate windows

9   **Help** menu—access the help system, an excellent reference guide

10 **Toolbox**—access tools for creating, marking, and transforming points,
    circles, and straight objects (segments, lines, and rays); also includes
    text and information tools

10a **Selection Arrow Tool** (Arrow)—select and transform objects

10b **Point Tool** (Dot)—draw points

10c **Compass Tool** (Circle)—draw circles

10d **Straightedge Tool**—draw line segments, rays, and lines

10e **Text Tool** (Letter A)—label points and write text

10f **Custom Tool** (Double Arrow)—create or use special "custom" tools

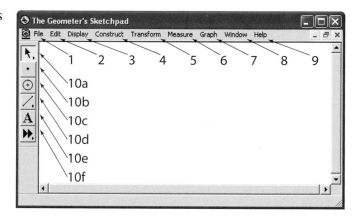

Creating a Sketch

- From the **File** menu, choose **New Sketch** to start with a new work area.

Opening an Existing Sketch

- From the **File** menu, choose **Open....**
  The Open dialogue box will appear.
- Choose the sketch you wish to work on.
  Then, click on **Open**.

  OR

- Type in the name of the sketch in
  the File name: entry box. Then,
  click on **Open**.

Saving a Sketch

If you are saving for the first time in a
new sketch:
- From the **File** menu, choose **Save As**.
  The Save As dialogue box will appear.
- You can save the sketch with the name
  assigned by *The Geometer's Sketchpad*®.
  Click on **Save**.

  OR

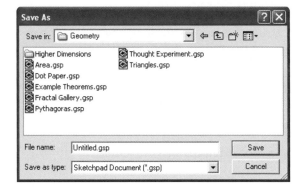

- Press the Backspace or Delete key to
  clear the name.
- Type in whatever you wish to name the
  sketch file. Click on **Save**.

If you have already given your file a name:
- Choose **Save** from the **File** menu.

Closing a Sketch Without Exiting *The Geometer's Sketchpad*®

- From the **File** menu, choose **Close**.

Exiting The Geometer's Sketchpad®

- From the **File** menu, choose **Exit**.

Setting Preferences

- From the **Edit** menu, choose **Preferences...**.
- Click on the **Units** tab.
- Set the units and precision for angles, distances, and calculated values such as slopes or ratios.

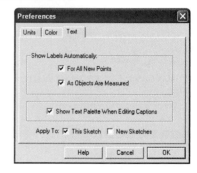

- Click on the **Text** tab.
- If you check the auto-label box For **All New Points**, then *The Geometer's Sketchpad®* will label points as you create them.
- If you check the auto-label box **As Objects Are Measured**, then *The Geometer's Sketchpad®* will label any measurements that you define.

You can also choose whether the auto-labelling functions will apply only to the current sketch, or also to any new sketches that you create.

Be sure to click on **OK** to apply your preferences.

Selecting Points and Objects

- Choose the **Selection Arrow Tool**. The mouse cursor appears as an arrow.

To select a single point:
- Select the point by moving the cursor to the point and clicking on it.

The selected point will now appear as a darker point, similar to a *bull's-eye* ⊙.

To select an object such as a line segment or a circle:
- Move the cursor to a point on the object until it becomes a horizontal arrow.
- Click on the object. The object will change appearance to show it is selected.

To select a number of points or objects:
- Select each object in turn by moving the cursor to the object and clicking on it.

To deselect a point or an object:
- Move the cursor over it, and then click the left mouse button.
- To deselect all selected objects, click in an open area of the workspace.

Constructing Line Segments

- Choose the **Point Tool**. Create two points in the workspace.
- Choose the **Selection Arrow Tool**, and select both points.
- From the **Construct** menu, choose **Segment**.

You can also use the **Straightedge Tool**:

- Choose this tool.
- Move the cursor to the workspace.
- Click and hold the left mouse button.
- Drag the cursor to the desired location.
- Release the mouse button.

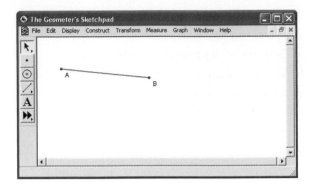

Constructing Triangles and Polygons

To construct a triangle:
- Choose the **Point Tool**. Draw three points in the workspace.
- Select the points.
- From the **Construct** menu, choose **Segments**.

You can construct a polygon with any number of sides.

To construct a quadrilateral:
- Draw four points.
- Deselect all points.
- Select the points in either clockwise or counterclockwise order.
- From the **Construct** menu, choose **Segments**.

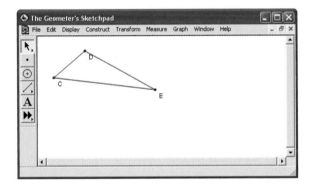

Constructing a Circle

- Select the **Compass Tool**.
- Move the cursor to the point where you want the centre of the circle.
- Click and hold the left mouse button. Drag the cursor to the desired radius.
- Release the mouse button.

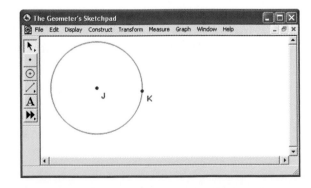

Constructing Parallel and Perpendicular Lines

To construct a line parallel to LM, passing through N:
- Select line segment LM (but not the endpoints) and point N.
- From the **Construct** menu, choose **Parallel Line**.

To construct a line perpendicular to LM, passing through N:
- Select line segment LM (but not the endpoints) and point N.
- From the **Construct menu**, choose **Perpendicular Line**.

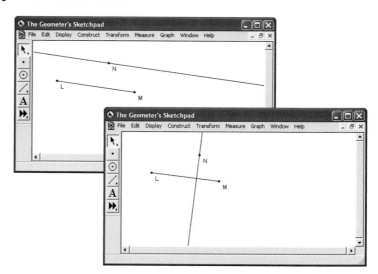

Constructing Rays

To construct a ray OP:
- Select point O and then point P.
- From the **Construct** menu, choose **Ray**.

   OR

- Click and hold on the Straightedge Tool on the left toolbar until a menu appears.
  Choose the option for a ray.
- Select point O and then point P.

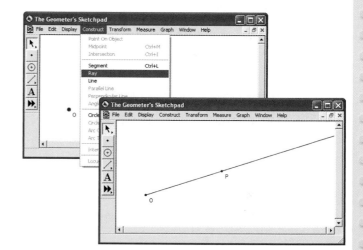

Constructing Midpoints

To construct the midpoint of line segment PQ:
- Select line segment PQ (but not the endpoints).
- From the **Construct** menu, choose **Midpoint**.

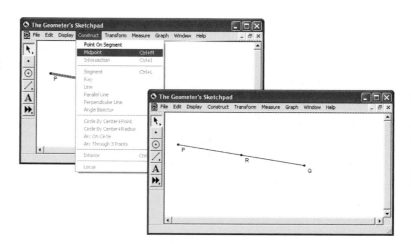

Using the Measure Menu

To measure the distance between two points:
- Ensure that nothing is selected.
- Select the two points.
- From the **Measure** menu, choose **Distance**.

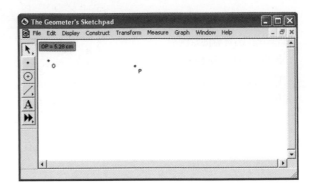

The Geometer's Sketchpad® will display the distance between the points, using the units and accuracy selected in **Preferences...** under the **Edit** menu.

To measure the length of a line segment:
- Ensure that nothing is selected.
- Select the line segment (but not the endpoints).
- From the **Measure** menu, choose **Length**.

To measure an angle:
- Ensure that nothing is selected.
- Select the three points that define the angle in the order Q, R, S. The second point selected must be the vertex of the angle.
- From the **Measure** menu, choose **Angle**.

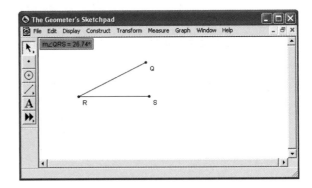

To calculate the ratio of two lengths:
- Select the two lengths be compared.
- From the **Measure** menu, choose **Ratio**.

Constructing and Measuring Polygon Interiors

The Geometer's Sketchpad® will measure the perimeter and the area of a polygon. However, you must first construct the interior of the polygon.

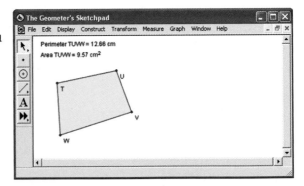

To construct the interior of this quadrilateral:
- Choose the four points of the quadrilateral, in either clockwise or counterclockwise order.
- From the **Construct** menu, choose **Quadrilateral Interior**. The interior of the quadrilateral will change colour.

To measure the perimeter:
- Select the interior of the polygon. It will have a cross-hatched appearance when selected.
- From the **Measure** menu, choose **Perimeter**.

The Geometer's Sketchpad® will display the perimeter of the polygon, using the units and accuracy selected in **Preferences...** under the **Edit** menu.

To measure the area:
- Select the interior of the polygon.
- From the **Measure** menu, choose **Area**.

Dilating and Rotating an Object

To dilate an object:
- Select a point to be the centre of the dilatation. Then, from the **Transform** menu, choose **Mark Center**.
- Select the object(s) to be dilated. From the **Transform** menu, choose **Dilate...**.
- In the Dilate dialogue box, enter the Scale Factor by which you want to dilate the object. Make sure that **Fixed Ratio** is selected. Click on **Dilate**.

To rotate an object:
- Select a point to be the centre of rotation. Then, from the **Transform** menu, choose **Mark Center**.
- Select the object(s) to be rotated. From the **Transform** menu, choose **Rotate...**.
- In the Rotate dialogue box, enter the number of degrees you want to rotate the object. Make sure that **Fixed Angle** is selected. Click on **Rotate**.

Changing Labels of Measures

- Right click on the measure and choose **Label Measurement** (or **Label Distance Measurement** depending on the type of measure) from the drop-down menu.
- Type in the new label.
- Click on **OK**.

Using the On-Screen Calculator

You can use the on-screen calculator to do calculations involving measurements, constants, functions, or other mathematical operations.

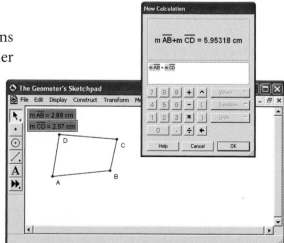

To add two lengths:
- From the **Measure** menu, choose **Calculate**. The on-screen calculator will appear.
- On the workspace, click on the first measure.
- On the keyboard, click on **+**.
- On the workspace, click on the second measure.
- Click on **OK**.

The sum of the measures will appear in the workspace.

OR

- Select the two measures. Then, choose **Calculate** from the **Measure** menu. This adds the measures to the drop-down list available by clicking on the **Values** button of the on-screen calculator.
- Click on the **Values** button. Select the first measure.
- Click on **+**.
- Click on the **Values** button. Select the second measure.
- Click on **OK**.

Coordinate System and Axes

The default coordinate system has an origin point in the centre of your screen and a unit point at (1, 0). Drag the origin to relocate the coordinate system and drag the unit point to change the scale.

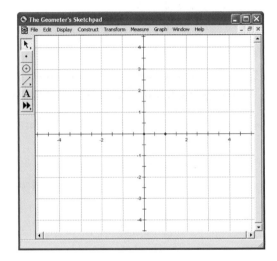

Creating Graphs

To plot a point on an *x*-*y* grid:
- From the **Graph** menu, choose **Plot Points...**.
- Ensure that Plot As is set to **Rectangular (x, y)**.
- Enter the *x*- and *y*-coordinates of the point.
- Click on **Plot**. A grid will appear with the plotted point. Click on **Done**.

You can plot additional points once you access the Plot Points dialogue box. Enter the coordinates of the next point and click on **Plot**. When you are finished plotting points, click on **Done**.

To graph an equation:
- From the **Graph** menu, select **Plot New Function**. A calculator screen with the heading **New Function** will appear.
- Using the calculator interface, enter the equation.
- Click on **OK**.

To plot a table of values:
- Select the table of data.
- From the **Graph** menu, select **Plot Table Data**.

Loading Custom Tools

Before you can use a **Custom Tool**, you must either create your own custom tools, or transfer the sample tools included with *The Geometer's Sketchpad*® program to the **Tool Folder**.

To transfer a sample custom tool:
- Open **Windows® Explorer**, and navigate to the **Sketchpad** directory, or whatever directory was used to install *The Geometer's Sketchpad*®.
- Choose **Samples**, and then **Custom Tools**. You will see a list of the custom tools provided with the program.
- Choose the sets of tools you want to use. Then, choose **Copy** from the **Edit** menu.
- Move back up two directory levels to the **Sketchpad** directory, and then choose **Tool Folder**. Choose **Paste** from the **Edit** menu.
- Open *The Geometer's Sketchpad*®. Choose the **Custom Tool**.

You will see the custom tool sets that you copied. Choose one of the tool sets, say **Polygons**. You will see a list of the individual tools available.

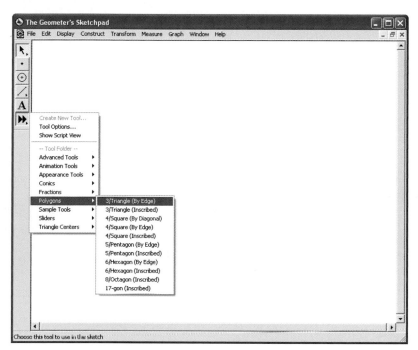

TI-83 PLUS AND TI-84 PLUS BASICS

The keys on the TI-83 Plus and TI-84 Plus are colour-coded to help you find the various functions.

- The grey keys include the number keys, decimal point, and negative sign. When entering negative values, use the grey $(-)$ key, not the blue $-$ key.
- The blue keys on the right side are the math operations.
- The blue keys across the top are used when graphing.
- The primary function of each key is printed on the key, in white.
- The secondary function of each key is printed in yellow and is activated by pressing the yellow 2nd key. For example, to find the square root of a number, press 2nd x^2 for [$\sqrt{\ }$].
- The alpha function of each key is printed in green and is activated by pressing the green ALPHA key.

Graphing Relations and Equations

- Press Y= . Enter the equation.
- To display the graph, press GRAPH .

For example, enter $y = \dfrac{3}{5}x - 2$ by pressing

Y= (3 ÷ 5) X,T,θ,n $-$ 2.

Press GRAPH .

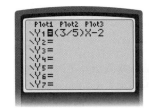
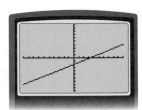

Setting Window Variables

The WINDOW key defines the appearance of the graph. The standard (default) window settings are shown.

To change the window settings:

- Press WINDOW . Enter the desired window settings.

In the example shown,

- the minimum x-value is -47
- the maximum x-value is 47
- the scale of the x-axis is 10
- the minimum y-value is -31
- the maximum y-value is 31
- the scale of the y-axis is 10
- the resolution is 1, so equations are graphed at each horizontal pixel

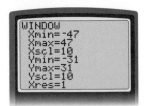

Setting Up a Table of Values

The standard (default) table settings are shown.
This feature allows the X's of the Table to be specified.

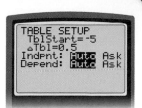

To change the Table Set-Up settings
- Press $\boxed{\text{2nd}}$ $\boxed{\text{WINDOW}}$. Enter the desired values.

In the example shown,
- The starting x-value of the table is –5.
- The change in x-values is 0.5.
- Press $\boxed{\text{2nd}}$ $\boxed{\text{GRAPH}}$.

The table values will appear as shown.

Setting Up the Display

The standard (default) graph screen display type is "FULL".
The standard (default) graph screen is shown.

To change to a Graph-Table (G-T) view
- Press $\boxed{\text{MODE}}$ $\boxed{\blacktriangledown}$ $\boxed{\blacktriangledown}$ $\boxed{\blacktriangledown}$ $\boxed{\blacktriangledown}$
  $\boxed{\blacktriangledown}$ $\boxed{\blacktriangledown}$ $\boxed{\blacktriangledown}$ $\boxed{\blacktriangleright}$ $\boxed{\blacktriangleright}$ $\boxed{\text{ENTER}}$.
- Press $\boxed{\text{GRAPH}}$.

 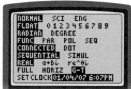 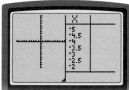

The vertical split-screen will appear as shown.

Tracing a Graph

- Enter a function using $\boxed{\text{Y=}}$.
- Press $\boxed{\text{TRACE}}$.
- Press $\boxed{\blacktriangleleft}$ and $\boxed{\blacktriangleright}$ to move along the graph.

The x- and y-values are displayed at the bottom of the screen.

If you have more than one graph plotted, use the $\boxed{\blacktriangle}$ and $\boxed{\blacktriangledown}$ keys to move the cursor to the graph you wish to trace.

You may want to turn off all STAT PLOTS before you trace a function:
- Press $\boxed{\text{2nd}}$ $\boxed{\text{Y=}}$ for [STAT PLOT]. Select **4:PlotsOff.**
- Press $\boxed{\text{ENTER}}$.

Using Zoom

The ZOOM key is used to change the area of the graph that is displayed in the graphing window.

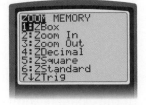

To set the size of the area you want to zoom in on:

- Press [ZOOM]. Select **1:Zbox**. The graph screen will be displayed, and the cursor will be flashing.
- If you cannot see the cursor, use the [▶], [◀], [▲], and [▼] keys to move the cursor until you see it.
- Move the cursor to an area on the edge of where you would like a closer view. Press [ENTER] to mark that point as a starting point.
- Press the [▶], [◀], [▲], and [▼] keys as needed to move the sides of the box to enclose the area you want to look at.
- Press [ENTER] when you are finished. The area will now appear larger.

To zoom in on an area without identifying a boxed-in area:

- Press [ZOOM]. Select **2:Zoom In**.

To zoom out of an area:

- Press [ZOOM]. Select **3:Zoom Out**.

To display the viewing area where the origin appears in the centre and the *x*- and *y*-axes intervals are equally spaced:

- Press [ZOOM]. Select **4:ZDecimal**.

To reset the axes range on your calculator:

- Press [ZOOM]. Select **6:ZStandard**.

To display all data points in a STAT PLOT:

- Press [ZOOM]. Select **9:ZoomStat**.

Setting the Format

To define a graph's appearance:

- Press [2nd] [ZOOM] for [FORMAT] to view the choices available.

The **Default Settings**, shown here, have all the features on the left "turned on."

To use Grid Off/Grid On:

- Select [FORMAT] by pressing [2nd] [ZOOM]. Cursor down and right to **GridOn**.
- Press [ENTER].
- Press [2nd] [ZOOM] for [QUIT].

Working With Fractions

To display a decimal as a fraction:
- Key in a decimal.
- Press $\boxed{\text{MATH}}$, and then select **1:▶Frac**. Press $\boxed{\text{ENTER}}$.

The decimal will be displayed as a fraction.

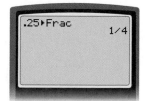

To enter fractions in calculations:
- Use the division key $\boxed{\div}$ to create fractions as you key them in.
- If you want the result displayed as a fraction, Press $\boxed{\text{MATH}}$, and then select **1:▶Frac**.
- Press $\boxed{\text{ENTER}}$.

For example, to calculate $\dfrac{3}{4} - \dfrac{2}{3}$:
- Press 3 $\boxed{\div}$ 4 $\boxed{-}$ 2 $\boxed{\div}$ 3.
- Then, press $\boxed{\text{MATH}}$, select **1:▶Frac**, and then press $\boxed{\text{ENTER}}$.

The result will be displayed as a fraction.

To calculate with mixed numbers:
- Use the $\boxed{+}$ and $\boxed{\div}$ keys to enter mixed numbers.
- If you want the result displayed as a fraction, press $\boxed{\text{MATH}}$, select **1:▶Frac**, and then press $\boxed{\text{ENTER}}$.

For example, to calculate $2\dfrac{3}{8} + 1\dfrac{3}{4}$:
- Press 2 $\boxed{+}$ 3 $\boxed{\div}$ 8 $\boxed{+}$ 1 $\boxed{+}$ 3 $\boxed{\div}$ 4.
- Then, press $\boxed{+}$, select **1:▶Frac**, and then press $\boxed{\text{ENTER}}$.

The result will be displayed as a fraction.

Entering Data Into Lists

To enter data:
- Press $\boxed{\text{STAT}}$. The cursor will highlight the **EDIT** menu.
- Press **1** or $\boxed{\text{ENTER}}$ to select **1:Edit…**.

This allows you to enter new data, or edit existing data, in lists **L1** to **L6**.

For example, press $\boxed{\text{STAT}}$, select **1:Edit…**, and then enter six test scores in list **L1**.
- Use the cursor keys to move around the editor screen.
- Complete each data entry by pressing $\boxed{\text{ENTER}}$.
- Press $\boxed{\text{2nd}}$ $\boxed{\text{MODE}}$ for [QUIT] to exit the list editor when the data are entered.

You may need to clear a list before you enter data into it.
For example, to clear list **L1**:

- Press `STAT` and select **4:ClrList**.
- Press `2nd` **1** for [L1], and press `ENTER`.

  OR

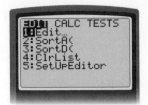

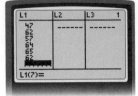

To clear all lists:

- Press `2nd` `+` for [MEM] to display the **MEMORY** menu.
- Select **4:ClrAllLists**, and then press `ENTER`.

Creating a Scatter Plot

To create a scatter plot:

- Enter the two data sets in lists **L1** and **L2**.
- Press `2nd` `Y=` for [STAT PLOT].
- Press **1** or `ENTER` to select **1:Plot1...**.
- Press `ENTER` to select **On**.
- Cursor down, and then press `ENTER` to select the top left graphing option, a scatter plot.
- Cursor down and press `2nd` **1** for [L1].
- Cursor down and press `2nd` **2** for [L2].
- Cursor down and select a mark style by pressing `ENTER`.
- Press `2nd` `MODE` for [QUIT] to exit the **STAT PLOTS** editor when the data are entered.

To display the scatter plot:

- Press `Y=` and use the `CLEAR` key to remove any graphed equations.
- Press `2nd` `MODE` for [QUIT] to exit the **Y=** editor.
- Press *z* and select **9:ZoomStat** to display the scatter plot.

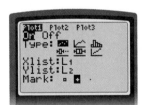

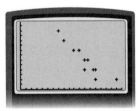

Line of Best Fit

You can add the line of best fit to a scatter plot by using the LinReg function:

- With the scatter plot displayed, press `STAT`. Cursor over to display the **CALC** menu, and then select **4:LinReg(ax+b)**.
- Press `2nd` **1** for [L1], followed by `,`.
- Press `2nd` **2** for [L2], followed by `,`.
- Then, press `VARS`, cursor over to display the **Y-VARS** menu, select **1:FUNCTION**, and then select **1:Y1**.

- Press `ENTER` to get the LinReg screen, and then press `GRAPH`.

The linear regression equation is stored in the **Y=** editor. If you press `Y=`, you will see the equation generated by the calculator.

Note: If the diagnostic mode is turned on, you will see values for **r** and **r²** displayed on the LinReg screen. To turn the diagnostic mode off:

- Press ⌈ 2nd ⌉ **0** for [CATALOG].
- Scroll down to **DiagnosticOff**. Press ⌈ENTER⌉ to select this option.
- Press ⌈ENTER⌉ again to turn off the diagnostic mode.

 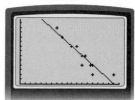

Finding an Intersection Point

There must be at least two equations in the calculator's Equation Editor.

- Press ⌈ Y= ⌉.

The example shows two linear equations.
An intersection point <u>must</u> be seen.

In the example, shown, an intersection point is seen.

- Press ⌈GRAPH⌉.

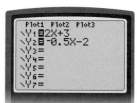

Note: If an intersection point is not seen adjust the **WINDOW** settings accordingly.
To find an intersection point,

- Press ⌈ 2nd ⌉ ⌈TRACE⌉ 5 ⌈ENTER⌉ ⌈ENTER⌉ ⌈ENTER⌉.

An intersection point will appear at the bottom of the screen.

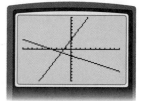

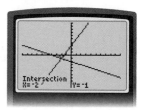

Finding a Zero or Maximum/Minimum Value

There must be at least one equation in the Equation Editor.

- Press ⌈ Y= ⌉.

The example shows a parabola.

To calculate a zero (x-intercept), maximum, or minimum there <u>must</u> be one seen.

- Press ⌈GRAPH⌉.

Note: If a zero (x-intercept), maximum, or minimum is not seen adjust the WINDOW settings accordingly.

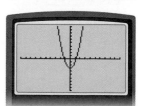

To find a zero,

- Press `2nd` [TRACE] 2.

Move to the left side of a zero (*x*-intercept) by pressing and holding the left cursor key.

- Press `ENTER`.

Move to the right side of a zero (*x*-intercept) by pressing and holding the right cursor key.

- Press `ENTER`.

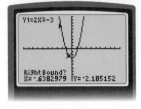

To find the value of a zero (*x*-intercept) using the calculator's guess,

- Press `ENTER`.

A zero (x-intercept) is shown at the bottom of the screen.

To find a minimum,

- Press `2nd` [TRACE] 3.

Move to the left side of a minimum by pressing and holding the left cursor key.

- Press `ENTER`.

Move to the right side of a minimum by pressing and holding the right cursor key.

- Press `ENTER`.

To find the value of a minimum using the calculator's guess,
- Press `ENTER`.

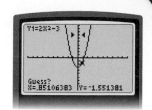

A minimum is shown at the bottom of the screen. Sometimes the values of X and/or Y are not exact because of the method used by the calculator to determine the values. The value for X, shown, is $-1.938E-6$. This means the number is -1.938×10^{-6}, in scientific notation. Moving the decimal six places to the left will give the number in standard form (0.000 001 938). In this case assume that the X of the minimum is 0 rather than 0.000 001 938.

To find a maximum,
Press `2nd` [TRACE] 4. Follow a similar procedure as above.

Using the CBR™ (Calculator-Based Ranger)

To access the CBR™ through the TI-83 Plus or TI-84 Plus:
- Connect the CBR™ to the TI-83 Plus or TI-84 Plus with the calculator-to-CBR cable.

Make sure both ends of the cable are firmly in place.
- Press `APPS`. Select **2:CBL/CBR**.
- When the CBL/CBR™ screen is presented, press `ENTER`.
- To access the programs available, select **3:Ranger**.
- When the **Ranger** menu is presented, press `ENTER`.

To record data from the CBR™:
- From the MAIN MENU screen, select **1:SETUP/SAMPLE**. All settings, except TIME (S), can be changed by using the cursor keys to position the `▶` beside the current option and pressing `ENTER` to cycle through the choices.

If the REALTIME option is set to YES, the sampling time is fixed at 15 s. To change the TIME (S) setting, you must first change the REALTIME option to NO, as shown. Then, cursor down to TIME (S), enter the desired value.

- Move the cursor up to START NOW at the top of the screen, and then press `ENTER`.

TI-89 TITANIUM BASICS

Accessing the Home Screen

The standard (default) screen for the TI-89 is shown.

To go to this screen,
• Press [HOME].

Pressing the [HOME] key will always take you back home screen.

Clearing the Home Screen

To clear the home screen,
• Press [F1] 8.

Clearing the Command Prompt Line

To clear the command prompt line,
• Press [CLEAR].

Clearing a Row of Information from the Home Screen or Re-computing a Command

In the example, rows of data exist for each command executed.

To go to any row from the home screen,
• Press the up arrow the appropriate number of times to highlight a row.

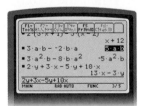

To delete a row from the home screen,
• Press [CLEAR]. Note that the row above has been deleted.

To re-compute a command from any row, highlight the row.
• Press the up arrow the appropriate number of times to highlight a row.

- Press [ENTER] [ENTER]. Note the first time you press enter the information is pasted in the command prompt line.

The second time you press enter the command is executed.

Clearing Out One-Character Variables

A letter may have a stored numerical value. This forces the calculator to compute a numerical answer if operations involving the letter are requested.

In the example, the calculator computed a value of 2 for the expansion of $x(x + 1)$ rather than the algebraic answer, $x^2 + x$, because x had a stored numerical value of 1.

To clear all one-character variables,
- Press [2nd] [F1] [ENTER] [ENTER].

In the example, the calculator provided the algebraic answer.

Accessing a Catalogue of Commands

To access an alphabetic catalogue of commands,
- Press [CATALOG].

To move to a different letter in the list of commands,
- Press [ALPHA] and the first letter of the command desired. Scroll down to the appropriate command and press [ENTER] to paste it to the command prompt line.

Collecting Terms with One Variable in Each Term

In the example, the calculator simplified $2x - 7x$.
To do this,
- Press 2 [X] [−] 7 [X] [ENTER].

In the example, the calculator simplified $3x - 4y + 7x + 8y$.

To do this,
- Press 3 [X] [−] 4 [Y] [+] 7 [X] [+] 8 [Y] [ENTER].

Collecting Terms with More than One Variable in Terms

When there are two variables next to each other there must be a multiplication sign between them otherwise the calculators treat groups of variables as separate items. In other words, the term xy would be treated differently than the term yx. They are not considered like terms unless there were a multiplication sign between both pairs of variables.

In the example, the calculator did not add the like terms of xy and yx until there was a multiplication sign between the variables.

To do this,

- Press $\boxed{X}$ $\boxed{Y}$ $\boxed{+}$ $\boxed{Y}$ $\boxed{X}$ $\boxed{\text{ENTER}}$.
- Press $\boxed{\text{CLEAR}}$ $\boxed{X}$ $\boxed{\times}$ $\boxed{Y}$ $\boxed{+}$ $\boxed{Y}$ $\boxed{\times}$ $\boxed{X}$ $\boxed{\text{ENTER}}$.

Collecting Terms with More than One Variable in Terms Containing Exponents

In the example, the calculator will collect the like terms $2x^2y^2 - 5y^2x^2$ even though there is no multiplication sign between the variables. This is because the variables are not directly beside each other.

To do this,

- Press 2 $\boxed{X}$ $\boxed{\wedge}$ 2 $\boxed{Y}$ $\boxed{\wedge}$ 2 $\boxed{-}$ 5 $\boxed{Y}$ $\boxed{\wedge}$ 2 $\boxed{X}$ $\boxed{\wedge}$ 2 $\boxed{\text{ENTER}}$.

In the example, the calculator will not collect the like terms $2xy^2 - 5y^2x$ because the x and y in the first term are side by side.

Only when there is a multiplication sign between the x and y in the first term, will the simplified answer be correct.

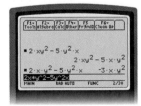

Expanding Expressions

To expand an expression,

- Press [F2] 3.

In the example, the calculator expanded $2(x + 3)$.

To do this,

- Press 2 [(] [x] [+] 3 [)] [)].
  Note the last bracket is essential.

In the example, the calculator expanded $2x(x + 3)$.

To do this,

- Press [F2] 3 2 [x] [×] [(] [x] [+] 3 [)] [)].

Note the multiplication sign is necessary to use when multiplying variables together.

In the example, the calculator expanded $(x + 3)(2x - 1)$.

To do this,

- Press [F2] 3 [(] [x] [+] 3 [)]
  [(] 2 [x] [−] 1 [)] [)].

Note a multiplication sign between brackets is not necessary.

Factoring Expressions

In the example the calculator factored $x^2 + 6x$.

To do this,

- Press [F2] 2 [x] [^] 2 [+] 6 [x] [)] [ENTER].

In the example the calculator factored $x^2 + 2x - 8$.

To do this,

- Press [F2] 2 [x] [^] 2 [+] 2 [x] [−] 8 [)] [ENTER].

Working with Fractions

In the example, the calculator added $\frac{1}{2} + \frac{7}{8}$.

To do this,

- Press 1 $\boxed{÷}$ 2 $\boxed{+}$ 7 $\boxed{÷}$ 8 $\boxed{\text{ENTER}}$.

In the example, the calculator converted an improper to a mixed fraction.

To do this,

- Press $\boxed{\text{F2}}$ 7 11 $\boxed{÷}$ 8 $\boxed{)}$ $\boxed{\text{ENTER}}$.

In the example, the calculator converted a fraction to a decimal.

To do this,

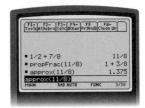

- Press $\boxed{\text{F2}}$ 5 11 $\boxed{÷}$ 8 $\boxed{)}$ $\boxed{\text{ENTER}}$.

Rounding Values

In the example, the calculator rounded the number to the nearest hundredth (two decimal places).

To do this,

- Press $\boxed{\text{2nd}}$ 5 $\boxed{▶}$ 3 11 $\boxed{÷}$ 8 $\boxed{,}$ 2 $\boxed{)}$ $\boxed{\text{ENTER}}$.
- Press $\boxed{\text{2nd}}$ 5 $\boxed{▶}$ 3 1.375 $\boxed{,}$ 2 $\boxed{)}$ $\boxed{\text{ENTER}}$.

Note that the 2 indicated the number of decimal places to round.

Finding a Common Denominator

In the example, the calculator found the common denominator for $\frac{3}{8} + 1\frac{1}{6} - \frac{1}{5}$ using the Least Common Multiple (lcm).
This command can only find the lcm for two numbers at a time.
Break the process into two steps. Find the lcm of the one first pair.
Find the lcm of the answer from one first pair with last value.

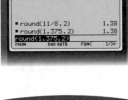

To do this,

- Press $\boxed{\text{2nd}}$ 5 $\boxed{▶}$ $\boxed{\text{ALPHA}}$ $\boxed{(}$ 8 $\boxed{,}$ 6 $\boxed{)}$ $\boxed{\text{ENTER}}$.
- Press $\boxed{▶}$ $\boxed{◀}$ $\boxed{◀}$ $\boxed{◀}$ $\boxed{◀}$ 24 $\boxed{,}$ 5 $\boxed{)}$ $\boxed{\text{ENTER}}$.

Note this command used the right arrow key to move the cursor to the right side of the command prompt and then the backspace key to remove text to the first bracket.

Answers

Note: Solutions to the Investigations, Discuss the Concepts questions, Achievement Check questions, Chapter Problem Wrap-up, Tasks, and some technology questions are provided in the *McGraw-Hill Foundations of Mathematics 10 Teacher's Resource*.

CHAPTER 1
Measuring Systems and Similar Triangles, pages 2–41

Get Ready!, pages 4–5

1. a) $\frac{5}{32}, \frac{3}{8}, \frac{1}{2}, \frac{3}{4}$ **b)** $\frac{1}{4}, \frac{5}{16}, \frac{11}{32}, \frac{7}{5}, 1\frac{1}{2}$ **c)** $\frac{5}{64}, \frac{3}{8}, \frac{9}{16}$

2. a) $\frac{9}{16}$ **b)** $\frac{53}{64}$ **c)** $-\frac{1}{16}$

d) $\frac{3}{8}$ **e)** $\frac{3}{32}$ **f)** $8\frac{3}{4}$

g) $\frac{3}{8}$ **h)** 52 **i)** $1\frac{7}{8}$

j) $\frac{3}{8}$

3. a) 3:1 **b)** 4:1 **c)** 2:3:6

4. a) $x = \frac{3}{5}$ **b)** $x = 15$ **c)** $p = 12$

d) $s = 2.5$ **e)** $p = 9, q = 15$

5. a) $x = 100°, y = 80°$ **b)** $x = 159°$
c) $x = 124°, y = 124°,$ **d)** $a = 122°, b = 58°$
$z = 56°$
e) $x = 41°$ **f)** $p = 48°$

1.1 Imperial Measure, pages 6–11

1. a) $2\frac{1}{2}$ in. **b)** $3\frac{3}{16}$ in. **c)** $2\frac{3}{16}$ in.

2. a) 2 pt, 1 qt **b)** 12 pt, 6 qt

c) 5 pt, 2.5 qt **d)** $6\frac{3}{4}$ pt, $3\frac{3}{8}$ qt

3. a) 16 gal **b)** 6.5 gal **c)** 6.25 gal

4. a) 160 fl oz **b)** 128 fl oz **c)** 384 fl oz **d)** 80 fl oz

5. a) 2 lb **b)** 28.5 lb

6. a) 48 oz **b)** 89.6 oz

7. In some cases, other answers are appropriate.
  a) book: inches; desk: feet/inches; lawn: yards/feet; airfield: miles/yards
  b) thimble: fluid ounces; glass: fluid ounces; pool: gallons; ocean: gallons
  c) paper: ounces; book: ounces; person: pounds; car: pounds/tons

8. 3.5 fl oz

9. $6\frac{2}{3}$ yd

10. $84\frac{3}{8}$ lb

11. 30 ft

12. $304.63

13. Answers will vary.

14. He will need to rent scaffolding because he will only reach a height of 14' 3".

15. a) 124 sq ft **b)** 318.47 sq ft **c)** 326.83 sq ft

16. $4351.28 after tax

17. a) total area $= 306\frac{83}{125}$ or 306.67 sq ft

  b) Need 2.788 qt, so need to buy 3 qt or $\frac{3}{4}$ gal.

1.2 Conversions Between Metric and Imperial Systems, pages 12–18

1. a) 16 km **b)** 3 yd **c)** 24 L **d)** 70.9 kg
  e) 30 mL **f)** 24 in. **g)** 4 qt **h)** 1.33 lb
  i) 70°F **j)** 25°C

2. 4.8 in.

3. Orlando, because 87°F is 30.6°C

4. 6 L

5. 366.9 km

6. a) approximation **b)** exact **c)** approximation
  d) approximation **e)** exact **f)** approximation/exact

7. A metric tonne, because 1 kg is approximately 2.2 lb. Thus, 1000 kg is about 2200 lb, and an imperial ton is 2000 lb.

8. Since 5 m is about 16.4 ft, only the Blackhaw viburnum should be planted under the hydro wires.

9. $0.80/L

10. Yes; $\frac{5}{16}$ in. is 0.794 cm and 5 mm is 0.5 cm, so it will fit, but the hole may be a little larger than necessary.

11. 1.35 kg red currants, 750 mL sugar, 255 mL water, 15 mL cornstarch

12. $6.59/kg is better because there are 2.204 kg in a pound, and 2.204 × $3.06 = $6.74/kg

13. 4 bottles per day.

14. a) 41°F to 140°F **b)** 65.56°C

16. 27.6 mpg

17. Baby is 4.218 kg; 2.5 mL/kg → 10.55 mL/4.218 kg baby → 2.1 tsp per 4 hours

18. 45.5 mpg

1.3 Similar Triangles, pages 19–29

1. a) $\angle A = \angle D, \angle B = \angle E, \angle C = \angle F$; AB ~ DE, AC ~ DF,
  BC ~ EF; $\frac{AB}{DE} = \frac{AC}{DF} = \frac{BC}{EF}$

b) ∠P = ∠U, ∠Q = ∠S, ∠R = ∠T; PQ ~ US, PR ~ UT,

QR ~ ST; $\dfrac{PR}{UT} = \dfrac{PQ}{US} = \dfrac{QR}{ST}$

2. a) ∠Y = 88°, ∠D = 45°, ∠F = 47°, EF = 10, XY = 4

   b) ∠C = 85°, ∠DBE = 32°, ∠D = 63°, DB = 16, BE = $13\frac{1}{3}$

   c) ∠C = 55°, ∠P = 33°, ∠Q = 92°, AB = 13.5, PR = 8.3

3. a) 19.5   **b)** 5

4. 7.4

5. 12.5

6. $b = 7.3$ cm, $d = 2.5$ cm

7. Answers will vary.

8. Yes, because $\dfrac{v}{p} = \dfrac{w}{q} = \dfrac{x}{r} = 1.4$.

9. ∠C = 40°, ∠P = 50°, ∠Q = 90°, ∠R = 40°, AC = 6.4 cm, QR = 15 cm, PR = 19.2 cm

10. PQ = 6.67 in.

11. a) 4.2 cm   **b)** Answers will vary.

12. Answers will vary.

14. a) Yes, because $\dfrac{AB}{DE} = \dfrac{AC}{DF} = \dfrac{BC}{EF} = \dfrac{1}{2}$.

   b) 10 sq units, 40 sq units

   c) Area (ABC) : Area (DEF) = 1:4. $\dfrac{1}{4} = \left(\dfrac{1}{2}\right)^2$

   d) The ratio comparing the areas of two similar triangles will be the square of the ratio comparing the lengths of corresponding sides.

   e)

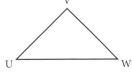

15. 128 cm²

16. 4:9

1.4 Solve Problems Using Similar Triangles, pages 30–37

1. Answers will vary. tree, building, flag pole, width of a river, CN Tower

2. Measure the shadow of the object and set up a proportion using the length of the shadow created by a metre stick.

3. Answers will vary.

4. 7 m

5. 83.7 m

6. 10 m

7. It reaches 6.4 ft further up the wall.

8.

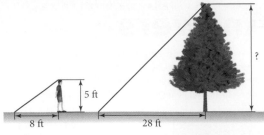

17.5 ft

9.

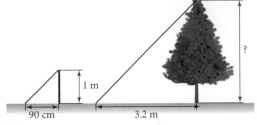

3.56 m

10. 43.3 m

11. 68.6 cm

12. 124.3 cm

14. 249.4 m

15. 10 cm

16. a) 40 000 km   **b)** same   **c)** 12 732.4 km

Chapter 1 Review, pages 38–39

1. a) imperial system

   b) ratio

   c) corresponding angles; corresponding sides

   d) proportional

2. a) matching sides in similar triangles

   b) matching angles in similar triangles

3. a) 30″   **b)** 6.25 qt   **c)** 12.5 lb

4. 77 ft 8 in.

5. 2 c

6. a) 3.72 mi   **b)** 1.5 gal   **c)** 71.6°F   **d)** 26.246′

7. One gallon for $3.58 is the better buy.

8. $257.04 after tax

9. 10.6 tbsp

10. a) ∠A = ∠D, ∠B = ∠E, ∠C = ∠F

   b) AB ~ DE, BC ~ EF, AC ~ DF

   c) $\dfrac{AB}{DE}, \dfrac{AC}{DF}, \dfrac{BC}{EF}$

   d) $\dfrac{AB}{DE} = \dfrac{AC}{DF} = \dfrac{BC}{EF}$

11. $\angle C = 30° = \angle D$, AB = 24, $\angle F = 35°$, FD = 29

12. $\triangle ZDE \sim \triangle ZXY$, XY = 16.53 cm

13. 33.3 cm

14.

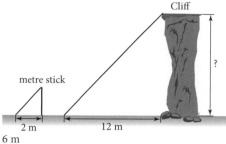

15. 30 m

16. 28 ft 9 in.

Chapter 1 Practice Test, pages 40–41

1. 4"

2. 1 lb

3. 144"

4. Yes; $\frac{3}{8}$ in. is 9.5 mm.

5. Yes; 6.5 L per 100 km is equivalent to 36 miles per gallon.

6. Yes; 1 L is 4 c of milk, which gives you 1200 mg of calcium.

7. a) $\angle Q = \angle X$, $\angle R = \angle Y$, $\angle S = \angle Z$

   b) QR ~ XY, QS ~ XZ, RS ~ YZ

   c) $\dfrac{QR}{XY}, \dfrac{QS}{XZ}, \dfrac{RS}{YZ}$

   d) $\dfrac{QR}{XY} = \dfrac{QS}{XZ} = \dfrac{RS}{YZ}$

8. $\triangle AEB \sim \triangle CED$; AE = 3.52 cm

9. $\triangle BDE \sim \triangle BAC$; BA = 17.5 cm

10.

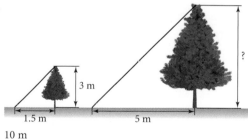

11.

[figure: Sean 6 ft, 10 ft, mirror, 30 ft, 18 ft, Cliff ?]

12. $\triangle ABC \sim \triangle DEC$; AB = 9.6 mm

CHAPTER 2
Right Triangle Trigonometry, pages 42–91

Get Ready!, pages 44–45

1. a) $x = 3$ **b)** $x = 2$ **c)** $x = 4$
   d) $x = 0.8$ **e)** $x = 6$ **f)** $x = 3$
   g) $x = 55$ **h)** $x = 8$ **i)** $x = 90$
   j) $x = 18$

2. a) $x = 3.6$ **b)** $x = 0.75$ **c)** $x = 0.9375$
   d) $x = 8$ **e)** $x = 132$ **f)** $x = 59.4$
   g) $x = 2.4$ **h)** $x = 11.25$ **i)** $x = 3.2$

3. a) 44°   **b)** 13°   **c)** 79°
   d) 58°   **e)** 78°   **f)** 90°
   g) 42°

4. a) 4.9   **b)** 2.3   **c)** 9.6
   d) 3.3   **e)** 5.4   **f)** 2.0
   g) 27.0

5. a) 2.3461   **b)** 0.0997   **c)** 3.4623
   d) 0.8563   **e)** 0.9091   **f)** 3.7564
   g) 31.6058

6. a) 576   **b)** 3136   **c)** 5041
   d) 144   **e)** 1444   **f)** 361
   g) 729

7. a) 5.2   **b)** 5.9   **c)** 13.7
   d) 16.9   **e)** 33.8   **f)** 7.9
   g) 23.3

8. a) 45   **b)** 50   **c)** 41
   d) 80   **e)** 19   **f)** 157
   g) 165

2.1 The Pythagorean Theorem, pages 46–53

1. AB = 10.8; BC = 5.8; CD = 10.8; AD = 12.0

2. a) 29.2 m   **b)** 11.7 cm   **c)** 12.6 in.   **d)** 42.5 m

3. a) 20 m   **b)** 8 m   **c)** 5 m   **d)** 36 m

4. a) 4.6 m   **b)** 5.1 m   **c)** 9.8 m

5. 174.0 m

6. a) 14.6 m
b) Answers may vary.

7. a) 16"
b) 42.4"
c) Answers may vary.
d) They may think that the measurement quoted is the width of the TV.
e) Answers will vary.

8. No, because the diagonal of the doorway is 92.3 in. and the drywall is 96 in. tall.

9. a) 44 cm
b) Answers will vary.

10. 127.3 ft

11. No, because the hypotenuse should be 5' not 5'3".

12. 27.3 cm

13. 4 ft.

14. a) 3.3 m
b) 3.0 m

15. 2.8 m

2.2 Explore Ratio and Proportion in Right Triangles, pages 54–62

1. a)

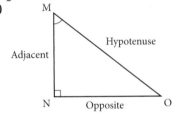

b)

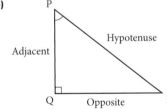

c)

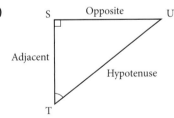

d)

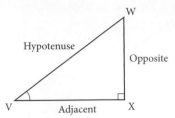

e)

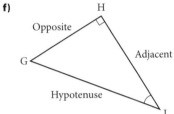

f)

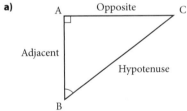

2. a)

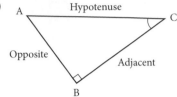

b)

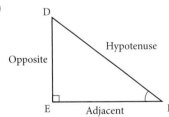

c)

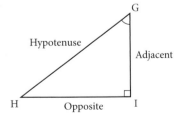

d)

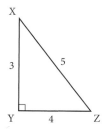

3. 5.8 : 10.4; 0.558

4. 12 : 13; 0.923

5. 24 : 29; 0.828

6. 12 : 17; 0.71

7. a) 2.1 : 3.5; 0.60   **b)** 3.1 : 3.5; 0.89

8. a) 0.53

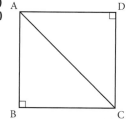

b) 0.6

9. Answers will vary.

10. a)
b)

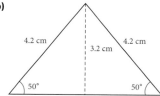

c)

Rate of Change	△ABC	△ACD
Opp. to ∠A	BC	DC
Adj. to ∠A	AB	AD
Opp. to ∠C	AB	AD
Adj. to ∠C	BC	DC

d) 3 : 3 = 1; Ratio is always 1.
e) No. It is only true in a square.

11. a) 0.71   **b)** 0.77   **c)** 0.64

12. a) 24.0   **b)** 17 : 17 = 1

13. a) XZ = 1.4   **b)** 0.71   **c)** 0.71

2.3 The Sine and Cosine Ratios, pages 63–73

1. a) 0.6691   **b)** 0.5446   **c)** 0.9455
   d) 0.9994   **e)** 0.2756   **f)** 0.7880
   g) 0.7071   **h)** 0.7431

2. a) 38°   **b)** 66°   **c)** 8°
   d) 51°   **e)** 67°   **f)** 17°
   g) 55°   **h)** 44°

3. a) 25.6 cm   **b)** 8.0 cm

4. 3.4 cm

5. 19.3 cm

6. 51°

7. 7.3 cm

8. 57°

9. 2.4 m

10. Yes. The ladder reaches 9.4 m above ground.

11. 1.5 m

12. 0.85 m

13. If triangle ABC has a right angle at B, then sin A = cos C and cos A = sin C.

14. 26 695 ft

16. a) 8.1 cm   **b)** 63°   **c)** 15.9 cm

17. a) 4.2 cm
b)

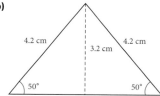

18. 41°

2.4 The Tangent Ratio, pages 74–82

1. a) 0.5317   **b)** 0.7265
   c) 1.0000   **d)** 3.0777

2. a) 19°   **b)** 66°
   c) 88°   **d)** 57°

3. 57.6 m

4. 51 m

5. 43 cm

6. 18 cm

7. 38 ft

8. a) SOH means that the sine ratio is opposite over hypotenuse, CAH means that the cosine ratio is adjacent over hypotenuse, and TOA means that the tangent ratio is opposite over adjacent.

b) Answers may vary.

9. Yes, because the ship is 2282 m, or 2.282 km, from the base of the cliff.

10. 211 cm; this measurement seems small for a house.

11. 2°

12. 7.2 m

13. 32°

15. 40°

16. a) 132°   **b)** 19.7 ft

2.5 Solve Problems Using Right Triangles, pages 83–87

1. 10.2 m

2. 85.9 m

3. 4.9 m

4. 2290 ft

5. 49 m

6. 72°

7. 101 m

8. 11 m

9. 13 m

10. 4.2 m

11. The shorter building is 10.1 m, and the taller building is 26.8 m.

12. 2.4 m

13. 12.8°

Chapter 2 Review, pages 88–89

1. Pythagorean theorem

2. sine ratio

3. cosine ratio

4. tangent ratio

5. 66.3 ft

6. 156.6 cm

7. 687.7 ft

8. a) 2.1 : 1.2
b) 2.1 : 1.2
c) The ratios are the same.

9. 42°

10. 57.4 km

11. 10.5 m

12. 16.1 cm

13. 16°

14. 59.6 ft

15. 2.1 m

16. 8.4 m

17. a) 66.6 ft   **b)** 22.4 ft

Chapter 2 Practice Test, pages 90–91

1. $a^2 + b^2 = c^2$, where a and b are the lengths of the legs and c is the length of the hypotenuse.

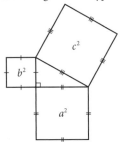

2. a)

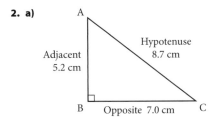

b) $\sin A = \dfrac{BC}{AC} = 0.8046$

3. a)

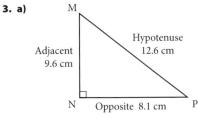

b) $\cos M = \dfrac{MN}{MP} = 0.7619$

4. a)

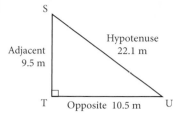

b) $\tan S = \dfrac{TU}{ST} = 1.1053$

5. 6.2 cm

6. 11.3 m

7. a) 7.3 cm   **b)** 5.4 cm

8. a) 12.2 cm   **b)** 10.0 cm

9. a) 85°   **b)** 54.8 m

10. 7.8 ft

Chapter 1 to 2 Review, pages 94–95
Chapter 1, page 94

1. a) 240 ft^2 **b)** $\dfrac{9}{16}$ ft^2

  c) 427   **d)** 18
  e) $2088

2. 4.53 h

3. $4.9/kg

4. a) AC = 60 cm; EF = 50.4 cm;
  ∠C = 31°; ∠E = 117°; ∠D = 32°
  b) GH = 11.4 in.; JI = 5.5 in.;
  ∠G = 67°; ∠JIK = 42°; ∠K = 67°

5. 34.6 m

6. 0.4 m

7. 84 ft

Chapter 2, page 95
8. a) 15 cm   **b)** 15.5 cm

9. a) 6.7 ft   **b)** 14.5 ft

10. a) $\sin A = \dfrac{8}{17}$; $\cos A = \dfrac{15}{17}$; $\tan A = \dfrac{8}{15}$
  b) $\sin E = \dfrac{13}{18}$; $\cos E = \dfrac{6}{9}$; $\tan E = \dfrac{13}{12}$

11. 12 ft

12. 90 m

13. 19 ft

14. 54.78 m

15. 146 m

CHAPTER 3
Linear Relations, pages 96–149

Get Ready!, pages 98–99

1. a) 3   **b)** 5   **c)** 3
  d) 4   **e)** 3   **f)** 1
  g) 7   **h)** 12

2. a) $\dfrac{4}{3}$ **b)** $\dfrac{2}{5}$ **c)** $\dfrac{1}{6}$
  d) $\dfrac{1}{4}$ **e)** $\dfrac{1}{3}$ **f)** $\dfrac{8}{15}$

3.

	Fraction	Decimal
a)	$\dfrac{1}{2}$	0.5
b)	$\dfrac{3}{5}$	0.6
c)	$\dfrac{3}{8}$	0.375
d)	$\dfrac{1}{4}$	0.25
e)	$\dfrac{1}{20}$	0.05
f)	$\dfrac{5}{8}$	0.625

4. a) 13   **b)** −2   **c)** −4
  d) −12   **e)** 4   **f)** 13

5. a) $-\dfrac{1}{2}$ **b)** −3   **c)** 3
  d) 2   **e)** $-\dfrac{1}{2}$ **f)** $-\dfrac{3}{11}$

6. A(4, 7), B(−3, 2), C(0, −5), D(−4, −1),
  E(−8, 5.5), F(6.5, 0)

7. a) −2   **b)** 4   **c)** −6
  d) −14   **e)** 14   **f)** 4

8. a) −9   **b)** 13   **c)** −3
  d) 6.5   **e)** −46   **f)** 0

3.1 Slope as a Rate of Change, pages 100–110
1. a) rise = 5, run = 5, slope = 1
  b) rise = 10, run = 5, slope = 2
  c) rise = 15, run = 10, slope = 1.5
  d) rise = 6, run = 12, slope = 0.5

2. a)

x	y	Rate of Change
0	5	
1	7	2
2	9	2
3	11	2
4	13	2

b)

x	y	Rate of Change
0	3	
1	4	1
2	5	1
3	6	1
4	7	1

c)

x	y	Rate of Change
0	−2	
1	2	4
2	6	4
3	10	4
4	14	4

3. a)

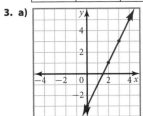

b)

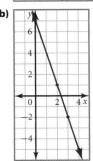

c)

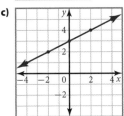

4. a) 2   **b)** −3

5.

Hours	Cost	Rate of Change
1	$2.50	
2	$5.00	$2.50
3	$7.50	$2.50
4	$10.00	$2.50
5	$12.50	$2.50

6. a)

x	y
0	−2
1	−1
2	0
3	1
4	2

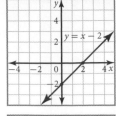

b)

x	y
0	−3
1	−1
2	1
3	3
4	5

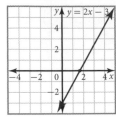

c)

x	y
0	1
1	4
2	7
3	10
4	13

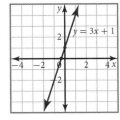

7. AB: rise = 6, run = 3, slope = 2;
CD: rise = −4, run = 8, slope = −0.5
EF: rise = 5, run = 5, slope = 1
GH: rise = 12, run = 3, slope = 4

8. a) $1.50 per basket
b)

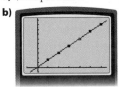

c) 1.5
d) The slope is the rate of pay in dollars that Bim earns for each basket of peaches he picks.

9. a)

Time (min)	Space Used (MB)	Rate of Change
1	1.4	
2	2.8	1.4
3	4.2	1.4
4	5.6	1.4
5	7.0	1.4
6	8.4	1.4
7	9.8	1.4
8	11.2	1.4
9	12.6	1.4
10	14.0	1.4

b)

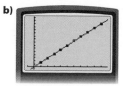

c) 1.4

10. rise = 1; run = 10; slope = $\frac{1}{10}$ = 0.1

11. a)

Distance Driven (km)	0	100	200	300	400
Earnings ($)	0	45	90	135	180

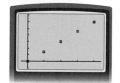

b) $y = 0.45x$; The equation of the line represents Jim's earnings for any distance he drives; x is measured in kilometres and y is measured in dollars.

12. a)

x	y	Rate of Change
0	−3.0	
1	−2.5	0.5
2	−2.0	0.5
3	−1.5	0.5
4	−1.0	0.5

b)

x	y	Rate of Change
0	−5	
1	−8	−3
2	−11	−3
3	−14	−3
4	−17	−3

c)

x	y	Rate of Change
0	0	
1	−0.5	−0.5
2	−1.0	−0.5
3	−1.5	−0.5
4	−2.0	−0.5

13. a)

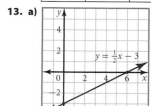

$y = \frac{1}{2}x - 3$

b)

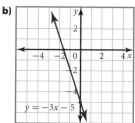

$y = -3x - 5$

c)

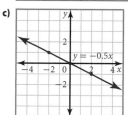

$y = -0.5x$

14. a) 0.5   **b)** −3   **c)** −0.5

16. a)

Date	Balance	Rate of Change
January 1	$67.00	
February 1	$62.50	−$4.50
March 1	$58.00	−$4.50
April 1	$53.50	−$4.50
May 1	$49.00	−$4.50
June 1	$44.50	−$4.50
July 1	$40.00	−$4.50

b)

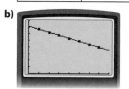

c) slope = −4.5   **d)** $y = -4.5x + 67$

3.2 Investigate the Slope and y-Intercept Using Technology, pages 111–117

1. a) 3   **b)** $-\frac{1}{4}$ **c)** 0.25   **d)** 2

2. a) 4   **b)** $\frac{3}{4}$ **c)** 0   **d)** 1.45

3. a)

b)

c)

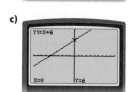

d)

4. a) $y = 3x + 7$ **b)** $y = x - 1$ **c)** $y = \frac{3}{4}x + \frac{1}{2}$
 d) $y = -4x$ **e)** $y = 4$

5. a)

b)

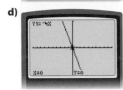

c)

d)

e)

6. a) $y = 2x + 1$ **b)** $y = -x + 2$
 c) $y = 3x - 4$ **d)** $y = -1.5x$

7. a) 125
 b) The slope represents the money saved each month.
 c) 1000
 d) The y-intercept represents the amount of money Marina started with.
 e) $y = 125x + 1000$

8. a) 1500; It represents his starting distance from home.
 b) -90; It represents the number of kilometres deducted from the distance home each hour.
 c) 960 km

9. a) $19.99 is the fixed cost to rent the car.
 b) The y-intercept would stay the same but the slope would be steeper.

10. a) In a standard window, Ymax $= 10$ but the y-intercept is 19.99 and the line has a positive slope. Therefore, the line would be graphed above the standard window.
 b) Change Ymax from 10 to larger number, such as 25.

3.3 Properties of Slopes of Lines, pages 118–127

1. PQ has a positive slope; QR has a negative slope

2. a) positive **b)** negative
 c) negative **d)** zero
 e) positive **f)** negative
 g) zero **h)** positive

3. a) line B **b)** line D
 c) line A **d)** line E
 e) line C

4. a)–d) Answers will vary.

5. a)–d) Answers will vary.

6. a) No, slopes are different.
 b) Yes, slopes are equal.
 c) Yes, slopes are equal.
 d) Yes, slopes are equal.
 e) Yes, slopes are equal.
 f) Yes, slopes are equal.
 g) No, slopes are different.
 h) No, slopes are different.

7. a)–d) Answers will vary.

8. a) Yes, rates of change equal 2.
 b) Yes, rates of change equal -3.
 c) No, neither relation is linear.
 d) Yes, rates of change equal 2.

9. a) AE, CD, FI and GH are parallel. ED, FG and HI are parallel.
 b) $\frac{4}{5}$ **c)** $-\frac{4}{5}$ **d)** 0

10. a) $5m$

b)

Vertical Change (m)	Horizontal Change (m)
0	0
50	1000
100	2000
150	3000
200	4000
250	5000

c)

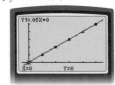

d) 0.05
e) $y = 0.05x + 0$

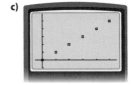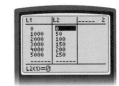

11. a)

x (weeks)	y (amount owing in $)
0	1000
1	950
2	900
3	850
4	800
5	750
6	700
7	650
8	600

b)

$y = -50x + 1000$

c) 1000 **d)** -50

e) The slope is negative because the amount owing is decreasing as time passes.

f) $y = -50x + 1000$

12. a) 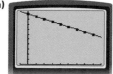 **b)**

13. a) 90°; perpendicular

b) i) $2, -\frac{1}{2}$ ii) $4, -\frac{1}{4}$ iii) $\frac{3}{4}, -\frac{4}{3}$ iv) $\frac{2}{3}, -\frac{3}{2}$; The slopes are negative reciprocals of each other.

c) Each pair of slopes has a product of -1.

14. Answers may vary.

a) $y = -\frac{1}{3}x + b$

b) $y = \frac{1}{2}x + b$

c) $y = \frac{5}{2}x + b$

15. $x = a$, where a can be any number, which will be the x-intercept of the line.

3.4 Determine the Equation of a Line, pages 128–137

1. a) i) 2 ii) 1 iii) $y = 2x + 1$

b) i) -1 ii) -3 iii) $y = -x - 3$

c) i) $\frac{3}{4}$ ii) 4 iii) $y = \frac{3}{4}x + 4$

d) i) $-\frac{5}{3}$ ii) $-\frac{7}{3}$ iii) $y = -\frac{5}{3}x - \frac{7}{3}$

2. a)   **b)**

c) 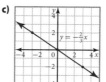 **d)**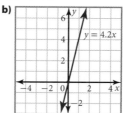

3. a) -1 **b)** 11

c) 0.5 **d)** 5

4. a) $y = 40x + 50$

b) 9

5. a) $y = 2x - 4$ **b)** $y = x + 4$

c) $y = -3x + 5$ **d)** $y = -5$

e) $y = -2x + 3$ **f)** $y = 3x + 7$

g) $y = 0.5x + 5$ **h)** $y = -1.5x - 4.5$

6. a) 2 **b)** 17 **c)** 95 **d)** -33

7. a) $y = 5x - 8$ **b)** $y = 1.5x + 5.5$ **c)** $y = -\frac{1}{2}x$

d) $y = 3x + 3$ **e)** $y = -\frac{2}{3}x - 6$ **f)** $y = -0.4x + 6$

8. a) $(1.5, 6.3)$

b)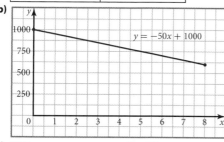

c) 4.2; 0

d) $y = 4.2x$

e) 8.4 km

9. $y = 55x + 65$

10. a) 3, 7 **b)** 16 **c)** $y = 3x + 1$

11. a) $175 **b)** $24 **c)** $y = 25x + 24$

12. a) $y = 2x + 40$ **b)** bolt: 2 g; container; 40 g

13. $E = 0.06s + 500$, where E represents earnings and s represents sales, both in dollars.

14. a) 3:30 pm **b)** 2.5 km

c) A(0, 0), B(0.25, 2.5), C(7, 2.5), D(8, 0)

d) AB: $y = 10x$; BC: $y = 2.5$, CD: $y = -2.5x + 20$

e) 10 km/h; 2.5 km/h

3.5 Graph Linear Relations by Hand, pages 138–145

1. a) slope: 3;
y-intercept: −4

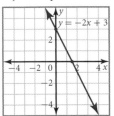

b) slope: 1
y-intercept: 3

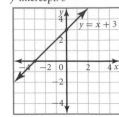

c) slope: −2;
y-intercept: 3

d) slope: −1
y-intercept: 0.5

e) slope: 0;
y-intercept: 7

2. a)

b)

c)

d)

e)

3. a)

b)

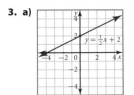

c)

d)

4. a)

b)

c)

d)

5.

6. Left side of roof: $m = \frac{2}{3}$, $b = 4$, $y = \frac{2}{3}x + 4$;
Right side of roof: $m = -\frac{2}{3}$, $b = 4$, $y = -\frac{2}{3}x + 4$

7. a)

b) 1070 m
c) 4 s
d) $y = 10x + 1000$

8. a)

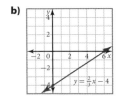

b) $y = 55x + 575$

9. a)

Envelopes Stamped	Remaining Balance ($)
0	40.00
10	34.50
20	29.00
30	23.50
40	18.00
50	12.50

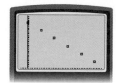

b) negative; The line slopes down to the right because the balance is decreasing

c) −0.55

d) $20.75

e) $y = -0.55x + 40$

f) 72; After 72 envelopes, the remaining balance is only $0.40 which means that no more envelopes can be stamped until the balance is increased.

11. a) $x = 4$ (In general, $x = a$, where a is a real number.)

b) Answers will vary; some number divided by zero

c) The calculator display will read "error" since division by zero is not possible.

12. a) b)

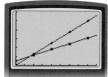

c) Cost: $y = 0.65x + 25$; Income: $y = 1.25x$

d) (41.67, 52.08)

e) This is the point where the school breaks even and can now start to make a profit.

Chapter 3 Review, pages 146–147

1. a) rate of change: change in one variable compared to the change in another variable

b) slope: the steepness of a line

c) linear relation: a relationship between two variables that appears as a straight line when graphed

d) y-intercept: the y-coordinate of the point where the graph intersects the y-axis

e) rise: the vertical distance between two points on a line

f) run: the horizontal distance between two points on a line

g) coefficient: a number that is multiplied by a variable

2. a) The rate of change in the y-values is 3.

b) They are the same.

c) 3

d) −2

e) $y = 3x - 2$

3. a)

Parking Time (min)	Cost ($)
15	0.25
30	0.50
45	0.75
60	1.00
75	1.25
90	1.50
105	1.75
120	2.00

b)

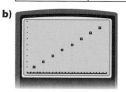

c) The rate of change beween the y-values is constant.

4. a) 2   **b)** −3   **c)** 0.3

5. a)    **b)**

c)    **d)**

6. a) a and d   **b)** b and c   **c)** −5, 2, 7, −1.5

d) Answers will vary, but must be of the following forms:

$y = 3x + b, y = -x + b, y = -0.25x + b,$ and $y = \frac{3}{4}x + b,$

where b is a y-intercept different from those listed in question 5.

e) Answers will vary, but must be of the following forms:

$y = -\frac{1}{3}x + b, y = x + b, y = 4x + b, y = -\frac{4}{3}x + b$ where b can be any number.

f) a, b, d, c

7. a) Yes, the rates of change are the same and the y-intercepts are different.

b) No, the rates of change are different and the y-intercepts are different.

8. a) $y = 3x, y = 3x - 12$

b) $y = -3x + 10, y = 3x - 7$

9. a) $y = 4x - 3$

b) $y = -2.7x + 6.3$

c) $y = 2.5$

d) $y = 2.5x$

10. a) $y = 2x + 2$
  b) $y = -3x + 11$
  c) $y = -2.5x$
  d) $y = \frac{3}{4}x + \frac{1}{2}$
  e) $y = -1.4x - 2.3$

11. a) $y = -0.5x + 4.5$
  b) $y = 1.5x - 2.5$
  c) $y = 500$
  d) $y = -2x - 1$

12. a) $6
  b)

Years	Value of Bond ($)
0	200
1	206
2	212
3	218
4	224
5	230

c)

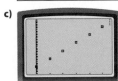

d) $y = 6x + 200$

13.

Chapter 3 Practice Test, pages 148–149

1. a) $m = 2, b = 5$ **b)** $m = -\frac{1}{2}, b = 3$ **c)** $m = 1, b = -7$
  d) $m = -3, b = -2.5$ **e)** $m = 1.8, b = 32$
  f) $m = 0, b = 6$

2. a) 2 **b)** 0 **c)** -3

3. a) $y = 3x + 1$ **b)** $y = -2x + 4$ **c)** $y = -9$

4. a)

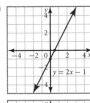

b)

c)

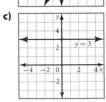

5. a)

Lesson Time (h)	Cost ($)
0.5	45
1.0	85
1.5	125
2.0	165

b)

c) $C = 80t + 5$
  d) $425

6. a) $y = 2x + 1$
  b) $y = -0.2x + 1.8$ **c)** $y = 5$

7. a) $y = -\frac{3}{4}x + 14$
  b) $y = -\frac{1}{5}x + \frac{19}{5}$

8. a) $y = 0.05x + 200$
  b) 200; base salary
  c) 0.05; commission
  d) $7000

9. a) $P = 240 - 0.8t$
  b)

c) 192 kPa
  d) 5 h

CHAPTER 4
Linear Equations, pages 150–193

Get Ready!, pages 152 - 153

1. a) 12 **b)** 10 **c)** 6
  d) 18 **e)** 30 **f)** 16
  g) 60 **h)** 18

2. a) 3 **b)** -1 **c)** -2
  d) -3 **e)** -10 **f)** -14

3. a) $2 + 7r + 4z$ **b)** $9y - 3$ **c)** $4r - 3$
  d) $x + 3y + 4$ **e)** $-5k - 3t$ **f)** $-8t + 22$
  g) $6x - 8y - 6z$ **h)** $4p + 4q - 1$

4. a) $3x + 6$ **b)** $13q + 6$ **c)** $-11p + 17$
  d) $11k - 11$ **e)** $10e - 6$ **f)** $20k + 24$
  g) $-7x + 20$ **h)** $7r + 11$

5. a) 5   **b)** 7   **c)** 1
d) −9   **e)** 0   **f)** 2.5

6. b)

c)

d)

e)

f)

4.1 Solve One- and Two- Step Linear Equations, pages 154–162

1. a) division   **b)** subtraction   **c)** addition
d) division   **e)** multiplication   **f)** addition

2. a) 8   **b)** 6   **c)** 12
d) 3   **e)** 143   **f)** 13

3. a) 4   **b)** 6   **c)** 17
d) 33   **e)** 2   **f)** 7

4. a) −1   **b)** 18   **c)** −4
d) 5   **e)** −30   **f)** 9

5. a) subtraction then division
b) addition then multiplication
c) addition then multiplication
d) addition then division

6. a) 2   **b)** 9   **c)** 1   **d)** 7

8. a) −14   **b)** 20   **c)** 10
d) −33   **e)** 18   **f)** −6
g) 15   **h)** −45

9. a) 18   **b)** 24   **c)** −3
d) −12   **e)** 12   **f)** 15

10. a) $y = 3.5x + 25$
b) m represents the cost per workbook; b represents the fixed cost.
c) 50

11. Answers may vary.

12. a) 1325 cm^2 **b)** 35 kg

13. 125

14. 58 m; Substitute the values of $w = 32$ and $P = 180$ into the equation for perimeter. Multiply the width by two. Next, subtract this multiplied value from each side of the equation. Finally, divide both sides by 2 to solve for l.

15. 6.1°F

16. a) $C = 30n$
b) No; $450 will only buy 15 uniforms.

17. 48; solve the equation $43 = \dfrac{38 + x}{2}$

18. a) $l - \dfrac{P}{2} - w$ **b)** $E - Pt$
c) $b = \dfrac{2A}{h}$ **d)** $h = \dfrac{V}{\pi r^2}$

19. a) Company Y
b) Yes, because $10 150 is less than $11 910 and $12 225.

4.2 Solve Multi-Step Linear Equations, pages 163–173

1. a) Divide 12 by 3 and subtract 5.
b) Multiply 5 by 2, add 5 and divide by 3.
c) Multiply 8 by 3, divide by 2 and add 4.
d) Divide 12 by 3 and subtract 4.
e) Multiply −3 by 4, divide by 3 and subtract 2.
f) Add 3 to 5, multiply by 5 and divide by 4.

2. a) −1   **b)** 5   **c)** 16
d) 0   **e)** −6   **f)** 10

3. a) 5   **b)** −15   **c)** 3
d) 1.2   **e)** −7   **f)** 0.25

4. a) −20   **b)** 0.5   **c)** −3
d) −1   **e)** 9   **f)** −4

5. a) 4   **b)** −9   **c)** 21
d) −4.25   **e)** $2\dfrac{2}{3}$ **f)** −13
g) 6   **h)** −3   **i)** −5
j) 80

6. No. While this approach may work in some cases, it would take too long in other cases. If the solution is a fraction, Minh may never guess the right fraction.

7. Answers may vary.

8. 50 years

9. $t = 3$; The cargo plane catches up with Flight 47 after 3 h.

10. a) $s = 20 - x$ **b)** $s = 20 + x$ **c)** 4 km/h

11. Jack takes 1 h 48 min; Diane take 1 h 3 min.

12. 24 h

13. a) $0.5n$
b) $75n + 100(0.5n) = 150\,000$; Species A: 1200; Species B: 600

14. a) 150   **b)** 160   **c)** 200

15. a) 1406.7 m/s   **b)** 127 602 m
c) No, double 53 km is 106 km, and the car travelled 127.6 km, which is an additional 21.6 km. This is because the car speeds up more and more, covering a greater distance in the second 30 s compared to the first 30 s.

16. 74

4.3 Model With Formulas, pages 174–183

1. a) $w = \dfrac{A}{l}$ **b)** $l = \dfrac{P - 2w}{2}$

c) $b = y - mx$ **d)** $r = \dfrac{C}{2\pi}$

e) $h = \dfrac{V}{lw}$ **f)** $h = \dfrac{2A}{b}$

2. a) 112.5 km **b)** $s = \dfrac{d}{t}$; 75 km/h

c) $t = \dfrac{d}{s}$; 1.75 h

3. \$136

4. \$2500

5. a) $t = \dfrac{I}{Pr}$ **b)** $r = \dfrac{I}{Pt}$ **c)** $P = \dfrac{I}{rt}$

d)

I	P	r	t
1980	2200	0.15	6
240	800	0.1	3
625	625	0.25	4
3300	2000	0.15	11
450	1800	0.05	5
4400	5000	0.04	22
450	600	0.025	30
522	725	0.08	9

6. \$3200

7. Graham: 45 km/h; Colin: 55 km/h

8. No, the two girls will be 13 km apart.

9. Answers will vary.

10. 85 words per minute

11. 10

12. a) $C = \dfrac{5(F - 32)}{9}$

b) 31.1°C

c) $C = \dfrac{F - 30}{2}$

d) 29°C

e) The graph shows that the lines are very close to each other.

13. 30 600 kPa

14. a) \$32 per person
  b) \$42 per person
  c) Since both halls charge \$16 800 for an event with 400 people, neither hall is a better deal than the other.

16. Raymond: 1.06, Jesse: 1.23, Tran: 1.26, Harvinder: 1.11, Igor: 1.23; The coach should choose Raymond, because he has the lowest WHIP.

4.4 Convert Linear Equations From Standard Form, pages 184–189

1. a) $m = -3, b = -6$; $y = -3x - 6$

  b) $m = \dfrac{1}{4}, b = 2$; $y = \dfrac{1}{4}x + 2$

  c) $m = \dfrac{5}{2}, b = -2$; $y = \dfrac{5}{2}x - 2$

  d) $m = 2, b = 1$; $y = 2x + 1$

2. a) $y = -2x + 1$
  b) $y = 3x - 5$
  c) $y = -2x + 4$
  d) $y = -5x - 8$

  e) $y = x + 1$
  f) $y = 2x - 3$

3. a) $y = 2x + 4$; $m = 2, b = 4$
  b) $y = -3x + 2$; $m = -3, b = 2$
  c) $y = x + 4$; $m = 1, b = 4$
  d) $y = -3x - 11$; $m = -3, b = -11$
  e) $y = 8x - 5$; $m = 8, b = -5$
  f) $y = -2x - 7$; $m = -2, b = -7$

4. a) $y = x - 3$; $m = 1, b = -3$
  b) $y = \dfrac{2}{3}x + 4$; $m = \dfrac{2}{3}, b = 4$
  c) $y = -2x + 5$; $m = -2, b = 5$
  d) $y = \dfrac{1}{2}x + 5$; $m = \dfrac{1}{2}, b = 5$
  e) $y = \dfrac{1}{5}x + 3$; $m = \dfrac{1}{5}, b = 3$
  f) $y = \dfrac{3}{4}x + 3$; $m = \dfrac{3}{4}, b = 3$
  g) $y = \dfrac{4}{3}x - 6$; $m = \dfrac{4}{3}, b = -6$
  h) $y = -\dfrac{1}{2}x - 3$; $m = -\dfrac{1}{2}, b = -3$

5. a) $3x + y = 750$, where x represents the number of adult tickets and y represents the number of children's tickets.
  b) $y = -3x + 750$
  c) 324

6. Subtract $3x - 3$ from both sides and then divide both sides by 2.

7. a)

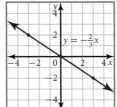

  b) $m = -\dfrac{2}{3}, b = 0$

  c) $y = -\dfrac{2}{3}x$

  d) If $C = 0$, then the graph passes through the origin.

8. -11

9. 5

10. -35

11. a) $1600

   b) $1800

   c) Answers will vary.

12. a) $y = -\dfrac{A}{B}x - \dfrac{C}{B}$

   b) $m = -\dfrac{A}{B},\ b = -\dfrac{C}{B}$

13. a) y-axis

   b) a sloping line that passes through the origin

   c) a vertical line that passes through the x-axis at $x = -\dfrac{C}{A}$

   d) a sloping line that does not pass through the origin

Chapter 4 Review, pages 190–191

1. a) Opposite operations are operations that "undo" one another.

   b) A variable term is a term that includes a letter or symbol to represent an unknown value.

   c) A constant term is a numerical term that cannot be changed.

   d) A formula describes an algebraic relationship between two or more variables.

   e) Standard form for a linear equation has the form $Ax + By + C = 0$.

2. a) i) divide   ii) 9

   b) i) subtract   ii) 4

   c) i) multiply   ii) 60

   d) i) subtract then divide   ii) −10

3. a) 3

   b) 20

   c) −32

   d) 14

4. $11.50

5. a) 2   **b)** 17

   c) 8   **d)** 10

   e) −65

6. 142.9 L of milk, 57.1 L of cream

7. a) subtract $2w$ from both sides, then divide both sides by 2

   b) divide both sides by 2π

8. a) $d = \dfrac{C}{\pi}$

   b) $m = \dfrac{y - b}{x}$

   c) $w = \dfrac{P}{2} - l$

   d) $h = \dfrac{S}{\pi r^2}$

9. 12 years

10. $36.29

11. Ari: 20 km/h; Lisa: 50 km/h

12. a) $y = -3x + 7;\ m = -3,\ b = 7$

   b) $y = 5x - 4;\ m = 5,\ b = -4$

   c) $y = x + 3;\ m = 1,\ b = 3$

   d) $y = -\dfrac{1}{14}x + 2;\ m = -\dfrac{1}{14},\ b = 2$

   e) $y = 6;\ m = 0,\ b = 6$

   f) $y = \dfrac{3}{8}x + 6;\ m = \dfrac{3}{8},\ b = 6$

13. 7

14. −12

Chapter 4 Practice Test, pages 192–193

1. a) 8   **b)** 1

   c) −4   **d)** −2

   e) 3

2. a) 2   **b)** −1

   c) 4   **d)** −9

   e) −3

3. 42

4. $r = \dfrac{A - P}{Pt}$

5. 35% solution: 46.7 mL; 80% solution: 23.3 mL

6. a) $m = \dfrac{1}{2},\ b = 3;\ y = \dfrac{1}{2}x + 3$

   b) $m = -2,\ b = -3;\ y = -2x - 3$

7. a) $y = -2x + 3;\ m = -2,\ b = 3$

   b) $y = 6x - 1;\ m = 6,\ b = -1$

   c) $y = -\dfrac{2}{3}x + 4;\ m = -\dfrac{2}{3},\ b = 4$

   d) $y = \dfrac{4}{5}x + 2;\ m = \dfrac{4}{5},\ b = 2$

   e) $y = -\dfrac{3}{2}x + 4;\ m = -\dfrac{3}{2},\ b = 4$

8. a) $a = \dfrac{P - b}{2}$ **b)** $r = \dfrac{A - P}{Pt}$ **c)** $b = \dfrac{2A}{h} - a$

9. a) 28   **b)** $I = A - \dfrac{P - 2}{2}$ **c)** 18

10. a) $C = 500 + 20p$ **b)** 1700   **c)** 83

CHAPTER 5
Linear Systems 194–229

Get Ready!, pages 196–198

1. a) $-2d - 4$ **b)** $5x + 3$

   c) $13y + 3$ **d)** $4m + 16$

   e) $c - 5$ **f)** $v + 10$

2. a) $y = \dfrac{3x}{8} + \dfrac{11}{8}$ **b)** $y = 3x - 4$

   c) $y = -4x + 9$ **d)** $y = 2x - 7$

   e) $y = \dfrac{5}{2}x - 3$ **f)** $y = -\dfrac{2}{3}x + \dfrac{1}{3}$

   g) $y = -\dfrac{2}{3}x + \dfrac{3}{2}$

3. a) $y = 2$ **b)** $y = 10$ **c)** $y = 9$

d) $y = 25$ **e)** $y = -6$ **f)** $y = \frac{1}{2}$

g) $y = -\frac{19}{5}$

4. a) $x = -\frac{11}{3}$ **b)** $x = \frac{9}{2}$ **c)** $x = 17$

d) $x = \frac{1}{2}$ **e)** $x = 8$ **f)** $x = 1$

g) $x = \frac{17}{2}$ **h)** $x = \frac{23}{13}$

5. a)

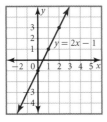

b)

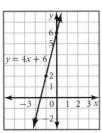

c)

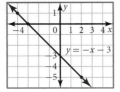

d)

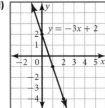

e)

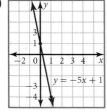

f)

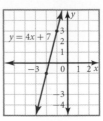

g)

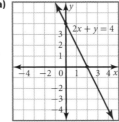

6. a)

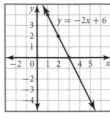

b)

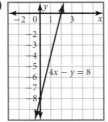

c)

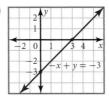

d)

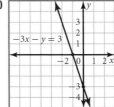

e)

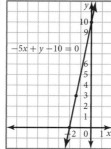

$-5x + y - 10 = 0$

f)

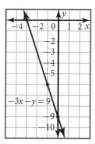

$-3x - y = 9$

g)

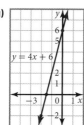

$y = 4x + 6$

7. a) $400 = 0.1n + 50$
  b) $8.50x = 52.00$
  c) $90 = 18 + 2.3x$
  d) $300 = 0.35d + 125$
  e) $450 = 270 + 12h$

5.1 Solve Linear Systems by Graphing, pages 198–204

1. a) $(2, 7)$ **b)** $(-3, -4)$
  c) $(2, 3)$ **d)** $(-3, 1)$

2. a) $\left(-\dfrac{1}{2}, -1\right)$ **b)** $(-24, -14)$
  c) $(-8, -19)$ **d)** $(-2.27, -14.09)$

3. a) $(1, 4)$

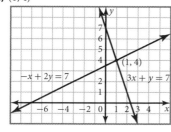

$-x + 2y = 7$ $3x + y = 7$

b) $(-1, -4)$

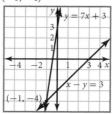

$y = 7x + 3$

$x - y = 3$

$(-1, -4)$

c) $(1, 2)$

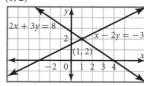

$2x + 3y = 8$ $x - 2y = -3$

$(1, 2)$

d) $(-1, -1)$

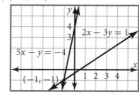

$2x - 3y = 1$

$5x - y = -4$

$(-1, -1)$

4. a) $(-1, 10)$

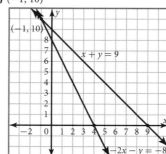

$(-1, 10)$

$x + y = 9$

$-2x - y = -8$

b) $(-1, -2)$

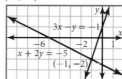

$3x - y = -1$

$x + 2y = -5$

$(-1, -2)$

c) $(0, 1)$

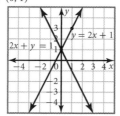

$2x + y = 1$ $y = 2x + 1$

d) $(3, 4)$

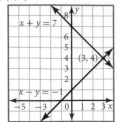

5. a) $C = 150 + 20m$

b) $C = 100 + 30m$

c)

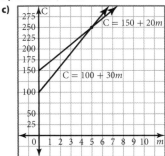

d) $(5, 250)$; This point represents the time when their costs are equal.

e) For Sherwood: $C = \$390$; for Coronation: $C = \$460$; I would join Sherwood.

6. a) $C = 10 + 3n$

b) $C = 7 + 4n$

c) $(3, 19)$

d) It represents point at which the rentals costs the same ($19) at both rental companies.

7. a) $C = 1000 + 75n$

b) $C = 1500 + 50n$

c) 20 guests

8.

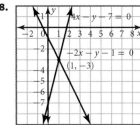

The solution is $(1, -3)$.

9. a) $C = 15n$

b) $C = 150$

c) If I expected to need my driveway cleared more than 10 times this winter, I would hire Morgan; otherwise I would hire Don.

11. a) $G = 80 + 10j$

b) $C = 110$

c) 3 jackets

12. $(4, -1)$

13. a) $C = 675 + 2n$

b) $R = 8.50n$

c) 104

14. a) No, the lines do not intersect.

b) It does not work and says "error: no sign change." It does not work because the lines are parallel.

15. a) Slope: 3; y-int: -4 ①
Slope: 3; y-int: -4 ②

b) They are the same line.

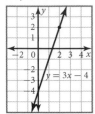

c) Infinite, because they line exactly the same line.

16. Infinite. Points on one line will always be on the other line too.

17. No. A linear system can only have no solutions, one solution, or infinitely many solutions.

5.2 Solve Linear Systems by Substitution, pages 205–211

1. a) $(-5, 8)$ **b)** $(3, 5)$ **c)** $(9, -1)$
d) $(1, 1)$ **e)** $(4, -3)$ **f)** $(1, 1)$
g) $(2, -1)$ **h)** $(2, -1)$

2. a) $(-0.8, -6.6)$ **b)** $(9.5, -15.5)$
c) $\left(\frac{2}{3}, \frac{1}{3}\right)$ **d)** $\left(\frac{1}{5}, -\frac{42}{5}\right)$

3. a) $(2, -4)$ **b)** $(6, -3)$
c) $(-1, 4)$ **d)** $\left(\frac{15}{4}, \frac{1}{2}\right)$

4. a) $M = 2S$ **b)** $M + S = 39$
c) Malcolm is 26 and Sundeep is 13.

5. a) $R = 500 + 15m$, $P = 410 + 18m$
b) 30 guests

6. a) $C = 825 + 2n$, $R = 7n$
b) 165 tickets
c) $7

7. If an equation has one variable isolated already, use it to substitute into the other equation and solve for the other variable.

8. a) $g + a = 63$, $g = a - 17$
b) 23 goals; 40 assists

9. $\frac{25}{18}$ or 1.39 h

10. $\left(\frac{69}{13}, -\frac{40}{13}\right)$

11. 8750 adults

12. a) $C1 = 80 + 0.22k$, $C2 = 100 + 0.12k$

 b) $k = 200$; The costs are the same when the truck is driven 200 km.

 c) Vito should hire Athena's Garage if the moving distance is less than 200 km. Conversely, Vito should hire City Truck Rental if the moving distance is more than 200 km.

13. 6

14. a) $C = 348 + 2t$

 b) $R = 5t$

 c) 116 dog tags

15. No, the point does not make both equations work.

16. a) There is no solution.

 b) The lines are parallel.

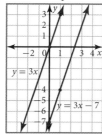

 c) The lines are parallel. There is no point of intersection.

17. a) The solution is $0x = 0$, which is always true.

 b) The two lines are the same.

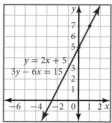

 c) There is an infinite number of solutions because the lines are coincident; that is, they yield the same line when graphed.

5.3 Solve Linear Systems by Elimination, pages 212–218

1. a) $(1, 1)$ **b)** $(-2, -1)$
 c) $(2, 4)$ **d)** $(-2, 2)$
 e) $(-1, -3)$ **f)** $(1, 5)$

2. a) $(2, 3)$ **b)** $(-1, 1)$
 c) $(2, -1)$ **d)** $(1, 1)$
 e) $(-1, 1)$ **f)** $(-2, -7)$

3. a) $(-2, 2)$ **b)** $(-1, 3)$
 c) $(-3, 2)$ **d)** $(3, -1)$

4. a) $\left(\frac{1}{4}, 1\right)$ **b)** $\left(\frac{7}{15}, \frac{1}{9}\right)$
 c) $(6, 9)$ **d)** $(1, 2)$

5. 20 g of cinnamon and 5 g of nutmeg

6. a) $a + c = 800$, $5a + 3c = 3600$

 b) 600 adult tickets

7. a) $s - w = 540$, $s + w = 680$

 b) The wind speed can be calculated by using the elimination method. When the equations are subtracted, s is eliminated. The left side is $-2w$ and the right side of the equation becomes -140. The next step is to divide both sides by -2 to find the wind speed.

8. a) $72 per day

 b) 65¢/km

9. a) $C = 120 + 8d$, $R = 16d$

 b) 15 customers

10. 36 h

11. $\frac{30}{11}$ or 2.73 h

12. 12.5 L

5.4 Solve Problems Involving Linear Systems, pages 219–225

1. 9 years; $35 000

2. $5000 at 3.25% and $3000 at 5%

3. $1050 at 8% and $2000 at 7.5%

4. a) 10 months

 b) Brant Gymnastics Club

 c) Jungle Gymnastics Club

5. $(4, 7)$; Substitution; y has been isolated already, so it can be substituted easily.

6. 30 medium-sized shirts

7. 21 cars; 31 vans

9. I would use the elimination method, since I could subtract the two equations and eliminate the y.

10. a) No, those dimensions produce a perimeter of 168 cm, which is far greater than the actual perimeter of 84 cm.

 b) 18 cm by 24 cm

11. This is possible because the lines are coincident. There are an infinite number of solutions.

12. a) $10 per meal

 b) $50 per day

13. a) $\frac{x}{80} + \frac{y}{60} = 5.5$; $x + y = 400$

 b) 280 km at 80 km/h and 120 km at 60 km/h

Chapter 5 Review, pages 226–227

1. a) A linear system is a set of two or more linear relations considered at the same time.

b) The point of intersection is the point at which two lines cross.

c) The substitution method is an algebraic method of solving a system of linear equations in which one equation is rearranged and substituted into the other.

d) The method of elimination is an algebraic method of solving a system of linear equations in which the equations are added or subtracted to eliminate one variable.

2. a)

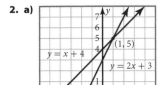

b)

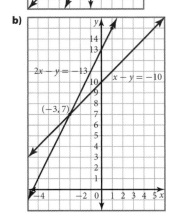

c)

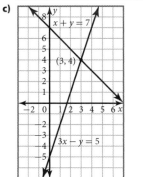

d)

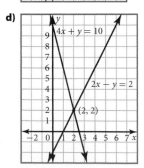

3. a) $(-1.29, 7.86)$ **b)** $(1.17, -0.13)$
c) $(-0.33, 2)$ **d)** $(1.56, -3.67)$

4. a) $(1, 8)$ **b)** $\left(\frac{1}{2}, 3\right)$
c) $(3, -4)$ **d)** $(2, 3)$

5. 5 ha of canola and 15 ha of corn

6. 17 softcover books and 11 hardcover books

7. a) $\left(2, \frac{1}{2}\right)$ **b)** $(4, 3)$
c) $(-1.25, 5.5)$ **d)** $\left(\frac{1}{3}, 3\right)$

8. a) $2(s + w) = 216$ **b)** $s = 90; w = 18$
$3(s - w) = 216$

9. 25 basketballs and 20 volleyballs

10. a) $\left(\frac{5}{2}, \frac{3}{2}\right)$ **b)** $(13, -1)$
c) $(1, 7)$ **d)** $(4, 0)$

11. $4000 at 8%
$2000 at 6%

12. For less than 300 mins per month, Doug should choose the second plan. Otherwise he should choose the first plan.

13. 33 dimes and 12 quarters

Chapter 5 Practice Test, pages 228–229

1. a) $(1, 5)$

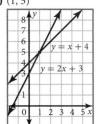

b) $(2, 2)$

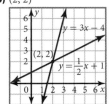

c) $(-1, 7)$

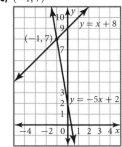

2. a) $(-1, -5)$ **b)** $\left(\frac{7}{3}, \frac{4}{3}\right)$ **c)** $(5, -1)$

3. a) $(-3, 7)$ **b)** $(1, 4)$ **c)** $\left(\frac{5}{3}, \frac{-13}{9}\right)$

4. $(2, -1)$; Methods will vary.

5. a) I would use the substitution method. I would replace the y in the second equation with $7x + 1$ and then find a value for x. Then, I would substitute that value back into the first equation to find a value for y.

   b) $(1, 8)$

6. a) $N = 10 + 4x$; $V = 40 + x$
   b) 10 items
   c) \$50

7. a) $A = 40 + 5x$
       $B = 100 + 2x$
   b) 20 shirts
   c) The cost is the same at 20 shirts for \$140. Ramona should choose the first company if fewer than 20 shirts are needed. The second company is less expensive for the production of more than 20 shirts.

8. a) $SA = 5 + x$
       $SZ = 7 + 0.5x$
   b) $(4, 9)$; The point of intersection means that the cost of renting equipment from the companies is the same, \$9, if one wishes to rent the equipment for 4 hours.
   c) It is cheaper to rent from snowbound Adventures if you wish to snow board for less than 4 hours.

9. a) 63 students
   b) \$675

10. 50 min per month

Chapters 3 to 5 Review, pages 232–233
Chapter 3, page 232

1. a) -3
   b) 2

2. a)

d	C = 0.35d + 2
0	2
1	2.35
2	2.7
3	3.05
4	3.4
5	3.75
6	4.1
7	4.45
8	4.8
9	5.15
10	5.5

   b)

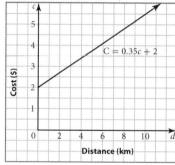

Cost of Taxi Trips

   c) slope $= 0.35$; the slope represents the additional cost per kilometre the taxi driver charges

3. a)

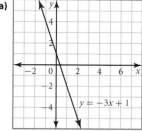

   b) rate of change $= -3$
   c) 1

4. a) $y = 2x + 4$ **b)** $y = \frac{3}{2}x - \frac{1}{4}$
   c) $y = -3x$ **d)** $y = \frac{1}{2}$

5. a) $y = x + 3$
   b) $y = 3x + 4$
   c) $y = -3x + 7.5$
   d) $y = -\frac{1}{4}x + 2$

6. a) $y = -4x - 10$
   b) $y = 5x - 11$
   c) $x = 1$

Chapter 4, pages 232–233

7. a) $x = 5$ **b)** $x = 12$
   c) $x = -1$ **d)** $x = -4$
   e) $t = 7$ **f)** $x = 2.5$

8. a) \$230
   b) 60 times

9. a) $l = \frac{P - 2w}{2}$ **b)** $r = \sqrt{\frac{A}{\pi}}$ **c)** $h = \frac{S}{2\pi r}$

10. \$5000

11. a) $y = -2x + 6$; slope $= -2$; y-int $= 6$
   b) $y = 3x + 4$; slope $= 3$; y-int $= 4$
   c) $y = \frac{4}{3}x - 2$; slope $= \frac{4}{3}$; y-int $= -2$

12. $B = 2$

Chapter 5, page 233

13. a) $(1, 0)$;

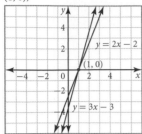

b) $(-1, -2)$;

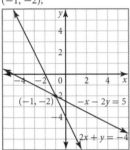

14. a) $(1, 5)$
b) $(-2, -3)$

15. a) $(-1, 1)$
b) $(0, 3)$

16. a) Primo Banquet Hall: $C = 2000 + 50n$, The Lookout Banquet Hall: $C = 1500 + 75n$
b) $(20, 2100)$
c) This point represents when the cost to invite the same number of people is the same at either hall.

17. a) $C = 700 + 3n$, $R = 10n$, where R represents the revenue
b) $n = 100$
c) total cost = \$1000

CHAPTER 6
Quadratic Relations, pages 234–275

Get Ready!, pages 236–237

1. a) 5
b) -2
c) -15
d) 12.75
e) -3.3

2. a) Answer provided in text.

b)

x	y
−3	9
−2	8
−1	7
0	6
1	5
2	4
3	3

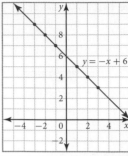

c)

x	y
−3	−7
−2	−5
−1	−3
0	−1
1	1
2	3
3	5

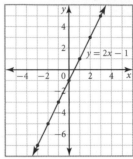

d)

x	y
−3	9
−2	7
−1	5
0	3
1	1
2	−1
3	−3

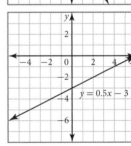

e)

x	y
−3	−4.5
−2	−4
−1	−3.5
0	−3
1	−2.5
2	−2
3	−1.5

3. a)

b)

c)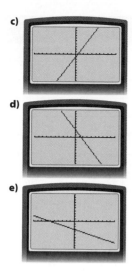

d)

e)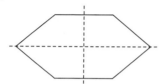

4. a) x-intercept: 2; y-intercept: -4
b) x-intercept: -2; y-intercept: -4
c) x-intercept: 2; y-intercept: 3
d) x-intercept: 1; y-intercept: -6

5. a) 2

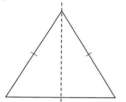

b) 1

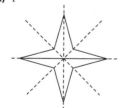

c) 4

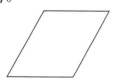

d) 0

6.1 Explore Non-Linear Relations, pages 238–244
1. a) curve; The points follow a U-shaped pattern.

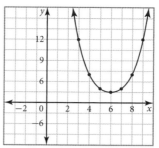

b) line; All points lie on the same line.

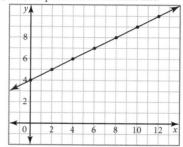

c) curve; The points follow a U-shaped pattern.

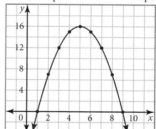

d) curve; The points follow a U-shaped pattern.

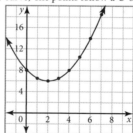

2. a)

Side Length (units)	Area (square units)
1	1
2	4
3	9
4	16
5	25

b)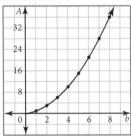

3. a)

Radius (cm)	Area (cm)
1	3.14
2	12.56
3	28.26
4	50.24
5	78.50

b)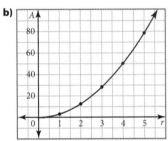

4. a)

Length (cm)	Width (cm)	Area (cm^2)
1	8	8
2	7	14
3	6	18
4	5	20

b)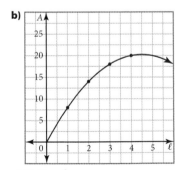

c) 20.25 cm^2

5. a)

Base	Height	Perimeter	Area
1	1	4	1
2	2	8	3
3	3	12	6
4	4	16	10
5	5	20	15
6	6	24	21
7	7	28	28
8	8	32	36

b) The relationship is linear, since the first differences are constant.

c) The relationship is quadratic, since the second differences are constant.

d) Area $= 15 + 14 + 13 + \ldots + 2 + 1 = 120$
Perimeter $= 4 \times 15 = 60$

6. a)

Width	Length	Area
1	2	2
2	4	8
3	6	18
4	8	32
5	10	50
6	12	72
7	14	98
8	16	128

b) Linear; the length of the figure is double the width.
c) Quadratic; Area = Length × Width = $2w \times w = 2w^2$.
d) Width = 8; Area = 128
e) 200 square units

7. a)

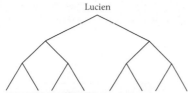

Lucien

b)

Number of People	Number of Conversations
1	2
2	4
4	8
8	16

c)

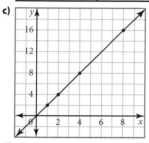

d) This is a linear relation.

Number of conversations = 2 × number of people

8. a)

Length	Width	Area
24	1	24
23	2	46
22	3	66
21	4	84
20	5	100
19	6	114
18	7	126
17	8	136
16	9	144
15	10	150

b)

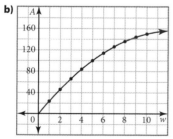

c) A curve of best fit is drawn in 8b).

d) The length and width should be 12.5 m by 12.5 m in order to maximize the area.

9. a)

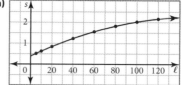

b) A curve of best fit is drawn in 9a).

c) quadratic

d) approximately 1.94 s

e) approximately 1.41 s

f) The longer the string the longer it will take for 1 swing to occur.

g) Theoretically, the results should be the same, however actual times and answers may vary.

6.2 Model Quadratic Relations, pages 245–253

1. a) quadratic   **b)** linear   **c)** quadratic

 d) quadratic   **e)** linear   **f)** quadratic

Quadratic relations have an x^2 term, linear relations have an x term but no x^2 term.

2. a) quadratic

b) linear

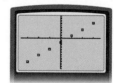

c) quadratic

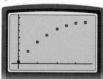

3.

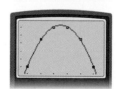

4 a)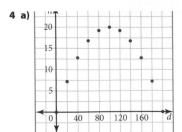

b) $y = -0.002x^2 + 0.4x$

c) It is a quadratic relation.

5. a)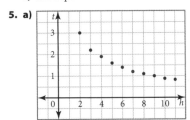

b) $y = 0.029\ 32x^2 - 0.5931x + 3.8854$

6. a)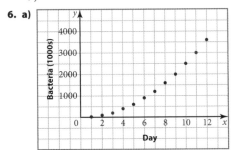

b) $y = 25.34x^2 - 4.90x + 2.84$

c) parabola   **d)** quadratic

8. a)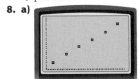

b)

c)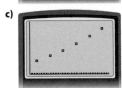

d) initial speed versus reaction distance: a linear relation fits best; initial speed versus braking distance: a quadratic relation fits best; initial speed versus total stopping distance: a quadratic relation fits best

e) The longer the skid mark, the faster the car was travelling.

9. a) Answers will vary.

b) Answers will vary.

10. Parabola and parable have similar names because both are meant to teach a truth. The parable is meant to teach truth through comparison or allegory. The parabola on the other hand is a mathematical comparison of two variables which are analyzed.

11. a)

x	y
−2	−9
−1	0
0	5
1	6
2	3
3	−4

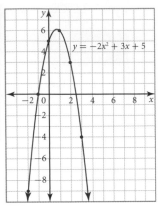

b)

x	y
−3	2
−2	−1
−1	−2
0	−1
1	2

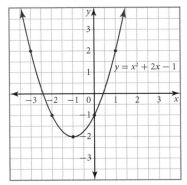

c)

x	y
−5	−1
−4	3
−3	5
−2	5
−1	3
0	−1

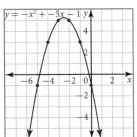

6.3 Key Features of Quadratic Relations, pages 254–263

1.

GRAPH A	
a) vertex	$(2, -1)$
b) axis of symmetry	$x = 2$
c) the y-intercept	3
d) maximum or minimum value	min $y = -1$
e) the x-intercepts	1, 3

GRAPH B	
a) vertex	$(-2, -1)$
b) axis of symmetry	$x = -2$
c) the y-intercept	3
d) maximum or minimum value	min $y = -1$
e) the x-intercepts	$-3, -1$

GRAPH C	
a) vertex	$(4, 6)$
b) axis of symmetry	$x = 4$
c) the y-intercept	2
d) maximum or minimum value	max $y = 6$
e) the x-intercepts	$-1, 9$

GRAPH D	
a) vertex	$(0, 2)$
b) axis of Symmetry	$x = 0$
c) the y-intercept	2
d) maximum or minimum value	max $y = 2$
e) the x-intercepts	$-2, 2$

GRAPH E	
a) vertex	$(1, 2)$
b) axis of symmetry	$x = 1$
c) the y-intercept	4
d) maximum or minimum value	min $y = 2$
e) the x-intercepts	none

GRAPH F	
a) vertex	$(0, -3)$
b) axis of symmetry	$x = 0$
c) the y-intercept	-3
d) maximum or minimum value	min $y = -3$
e) the x-intercepts	$-1.7, 1.7$

2. a)

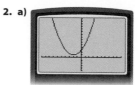

b) $(-2, 1)$ **c)** $x = -2$ **d)** 3
e) min: $y = 1$ **f)** none

3. a)

b) $(-1, -1)$ **c)** $x = -1$
d) -3 **e)** maximum: $y = -1$
f) none

4. a) $(3, 18)$
    b) The maximum height of the doorway is 18 ft.
    c) 0
    d) 0, 6
    e) The base of the doorway is 6 ft wide.
    f) Parabolas create arches which are very strong entrance structures.

5. Answers will vary.

6. a) approximately $(6, 13)$ **b)** $x = 6$
    c) depth is approximately 13 cm
    d) 0, 12   **e)** 12 cm

8. a)

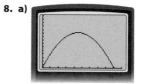

    b) 45 yards   **c)** Answers may vary.
    d) No, the field goal will not be successful because at the 10 yd from the kicker, the ball is only 7 ft high, not 13.2 ft, which is the height of the posts.

6.4 Rates of Change in Quadratic Relations, pages 264–271

1. a) $y = x^2 - 6x + 8$

x	y
0	8
1	3
2	0
3	-1
4	0
5	3
6	8

This relation is quadratic.

b) $y = x^2 + 7x + 12$

x	y
−7	12
−6	6
−5	2
−4	0
−3	0
−2	2
−1	6
0	12

This relation is quadratic.

c) $y = x^2 - 3x + 10$

x	y
−2	20
−1	14
0	10
1	8
2	0
3	10
4	14
5	20

This relation is quadratic.

d) $y = x^2 + 3x - 18$

x	y
−6	0
−5	−8
−4	−14
−3	−18
−2	−20
−1	−20
0	−18
1	−14
2	−8
3	0

This relation is quadratic.

2. a) neither **b)** neither **c)** linear

3. a) Answers may vary.

x	y
0	0
1	0.96
2	1.84
3	2.64
4	3.36
5	4

b)

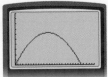

c) The first differences are not constant since the relation is not linear.

d) The second differences are constant, which are −0.08; because the relation is quadratic.

e) 75 kg; 79.56 kg

4. a) The values in the following table are approximate values.

x	y
0	0
20	4900
40	7000
60	7800
80	7400
100	5600
120	1900

b) $y = -1.93 x^2 + 245.18x + 276.19$ (answers may vary slightly)

5. If the second differences are constant then the relation is quadratic.

7. a)

Number of Sides	Number of Diagonals
4	2
5	5
6	9
7	14

b)

Number of Sides	Number of Diagonals
8	20
9	27

c) $y = 0.5x^2 - 1.5x$

d) 170

8. a) Answers will vary.
  b) Answers will vary.
  c) Answers will vary.

Chapter 6 Review, pages 272–273

1. a) parabola
   b) minimum
   c) vertex
   d) axis of symmetry

2. a)

Figure	Triangular Number
1	1
2	4
3	9
4	16
5	25
6	36
7	49
8	64

b)

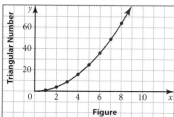

3. a)

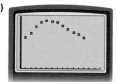

b) $y = -1.11x^2 + 13.61x + 56.16$

4. a) $(-1, -3)$ **b)** $x = -1$
   c) y-int: -1 **d)** min: -3
   e) $-2.225, 0.225$

5. a)

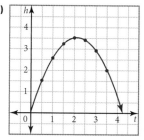

b) A curve of best fit is drawn in 5a).
c) a parabola
d) After 2 s the arrow has gone 11.42 m.
   After 3 s the arrow has gone 17.13 m.
   Divide the distance, 20 m, by the time the arrow hit the target to solve for the speed. Then multiply each specific time by the speed to calculate how far the arrow travelled.

6. a)

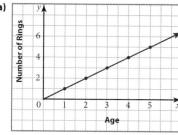

b) It is linear.
c) Linear, since one more ring is created for every year the tree is alive.
d) 3.14 cm/year
e) Theoretically, yes. Divide the radius by 0.5 cm, to tell the number of rings the tree has, which is the age of the tree. However, there may be differences from year to year. If a certain summer is dry, the tree will not grow as much, compared to a relatively wet summer.

7. a), b)

d	h	First Differences	Second Differences
-5	1.15		
-4	1.87	-0.72	
-3	2.43	-0.56	-0.16
-2	2.83	-0.40	-0.16
-1	3.07	-0.24	-0.16
0	3.15	-0.08	-0.16
1	3.07	0.08	-0.16
2	2.83	0.24	-0.16
3	2.43	0.40	-0.16
4	1.87	0.56	-0.16
5	1.15	0.72	-0.16

c) parabola
d)

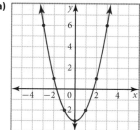

Chapter 6 Practice Test, pages 274–275

1. a)

b)

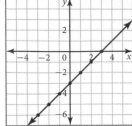

c)

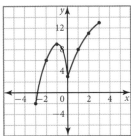

Data set a) is quadratic.

2. a) quadratic; smooth U-shaped curve
b) not quadratic; the shape is not a smooth "U"
c) quadratic; smooth U-shaped curve
d) not quadratic; the figure is an oval shape.

3. a)

b) $y = 0.0036x^2 - 0.27x + 5.71$
c) The relationship is best modelled by a quadratic relation because the data do not have a linear trend, they form a curve.

4. a)

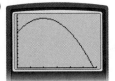

b)

d	h	First Differences	Second Differences
0	10		
10	13	-3	
20	14	-1	-2
30	13	1	-2
40	10	3	-2
50	5	5	-2
60	-2	7	-2

5. a) (3, 4)
b) $x = 3$
c) -5
d) max: $y = 4$
e) 1, 5

6. a) Answers may vary.
b) Answers may vary.
c) Answers may vary.
d) Answers may vary.

CHAPTER 7
Quadratic Expressions, pages 276–315

Get Ready!, pages 278–279

1. a) -5 **b)** 6   **c)** 2   **d)** -7

2. a) binomial   **b)** monomial
   c) trinomial   **d)** polynomial

3. a) $-6p$ **b)** $20q$ **c)** $18r^2$
   d) $-2x$ **e)** $6x$ **f)** -2

4. a) $-2x + 14$ **b)** $x^2 + 8x + 15$
   c) $8x^2 + 3x$ **d)** $x^2 - 3x - 5$

5. a) $2x - 6$ **b)** $-4x^2 - 12x + 20$
   c) $10x^2 + 15x$ **d)** $-3x^2 + 6x + 3$

6. a) -10 **b)** 28
   c) 10   **d)** -21

7. a) $34x$ **b)** $24x$
   c) $2x + 14$

8. a) 16   **b)** $49x^2$
   c) $9x^2$ **d)** $81x^2$

9. a) 24   **b)** 3
   c) 65   **d)** 55

10. 319 cm^2

7.1 Multiply Two Binomials, pages 280–289

1. a) $x^2 + 5x + 6$ **b)** $x^2 + 9x + 20$
   c) $x^2 + 9x + 8$ **d)** $x^2 + 5x + 6$
   e) $x^2 + 12x + 27$ **f)** $x^2 + 11x + 30$

2. a) $6x^2 + 17x + 7$ **b)** $9x^2 + 3x - 20$
   c) $5x^2 - 7x - 6$ **d)** $6x^2 - 13x + 6$

3. a) $x^2 + 10x + 25$ **d)** $x^2 + 14x + 49$
   c) $x^2 + 6x + 9$ **d)** $x^2 + 12x + 36$
   e) $x^2 + 16x + 64$ **f)** $x^2 + 8x + 16$

4. a) $4x^2 + 4x + 1$ **b)** $16x^2 - 8x + 1$
   c) $9x^2 + 12x + 4$ **d)** $25x^2 - 20x + 4$

5. a)
   $4x + 5$
   $x + 3$

b) $4x^2 + 17x + 15$

6. a) $x^2 + 7x + 10$ **b)** $x^2 + 3x - 10$
  c) $x^2 - 3x - 10$ **d)** $x^2 - 7x + 10$

7. a) no
  b) b is the sum of the two constants, c is the product of the two constants.

8. $x^2 + 6x + 9$

9. $5x^2 + 26x + 24$

10. a) $20x^2 + 7x - 6$ **b)** $18x + 2$

11. a) $4x^2 + 30x + 50$ **b)** 6000 ft^2 **c)** 2400 ft^2

12. a) $2x^2 - 18$ **b)** 224 m^2 **c)** \$1117.76

13. Answers will vary.

14. a) $x^2 + 5x + 6.25$ **b)** 10.5625 m^2
15. -4

16. a) **i)** $8x^2 + 32x + 30$
    ii) $21x^2 - 74x + 65$
    iii) $13x^2 - 106x + 35$
  b) photograph: 2310 cm^2
  mat: 3680 cm^2
  visible mat: 1370 cm^2
  yes; it does follow the guideline, only 62.8% of the mat is covered by the photo.

7.2 Common Factoring, pages 290–297

1. a) 2   **b)** 5   **c)** $4x$ **d)** $4x$

2. a) $3(x + 5)$ **b)** $4x(x + 2)$ **c)** $5x(x - 2)$ **d)** $-7x(1 - 3x)$

3. a) $3(x^2 - 4x + 6)$
  b) $-10(x^2 - 2x + 3)$
  c) $-3(3x^2 + x - 3)$
  d) $2(2x^2 - 3x + 4)$

4. a) $6x(x + 2)$ **b)** $9x(x + 2)$
  c) $4x(x + 6)$ **d)** $15x(x + 2)$

5. a) yes   **b)** binomial

6. a) $8(x - 3)$ **b)** $x(x + 5)$
  c) $x(x - 10)$ **d)** $4(x^2 + 4x + 6)$

7. a) $x(x + 5)$ **b)** 2 m by 7 m
  c) 18 m

8. a) $3x, 7x + 1$ **b)** $2x, x + 9$

9. a) $x^2 + 40$
  b) 40, 41, 44, 49, 56, 65, 76, 89, 104
  c) $0 \le x \le 7$
  d) $x \ge 8$

11. a) $4x^2 + 16x$ **b)** $4x(x + 4)$
  c) 52 m by 17 m

12. Answers will vary. For example, $5x^2 + 125x - 10$ and $15x^2 - 65x + 5$.

13. Answers will vary. For example, $6x^2 + 72x$ and $78x^2 + 42x$.

14. a) $14x(x - 2)$ **b)** yes
  c) yes   **d)** $3x(x + 13)$

15. division and multiplication; answer will vary.

16. $7x$ by $x + 6$; 7 m by 7 m

17. a) $4y(2x - 1)$
  b) $2x^2(x - 2)$
  c) $-3x(3x^2 - 5x + 7)$
  d) $5xy(x - 2 + 3y)$

18. 14 cm by 19 cm

7.3 Factor a Difference of Squares, pages 298–305

1. a) 7   **b)** 9   **c)** 10

2. a) 5^2 **b)** 6^2 **c)** 4^2

3. a) yes, both perfect squares and one positive term and one negative term
  b) no, both terms are positive
  c) yes, both perfect squares and one positive term and one negative term

4. a) $(x + 9)(x - 9)$ **b)** $(x + 11)(x - 11)$
  c) $(x + 12)(x - 12)$ **d)** $(20 + x)(20 - x)$
  e) $(5 + x)(5 - x)$ **f)** $(7 + x)(7 - x)$
  g) $(10 + x)(10 - x)$ **h)** $(15 + x)(15 - x)$
  i) $(4x + 11)(4x - 11)$

5. a) $x^2 - 36$ **b)** $(x + 6)(x - 6)$ **c)** 16 cm by 4 cm

6. a) $x + 7, x - 7$ **b)** 576 cm^2

7. a) $10 - x$ **b)** 14 ft by 6 ft   **c)** 84 ft^2

8. yes, both perfect squares and one positive term and one negative term

9. a) $9 - x^2$; $(3 + x)(3 - x)$ **b)** $25 - 4x^2$; $(5 + 2x)(5 - 2x)$
  c) $81 - 16x^2$; $(9 + 4x)(9 - 4x)$

10. $x^2 + 1$ is the sum of two squares. $x^2 - 1$ is a difference of squares because both terms are perfect squares and they are subtracted.

11. $x^2 + 25$ cannot be factored.

12. $2x^2 - 18$ is not a difference of squares. However, after the common factor 2 is removed, the other factor is a difference of squares.

13. a) $2(2x + 3)(2x - 3)$
  b) $3(4x + 3)(4x - 3)$
  c) $5(x + 3y)(x - 3y)$

14. 20 m by 20 m

7.4 Factoring Trinomials of the Form $x^2 + bx + c$,
pages 306–311

1. a) 4, 5   **b)** 2, 9
    c) $-3, -4$ **d)** $2, -7$

2. a) $(x + 6)(x + 6)$ **b)** $(x - 3)(x - 9)$
    c) $(x + 10)(x - 3)$ **d)** $(x - 18)(x + 2)$

3. a) $(x + 2)(x + 2)$ **b)** $(x - 5)(x + 1)$
    c) $(x + 11)(x - 2)$ **d)** $(x - 4)(x - 5)$

4. $x + 1, x + 1$

5. a)

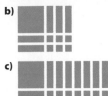

b)

c)

6. a) $x + 10$ by $x + 2$ **b)** $x + 2$ by $x + 3$
c) $x + 2$ by $x + 7$

    a) $(x + 10)(x + 2)$ **b)** $(x + 2)(x + 3)$
    c) $(x + 2)(x + 7)$

7. a) $(x + 3)(x + 5)$ **b)** 9 cm by 7 cm

8. a) $(x - 5)(x + 2)$ **b)** $(x - 2)(x - 3)$

9. No, $(x - 12)(x + 2)$ is the correct answer. $(x - 6)(x - 4)$ is $x^2 - 10x + 24$

11. $x^2 - 3x - 28$

12. Answer will vary. $6, -6, -126$.

13. $12, -12$

14. It forms a rectangle, $x + 2$ by $x + 1$.

The tiles cannot be arranged to form a rectangle.

15. a) $(x + 6)(x + 6)$
    b) square, because both factors are equal
    c) 7 m by 7 m

16. a) $3(x + 2)(x + 5)$
    b) $4(x + 3)(x - 6)$
    c) $-(x - 3)(x - 1)$
    d) $2(x + 1)(x + 1)$

17. 12.5 cm by 3.5 cm

Chapter 7 Review, pages 312–313

1. a) iv   **b)** iii   **c)** i   **d)** ii

2. a) $x^2 - x - 72$ **b)** $2x^2 - 7x - 15$
    c) $6x^2 - 11x + 3$ **d)** $x^2 - 36$

3. a) $x^2 + 10x + 25$ **b)** $x^2 - 14x + 49$
    c) $4x^2 + 12x + 9$ **d)** $9x^2 - 12x + 4$

4. Enrico is incorrect. The answer should be $2x^2 + 11x - 21$.

5. a) $5x^2 + 53x + 30$ **b)** 3090 cm²   **c)** yes

6. $(5x - 2)(x + 3) - (x + 2)(x + 1)$

7. a) $5(x - 5)$ **b)** $4x(2x + 5)$ **c)** $-3(2x^2 - 5x - 9)$

8. a) $4(x - 5)$ **b)** $3x(2x + 5)$ **c)** $7(x - 3)(x + 1)$

9. a) x by $x + 51$ **b)** $4x + 102$

10. a) $2x(7x - 6)$ **b)** $-5y^2(2 - 3y)$ **c)** $6x(5x^2 - 4x + 2)$

11. a) $(x + 4)(x - 4)$ **b)** no
    c) $(7 + 3x)(7 - 3x)$ **d)** $(2 + 5x)(2 - 5x)$

12. a) $(x + 5)(x - 5)$ **b)** $(9x + 10)(9x - 10)$
    c) $(8 + 11x)(8 - 11x)$ **d)** $(x + 6)(x - 6)$

13. a) $9x^2 - 16$ **b)** $(3x + 4)(3x - 4)$

14. $(x^2 + 12x + 36) - (x^2 + 2x + 1) = 10x + 35$

15. a) 2, 5   **b)** $-3, -3$ **c)** $-1, 9$ **d)** $-9, -4$

16. a) $(x + 9)(x - 3)$ **b)** $(x + 5)(x + 5)$

Chapter 7 Practice Test, pages 314–315

1. a) $x^2 + 12x + 27$ **b)** $2x^2 + 9x - 5$
    c) $x^2 + 12x + 36$ **d)** $x^2 - 49$

2. a) $x^2 + 6x + 8$ **b)** $2x^2 + 5x - 3$

3. a) $8x(2x - 3)$ **b)** $5x(3x + 4)$
    c) $-2x(7x + 3)$ **d)** $7(3x + 1)(x - 1)$

4. a) $(x + 3)(x + 7)$ **b)** $(x - 4)(x + 1)$
    c) $(x - 5)(x - 5)$ **d)** $(x + 10)(1x - 10)$

5. 426 cm

6. because the two factors are the same. $(x + 7)(x + 7)$

7. a) $25x^2 - 9$
    b) $(5x + 3)(5x - 3)$
    c) 8 m × 2 m

8. a) $9a(a - 2)$; $9(a^2 - 2a)$; $3a(3a - 6)$
    b) $9a(a - 2)$, because it cannot be factored any further

9. a) $8x^2 + 32x$
    b) 49.92 m²

CHAPTER 8
Represent Quadratic Relations, pages 316–355

Get Ready!, pages 318–319

1. a)

b)

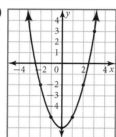

c)

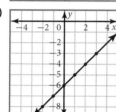

d)

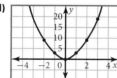

2. a) Linear. We know this because the first differences are constant.
b) Quadratic. We know this because the second differences are constant.
c) Linear. We know this because the first differences are constant.
d) Quadratic. We know this because the second differences are constant.

3. a) $(-1, 4)$ **b)** $(1, 5)$

4. a) vertex: $(1, 9)$; axis of symmetry: $x = 1$; x-intercepts: $-2, 4$; y-intercept: 8
b) vertex: $(-3, -4)$; axis of symmetry: $x = -3$; x-intercepts: $-5, -1$; y-intercept: 5
c) vertex: $(0, 3)$; axis of symmetry: $x = 0$; x-intercepts: none; y-intercept: 3
d) vertex: $(0, -4)$; axis of symmetry: $x = 0$; x-intercepts: none; y-intercept: -4

5. a) -3 **b)** 10   **c)** ± 3

6. a) $-4x^2 + 8x$ **b)** $x^2 + 8x + 15$ **c)** $x^2 - 2x - 3$

7. a) $-5(x^2 - 2)$ **b)** $3x(x - 5)$ **c)** $(x + 9)(x - 2)$

8.1 Interpret Quadratic Relations, pages 310–328

1. a) 4 m   **b)** 2 m   **c)** 4.25 m
d) 0.5 m   **e)** 1 m

2. a) 20 m   **b)** 2.5 s   **c)** 5 s

3. a)

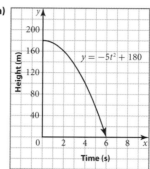

b) 180 m   **c)** 118.75 m

4. a)

b) $y = -0.0083x^2 + 1.0007x - 0.0029$
c) 120 m   **d)** Yes

5. a)

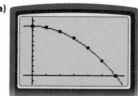

b) $y = -1.119x^2 + 0.021x + 9.990$
c) 3 s   **d)** 10 m

6. a)

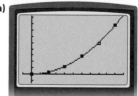

b) Yes, the points appear to form half a parabola.
c) $y = 3.14x^2$ **d)** 314 cm^2

7. a)

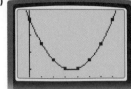

b) Yes, the points appear to be quadratic since the second differences are constant.

c) because the height of the bridge decreases first, then increases

8. a)

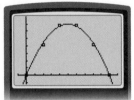

b) $y = -0.112x^2 + 5.607x - 0.714$

c) 25 m

9. a)

Price of Ticket ($)	Attendance	Revenue ($1000s)
40	8000	320
41	7850	321.85
42	7700	323.40
43	7550	324.65
44	7400	325.60
45	7250	326.25
46	7100	326.60
47	6950	326.65
48	6800	326.40
49	6650	325.85
50	6500	325.00
51	6350	323.85
52	6200	322.40

b)

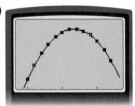

c) 47

10. a) 3 s

b) 270 m

11. a)

Width (m)	Length (m)	Area of Garden (m²)
1	13	13
2	12	24
3	11	33
4	10	40
5	9	45
6	8	48
7	7	49
8	6	48
9	5	45
10	4	40
11	3	33
12	2	24
13	1	13

b)

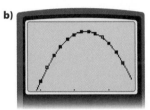

c) 7 m by 7 m

13. a)

w (cm)	d (cm)
0	0
25	11
50	20
75	27
100	32
125	35
150	36

b)

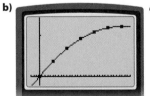

$d = -0.0016w^2 + 0.48w$

c) $d = -0.0016w^2 + 0.48w = -0.0016w(w - 300)$

8.2 Represent Quadratic Realations in Different Ways, pages 329–335

1. a) $-2, -3$ **b)** $-9, 2$ **c)** 4, 6

2. a) minimum   **b)** -4 **c)** $-4, 1$

3. a) minimum: -1 **b)** maximum: 1   **c)** 18.75

4. a

5. 56.25 m^2

6. a) $y = (x - 2)(x - 8)$
   b) 2, 8
   c) 6 m

7. a) $10 000   **b)** 3 hours   **c)** $15 400

8. a) $120 000   **b)** 7000

9. Companies can maximize their profit by calculating the necessary production level that corresponds with the maximum value in the quadratic relation that models their profit.

10. a)

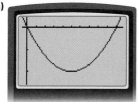

   b) 2 m
   c) 5 m
   d) 10 m

11. 30 yd

12. zeros: 1, 5; maximum: 8

13. Haley's method works because parabolas are symmetrical. The vertex's x-coordinate is equal to the average of the zeros.

8.3 The Quadratic Relation $y = ax^2 + c$, pages 336–343

1. a) $y = 3x^2 - 7$, $y = x^2 - 7$, $y = \frac{1}{3}x^2 - 7$

   b) $y = -4x^2 + 5$, $y = -0.75x^2 + 5$, $y = -\frac{1}{2}x^2 + 5$

2. a) -4; minimum
   b) 7; minimum
   c) 45; maximum
   d) -8; maximum
   e) 3; maximum
   f) 5; maximum

3. a) $y = x^2 - 4$ **b)** $y = 3x^2 + 7$

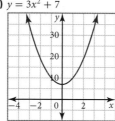

c) $y = -5x^2 + 45$

d) $y = -2x^2 - 8$

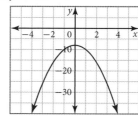

e) $y = -\frac{1}{3}x^2 + 3$

f) $y = -\frac{1}{2}x^2 + 5$

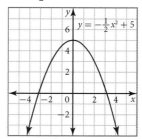

4. a) 45 m
   b) 3 s

5. a) 250 ft deep
   b) 10 s
   c) yes; since $10 < 20$

6. a)

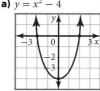

   b) The graphs are the same. When you expand $-3(x + 3)(x - 3)$ you get $-3x^2 + 27$.

7. a) 1.5 m
   b) approximately 9.5 m

8. a) 25 m²

    b) 10 m by 10 m

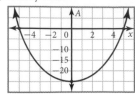

9. a) 20 m

    b) approximately 120 m

10. $a = 4$

11. $c = 60$

12. Parabolas are used in bridges, doorways, in historical buildings, and tunnels.

13. a) $h = -\dfrac{5}{6}t^2 + 100$

    b) approximately 4.5 s

    c) approximately 11 s

8.4 Solve Problems Involving Quadratic Relations, pages 244–351

1. a) revenue = $3600; ticket price = $6.00

    b) $3500

    c) c, the constant part of the quadratic relation represents the original revenue.

2. a) 15 m   **b)** 335 m

    c) 515 m   **d)** 10 s

    e) 13.11s   **f)** 20.15 s

3. a) The first quaterback threw it by 4.15 yd further.

    b) The first quaterback threw it higher.

    c) Answers may vary.

4. a) 13 m

    b) 472.9 m

    c) 523.20 m

    d) 10.20 s

    e) 10.03 s

    f) 20.54 s

5. a) No. Only the second shot is able to score. The ball from the first shot has a height of 2.625 m at the goal, so the shot is above the crossbar and will not go in the goal. The ball from the second shot has a height of 1.875 m at the goal and is below the crossbar.

    b) No. Only the second shot is able to score.

7. a) $484 000

    b) $0.20

    c) $2.20

    d) 210 000 people

8. a) $32.50

    b) 8000 barrels

    c) $176.50

9. a) 0.75 yd   **b)** 25.95 yd

    c) 32 yd   **d)** 25 yd

    e) 50.30 yd

10. a) 7 ft   **b)** 67 ft

    c) 87 ft   **d)** 4 s

    e) 3.69 s   **f)** 8 s

11. a) 87 L

    b) 28.65 L

    c) 9.2 L at 100 km/h

    d) Answers may vary.

12. The lower one is 18.7 m, the other one is 22.35 m.

13. 5625 m²

Chapter 8 Review, pages 352–353

1. zeros

2. a)

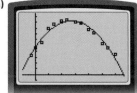

    b) $y = -0.2488x^2 + 6.7671x + 46.3705$

    c) 12°C or 13.6°C (from the graph)

3. a)

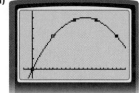

    b) $y = -0.032x^2 + 0.8x$

    c) maximum height = 5 ft; horizontal distance = 12.5 yd

4. a) Area $= -w^2 + 20w$

    b) $w = 10$

5. 12 ft apart. It is twice the distance from one tree to the centre of the rope.

6. a) 13 m   **b)** 1.63 s   **c)** 1 s

7. a) 15 ft   **b)** 20 ft   **c)** 7.75 ft

8. a) 14.532 ft   **b)** 10.5 ft

    c) Yes. When the jump shot is taken 24 ft from the basket, by the time the ball reaches the basket it has a height of 10.5 ft and will be above the rim, thus, able to go into the basket.

9. a) $2812.50
  b) 5
  c) $7.50

Chapter 8 Practice Test, pages 354–355

1. a) 0; 0; maximum: 0
  b) -2; -2, 1; minimum: -2.25
  c) -49; -7, 7; minimum: -49
  d) 0; -4, 0; minimum: -4

2. a)

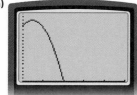

  b) $y = -0.035x^2 + 0.875x + 6.25$
  c) 11.72 ft
  d) 12.5 yd
  e) 4.36 ft

3. a) 21.5 m
  b) 22.725 m; 0.5 s
  c) 17.825 m
  d) approximately 2.65 s

4. a)

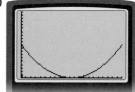

  b) 136.73 ft
  c) 1207.55 ft or 2992.45 ft

5. a) $1 800 000
  b) 60 000
  c) 30 000 to 90 000; The profit will be less than zero when the manufacturer produces less than 30 000 or more than 90 000.

6. Good. $h = -0.03(42)^2 + 1.50(42) = 10.08$
  Since $10.08 > 10$ the field goal was good.

Chapter 6 to 8 Review, pages 358–359
Chapter 6, page 358

1. a)

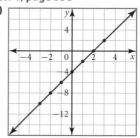

  b)

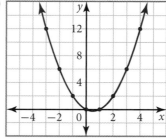

2. a)

x	y
0	0
1	8
2	12
3	12
4	8
5	0

  b) $y = -2x^2 + 10x$

  c)

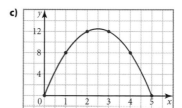

  d) Vertex: (2.5, 12.5); Axis of symmetry: $x = 2.5$

3. a)

x	$y = 4x^2 - 10x + 1$
0	1
1	-5
2	-3
3	7
4	25
5	5

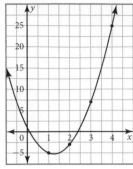

b) y-int: $y = 1$; x-ints: $x = 0.104$, $x = 2.396$;
   vertex: $(1.25, -5.25)$

Chapter 7, page 358

4. a) $x^2 + 2x - 8$
   b) $x^2 - 6x + 9$
   c) $4x^2 + 4x - 3$
   d) $9x^2 - 6x + 1$

5. $12^2 - x^2$

6. a) GCF: 3; $3(x + 6)$
   b) GCF: $5x$; $5x(x - 2)$
   c) GCF: 3; $3(x^2 + 3x - 6)$
   d) GCF: $14x$; $14x(x^2 + 2)$

7. a) $A = 10x(x + 50)$
   b) $P = 2(x + 50) + 2(10x)$ or $P = 22x + 100$
   c) $A = 6000 \text{ m}^3$, $P = 320 \text{ m}$

8. a) $(x + 3)(x - 3)$
   b) $(5 - x)(5 + x)$

9. a) $(x - 6)(x + 3)$
   b) $(x - 9)(x - 2)$
   c) $(x + 6)(x + 5)$
   d) $(x - 5)(x + 1)$

Chapter 8, page 359

10. 41.47 ft

11. a)

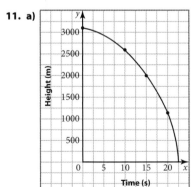

b) $y = -4.9x^2 + 3100$
c) 21.99 s

12. a) 5 s
   b) 2.5 s
   c) 31.25 m

13. 15 625 ft^2

14. a) \$11 760
   b) \$280

CHAPTER 9
Volume and Surface Area, pages 360–409

Get Ready!, pages 362–363

1. a) $b = 5.9$ in.
   b) $k = 379.7$ mm
   c) $f = 12.0$ cm
   d) $d = 6.3$ m
   e) $c = 4.9$ cm
   f) $x = 5.2$ cm
   g) $p = 6.5$ mm

2. a) rectangular prism
   b) triangular prism
   c) cube
   d) square-based pyramid
   e) cylinder
   f) pentagonal pyramid

3. a) 10.5 ft
   b) 2.41 m
   c) 7500 mL
   d) 44 pints
   e) 567 ft^3
   f) 0.117 54 m^2

4. a) 32 cm^2
   b) 3.14 yd^2
   c) 6 m^2
   d) 64 cm^2

9.1 Volume of Prisms and Pyramids, pages 364–371

1. a) 60 000 cm^3
   b) 20 ft^3
   c) 9.548 m^3
   d) 24 yd^3

2. a) 1386 in^3
   b) 1.54 m^3

3. a) 16 464 ft^3
   b) 160 160 mm^3
   c) 10 800 yd^3
   d) 12 cm^3
   e) 81 312 cm^3
   f) 20 720 in^3

4. a) 18 943.75 cm^3
b) 1866.48 in^3
c) 12.1 ft^3
d) 10.8 m^3

5. a) 720 in^3
b) 3.30 m^3
c) 2.95 m^3

6. a) 700 000 ft
b) 9930.67 in.

7. The cube has greater volume. The cube has volume 64 in^3 and the rectangular prism has volume 60 in^3.

8. Answer will vary.

9. a) Design 1 because it has less surface area and will be cheaper to make.
b) Answers will vary.
c) Vanessa should use Design 1 because it has less surface area and will be cheaper to make.

10. a) 91 152 065 ft^3
b) 83 068 742 ft^3
c) 8 083 323 ft^3

11. a) 50 000 cm^3
b) 30 000 cm^3
c) Yes, because it can hold 50 000 cm^3, which is more than 30 000 cm^3.

13. 64 ft^3

14. a) The volume will increase by a factor of 4.
b) There is no change in the volume.
c) The volume will increase by a factor of 8.
d) The volume will be 75% of its original value.
e) The volume will increase by a factor of 3 because $V = (3\ell)(w)(h) = 3\ell wh$.

9.2 Surface Area of Prism and Pyramids, pages 372-380
1. a) 1608 in^2

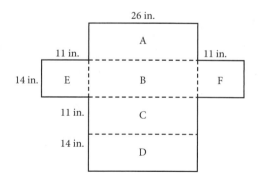

b) 112 yd^2

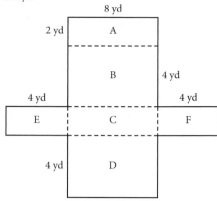

c) 21.42 m^2

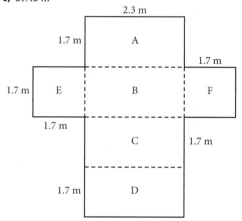

d) 1312 cm^2

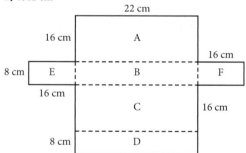

e) 16.94 yd^2

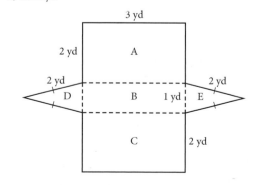

f) 2069.2 cm^2

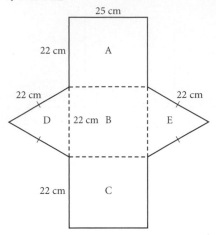

2. a) 1046.4 m^2

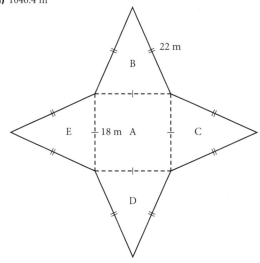

b) 995.9 ft^2

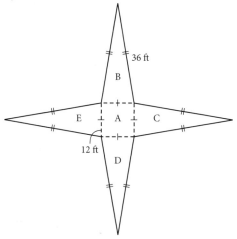

c) 106 447.2 mm^2

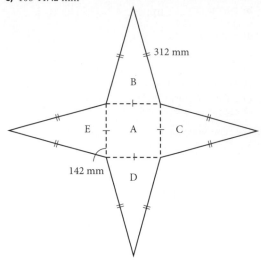

d) 117.2 in^2

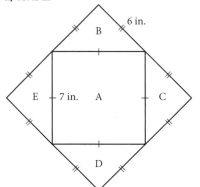

3. a) 318.2 cm^2 **b)** 2154 in.^{2}
    c) 3079.3 m^2 **d)** 37.6 ft^2

4. a) 1344 yd^2 **b)** 480 cm^2
    c) 384 m^2 **d)** 79.5 in.^{2}

5. a) 512 ft^2 **b)** 631.4 in.^{2}

6. She needs enough sealant to cover 2044 ft^2.

7. The right triangular prism has greater surface area. The right triangular prism has surface area 401 cm^2 and the isosceles triangular prism has surface area 375 cm^2.

8. a) 1975.3 m^2 **b)** $632.10

9. You would need to add up the surface areas of the four triangles that make up the roof and the four squares that make up the sides of the doghouse.

10. $32.60

11. a) inner pyramid: 50.91 in.^{2}; outer pyramid: 69.97 in.^{2}
    b) The total cost is $28.18 per package.

12. $148.50

13. a) 1700 m^3 **b)** \$193 876 **c)** 3 workers

14. a) 10.6 cm **b)** 224.7 cm^3 **c)** 282 cm^2

15. 10.3 cm

9.3 Surface Area and Volume of Cylinders, pages 381–390

1. a) $SA = 8017.3$ cm^2; $V = 54\,739.1$ cm^3
 b) $SA = 339.3$ ft^2; $V = 424.1$ ft^3
 c) $SA = 25.64$ m^2; $V = 9.95$ m^3
 d) $SA = 11.4$ m^2; $V = 2.92$ m^3

2. a) 19 704.1 cm^2 **b)** 3342.7 in.^{2}
 c) 1924.2 cm^2 **d)** 169.6 ft^2

3. a) 239 342.9 cm^3 **b)** 5154.2 in.^{3}
 c) 196.9 yd^3 **d)** 26 146.3 cm^3

4. a) 15.8 cm^3 **b)** 11.0 cm^3 **c)** 4.8 cm^3

5. 791.7 in.^{3}

6. 2.5 cm

7. 0.4 in.

8. a) 0.392 m^2 **b)** 10.59 m^2

9. 211 492 m^3

10. a) 1006 cm^3
 b) Yes, because the can will hold 1006 mL, which is more than 972 mL.
 c) Answers will vary.

11. a) radius = 2.78 cm; height = 8.5 cm
 b) $SA = 197.03$ cm^2
 c) \$689 605.00

12. The shorter cylinder has greater volume. The shorter cylinder has volume 81.8 in.^{3} and the longer cylinder has volume 63.2 in.^{3}.

13. Answers will vary.

14. a) 35.4 m **b)** 981.8 m^2

15. a) The volume also doubles.
 b) The volume increases by a factor of 9.
 c) The volume also decreases to $\frac{1}{3}$ of its original value.
 d) The volume increases by a factor of 8.
 e) The volume increases by a factor of 4.

9.4 Volume of Cones and Spheres, pages 391–397

1. a) 5486.3 cm^3 **b)** 3694.5 in.^{3} **c)** 8.4 ft^3
 d) 261.8 m^3 **e)** 28 735.1 mm^3 **f)** 0.8 yd^3

2. a) 137.3 m^3 **b)** 268.1 ft^3 **c)** 3053.6 in.^{3}
 d) 57.9 yd^3 **e)** 150.5 mm^3 **f)** 1022.65 cm^3

3. a) 366.5 cm^3 **b)** 2.8 cm

4. a) $V_{large} = 11\,494$ cm^3; $V_{small} = 11.494$ cm^3
 b) 1000 times larger

5. a) 38 792.4 mm^3 **b)** 381.7 in.^{3}
 c) 1 047 394.4 mm^3 **d)** 4849.0 cm^3

6. a) 1728 in.^{3} **b)** 12 in.
 c) 904.8 in.^{3} **d)** 823.2 in.^{3}

7. Answers may vary.

8. 6.4 cm

9.

	Volume	Radius	Height
a)	227 cm^3	27 mm	29.7 cm
b)	775 in^3	4.5 in.	3 ft
c)	188 yd^3	9 ft	19.9 yd
d)	56 m^3	6.5 m	126 cm

10. 36 scoops

11. 885.9 mL

12. a) 3.1 cm **b)** 0.8 yd
 c) 8.6 in **d)** 30.8 mm

9.5 Solving Problems Involving Surface Area and Volume, pages 398–405

1. a) 3.5 ft **b)** 31.5 ft
 c) 1212.3 ft^3 **d)** 89.8 ft^3
 e) 1302.1 ft^3

2. a) corner: 7.95 in.^{3}; side: 14.1 in.^{3}
 b) 5.3 ft^3
 c) 882.7 lb

3. 3.0 m^2

4. a) 600 cm^3 **b)** 575.4 cm^3

5. a) 29 791 000 ft^3
 b) 7 799 265.6 ft^3
 c) 37 590 265.6 ft^3

6. a) 982.1 cm^2 **b)** 2150.4 cm^3

8. a) 30.75 ft^2 **b)** 2.7 L

9. 332 in.^{2}

10. Answers will vary.

11. 1493.2 cm^3

12. a) 1.9 m^3 **b)** 0.4 m^3
 c) 79% decrease

Chapter 9 Review, pages 406–407

1. a) prism **b)** pyramid
 c) sphere **d)** cone
 e) volume **f)** cylinder
 g) surface area

2. a) 4 yd^3 **b)** 113 792 cm^3

3. Volume is also doubled.

4. a) 539.5 ft^2 **b)** 6849 cm^2

5. a) $SA = 11\,272.0$ cm^2; $V = 66\,366.1$ cm^3
   b) $SA = 2551$ ft^2; $V = 7850.8$ ft^3

6. a) 2488.1 in.^{3} **b)** 19 905.1 in.^{3}

7. a) 1272.3 ft^3 **b)** 84 759.4 m^3

8. a) $V_{cube} = 3375$ in.^{3}; $V_{prism} = 19\,440$ in.^{3}
   b) 16 065 in.^{3}

9. a) 58 782.3 in.^{3} **b)** 19 594.1 in.^{3} **c)** 53.4 in.

10. 7681.8 in.^{2}

Chapter 9 Practice Test, pages 408–409

1. a) $SA = 6328.8$ cm^2; $V = 24\,166.7$ cm^3
   b) $SA = 980.2$ yd^2; $V = 1759.3$ yd^3

2. a) 3053.6 in.^{3} **b)** 5131.3 cm^3

3. a) 34 636.1 ft^3 **b)** 40.4 ft

4. a) The cube has the greater volume. The cube has volume 5832 in.^{3} and the rectangular prism has volume 5760 in.^{3}.
   b) The rectangular prism has the greater surface area. The rectangular prism has surface area 2592 in.^{2} and the cube has surface area 1944 in.^{2}.

5. a) 955.0 in.^{3} **b)** 25 balloons

6. The volume of each block is 384 cm^3, so only 2 will fit in the box.

7. a) 1050.6 in.^{2} **b)** 7

Chapters 1 to 9 Review, pages 412–415
Chapter 1, page 412

1. $857.03

2. $j = 24$ cm; $y = 19$ cm

3. 4.68 m

Chapter 2, page 412

4. a) 40.3 cm
   b) 37.4 cm

5. 16.5 m

Chapter 3, page 412

6. slope of AB $= \dfrac{4}{3}$; slope of CD $= -4$; slope of EF $= 0$;

7. a) $y = \dfrac{1}{2}x + 4$ **b)** $y = \dfrac{1}{2}x - 6$ **c)** $y = -x - 6$

8. a)

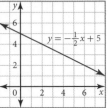

   b)

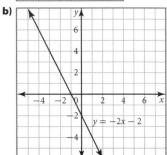

9. a)

Time (h)	Cost ($)
1	80
2	105
3	130

   b)

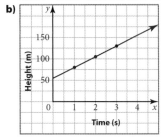

   c) $y = 25x + 55$
   d) $155
   e) $92.50

Chapter 4, page 413

10. a) $x = 3$ **b)** $k = 20$ **c)** $y = 21$ **d)** $z = 2$

11. a) $y = 4x + 5$ **b)** $y = -6x + 3$
   c) $y = \dfrac{4}{15}x + 2\dfrac{2}{5}$

12. $C = -23$

13. $(-2, -6)$

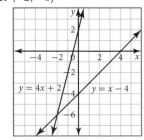

Chapter 5, page 413

14. a) $(-16, -28)$ **b)** $(1, 1)$

15. a) $(-2, 4)$ **b)** $(5, 1)$

16. \$9500 and \$5500 respectively

Chapter 6, page 413

17.

x	y	First Differences	Second Differences
−3	31		
−2	18	−13	
−1	9	−9	4
0	4	−5	4
1	3	−1	4
2	6	3	4

18. a) $(-6, 18)$ **b)** $x = -6$
    c) x-intercepts: $(-9, 0)$, $(-3, 0)$; y-intercept: $(0, -54)$
    d) max: 18

Chapter 7, page 414

19. a) $x^2 - 2x - 15$
    b) $2x^2 - x - 1$
    c) $4x^2 - 12x + 9$

20. a) GCF: 9; $9(2x - 3)$ **b)** GCF: x; $x(5x + 1)$

21. a) $l = 4x$; $w = x + 50$ **b)** $10x + 100$
    c) $P = 600$ m; $A = 20\ 000$ m^2

22. no; $(x + 7)(x - 6)$

23. a) $(x + 6)(x - 6)$ **b)** $(x + 7)(x - 1)$
    c) $(x - 7)(x + 4)$ **d)** $(x + 5)(x - 1)$

Chapter 8, page 414

24. a)

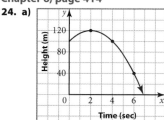

b) 100 m   **c)** 120 m; 2 s

25. a)

b) $(-4, 0)$, $(4, 0)$
c) 8 m

Chapter 9, page 415

26. a) Surface Area: 1088 cm^2; Volume: 2112 cm^3
    b) Surface Area: 3204.4 in.^{2}; Volume: 12 880.5 in.^{3}
    c) Surface Area: 96 m^2; Volume: 48 m^3

27. a) 1180.2 cm^3 **b)** 33.5 in.^{3}

28. a) 66 yd^2 **b)** \$207.90

Skills Appendix

Add and Subtract Integers, page 416
1. a) 17   **b)** 0   **c)** 8
2. a) 23   **b)** 11   **c)** −3
3. a) 42   **b)** 5   **c)** −17   **d)** 10

Algebra Tiles, page 417
1. a)

b)

c)

Angle Properties, pages 417–418
1. a) 115°   **b)** 50°   **c)** 160°
    d) 102°   **e)** 90°   **f)** 172°

2. a) $x = 75°$, $y = 105°$
    b) $x = 145°$, $y = 35°$
    c) $x = 130°$, $y = 50°$, $z = 130°$

Area, page 419
1. a) 7.5 mm^2 **b)** 4 mm^2
    c) 11 cm^2 **d)** 12.53 cm^2

Common Factors, 420
1. a) 1, 2, 4; GCF: 4
    b) 1, 2, 4, 8, 16; GCF: 16
    c) 1, 2, 3, 5, 6, 10, 15, 30; GCF: 30

2. a) 1, 3; GCF: 3   **b)** 1, 5; GCF: 5
    c) 1; GCF: 1   **d)** 1, 3; GCF: 3

Convert Fractions to Decimals, 420–421
1. a) 0.2   **b)** 0.35
    c) 0.375   **d)** 0.7
    e) 0.65   **f)** 0.25

2. a) 0.7   **b)** 0.2
    c) 0.4   **d)** 0.8

Convert Measurements, page 421

1. a) 138 000 mL   **b)** 0.000 45 km
  c) 0.58 mL   **d)** 72 ft
  e) 0.7 m^2 **f)** 189 ft^3

Evaluate Expressions, page 422

1. a) −2   **b)** 10   **c)** 10   **d)** −1

2. a) 13   **b)** 5   **c)** −5   **d)** 67

3. a) 24   **b)** 10   **c)** −50   **d)** −7

Fractions, pages 422–424

1. a) $\frac{5}{6}$ **b)** $\frac{4}{5}$ **c)** $\frac{3}{4}$ **d)** $\frac{5}{6}$

2. a) $\frac{3}{20}$ **b)** $\frac{2}{3}$ **c)** $\frac{1}{6}$ **d)** $-\frac{1}{10}$

3. a) $\frac{10}{63}$ **b)** $\frac{1}{25}$ **c)** $\frac{9}{25}$ **d)** $\frac{3}{20}$

4. a) $\frac{4}{15}$ **b)** $\frac{3}{4}$ **c)** $\frac{25}{42}$ **d)** $\frac{25}{27}$

Graph Coordinates, 424–425

1. a) 2   **b)** −1   **c)** 5   **d)** 0

2. a) 7   **b)** −2   **c)** −3   **d)** 20

3.

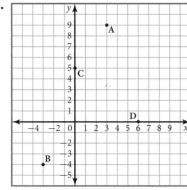

4. A(2, −4), B(5, −1), C(−4,1), D(0, 3)

Graph Linear Relations, pages 425–426

1. a)

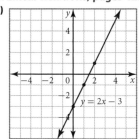

b)

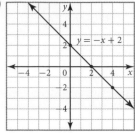

c)

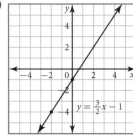

2. a)

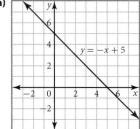

b)

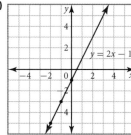

c)

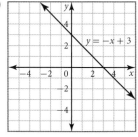

Intercepts, pages 426–427

1. a) x–int: -3, y–int: -1 **b)** x–int: 3, y–int: -4

2. a)

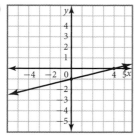

b)

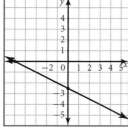

Isolate a Variable, 427

1. a) $y = -\dfrac{8}{3}x + \dfrac{2}{3}$

b) $y = \dfrac{3}{2}x - \dfrac{7}{4}$

c) $y = 2x - 13$

d) $y = \dfrac{5}{6}x + \dfrac{11}{6}$

Least Common Denominator, page 428

1. a) 30 **b)** 28 **c)** 36 **d)** 30

2. a) 10 **b)** 24 **c)** 100 **d)** 72

Linear and Non-Linear Relations, pages 429–430

1. a)

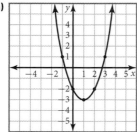

non-linear

b)

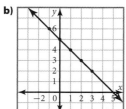

linear

2. a)

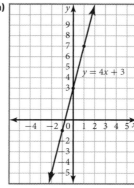

linear

b)

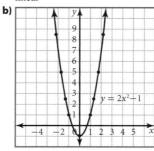

non-linear

Lines of Symmetry, pages 430–431

1. a)

b)

2. a)

b)

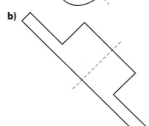

Lowest Terms, 432

1. a) $\frac{1}{2}$ **b)** $\frac{3}{5}$

   c) $\frac{3}{8}$ **d)** $\frac{1}{20}$

Multiply and Divide Expressions, pages 432–433

1. a) $15y$ **b)** $60p^2$
   c) $-2x^2$ **d)** $-48k^2$

2. a) $-4x$ **b)** $3k$
   c) $-3y$ **d)** -5

3. a) $-8x - 6$
   b) $-3y^2 - 18y + 3$
   c) $35a - 10a^2$
   d) $-12p^2 + 28p - 20$

Nets, page 433

1. a) cube
   b) cone
   c) triangle-based pyramid

Polynomials, page 434

1. a) binomial
   b) trinomial
   c) polynomial
   d) trinomial

2. a) -5 **b)** 8
   c) -1 **d)** 24

Properties of Triangles, pages 435–436

1. a) 68°   **b)** 45°

2. a) 120°   **b)** 60°
   c) 45°   **d)** 95°
   e) 82°   **f)** 37°

3. a)

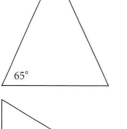

b)

c)

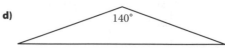

d)

Proportions, page 436

1. a) $x = 48$ **b)** $x = 20$
   c) $x = 2$ **d)** $x = 66$

2. a) $x = 1$ **b)** $x = 4000$
   c) $x = \frac{100}{17}$ **d)** $x = 3$

Pythagorean Theorem, page 437

1. a) $w \doteq 2.8$ cm
   b) $x \doteq 2.4$ mm
   c) $c \doteq 2.2$ cm

Ratios, page 438

1. a) $5 : 6$ **b)** $2 : 7$
   c) $1 : 4$ **d)** $6 : 5$

Rounding, pages 438-439

1. a) 4   **b)** 10
   c) 9   **d)** 2

2. a) 7.9   **b)** 8.4
   c) 10.8   **d)** 101.0

3. a) 5.89   **b)** 0.14
   c) 11.70   **d)** 0.00

Simplify Expressions, page 439

1. a) $4b + 13$ **b)** $10k - 11$
   c) $-4f + 8$ **d)** $2t + 2$

2. a) $7y + 4z - 6$ **b)** $10a + 7b$
   c) $13p - q - 4$ **d)** $3t + 3u + 3$

Solve Equations, page 440

1. a) $x = -5$ **b)** $x = 5$
   c) $x = \frac{40}{3}$ **d)** $x = -24$

2. a) $x = -1$ **b)** $x = -32$
   c) $x = \frac{20}{3}$ **d)** $x = 10$

Solve Linear Systems by Graphing, page 441

1. a) $(-1, -4)$ **b)** $(1, 7)$

Squaring, pages 441–442

1. a) 25   **b)** 9   **c)** 36

2. a) 97   **b)** 68   **c)** 101

3. a) 60   **b)** 45   **c)** 300

4. a) 54   **b)** 107   **c)** 32

Square Roots, pages 442–443

1. a) 6   **b)** 8   **c)** 10
   d) 3

2. a) 4.5   **b)** 13.4   **c)** 9.9
   d) 11.4

Word Problems, page 443

1. a) Let x represent the number of jeans Damian bought.
So, $45x = 225$.

b) Let y be the number of CDs Ming sold.
So, $8y = 136$

c) Let z be the number of diapers Terry changed.
So, $2z + 25 = 31$.

Glossary

A

adjacent side The side that forms one of the arms of the angle being considered in a right triangle, but is not the hypotenuse.

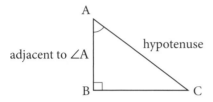

algebraic expression A mathematical phrase made up of numbers and variables.

$3x - 2, 5m,$ and $12xy + x + 14y$

angle of depression The angle between the horizontal and the line of sight down to an object.

angle of elevation The angle between the horizontal and the line of sight up to an object. Also known as an angle of inclination.

angle of inclination The angle between the horizontal and the line of sight up to an object. Also known as an angle of elevation.

area The number of square units needed to cover a two-dimensional region.

axis of symmetry A vertical line that passes through the vertex of a parabola. The equation of the axis of symmetry is $x = a$, where a is the x-coordinate of the vertex.

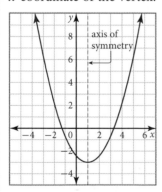

B

binomial A polynomial that has two terms.

$4x^2 + 2$ is a binomial.

break-even point The point at which total cost equals total revenue.

C

circumference The perimeter of a circle.

coefficient A number that is multiplied by a variable.

In $y = -2x$, the coefficient of x is -2.

common factor A number that is a factor of all the numbers in a set.

7 is a common factor of 14, 21, and 42.

complementary angles Angles whose sum is 90°.

composite figure A figure that is made up of two or more geometric figures.

cone A three-dimensional object with a circular base and a curved surface that tapers to a point.

congruent Identical in shape and size.

consecutive numbers Successive numbers that follow in order.

5, 6, 7, 8, ... are consecutive numbers.

constant term A numerical term which cannot change; that is, it remains constant. In the equation $7x + 3 = -5$, the constant terms are 3 and -5.

coordinate grid A grid formed by perpendicular number lines. Used for graphing points as ordered pairs.

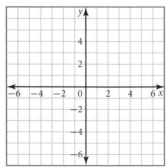

coordinates The numbers in an ordered pair that locate a point on a coordinate grid.

corresponding angles Angles that have the same relative position in a pair of similar triangles. Corresponding angles are equal.

corresponding sides Sides that have the same relative position in a pair of similar triangles. Lengths of corresponding sides are proportional.

cosine ratio The ratio comparing the length of the side adjacent to the angle to the length of the hypotenuse in a right triangle.

$$\cos A = \frac{\text{length of side opposite A}}{\text{length of hypotenuse}}$$

cube A prism with six congruent square faces.

curve of best fit A curve that passes through, or as near as possible to, the points on a scatter plot.

cylinder A three-dimensional object with two parallel circular bases.

denominator The number of equal parts in the whole or the group. In a fraction, the denominator is the bottom number.

diagonal A line that joins two vertices of a polygon, but is not a side.

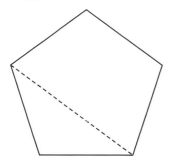

diameter A line segment that passes through the centre of a circle and joins two points on the circumference of the circle.

difference of squares A binomial in which a square term is subtracted from another square term. The factors of a difference of squares are binomials with identical terms but opposite operations.

dimension In geometry, the length, width, or height of a figure or object.

distributive property When a polynomial is multiplied by a monomial, the monomial multiplies each term in the polynomial.

$$a(x + y) = ax + ay$$

elimination method An algebraic method of solving a system of linear equations. The equations are added or subtracted to eliminate one variable.

equation A mathematical statement that two expressions are equal.

$6x - 1 = 4x$ is an equation.

equilateral triangle A triangle with all sides equal and all angles equal.

expand Multiply, often using the distributive property.

factor A number or expression that divides evenly into another number or expression.

first differences The difference between consecutive y-values in a table of values with evenly spaced x-values. First differences are constant for a linear relation.

formula An equation that describes an algebraic relationship between two or more variables.

greatest common factor (GCF) The greatest number that is a factor of two or more numbers. The GCF of 36, 48, and 72 is 12.

height of an object The perpendicular distance from the base of the object to the opposite face or vertex.

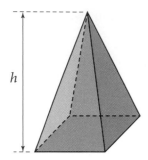

hypotenuse The longest side of a right triangle. The side opposite the right angle in a right triangle.

imperial system A system of measurement based on British units.

integer A number in the sequence ..., −3, −2, −1, 0, 1, 2, 3, ...

intercept The distance from the origin of a coordinate grid to the point at which the line or curve crosses a given axis.

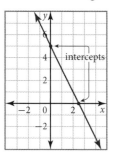

isosceles triangle A triangle with exactly two equal sides.

least common denominator (LCD) The least common multiple of the denominators of two or more fractions.

The LCD of $\frac{1}{4}$, $\frac{1}{6}$, and $\frac{1}{3}$ is 12.

least common multiple (LCM) The least number that is a multiple of two or more numbers. The LCM of 2, 3, and 5 is 30.

legs The two shorter sides of a right triangle. The sides adjacent to the right angle.

like terms Terms that have the same variables raised to the same exponent.

$4x$ and $-6x$ are like terms.

line of best fit A line that passes through, or as near as possible to, the points on a scatter plot.

linear equation An equation that relates two variables so the ordered pairs that satisfy the equation lie in a straight line on a graph.

linear relation A relation between two variables that appears as a straight line when graphed.

linear system A set of two or more linear equations that are considered at the same time.

line of symmetry A line that divides a figure into two congruent parts that are reflections of each other in the line.

line segment The part of a line that joins two points.

mass A measure of the quantity of matter in an object.

maximum value The greatest value of a quadratic relation represented by a parabola that opens downward. The y-value at the vertex of a parabola.

metric system A system of measurement in which all units are based on multiples of 10.

minimum value The least value of a quadratic relation represented by a parabola that opens upward. The y-value at the vertex of a parabola.

mnemonic A memory aid, such as BEDMAS, to remember the order of operations or SOH CAH TOA to remember the trigonometric ratios.

monomial A polynomial with one term, such as $5x^2$.

multiple The product of a given number and a natural number. Some multiples of 7 are 7, 14, 21, 28, ...

net A two-dimensional pattern that can be folded to make a three-dimensional object. This is a net for square-based pyramid.

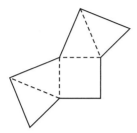

non-linear relation A relation between two variables that does not appear as a straight line when graphed.

numerator The number of equal parts being considered in the whole or the group. In a fraction, the numerator is the top number.

opposite angles The pairs of angles formed on either side when two lines intersect.

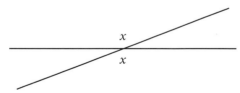

opposite operations Operations that "undo" one another. Addition and subtraction are opposite operations. Multiplication and division are opposite operations.

opposite side The side across from the angle being considered. The side that does not form one of the arms of the angle being considered.

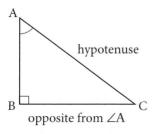

order of operations The convention for evaluating expressions with more than one operation: **B**rackets, **E**xponents, **D**ivision, **M**ultiplication, **A**ddition, and **S**ubtraction (BEDMAS).

ordered pairs A pair of numbers used to locate a point on a coordinate grid. The first number indicates the horizontal distance from the y-axis. The second number indicates the vertical distance from the x-axis.

origin The point of intersection of the x- and y-axes on a coordinate grid. The point $(0, 0)$.

parabola The graph of a quadratic relation. A symmetrical U-shaped graph.

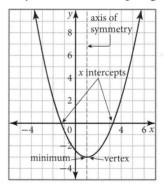

parallel lines Lines in the same plane that do not intersect. Parallel lines have the same slope.

perfect square trinomial The result of squaring a binomial.

perimeter The distance around a closed figure.

perpendicular lines Lines that intersect at right angles.

point of intersection The point at which two lines cross. The coordinates of the point of intersection satisfy both equations.

polynomial An algebraic expression made up of one or more terms, separated by addition or subtraction.

prism A three-dimensional object with two parallel, congruent polygonal bases. A prism is named by the shape of the base.

product The result of multiplication.

profit Total revenue minus total costs.

proportional Quantities are proportional if they have the same ratio. The side lengths of two triangles are proportional if there is a single value that will multiply each side length of the first triangle to give the side lengths of the second triangle.

pyramid A three-dimensional object with one polygonal base and triangular faces that meet at a common vertex. A pyramid is named by the shape of the base.

Pythagorean theorem In a right triangle, the square of the hypotenuse is equal to the sum of the squares of the legs. For a right triangle with legs a and b and hypotenuse c, $c^2 = a^2 + b^2$.

quadratic equation An expression of the form $ax^2 + bx + c$, where $a \neq 0$.

quadratic relation A relation between two variables that appear as a parabola when graphed. A relation of the form $y = ax^2 + bx + c$, where $a \neq 0$.

radius A line segment joining the centre of a circle to a point on the circumference, or the length of this line segment.

rate of change A change in one quantity relative to the change in another quantity.

ratio A comparison of two quantities measured in the same units.

rectangle A quadrilateral with two pairs of equal opposite sides and four right angles.

rectangular prism A three-dimensional object with three pairs of congruent parallel rectangular faces.

rectangular pyramid A three-dimensional object with a rectangular base and two pairs of congruent triangular faces.

relation An identified pattern, or relationship, between two variables. A relation can be represented by an equation, a graph, a set of ordered pairs, or a table of values.

revenue Total income from sales.

right angle A 90° angle.

right triangle A triangle that contains one 90° angle.

rise The vertical distance between two points on a line.

run The horizontal distance between two points on a line.

scatter plot A graph that compares two sets of related data. Shows two-variable data as points plotted on a coordinate grid.

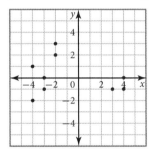

second differences The difference between consecutive first differences. For a quadratic relation, second differences are constant.

similar triangles Triangles in which the ratios of the lengths of corresponding sides are equal and corresponding angles are equal.

$$\triangle ABC \sim \triangle DEF$$

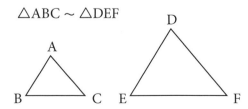

simplify Find a simpler and shorter equivalent expression. Usually involves collecting like terms.

sine ratio The ratio comparing the length of the side opposite the angle to the length of the hypotenuse in a right triangle.

$$\sin A = \frac{\text{length of side opposite A}}{\text{length of hypotenuse}}$$

slant height In a pyramid or a cone, the slant height is the least distance from the edge of the base to the vertex.

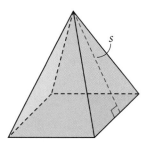

slope A measure of the steepness of a line. Compares the vertical distance to the horizontal distance between two points.

$$\text{slope} = \frac{\text{rise}}{\text{run}}.$$

slope *y*-intercept form A linear equation of the form $y = mx + b$, where m is the slope of the line and b is the *y*-intercept.

solution The value of the variable that makes an equation true.

sphere A three-dimensional ball-shaped object. Every point on the surface is an equal distance from a fixed point (the centre).

square-based prism A prism with two congruent, parallel square bases and four congruent rectangular faces.

square-based pyramid A pyramid with a square base and four congruent triangular faces.

square root A number that is multiplied by itself to give another number.

standard form of the equation of a line A linear equation of the form $Ax + By + C = 0$ where A is a whole number, B and C are integers, and A and B cannot both equal zero.

substitution method An algebraic method of solving a system of linear equations. One equation is solved for one variable, then that value is substituted into the other equation.

sum The result of addition.

supplementary angles Angles whose sum is 180°.

surface area The number of square units needed to cover the surface of a three-dimensional object.

 T

table of values A table used to record the coordinates of points in a relation.

x	y
0	1
1	4
2	7
3	10
4	13
5	16

tangent ratio The ratio comparing the length of the side opposite the angle to the length of the side adjacent to the angle in a right triangle.

$$\tan B = \frac{\text{length of side opposite B}}{\text{length of side adjacent to B}}$$

term A number or a variable, or the product of numbers and variables.

tessellation A tiling pattern in which congruent figures cover a surface with no gaps or overlaps.

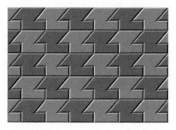

theorem A mathematical statement that has been proved.

triangle A three-sided polygon.

triangular prism A three-dimensional object with two congruent, parallel triangular bases and three rectangular faces.

triangular pyramid A three-dimensional object with a triangular base and three triangular faces.

trigonometry Means *triangle measurement*. Used to calculate lengths of sides and measures of angles in triangles.

trinomial A polynomial with three terms. $x^2 + 2x + 1$ is a trinomial.

variable A letter used to represent a value that can change. In the expression $5p + 4$, p is the variable.

variable term A term that includes a letter or symbol to represent an unknown value. In the equation $7x + 3 = -5$, the variable term is $7x$.

Venn diagram A diagram using circles to show the relationships between sets.

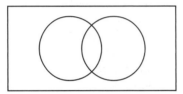

vertex (of a polygon) A point at which two sides of a polygon meet.

vertex (of a parabola) The point at which the parabola changes from decreasing to increasing or from increasing to decreasing.

volume The amount of space occupied by an object. Volume is measured in cubic units.

weight The force of attraction between an object and the Earth or other planet.

x-axis The horizontal number line on a coordinate grid.

x-coordinate The first number in an ordered pair, which represents the horizontal distance from the y-axis on a coordinate grid.

x-intercept The x-coordinate of a point at which the graph of a relation crosses the x-axis. The value of x when $y = 0$.

y-axis The vertical number line on a coordinate grid.

y-coordinate The second number in an ordered pair, which represents the vertical distance from the x-axis on a coordinate grid.

y-intercept The y-coordinate of the point at which the graph of a relation crosses the y-axis. The value of y when $x = 0$.

zeros The x-intercepts of a quadratic relation. The value(s) of x when $y = 0$.

Index

A

acute angle, 59
adjacent side, 58
   opposite side, 63–73
   problems, 59–63
aerospace technologists, 235
aesthetics, 195
algebra, 155
algebra tiles, 153, 280, 282, 283,
   306–307
   greatest common factor, 290
algebraic expressions, 152, 196,
   278
   evaluation, 153, 236
   simplification, 152
allegory, 253
angle of depression, 84
angle of elevation, 84
angles, 56, 65
   measurement, 70
   measuring with
   clinometer, 83–84
   opposite, 5
   properties of, 5
   right triangle, 58
   sides, 22
   supplementary, 5
applications, See specific
   applications
approximately, 22
arch, 321, 332
   problems, 341–343
archeology, 236
architecture, 262
   quadratic relations, 267–268
area, 363
   circle, 242
   problems, 286–289, 310–311
   rectangle, 238, 242, 278, 280,
   281, 285, 363
   square, 241, 301
   triangles, 240
astronauts, 254
axis of symmetry, 256
   problems, 260–263
   quadratic relation, 257–259,
   318

B

bacterial culture (growth), 251
barn, 400
base of triangles, 240
binomials, 278
   distributive property, 284
   greatest common factor, 292
   modelling, 282
   multiplication, 280–289, 312
   problems, 286–289,
   294–297, 310–311
   squaring, 283, 284
Blom, Pieter, 320
body surface area, 161
box, 362
break-even point, 184, 208
   problems, 204
bungee jumping, 154
Burlington Skyway, 351

C

calipers, 7
camera obscura, 35
Canadian Football League, 280
Canadian Standards
   Association, 73
Capilano Bridge, 325
cardiorespiratory fitness, 173
carpenter, 43
Cathedral Bluffs, 82
Celsius, 12, 114, 157, 352
   conversion, 12–18
   problems, 182–183
centimetre, 12
   conversion, 12–18
circle
   area, 242
   perimeter, 242
   radius, 242
circumference, 27, 37
civil engineering
   technologist, 317
clinometer, 83
coefficient, 121
coffee, 397
commission, 137
common factors/factoring,
   98, 312

comparison, 253
composite solids
   problems, 402–405
   surface area, 398–405, 407
   volume, 398–405, 407
computer aided design
   (CAD), 317
Computer Algebra System
   (CAS), 167–168, 178–179,
   281, 291
computer graphic artist, 361
cone, 82, 391
   problems, 394–397
   volume, 391–397, 407
constant in a linear
   equation, 213
constant terms, 165
coordinate grid, 99
corresponding angles, 21
   similar triangles, 25–29
corresponding sides, 21
cosine, 63–73
cosine ratio, 63–73, 67, 89
   problems, 71–73
cost, 8
cube
   problems, 379
   surface area, 320
   volume, 369
cup, 6, 7
curve of best fit, 239
   problems, 241–244, 252
cylinder, 381, 401
   problems, 386–390,
   402–405
   surface area, 381–390, 407
   volume, 381–390, 391–397,
   407

D

data collection, 245–246
decimal, 98
   linear equations, 156–157
degree, 6, 12, 114, 157
design, 259
   parabola, 259
diagonals in polygons, 270–271
diameter, 27, 37

parable, 253
parabola, 238, 253, 254–258, 318, 319
  design, 259
  features of, 256–259
  maximum, 256
  minimum, 256
  problems, 333–335
parabolic arch
  (problems), 341–343
  see also arch
parallel lines, 123, 211
  problems, 124–127
  similar triangles, 23–24
patterns, 299
pedometer, 135
pendulum, 244
perfect square trinomial, 284, 314
perimeter
  circle, 242
  rectangle, 161, 238, 242, 293–294
period, 244
perpendicular line, 56, 64, 65
Pharoah Khufu, 370
Pi (π), 382
pill capsule, 399
pinhole camera, 35
pint, 6, 7, 8, 12
  problems, 10–12
pitch, 138
point
  equation of a line, 131, 132
  problems, 134–137
point of intersection, 198, 199
  problems, 201–204
polygons, 191
  diagonals, 270–271
polynomials, 278
pound, 6, 7, 12
  conversion, 12–18
  problems, 10–12
powers (numbers), 300
pressure (problems), 182–183
principal, 177
prism, 364
  equilateral triangular, 366
  problems, 367–371, 376–380
  square, 365
  surface area, 372–380, 406

volume, 364, 367–371, 406
problem solving, 347–351
profit, 184, 355
  problems, 334, 348–351
projectile motion, 276
projectiles, 316
proportion, 4, 44
  right triangles, 54–62, 88
proportional, 21, 22
PST, 178–179
pyramid, 364
  problems, 367–371, 376–380
  rectangular, 365
  surface area, 372–380, 406
  volume, 364, 367–371, 406
Pyramids of Giza, 370
Pythagoras, 46
Pythagorean theorem, 42, 46, 47, 88, 362, 366
  problems, 49–53

Q

quadratic expression, 276, 280
quadratic relation, 234, 238, 352
  analyzing, 331–332
  architecture, 267–268
  axis of symmetry, 257–259, 318
  factoring, 330
  first differences, 264–266, 273
  form $y = ax^2 + c$, 336–343, 352–353
  graph, 257, 321, 329–331
  interpretation, 320–328, 332, 352
  key features, 254–263, 272–273
  maximum, 257
  minimum, 257
  modelling, 245–253, 272
  problems, 249–253, 260–263, 269–271, 323–328
  rate of change, 264–271, 273
  representing, 316, 329–335, 352
  second differences, 264–266, 273

shape of, 254–256
solving problems, 344–351, 353
vertex, 257, 318
x-intercept, 257, 318, 330
y-intercept, 257, 318
quart, 6, 7, 12
  problems, 10–12

R

radius (circle), 242
Rainbow Bridge, 263
ramp, 319
  problems, 335
rate of change, 100, 184
  calculating, 103
  earnings, 104–105
  problems, 106–110
  quadratic relation, 264–271
  slope, 146
ratio, 4, 21
  cosine, *see* cosine ratio
  problems, 59–63
  right triangles, 54–62, 88
  side length, 54–62
  simplest form, 4
  sine, *see* sine ratio
  tangent, *see* tangent ratio
ray, 55
rectangle
  area, 238, 242, 278, 280, 281, 285, 363
  dimensions, 293–294, 306, 307, 308–309
  perimeter, 161, 238, 242, 293–294
  problems, 294–297, 310–311
rectangular prism, 401
  nets, 362
  surface area, 373
  volume, 369, 370
rectangular pyramid
  problems, 376–380
  right triangular prism
  surface area, 374, 375
  volume, 365
relations (graph), 318

revenue (maximum), 344–345
  See also break-even point,
  interest, investments, simple
  interest
right isosceles triangle, 240
right triangle, 240
  adjacent side, 58
  angles, 58
  hypotenuse, 362
  leg, 362
  opposite side, 58
  problems, 59–63, 86–87
  proportion, 54–62, 88
  ratios, 54–62, 88
  sides, 58
  solving problems using,
  83–87, 89
right triangular prism
  (problems),
  378
rise, 101
robotics, 276
roof truss, 47
rounding, 44
ruler, 7
run, 101

satellite dishes, 261, 328
scale drawings, 138
scatter plot, 251
Science North, 276
second differences, 266
  problems, 269–271
  quadratic relations, 264–266
segment, 55, 64, 65
service charges, 178–179
side lengths, 54–62
sides
  angles, 22
  right triangle, 58
silos, 385, 402
similar triangles, 21, 38
  corresponding angles, 25–29
  Geometer's Sketchpad,
  20–21
  height, measuring, 30–37
  length, measuring, 30–37
  opposite angles, 22–23

parallel lines, 23–24
  properties of, 19–29
  side lengths, 24
simple interest, 177
  see also interest, investment
  formula, 177
  problems, 181–183
simplification of algebraic
  expressions, 152
sine, 63–73
sine ratio, 63–73, 66, 89
  problems, 71–73
slant height, 375
slope, 100, 101, 197
  equation, 104
  equation of a line, 130, 131
  fraction, 140
  graph, 138–145
  graphing calculator,
  111–112
  line, 102
  linear equation, 185
  linear relation, 113, 114
  negative, 122
  positive, 122
  problems, 106–110, 115–
  117, 124–127, 134–137,
  187–189
  properties of, 118–119, 147
  rate of change, 146
  y-intercept, 146
Snowbirds, 219
solar oven, 261
space probe, 176
speed, 171
  formula, 176
  problems, 180–183
sphere, 392
  problems, 394–397
  volume, 392–397, 407
square prism (volume), 365
square roots, 45, 300
  problems, 302
square-based pyramid
  net, 377
  problems, 376–380
  surface area, 374
  volume, 369
squares, 45
  area, 241, 301
  difference of two, 298–305

stairs, 404
standard form, 184
storage tanks, 384, 385
substitution
  linear system, 205–211,
  220–221
  linear systems, 226
  problems, 209–211
substitution method, 205
  linear system, 219–220
  problems, 209–211
sundials, 245
supplementary angles, 5
supply and demand, 207
surface area, 360, 372
  composite solid, 398–405,
  407
  cube, 320
  cylinders, 381–390, 407
  prism, 372–380, 406
  problems, 376–380, 386–390
  pyramid, 372–380, 406
  rectangular prism, 373
  rectangular pyramid, 374,
  375
  square-based pyramid, 374
surveyor, 83
suspension bridge, 325
  problems, 334
Sydney Harbour Bridge, 275
symmetry, 237
  lines, 236

tablespoon, 6
tangent ratio, 74–82, 77, 89
  problems, 79–82
taxes, 178–179
teaspoon, 6
technology and data collection,
  245–246
temperature, 12, 157, 352
  conversion, 12–18
  linear relation, 114
  measurement, 6
  problems, 182–183, 250
tesselations, 28

Credits

Photo Credits

iv (top)NASA/JPL, (bottom) Jeff Greenberg/Index Stock Imagery; v (top) Peter Bowater/Photo Researchers, Inc, (bottom) Karl Weatherly/Getty Images; vi (top) © Jim Sugar/CORBIS, (bottom) ©Don Johnston/Alamy; vii (top) ©SHOTFILE/Alamy, (bottom) © Richard Cummins/CORBIS; x (top) © Digital Vision Ltd./SuperStock, (bottom) © Momentum Creative Group/Alamy; p2–3 Royalty-Free/CORBIS; p3 (top right) © Bill Varie/CORBIS; p5 (top right) Reza Estakhrian/The Image Bank/Getty Images; p6 (top) Blair Seitz/Photo Researchers, Inc.; p7 (top) Dennis MacDonald/PhotoEdit, Inc., (top center) Image Source/Getty Images, (bottom left) © Photodisc/Getty Images, (bottom) Peter Watson/Intuition Photography, (bottom right) Peter Watson/Intuition Photography; p11 Photodisc Collection/Getty Images; p12 NASA/JPL; p19 Geostock/Getty Images; p28 M.C. Escher's "Symmetry drawing E78" ©2006 The M.C. Escher Company - The Netherlands. All rights reserved. www.mcescher.com; p30 © Bjorn Backe; Papilio/CORBIS; p35 © David Lees/CORBIS; p37 Visual Arts Library (London)/Alamy; p41 Greg Pease/The Image Bank/Getty Images; p42–43 Ilene MacDonald/Alamy; p43(top right), © Ariel Skelley/CORBIS; p45 Jeff Dunn/Index Stock Imagery; p46 STS-110 Shuttle Crew, NASA; p54 Ocean Drilling Program/NOAA; p63 Jeff Greenberg/Index Stock Imagery; p73 ©JOHN SANFORD/Grant Heilman Photography; p74 Layne Kennedy/Corbis; p83 (top) © Joel Benard/Masterfile, (bottom) © Bettmann/CORBIS, (center left) Frank Vetere/Alamy, (bottom right) Thomas Shjarback/Alamy; p91 (top) Photo courtesy of Barbara Canton, (bottom) Royalty-Free/CORBIS; p95 Yvette Cardozo/Index Stock Imagery; p96–97 Peter Bowater/Photo Researchers, Inc; p97 (top right) © Royalty-Free/Corbis; p99 © Bill Barley/SuperStock; p100 © Royalty-Free/Corbis; p110 © Michael S. Yamashita/CORBIS; p111 © Brand X/SuperStock; p117 Mark Segal/Index Stock Imagery; p118 © Royalty-Free/Corbis; p128 © Royalty-Free/Corbis; p135 David Young-Wolff/PhotoEdit, Inc.; p136 (top right) M Stock/Alamy, (bottom left) Hemera Technologies/Alamy; p137 © Steve Prezant/CORBIS; p138 Peter Horree/Alamy; p144 Hugh Threlfall/Alamy; p145 Royalty-Free/CORBIS; p149 Reimar Gaertner/Alamy; p150–151 Royalty-Free/CORBIS; p151 (top right) Flying Colours Ltd/Getty Images; p153 BananaStock/Alamy; p154 (top) © Paul A. Souders/CORBIS, (bottom) Craig Lovell/Eagle Visions Photography / Alamy; p160 Karl Weatherly/Getty Images; p161 © Newstockimages/SuperStock; p162 (top) © James Marshall/CORBIS, (bottom) Jeff Greenberg/PhotoEdit, Inc.; p163 Ralph Ginzburg/Peter Arnold, Inc.; p171 Chuck Carlton/Index Stock Imagery; p173 © SuperStock, Inc./SuperStock; p174 AP Photo/Roberto Borea; p176 NASA Langley Research Center (NASA-LaRC); p177 Keith Brofsky/Getty Images; p178 Jochen Tack/Peter Arnold, Inc.; p181 Otto Stadler/Peter Arnold, Inc.; p182 © Alan Porritt/epa/Corbis; p183 Rudi Von Briel/PhotoEdit, Inc.; p184 © Royalty-Free/Corbis; p188 © Wolfgang Kaehler/CORBIS; p190 ©Rudy Sulgan/Corbis; p191 © Royalty-Free/Corbis; p193 FogStock LLC/Index Stock Imagery; Chapter 5 p194–195 © SuperStock, Inc./SuperStock; p195 (top right) © ELDER NEVILLE/CORBIS SYGMA; p197 Image Source/SuperStock; p198 ©Robert Stainforth/Alamy; p202 © BananaStock/SuperStock; p203 ©Ingram Publishing/SuperStock; p205 © Angelo Cavalli/SuperStock; p211 © Spencer Grant/PhotoEdit; p212 © Muriot/photocuisine/Corbis; p218 (bottom) © Tom Stewart/CORBIS, (top) Image Source/Getty Images; p219 Air Force Public Affairs/Department of National Defence; p220 © Ingram Publishing/SuperStock; p224 ©John T. Fowler/Alamy;

p225 ©Travel Ink/Index Stock Imagery; p226 Larry MacDougal/Peter Arnold, Inc.; p227 ©ThinkStock/SuperStock; p229 Renee DeMartin/Photonica/Getty Images; p230 © Michelle Pedone/zefa/Corbis; p231 © Royalty-Free/Corbis; p234–235 Steve Allen/Getty Images; p235 (top right) WorldFoto/Alamy; p237 (top) Robert J. Blumenschine, (bottom) The Natural History Museum/Alamy; p238 Paul Thompson Images/Alamy; p244 ©Maria Ferrari/SuperStock; p245 ©Photo Researchers, Inc.; p250 Big Cheese Photo/Index Stock Imagery; p253 Jessica Addams/Wolf Park, www.wolfpark.org; p254 © Jim Sugar/CORBIS; p259 Peter Watson/Intuition Photography; p262 (top) FirstShot/Alamy, (bottom)The Natural History Museum/Alamy; p263 © Galen Rowell/CORBIS; p264 (top) © PICIMPACT/CORBIS, (center right) © Royalty-Free/Corbis; p265 Ross Woodhall/Photographer's Choice/Getty Images; p268 ©David Prichard/First Light; p273 © BIOS Klein & Hubert / Peter Arnold, Inc.; p275 (bottom) Matthew Wellings/Alamy, (top) Robert J. Blumenschine, (center right) The Natural History Museum/Alamy; p276-277 ©Don Johnston/Alamy; p277 (top right) Royalty-Free/CORBIS; p279 ©Royalty-Free/Corbis; p280 ©Iconotec/Alamy; p288 Stan Liu/Iconica/Getty Images; p290 AP PHOTO/CP, Francois Roy; p296 ©Eurostyle Graphics/Alamy; p297 ©Patti McConville/Grant Heilman Photography, Inc.; p298 ©Royalty-Free/Corbis; p304 © Pawel Libera/Corbis; p306 © Ingram Publishing/SuperStock; p314 ©Ross M. Horowitz/Getty; p315 ©David H. Wells/Corbis; p316–317 © SHOTFILE/Alamy; p317 (top right) ©Cindy Charles/PhotoEdit; p320 © Robert Harding Picture Library Ltd/Alamy; p323 © Alex Bartel/SuperStock; p328 (c) Stockbyte/PunchStock; p329 © Richard T. Nowitz/Corbis; p334 (top) Skip Nall/Getty Images, (bottom) ©Lee F. Snyder/Photo Researchers, Inc.; p336 (top) © Peter Watson/Intuition Photography; p339 © Peter Watson/Intuition Photography; p342 Mike Mesgleski /Index Stock; p343 ihoe/Alamy; p344 © Gideon Mendel/Corbis; p345 Bill Aron/PhotoEdit; p349 Keith Alstrin /Index Stock Imagery; p350 Troy+Mary Parlee/Index Stock Imagery; p351 © Peter Watson/Intuition Photography; p353 FAN travelstock/Alamy; p354 Eric Figge/Index Stock Imagery; p357 ©PhotoLink/Getty Images; p359 Barry Winiker/Index Stock; p360–361 Royalty-Free/CORBIS; p361 (top right) ImageState/Alamy; p363 Royalty-Free/CORBIS; p364 © Robert Holmes/CORBIS; p370 Daryl Benson/The Image Bank/Getty Images; p372 Rimmington CE, photographersdirect.com; p374 © Tibor Bognár/CORBIS; p379 Andrew Ward/Life File/Getty Images; p381 Richard Elliott/Stone/Getty Images; p385 ©Wally Bauman/Alamy; p391 © Richard Cummins/CORBIS; p392 © Myrleen Ferguson Cate/PhotoEdit; p393 (c) Photodisc/PunchStock; p397 Howard Birnsthil Photography, photographersdirect.com; p398 (top) © Peter Finger/CORBIS, (bottom) © Curtis R. Lantinga/Masterfile; p409 Royalty-Free/CORBIS; p410 © Image Source/SuperStock; p411 ©Royalty-Free/Corbis;

Illustration Credits

Pronk&Associates

Technical Art

Pronk&Associates